中国可再生能源政策变迁机制研究：国际气候变化机制与国内可再生能源政策倡议联盟的互动

Renewable Energy Policy Change in China: Interlinking the Climate Change Regime and Domestic Pro-Renewable Energy Coalition

李昕蕾　著

山东大学出版社

总　序

2011年是山东大学建校110周年。作为中国近代第二所官办大学——“山东大学堂”，山东大学的积累之悠久，底蕴之深厚，堪可感慨系之。

晚清光绪二十七年(1901年)，山东巡抚袁世凯奏呈朝廷并由光绪帝御批的《山东大学堂章程》中，就山东大学堂的办学宗旨作了这样的阐述：

公家设立学堂，是为天下储人才，非为诸生谋进取；
诸生来堂肄业，是为国家图富强，非为一己利身家。

在20世纪初叶，在东渐之西学纷至沓来的近代中国，袁氏奏呈的“办学章程”有着某种意义上的传承性与超越性。愚以为，袁氏立意“天下”、“国家”，绝非其偶然心念一动，在这一理念的背后，当是数千年孔孟儒学传统文化精粹的蕴聚与支撑。为了“天下”、“国家”，而非“一己”之“进取”的办学理念，在那个中华羸弱、列强环伺的年代，越发彰显着山东大学的历史使命与民族责任，成为山东大学立足与发展的价值础石。正是基于这样的理念，山东大学在伴随着时代动荡、社会变迁的百余年行进途中，尚能安然把握着方向与节奏，使之得以在不同的历史阶段，均能汇聚时代的学术精英，渐次积淀了丰厚的学术内涵和大学文化底蕴。迄今，亦能风雨无阻，依然跻身于全国高校第一方阵的前排。

政治学与公共管理学院是山东大学百余年行程过半的时候才得以组建的，如今业已年过而立。作为全国政治学与公共管理学在山东区域的一方重镇，其或发展或进步或逡巡或蹒跚，总会令人瞩目，引人关注。作为山东大学不可割舍的肌体，政管学院之举手投足、一笑一颦，往往事关全校的布局与发展，甚或波及百年山大之盛誉。于是兹事体大，吾侪不敏，遂以《论语·泰伯》之教训为警醒："士不可以不弘毅，任重而道远！"为此，于2009年即谋划聚合全院教师，协同努力，做一学术振兴。列为其重要举措之一，即出版学术著作若干，自成体系，冠名曰"政治发展与治理研究系列丛书"，为的是既能涵盖学院诸多学科，又能与主体方向不离不弃——推动山东大学政治学学科建设与发展而积累学术内涵；同时，在这样的操练过程中，不断推出青年才俊，实现个体与整体的同步迈进。

我们肩负着学界前辈的成就与希冀，我们延续着百年山大的底蕴和盛誉。在当下学术与世俗混而难分、盛名与实学真伪莫辨的"转型时代"，我们当以山大人的真诚与辛劳，为学界奉上这组系列文字。目的是弘扬学术，以文会友，抑或移风易俗，振兴我山东大学之政治学学科。

是为序。

葛　荃

山东大学政治学与公共管理学院教授兼院长

2012年12月17日　重识于巢舍

Book Sketch

The energy supply mix in China is characterized by a coal-dominated pattern; over 70% energy consumption is from coal and over 80% electricity is from coal thermal plants. The main puzzle of this book is that, against the backdrop of a heavy carbon lock-in energy structure, why has China made remarkable progress in renewable energy development and become a world leader in this area within one decade; what are the hidden dynamics for China's renewable energy policy change? Although existing researches have pointed out that the rapid growth of renewable energy is mainly due to the convergence of energy security concerns, the climate change concerns, environmental protection concerns and economic growth concerns, these studies oversimplify the strong resistance of conventional interest groups in the energy sector and fail to explain how the formerly-weak pro-renewable energy (pro-RE) actors strengthen their position in the policy-making system to push the renewable energy policy change. This book attempts to investigate how the climate change regime, as an external impetus, has an impact on the institution building and resource allocation among different domestic stakeholders, and makes a breakthrough in the coal lock-in structure to promote RE policy change in China.

The primary aim of this book is to analyze how the capacity building of the pro-RE coalition gets enhanced through climate change socialization process and how the strengthened pro-RE coalition competes with the conventional energy forces to spur renewable energy policy change: from a vacant position to the introduction of the tendering system beginning in 2003, then the development of the feed-in tariff policy beginning in 2005 by issuing the Renewable Energy Law, and finally attempting to combine the quota system with feed-in tariff policy in order to solve the bottlenecks of grid-connection and curtailment. Through combining the socialization theory with Sabatier's advocacy coalition framework (ACF), I draw up a systematic theoretical framework to interlink the influence of climate change socialization with the strengthening of the pro-RE coalition. Along with the increasing salience of climate change in the past two decades, China as the largest GHG emitter has gradually softened its stance and shown more socializing tendency in the climate change negotiations in order to get more material incentives, boost the national reputation, reduce the international pressure and stimulate its own low-carbon transformation. In this process, the role playing and the strategic calculation micro-processes of climate change socialization have strengthened the capacity building of the pro-RE coalition through institutional anchoring and resource reallocation mechanisms at the domestic level. The pro-RE coalition has gained more governmental and societal supporters, expertise, legal authority, financial support to compete with conventional energy interests, and to promote renewable energy policy change by means of policy-oriented learning and argumentative persuasion. This book concludes that the capacity building of the pro-RE coalition is a key link-up to bridge the climate change regime and domestic renewable energy policy change; without external dynamics from the climate change socialization process, the pro-RE coalition could not have obtained sufficient resources to promote rapid renewable energy growth within only one decade.

Acknowledgements

This book is based on my PhD dissertation written at the Free University of Berlin, Germany. I would like to call this book my little "brain-child", since it was cultivated in a bitter-sweet process with four-year arduous efforts. Walking in a bumpy road of dissertation-writing, I luckily received numerous supports from many people.

First of all, I would like to show my great appreciation to my supervisors, Prof. Martin Jänicke and Prof. Miranda Schreurs, who provided me with a precious opportunity to learn how to become a qualified political scholar focusing on environmental policy analysis. Prof. Martin Jänicke is a Founding Director of the Environmental Policy Research Center and well-known as a founder of Ecological Modernization Theory. In the early stage of my dissertation-writing, thanks to his patient guidance and warm-hearted encouragement, I was finally determined to engage in the research of China's renewable energy policy change. Prof. Martin Jänicke is also a foreign expert in the Task Forces Group of China Council for International Cooperation on Environment and Development (CCICED) and has rich research experience in renewable policy as well as policy innovation of China. During our regular research discussions, I benefited a lot from his trenchant comments and thought-provoking suggestions. Whenever my thoughts came to a standstill or even into a dead-lock, he was always there to support, guide and encourage me to overcome all kinds of difficulties.

Before starting my PhD study in Berlin, I once luckily met Prof. Miranda Schreurs, Director of FFU, in a summer school jointly held by FU Berlin and Fudan University in Shanghai in 2007. The wonderful lecture given by Prof. Schreurs stimulated my interest in environmental politics and broadened my horizons to consider studying abroad. During four-year PhD study in FFU since 2009, I really benefited a lot from inspired discussions of every-week colloquiums led by Prof. Schreurs. She helped to change my research from a "fact-finding mission" into a scientific study. Her sharply critical but instructive remarks and suggestions spurred me to revise and improve my research time and time again. What impressed me most is that, as a native speaker but a super-busy professor, she even sacrificed her rest time and tried her best to proofread my dissertation during her traveling, which made this dissertation easier to read.

I am also grateful to Prof. Klaus Segbers, the leader in the Graduate School of Global Politics (GSGP). With his support, I won a chance to become one of the first enrollment PhD students in the Center for Global Politics. Within this well-structured project, I found it so beneficial to join in those theoretical courses, academic seminars and online discussions. Meanwhile, my student advisors in GSGP, Claudia Kissling, Bettina Rollow, Sabine Pag and Daniela Schmidt provided lots of generous help for my study. My thanks also go to my GSGP classmates Wang Xiaoguang, Frauke Austermann and Ren Lin. The heated discussions with them in seminars drove me to make continuous improvement to my dissertation proposal. With an outstanding teamwork, we successfully organized the First International GSGP Workshop—"China and Europe in the 21st Century Global Politics: Partnership, Competition or Co-Evolution?"—in Renmin University of China in 2012.

There were also many people from outside of FU Berlin without whose support this book would have never been ready. I want to express my gratitude to Prof. Huan Qingzhi and Prof. Zhang Haibin in Peking University, Ren Dongming, the Director of Center for Renewable Energy Development Center (CRED) in NDRC and Zhang Lei in Brussels Institute of Contemporary China Studies, Vrije Universiteit Brussel. I had interviews with them for several times respectively, face to face or by emails. They showed their great patience and kindness to provide me with their keen insights and authoritative advice. I am also grateful to my friends who agreed to spend their valuable time in answering many questions that came up in the process of dissertation writing. I would like to extend my great thanks to Li Huiming, Zhan Xin, Zhou Na and Huang Dong, since they gave me valuable suggestions to my research and encouraged me to move on. Furthermore, I want to show my special appreciation to CSC (Chinese Scholarship Council), which provided me with a generous financial support during last four years.

Finally, I want to say that I could not finish this book without wholeheartedly comforting support and encouragement from my husband, Ren Xiangrong. Although we were separated by thousands of miles, I could still feel his soul accompanying me during this particularly stressful and challenging period of time in my life. I would like to extend my final special thanks to my parents, Li Lianshun and Li Bingying. They are my warm soul harbor forever. Every time when I felt frustrated and lost confidence, they were ready to cheer me up and give me sufficient energy to rebuild my life and look ahead. I want to contribute this book to them to be grateful for their fostering. Without my family, I definitely wouldn't be there, were I am now.

Li Xinlei
Summer of 2015

List of Abbreviations

ACF	Advocacy Coalition Framework
ADP	Durban Platform for Enhanced Action
AOSIS	Alliance of Small Island States
APEC	Asia-Pacific Economic Cooperation
AQSIQ	Administration of Quality Supervision, Inspection and Quarantine
BAU	business as usual
BNEF	Bloomberg New Energy Finance
BRIC	Brazil, Russia, India and China
CAEP	Chinese Academy for Environmental Planning
CAREI	China Association of Rural Energy Industry
CAS	China Academy of Science
CASS	Chinese Academy of Social Sciences
CBDR	Common but Differentiated Responsibilities
CCF	Green Climate Fund
CCICED	China Council for International Cooperation on Environment and Development
CCS	Carbon Capture and Storage
CDM	Clean Development Mechanism
CDMFUND	China Clean Development Mechanism Fund
CECA	China Energy Conservation Association
CERs	Certified Emission Reductions
CIF	Clean Investment Funds (World Bank)
CMA	China Meteorological Administration
CNOOC	China National Off-shore Oil Corporation
CNPC	China National Petroleum Corporation

CNREC	China National Renewable Energy Center
CO_2	carbon dioxide
COACH	Cooperation Action within CCS China-EU
COP	Conference of the Parties (to the UNFCCC)
CPC	the Communist Party of China
CRED	Center for Renewable Energy Development
CREIA	Chinese Renewable Energy Industries Association
CRES	Chinese Renewable Energy Society
CRESP	China Renewable Energy Scale-up Programme
CSDR	China Sustainable Development Report
CSG	China Southern Power Grid Company
CTCN	Climate Technology Centre and Network
CWEA	Chinese Wind Energy Association
DNERE	Department of New Energy and Renewable Energy
DRC	Development Research Center (of the State Council)
DRCEP	Department of Resource Conservation and Environmental Protection
EB	Executive Board (of the CDM)
EC2	Europe-China Clean Energy Center
ERI	Energy Research Institute
ETS	Emissions Trading Scheme
EU	European Union
FIT	Feed-in Tariff
FYP	Five-Year Plan
G20	Group of Twenty
G8	Group of Eight
GDP	Gross Domestic Production
GEF	Global Environmental Facility
GHG	Green House Gas
GWEC	Global Wind Energy Council
IEA	International Energy Agency
IMF	International Monetary Fund
IPCC	Intergovernmental Panel on Climate Change
IPE	Institute of Public & Environmental Affairs
JI	Joint Implementation
MEP	Ministry of Environmental Protection
MIIT	Ministry of Industry and Information Technology
MOA	Ministry of Agriculture

MOF	Ministry of Finance
MOFA	Ministry of Foreign Affairs
MOHURD	Ministry of Housing and Urban-Rural Development of China
MOLAR	Ministry of Land and Resources
MOST	Ministry of Science and Technology
MOT	Ministry of Transport
NBS	National Bureau of Statistics of China
NCOCC	National Communication on Climate Change
NCSC	China National Center for Climate Change Strategy and International Cooperation
NDRC	National Development and Reform Commission
NEA	National Energy Administration
NEB	National Energy Bureau (2003-2008)
NEC	National Energy Commission
NGO	Non-governmental Organization
NLGCC	National Leading Group on Climate Change
NPC	National People's Congress
NZEC	UK-China Near Zero Emissions Coal initiative
ODA	Official Development Assistance
OECD	Organization for Economic Cooperation and Development
OPEC	Organization of the Petroleum Exporting Countries
PCF	Prototype Carbon Fund
PV	Photovoltaic
R&D	Research and Development
RCEECC	Research Center for Energy Environment and Climate Change
RE	Renewable Energy
RED	Sino-Danish Renewable Energy Development Programme
REDP	China Renewable Energy Development Project
REEEP	Renewable Energy & Energy Efficiency Partnership
RMB	renminbi (China's currency unit)
RPS	Renewable Portfolio Standards
SAC	Standardization Administration of China
SASAC	State-owned Asset Supervision and Administration Commission
SAT	State Administration of Taxation
SC	State Council of China
SCLGECER	State Council Leading Group for Energy Conservation and Emission Reduction

SCSC	Standing Committee of the State Council
SDPC	State Development Planning Commission (1998-2003)
SEAC	State Expert Advisory Committee
SEPA	State Environmental Protection Administration (1988-2008)
SERC	State Electricity Regulatory Commission of China
SETC	State Economic and Trade Commission
SGCC	State Grid Corporation of China
Sinopec	China Petroleum and Chemical Corporation
SO_2	sulfur dioxide
SOA	State Oceanic Administration
SOEs	State-owned Enterprises
SPC	State Planning Committee (1951-1998)
SWH	Solar Water Heating
TRECs	Tradable Renewable Energy Credits
U. K.	United Kingdom
U. S.	United States
UN	United Nations
UNDP	United Nations Development Programme
UNEP	United Nations Environment Programme
UNFCCC	United Nations Framework Convention on Climate Change
WB	World Bank
WMO	World Meteorological Organization
WSSD	World Summit on Sustainable Development
WTO	World Trade Organization

Units of Measure

btce	billiontonnes of coal equivalent
btoe	billiontonnes of oil equivalent
gce	gram of coal equivalent
Gt	gigatonne
GW	gigawatt (1 gigawatt = 1 million kilowatts)
kW · h	kilowatt hours
Mt	megatonne
Mtce	millionton of tce
Mt CO_2/yr	megatonne of CO_2 per year
Mtoe	milliontonnes of oil equivalent
MW	megawatt
tce	standard coal equivalents
TW	terawatt(1 terawatt = 1 trillion watts)
TW · h	tera watt hour(s)

Contents

Chapter 1
Introduction

The energy supply mix in China relies heavily on fossil fuels (over 90%). Coal, oil and natural gas accounted for 68%, 19% and 4.4% of the energy supply, respectively in 2010 (Zhang et al. 2012: 1). The coal-dominated energy structure has changed little during the past decade, presenting a heavy path dependency on "black energy". Coal-based electricity has occupied the dominant position; 78.7% of China's electricity supply was produced from coal in the power sector in 2009 and over 82% in 2011 (Leung 2011). The interest groups behind coal and oil and state-owned power and grid enterprises have strong vested interests in the current coal-dominated energy mix. The fossil fuel-dominated energy supply structure has caused severe local and regional environmental pollution since at least the late 1980s. Although the government took some pollution control measures to internalize environmental costs, it failed to stimulate a fundamental reform in the energy structure—the de-carbonization of the energy supply mix did not make itself onto the political agenda.

For over 30 years since the economic reforms started in 1978, China has had an average annual 8%-10% economic growth rate. Much of this economic growth is dependent on highly energy-intensive industries in the coal-dominated energy mix (Lee 2012: 7). When China became a net oil importer in 1993, its leaders began to give a higher priority to maintaining oil-supply continuity and developing a "go-out" strategy to encourage state-owned oil companies to search for oil abroad. Supply-side management has become the main focus of energy security in China, and this has contributed to a continued high degree of oil dependency. In 2009, the ratio of China's dependency on foreign oil reached 53.7%, exceeding 50% for the first time in history (IEA 2010). In 2010, China surpassed Japan to become the second largest economic entity, and overtook the U. S. as the top energy consumer in the world (Cheng 2008: 301).

The Chinese government is being forced to reconsider its supply-biased energy security approach, and to pay more attention to energy efficiency and energy diversification. Domestically produced and environmentally friendly renewable energy (RE) can provide a reliable source of energy to benefit the country's energy security. However, a green transition to renewable energy and energy efficiency in the energy sector is not an easy path to take. The traditional coal and oil coalitions in China have a strong interest in keeping their dominant positions in the energy sector. The opposition from these conventional interest groups to renewable energy development cannot be underestimated. There is also strong resistance from the state-owned grid corporations to RE power connection and transmission. These corporations contend that ambitious renewable targets will threaten national grid stability.

Significantly, despite this carbon locked-in energy structure, China has had a remarkably rapid development of renewable energy capacity. Historically speaking, China is a latecomer in RE development, having started about 10 years later than many pioneering countries, such as Germany, the Netherlands and Denmark. Within one decade—as of 2010, China came to rank at the top in terms of its RE investment and became the world leader in installed wind power capacity, solar panels/cells manufacturing, and solar water heating utilization (Zhang et al. 2012: 1). Especially in the 11th Five-Year Plan① period (2006-2010), the issuing of the Renewable Energy Law (RE Law) in 2005 provided a great boost to RE. Considering the strong conventional vested interest groups in the energy sector of China, the successful performance of renewable energy contributed a lot to making a breakthrough in the coal-dominated development pattern. The *main research puzzle of this book* is to explain why a heavily coal-dominated country like China with an energy security strategy that focuses on securing fossil fuel supply, has become a leading country in the renewable energy field within only ten years. What explains the country's rapid renewable energy development?

Renewable energy development is usually understood as a domestic green energy issue. It is mainly driven by energy security and economic development concerns at the domestic level. China, as the biggest energy consumer, relies heavily on coal and oil imports. This high energy dependency rate has forced national leaders to find alternative energy to guarantee its long-term energy security. Therefore, promoting RE development has become an inevitable choice for China's national energy strategy.

① Five-Year Plan (FYP) refers to a series of social and economic strategic development initiatives to map the strategies for economic development, set the growth targets, and launch the structural reforms, which provides a significant blueprint or signpost for the immediate future. Since China launched its 1st FYP in 1953, China's five-year plans have played pivotal role in guiding the general economical and social development.

Greater reliance on RE power could reduce environmental pollution from coal-fired power plants. Energy security and environmental protection concerns at the domestic level are indispensable factors to understand RE development. Domestic renewable energy policy change must, however, be understood as being influenced by international factors, especially the impact of the climate change regime, a factor that has yet not been properly studied. Economy and Schreurs (1997: 4-5) emphasized the internationalization tendency of environmental politics and the impact of linkages among international and domestic politics on domestic policy. As mentioned above, considering the strong resistance to RE development from the conventional interest groups in the coal-dominated energy mix, the external dynamics from the international level have been of great importance for breaking the carbon lock-in energy structure and promoting the rapid development of RE, especially as it has paralleled by an increasing interest convergence between domestic and international level.

The rapid growth of energy consumption in China has led to soaring green house gas (GHG) emissions. China surpassed the U. S. to become the largest emitter of GHGs in 2007, and as a result has been confronted with greater international pressure to take on legally binding GHG emission reductions commitments within the climate change regime. Although China has refused to take on a legally binding commitment to reduce the GHG emissions, China's leaders have made some voluntary carbon-intensity reductions and RE development commitments in the climate negotiations in order to boost the national image and avoid the loss of national reputation. These commitments made by national leaders have formed a "carbon reduction pressure" mechanism (People Net 2010a) to force structural reform in the energy mix through aggressively promoting RE development and exploring low-carbon development approach. Especially since 2011, the governmental discourse on climate change has undergone a great change from statements of being "confronted seriously with the climate change challenge" to "treat the climate change as an opportunity to restructure the economy positively" (Xinhua News 2009b).

Beyond international reputational pressure, the climate change regime provides China with access to material incentives (international green fund, technological transfer and cooperative projects), knowledge and ideas about best practices, which China can use to avoid the vicious circle of the "black growth trap" and to readjust its policy system in a greener orientation. China's leadership has performed in a pragmatic way to take advantage of international material incentives to promote RE development, becoming the largest beneficiary of projects under the Clean Development Mechanism (CDM) and closely cooperating with the World Bank (WB) and the Global Environment Facility (GEF) in the cooperative frameworks of China Renewable

Energy Development Project (REDP), and the China Renewable Energy Scale-up Program (CRESP) under the climate change regime. These international resources have stimulated national capacity building, such as the institutional changes for RE governance, and have had an influence on domestic resource reallocation in the direction of the pro-RE actors at the domestic level. During this process, the number of pro-renewable energy actors has increased gradually and these actors have gained more political resources to compete with the conventional interest groups in the energy sector. There have been profound policy changes in relation to RE and the setting of ambitious RE targets in the past decade that has led to soaring growth rates in RE. Renewable energy, as one of the key components of green growth and low-carbon development, has a strategic position in the national 12th Five-Year Plan (2011-2015). According to the planning guidance of the 13th Five-Year Plan (2016-2020) issued in 2015, RE plays a pivotal substitution role in energy structure optimization.

What is behind China's compliance in the climate change regime and its increasing domestic green transformation tendencies? How are the international factors encouraging policy change linked to the interactions of different stakeholders in the RE policy-making process? How has domestic RE policy change promoted rapid RE development? There is a rich research literature concerning China's climate change negotiation stance (climate change policy) and approach to mitigation. ① There are also RE development reports and policy assessments for China. ② There is not sufficient work, however, addressing the influence of the climate change regime as well as that of domestic pro-renewable energy actors. It is argued that this is necessary to be looked at to explain China's RE policy change and rapid RE development. In order to explore China's rapid RE development despite the coal-dominated energy mix, there is need for a systemic framework to investigate how international sources influence the

---

① There is a rich research literature concerning China's climate change policy and its position in the climate change negotiations. See Chan 2006; Harris 2003; Harris 2006; Harris 2007; Harris 2009; Harris 2011a; Harris 2011b; Lewis 2008; Lewis 2009; Lewis 2011; Li and Xu 2010; Liang 2010; Ojekunle et al. 2009; Richerzhagen and Scholz 2008; Teng and Gu 2007; Vandenbergh 2007; Wiener 2007; Ye et al. 2007; Yu 2004a; Yu 2004b; Zhang 2006; Zhang 2007; Zhang 2010a; Zhuang 2009.

② Many international institutions, academic institutes, NGOs, and governmental institutions have published special reports on China's RE development with sufficient data and up-dated information. See the global and regional reports from RE Network for the 21st Century (REN21) related to the RE industry in China (REN21 2006, 2009a, 2009b, 2011, 2012, 2013); a series of RE development reports and books published by the China Renewable Energy Scale-up Program (CRESP) and the Center for Renewable Energy Development (CRED) (Ren et al. 2009; Gao et al. 2009; Wang, Z. et al. 2010; Wang, Z. et al. 2012). In addition, international institutions (such as IEA, World Bank, Global Environmental Facility) have published reports (partly) related to RE development in China. For example, the Clean Energy Progress Report issued by the IEA, and the Medium-Term RE Market Report 2012: Market Trends and Projections to 2017 issued by the IEA.

interaction of stakeholders in China's green transformation. Through combining the socialization theory and the advocacy coalition framework (ACF), I attempt to analyze how external dynamics have helped to strengthen the pro-RE actors at the domestic level in the policy-making system (the building of institutional capacity, the institutional anchoring in RE development and political resource reallocation in the direction of pro-RE actors) and how pro-RE actors have competed with the conventional energy forces in order to promote policy change and rapid RE development.

1.1 What is behind the rapid development of renewable energy in China?

According to the Renewable Energy Law issued in 2005, the definition of renewable energy (RE) refers to non-fossil energy sources, including wind energy, solar energy, biomass energy, geothermal energy, hydropower, and ocean energy. Hydropower is already a well commercialized technology in China, so hydropower is no longer as much a focus of RE policy discussions as are such non-hydro renewable energies as wind power, biomass and solar energy (Zhang et al. 2012: 1).① This book only focuses on the development of non-hydro RE, especially from wind, solar and biomass.

Until China signed the Kyoto Protocol in 1998 and finally changed its suspicious attitude towards the CDM projects that were introduced by the climate change regime around 2001 (Hatch 2003; Heggelund 2007)②, the large scale exploitation of RE (wind, solar and biomass) did not get much political or financial support. More

① Hydropower development is usually constrained by the national geographical conditions, and the large-scale hydropower projects might cause unexpected negative ecological impacts. Local environmental NGOs are quite cautious to the ecological destruction caused by hydropower construction, such as environmental movements against the Nujing Hydropower Dam project.

② During the interview with Prof. Zhang Haibin, Professor in School of International Studies, Peking University, focusing on climate change policy and energy security (7 August 2010, in Beijing), he also mentioned the attitude change of China towards the CDM in the beginning of the 21st century, because at first stage the officials from China's Ministry of Foreign Affairs had concerns that the CDM would only serve the interests of the industrialized world. However, the National Development and Reform Commission (NDRC) and the Ministry of Science and Technology showed more interest for technology transfer under the CDM.

recently, a RE policy system① has gradually been established. One of the key milestones was the issuing of the Renewable Energy Law in 2005 (taking effective in 2006), which stimulated RE investment and guaranteed a more favorable environment for RE development. From 2006 to 2010 in the 11th Five-Year Plan (FYP) period, RE experienced an incredibly rapid growth rate. China's wind capacity installation doubled every year for five years in a row (Wang, F. et al. 2010: 1832) and small hydroelectric capacity increased by 4-6 GW annually from 2004 to 2008 (Givner 2010). According to REN21, China is the global leader in wind power capacity, solar water heating and solar panel/cell production, and has ranked at the top place in RE investment since 2010 (see Table 1.1). In 2012, wind power generation increased more than the generation of electricity from coal and passed nuclear power output for the first time (REN21 2013:4). If the ambitious renewable targets of the 12th FYP issued in 2011 are realized, China could become the largest country in solar photovoltaic (PV) power generation by 2015.

Table 1.1 Top five countries-total RE capacity as of end-2012

	RE power capacity (not incl. hydro)	Wind power capacity	Solar hot water/heat capacity	Solar PV capacity	Biomass power capacity	Hydro power capacity	New capacity investment (2012)
1	China	China	China	Germany	U.S.	China	China
2	U.S.	U.S.	Germany	Italy	Brazil	Brazil	U.S.
3	Germany	Germany	Turkey	U.S.	China	U.S.	Germany
4	Spain	Spain	Brazil	China	Germany	Canada	Japan
5	Italy	India	India	Japan	Sweden	Russia	Italy

Source: REN21(2013: 8).

RE is starting to make inroads into the fossil fuel dominated energy system. Nevertheless, due to the rapid growth of fossil fuel consumption, the RE percentage in the energy supply mix is still rather low: excluding nuclear and hydropower, the

① The RE policy system in China includes three levels: the first level are basic laws issued by National People's Congress (NPC), such as the RE Law issued in 2005, the RE Law Amendment in 2009; the second level includes key administrative regulations especially Five-Year Plans (FYPs) issued by the State Council, like the 12th FYP issued in 2011, the 12th FYP for RE development in 2012 and the 12th FYP for the Energy development in 2013; the third level includes supportive administrative regulations by ministries and local governments, like the Notice on Policy to Improve Grid-Connected Power Pricing for Wind Power in 2009 and the Regulation for Management of Renewable Power Quotas (Draft Version) in 2012.

percentage of wind, solar and biomass power in the electricity mix only accounted for 3% in 2010 (Wang, Z. et al. 2012). Since the second half of 2010, the potential drawbacks of the rapid RE development approach gradually became apparent. Problems have included a grid connection bottleneck for renewable power, wind turbine grid disconnection accidents, renewable power curtailment, overcapacity and vicious competition of wind turbines as well as solar panels. Meanwhile at the international level, due to the Euro crisis and sluggish progress in the international climate change negotiations, the carbon market (especially the EU's Emission Trading System) has suffered from low prices. The carbon price collapsed from its peak of 30 Euros in July 2008 to less than 7 Euros in September 2012, further worsening the situation of CDM projects (Shankar 2012). As the largest beneficiary of CDM projects, China has been confronted with increasing difficulties in getting further international incentives from the climate change regime. What is worse, the United States has begun to set an anti-dumping duty and anti-subsidy tariffs on solar panels/cells imported from China since 2012 (Wingfield 2012), which means the price competitive advantage of the Chinese solar panel industry has been largely lost. Following the introduction of these measures in the United States, in September 2012, the European Union launched an anti-dumping investigation into China's solar panel exports to Europe (EC 2012). Compared with the United States, the EU anti-dumping investigation has a much greater influence on China's solar panel industry because the EU is the largest PV export market for China (accounting for 80%).

Against this background, some scholars have pointed out that China's RE development has entered a period of adjustment and RE development should focus more on renewable power quality rather than installation quantity. In particular, there should be efforts to solve the grid-connection and curtailment problems. The strategic position of RE has not been weakened by these domestic and international adversities due in part to ambitious RE development targets. According to the 12th FYP for RE Development, electricity generation from renewable sources should account for more than 20% of total electricity generation by 2015 (NEA and CNREC 2012). The 2015 target for the on-land wind energy is set as 100 GW, and according to the China Wind Power Outlook 2012, on-land wind power can reach 200-300 GW by 2020 and more than 400 GW by 2030 (CREIA et al. 2012). In the 12th FYP for RE Development, the installations of solar PV power systems will reach 21 GW by 2015 and 50 GW by 2020 (NEA 8/2012; Wang, Z. et al. 2012). If the policy implementation of this target can be fostered effectively, China will become the largest solar PV generation nation and provide a promising domestic market for digesting the overcapacity in solar panel products.

There are several approaches to analyze rapid renewable energy development in China. It is usually understood as a domestic energy issue related to energy security, environmental protection and economic development concerns. However, the mere domestic approach oversimplifies the strong resistance from the conventional energy forces in the carbon lock-in structure. This book tends to treat China's participation in the climate change regime as a significant external impetus to influence the interaction of stakeholders in the renewable energy development. The *main research question* is:

Why is China promoting such strong renewable energy development and how has it become a world leader in renewable energy development in the time span of one decade? Why and how does China's participation in the climate change regime exert an influence on domestic energy policy change towards renewable energy?

Three further sets of questions are raised:

(1) Why has China's participation in the climate change regime mattered for domestic RE policy change? How has China's participation in the climate change regime influenced the interaction of domestic stakeholders in the energy system?

(2) How could pro-RE actors strengthen their position in a system which is dominated by coal and increase their ability to influence RE policy change? How have socialization processes contributed to the capacity development of the pro-RE coalition?

(3) How have pro-RE actors taken advantage of international and domestic resources to compete with conventional energy forces and promote their own goals?

1.2 Renewable energy policy change as the dependent variable

No doubt, rapid RE development cannot occur without strong renewable energy policy support and a favorable social-political context. Compared with traditional fossil fuels like coal, oil and natural gas, renewable energies do not have competitive advantages in production costs nor are they a stable source for the electricity supply, especially in the initial stages of their development. Favorable governmental support is an indispensable precondition for the promotion of RE projects and the acceleration of technological innovation. The gradual RE policy changes of the past decade have provided a strong basis for the rapid growth of RE. What is of special interest is that these changes have occurred despite the dominance of conventional interest groups in the still heavily coal-dominated energy sector. There has been a continuous process of RE policy change from the introduction of a tendering system and the development of a feed-in tariff (FIT) system①, to the introduction of the Renewable Portfolio Standard (RPS) / quota system②. Behind these policy changes, there has been competition between the pro-RE actors and the conventional energy forces in the RE policy-making process.

As mentioned above, China is a late-comer in RE development. Before the 1990s, RE (especially biogas, solar stove and solar water heating) was only regarded as a supplementary measure for energy development in rural areas. The strategic development of large-scale modernized RE projects (like wind power, solar PV and bio-fuels) did not get much attention for quite a long time. After China became an oil net importer in 1993, energy diversification gained more weight and RE development became more important. In 1995, the Guideline for the Development of New Energy and RE in China (1996-2010) was issued; however, there was no specific governmental institution responsible for designing the concrete policy instruments to promote RE. In 2003, China issued the Wind Power Concession Program (NDRC 2003) following the example of the former U. K. tendering policy model, in order to create incentives for international and domestic investors to develop large-scale wind farms and to encourage a reduction in the price of wind power through the government-overseen competitive processes. In order to avoid vicious competition and guarantee a profitable space for renewable production, China learned from Germany and introduced the feed-in tariff model. This was done with the issuing of the RE Law in 2005. The facts have shown that the RE Law has played a significant role in promoting rapid RE development. There was a five-year long boom in RE growth from 2006-2010.

As a result of problems tied to RE development, like grid-connection, wind power curtailment, grid disconnection accidents and loopholes in policy coordination, there has been increasing voice for amending the RE Law and exerting more pressure on the state-owned grid corporations. Due to the efforts of pro-RE actors in China, the U. S. model of the Renewable Portfolio Standard (RPS) / quota system policy has been gradually introduced to combine with the FIT. This tendency has been manifested in the RE Law Amendment in 2009 and has been further embodied in the 12th FYP for RE Development since 2011. Still not satisfied with the abstract clauses in

① The feed-in tariff (FIT) refers to a price-based policy which offers RE developers a guaranteed power sales price, coupled with a purchase obligation (a guaranteed market) by electric utilities in relatively long time (such as 20 years).

② The Renewable Portfolio Standard (RPS) or the quota system is defined as a market-based mechanism that generally places an obligation on electricity supply companies to produce a specified fraction of their electricity from RE sources.

the RE Law Amendment in 2009, pro-RE actors backed the Regulation for Management of Renewable Power Quota (Exposure Draft), which was released in May 2012. In this draft, it can be seen that the renewable power quotas, as mandatory quantitative indicators for grid companies, power companies and provincial governments, have equipped the RE Law Amendment with "new teeth". Since RE quotas challenge more conventional interest groups in the energy sector, this policy change needs strong support in the form of supportive governmental regulations.

The goal of this book is to investigate how the capacity of the pro-RE coalition was enhanced through what could be called a climate change socialization process. What is clear is that the RE coalition has gained more political resources to compete with the conventional energy forces and has used this to promote RE policy change and rapid RE development. The *dependent variable* in this book is RE policy change in China. Through combining insights from socialization theory and the advocacy coalition framework, I aim to provide a systemic theoretical framework for exploring the dynamics behind RE policy change in China.

1.3 The role of the climate change regime in the renewable energy policy change

Before exploring the role of the climate change regime in domestic RE policy change, it is necessary to examine the domestic factors responsible for RE development. Energy security and economic development concerns are two main driving forces behind RE development at the domestic level. These factors are explored below.

Energy security concerns at the domestic level

Although China's abundant reserves of coal and modest reserves of petroleum have provided the foundation for the country's energy consumption, they have never been able to fully satisfy the country's total energy demands. In recent years China has been forced to import ever larger amounts of coal and oil from abroad. China has expanded its coal imports, becoming the largest coal-importer in the world in 2009. This has been due to the rapid growth in energy consumption. The Chinese government has been paying more attention to national strategic oil reserves and oil diplomacy (Finance Eastday 2011), and has encouraged state-owned enterprises to search for oil in Africa, Latin America, the Middle East and Central Asia. Although the supply-biased energy security is still dominant, the increasing energy dependency challenges the government's control of the fuel supply and causes uncertainties in terms of energy security. Chinese leaders have realized that low energy efficiency and the huge environmental pollution problems caused by fossil fuel consumption have led to many negative effects on the energy system. Therefore, promoting RE is regarded as a kind of national energy strategy to guarantee long-term energy security. Although energy security concerns are an indispensable part of the explanation behind RE development, the strong resistance from the conventional interest groups in the energy sector cannot be ignored. The bottlenecks in wind power development, such as grid-connection and curtailment problems are mainly due to the resistance of powerful state-owned grid enterprises. According to the statistics of CWEA, the percentage of off-grid wind power is still quite high in 2010 (around 20%-30%) due to the grid-connection problem (CREIA et al. 2012). The top 10 provinces for wind generation have lost over 17% wind power production due to the wind curtailment problem in 2011 (CREIA et al. 2012).① In the bio-fuel production field, the problem is similar: it is hard for biofuels to enter the fuel transportation and fuel sales system. This is mainly due to the strong hindrance from the conventional interest groups in the state-owned oil enterprises. The Exposure Draft of Energy Law was issued in 2007 for social-wide discussion. However, after five years, the Energy Law was still not ratified. One significant reason behind this phenomenon is that conventional energy interest groups refused to put much priority on RE development and electricity market reform in the Energy Law. As a result, it is too rash to conclude that only energy security concerns led to China's RE rapid development.

Apart from the resistance from conventional coal, oil and grid state-owned enterprises to RE development, nuclear power companies cannot be overlooked. In China, nuclear power is treated as a significant clean energy that can help guarantee energy security and reduce the pressure of GHG emission reductions. Powerful nuclear supporters have lobbied the paramount leaders, arguing that investing in the development of nuclear power has more strategic importance than developing RE, since the former is more steady and efficient. However, Japan's Fukushima nuclear accident in March 2011 was a warning signal to the rapid growth tendency of nuclear power. Under current plans nuclear capacity is to be increased by an additional 40 GW from the current level of 10 GW. Due to the shocking effect of the Fukushima disaster, national leaders called for a pause to the construction of nuclear projects in order to check the security situation. They also attached a higher priority on RE development.

① Grid curtailment means a reduction of grid companies in the scheduled capacity of RE power delivery. See GWEC 2012.

Economic growth concerns at the domestic level

Some scholars argue that the development of the RE industry may represent just another example of deliberate efforts by the government to grow an industry facilitating national economic growth (Givner 2010: 26). Scholars have amassed considerable evidence that China often promotes particular RE industries in pursuit of economic and developmental goals, so that positive environmental outcomes may just be welcome byproducts of economic growth oriented policies rather than policy goals in and of themselves (Givner 2010: 28-29). Furthermore, the RE industry will provide more employment opportunities. Especially at the local level, some local governments rush to develop this "Green Gold" in order to promote local economic development and earn more credits for their political performance. Some local governments only care for the economic and development goals when developing local solar-panel industries, and do not show concern for the serious environmental pollution from the poly-silicon production process. However, this developmental approach fails to explain where the "green windfall" comes from. The introduction of feed-in tariff policy embodied in the RE Law has provided sufficient profitable space for the RE industry, and provides great dynamics for the "green rush". Therefore, this approach does not give a causal chain to explain RE policy change: what are the other factors responsible for the emergence of the RE Law and the RE Law Amendment? As has been argued by Boyd, "the motivations for China's recent energy and climate change policies are far more complex than the stereotypical view of China as a country bent on the pursuit of economic growth at all costs would allow" (Boyd 2012b: 2).

The climate change regime as a significant external impetus for RE policy change

Some scholars argue that major policy initiatives, such as China's huge investment in renewable energy, are primarily motivated by domestic political and economic concerns and only peripherally related to international pressures tied to the climate change negotiations. Due to its political nature, "the Chinese government is eminently capable of actively developing particular industries for political and economic goals entirely independent of foreign influence" (Givner 2010: 26). On the one hand, clearly domestic factors, especially energy security concerns, are responsible for China's rapid RE development; on the other hand, it must be recognized that external pressures tied to the climate change regime have played a significant role in breaking the carbon lock-in energy structure. Over time, pro-renewable energy actors have become stronger. This can be seen in their institutional anchoring and the reallocation in their direction of political resources. They now have a louder voice in the policy-making system when competing with conventional energy forces.

After two decades of efforts, climate change is ranked as a "top global green issue" in the international system and climate change mitigation is a truly global affair that has won worldwide recognition. The influence of the climate change regime, which mainly refers to the UN legal regimes of the United Nations Framework Convention on Climate Change (UNFCCC), the Kyoto Protocol, and the GEF, has expanded or spilled over onto the agenda of many other international institutions, such as the G20, the G8 +5, the World Bank, the UNDP, as well as bilateral and multilateral international cooperation initiatives, such as the EU-China Climate Partnership and the Sino-US Cooperative Framework on Environment and Energy. Keohane and Victor define this kind of agenda-based network as "climate change regime complex" (Keohane and Victor 2010: 2). The salience of climate change in more international institutions has further enhanced the influence of this "top green issue" in the international community.

China took part in the United Nations Conference on the Environment and Development (UNCED) and ratified the UNFCCC in 1992, and then issued Local Agenda 21 of China in 1994. This marked a milestone in China's participation in the climate change regime (Harris and Yu 2005).① Due to the country's rapidly increasing GHG emissions linked to the country's rapid economic growth, China has been confronted with increasing international pressure. This has been especially true since China surpassed the U. S. to become the biggest emitter in 2007. Heggelund points out that China is a key figure in the international climate regime for two reasons: *first*, considering that it is responsible for the largest share of GHG emissions, any global GHG emission reduction agreement cannot achieve its goal without China's contribution; *second*, as the largest developing country in the world with an influential voice in the UN Security Council, "its status and influence in the G-77 of Third World states give China prominence in climate negotiations" (Heggelund 2007). According to the latest data from PBL Netherlands Environmental Assessment Agency, China's emission share in 2011 is 29%, which is much higher than the U. S. (16%) and the EU (11%) (Olivier et al. 2012: 6). The spilt among the G-77 Group has grown. Emission reduction pressures on major developing countries are not only coming from developed countries but also from other developing and the least developed countries. Under great international pressure, China's leaders have begun to admit that a more flexible stance needs to be taken and that conventional means

---

① Harris and Yu (2005: 50) think Local Agenda 21 of China has included climate change as one priority for attention, and it served as one guide to China's national economic and social development plans for the period 1996-2005.

alone are not enough. China's leaders recognize that if they do not take action, the country's national reputation and soft power will be greatly damaged.

China has acted in a pragmatic way in the climate change negotiations, on the one hand refusing to take on any legally binding GHG emission reduction responsibility but on the other, taking some domestic voluntary low-carbon initiatives to reduce the international pressure and keep a benign national image. Harris argues that even though China has carried out many domestic policies related to climate change (energy efficiency and alternative energy production), "those policies are driven by objectives other than fighting climate change, such as energy security, technology innovation to enhance economic competitiveness, and profiting from the Kyoto Protocol's Clean Development Mechanism" (Harris 2011a: 8). Nevertheless, even from this critical realist perspective, it cannot be denied that RE development has been facilitated by international resources (fund and technological transfer, knowledge and best practices) provided by the climate change regime.

The increasing salience of "climate politics" has provided external dynamics and formed a context of carbon constraints on domestic policy making. There is a close relationship between climate change policy and energy policy. This has especially been the case since the NDRC (the most powerful governmental agency in energy regulation) took over the main responsibility for climate change negotiations in 1998. The voluntary commitment (40%-45% carbon-intensity reduction and 15% non-fossil energy consumption by 2020) made by China before the 2009 Copenhagen Conference officially combined a RE development target with the climate mitigation mission (Carraro and Tavoni 2010). Furthermore both the GHG emission reduction target and RE development target have been devolved onto the provincial level. These "green indicators" have gradually been included into the performance assessment system for local officials. Also significant is that the NDRC issued the Notice on Carbon Trading Trials Scheme in October 2011 to initiate a group of municipal and provincial-level carbon-trading trials (Wang, T. 2012). During the lifetime of the 12th Five-Year Plan (that is, by 2015), a cap-and-trade mechanism is to be introduced nationwide. In May 2012, China published the *Climate Change Law* (*Exposure Draft*) after a three-year effort (Point Carbon 2012). The main goal of this first climate change law is to provide a legislative position for three key mechanisms: a coal consumption cap, a domestic carbon trading system and a carbon tax, and to assign tasks and obligations to both governmental institutions and corporations (China News 2012a; China News 2012c). The efforts to promote a carbon trading system provide a strong dynamic for the implementation of the RPS/quota system and subsequently should help guarantee rapid RE development in the long run. In June

2015, China mapped out how it will try and peak greenhouse emissions by 2030 or before and submitted its *Intended Nationally Determined Contribution* (*INDC*) document to UN: China planned to reduce the carbon intensity of its economy 60%-65% per unit of GDP by 2030, compared with 2005 levels, and reiterated a previously-announced aim that RE should make up 20% of its primary energy supply by the same date (China dialogue 2015). Shi Pengfei, the vice chairman of the Chinese Wind Energy Association, has pointed out that "meeting the international climate change mitigation commitments is a main driver of China's RE policy in the next decade" (China News 2012d). Andrews-Speed points out that "there is increasing evidence that the top leaders do indeed take low-carbon transition seriously, for two reasons: first, because large areas of China are projected to suffer from the effects of climate change; and, second, because the external pressure on China to pursue low-carbon policies can be used by the government to push forward efforts to restructure the economy" (Andrews-Speed 2012: 220), such as developing the RE industry.

1.4 Strengthening of the pro-renewable energy coalition and main assumption

Although I have put emphasis on the role of the climate change regime in domestic RE policy change, the question here is how to bridge the international and domestic sources of RE policy change. It is necessary to go deeper into the sub-national level to analyze key actors who can exert influence in the RE policy-making process. In China, the authoritarian system is not a monolithic decision-making system; instead, different interest groups in various policy subsystems try to influence the politburo. The final decision-making process on key strategic issues is based on a consensus building mechanism among the seven to nine members of the politburo standing committee. A "fragmented authoritarianism framework" is usually applied to illustrate the rules of the policy-making process (Mertha 2009: 995). It also should be noted that there has been an increasing pluralization of the policy-making process and the barriers to entry have been lowered. Certain actors, such as formerly marginalized bureaucratic institutions, newly-established governmental institutions, policy research institutions, academic institutes, industry associations, non-governmental organizations, and media power, now have a more favorable political opportunity structure to show their views and provide policy proposals in the policy-making system (Mertha 2009: 995). The goal of this book is to investigate how the strengthening of the pro-RE coalition occurred as a result of climate change socialization and how they worked to promote RE policy change.

The advocacy coalition framework (ACF) which was put forward by Sabatier and Jenkins-Smith (Sabatier 1988; Sabatier 2007; Sabatier and Jenkins-Smith 1993a) provides a systematic theoretical approach for exploring how policy change takes place through the interaction of different stakeholders in a specific policy domain. According to Sabatier, the *advocacy coalition* refers to "people from various governmental and private organizations who share a set of same normative and causal values in their belief systems and who often act in concert" within a certain subsystem facing the same policy problem (Sabatier and Jenkins-Smith 1993a: 18). They contend that one subsystem usually contains two or more advocacy coalitions and policy change depends on the competition process between different advocacy coalitions. In other words, an advocacy coalition is a set of governmental and societal actors with the same causal values who promote policy change, rather than a specific governmental institution.

Based on the ACF framework of Sabatier, the *pro-renewable energy coalition* in this book is defined as a set of actors from various governmental institutions and societal actors who share a set of similar normative and causal values in RE development and who often act in concert to promote RE policy change. To be more specific, the pro-RE coalition set includes paramount leaders and bureaucratic actors supporting RE development, especially newly established governmental institutions responsible for RE regulation, RE research institutions and think tanks, key RE policy scholars and experts, RE industry associations, and related media, especially professional RE websites. These actors are "policy entrepreneurs" and "policy supervisors" in RE development. They have challenged the old energy pattern dominated by fossil fuel, provided ideas about RE policy instruments and RE development proposals to key energy regulatory actors, and exposed loopholes in the current RE development process. As a result of its strengthened power and the increased pluralization of China's "fragmented authoritarianism", the pro-RE coalition has gained more voice in the energy policy-making system.

Compared with conventional vested interests, the pro-RE coalition is still in a comparatively weaker position. The conventional energy coalition tries to control political resource allocation and constrain the resource accessibility of the pro-RE coalition. As a minor coalition in the subsystem, the capacity buildup of the pro-RE coalition is of great importance. Sabatier points out that the capability of an advocacy coalition to promote policy change depends upon its resources, which include "money, expertise, number of supporters, and legal authority" (Sabatier and Jenkins-Smith 1993b: 29). The growth of the pro-RE coalition is reflected in several ways: *first*, they have been able to gain more resources; *second*, this has been done through various enlargements of pro-RE agencies, like the newly established governmental institutions, governmental RE research agencies and societal RE academic institutions, and the RE industry associations; *third*, through the degree of involvement of pro-RE agencies in the policy-making process and upgrading hierarchy level of pro-RE agencies in the bureaucratic system.

Through combining socialization theory and the advocacy coalition framework (ACF), this book aims to explore how international sources of pressure emanating from the climate change regime have influenced pro-RE coalition building through role playing① and strategic calculation② mechanisms (leading to the institutional anchoring and resource reallocation), and how the strengthening of the pro-RE coalition promotes RE policy change through policy-oriented learning and argumentative persuasion. Due to the external dynamics from the climate change regime, more new RE supportive agencies have come into being and meanwhile they have gained more political resources to increase their voice in the RE policy-making process. According to the line of argumentation made above, the *main assumption of this book* is that the strengthening of the pro-renewable energy coalition in the socialization process of climate change (by means of institutional anchoring and resource reallocation) and its competition with the conventional energy forces in the renewable energy policy-making process are significant dynamics to promote RE policy change and rapid RE development.

1.5 Plan of this book

The main goal of this book is to combine socialization theory with the advocacy coalition framework (ACF) to explore how the pro-RE coalition was strengthened through the socialization process that took place through participation in the climate change negotiations and analyze how the strengthening of the pro-RE coalition made it possible for it to compete with the status quo forces to promote RE policy change and rapid RE development.

---

① "Role playing", a concept introduced by Checkel means "non-calculative behavioral adaptation of agents due to the bounded rationality, but without reflective internalization process" (Checkel 2005: 810). This concept is similar to "mimicking" proposed by Alastair I. Johnston, which refers to "a pro-group mechanism whereby a novice initially copies the habits, procedural rules—including discursive practices—of the group to navigate through an uncertain environment" (Johnston 2005: 1021-1022). See more details in Chapter 2.

② Checkel puts forward the concept of "strategic calculation" to describe that the dynamics behind the socialization process is from the agents' interest calculation (constraints and incentives) (Checkel 2005: 808). Johnston (2001) has enriched the concept by emphasizing social influence, which refers to "a class of micro-processes that elicit pro-norm behavior through the distribution of social rewards and punishments" (Johnston 2001: 499-501). See more details in Chapter 2.

The theoretical framework and critical arguments will be presented in the next chapter. The main aim of Chapter 2 is to construct a comprehensive theoretical framework to explain the strengthening of the capacity of the advocacy coalition. This is done by combining socialization theory and Sabatier's Advocacy Coalition Theory (ACF). Through strategic calculation and institutional anchoring, international sources can couple with domestic sources to promote institutional, procedural and discursive lock-in effects and resource reallocation among different domestic actors. Therefore, it is possible to interlink the ACF with the socialization theory to explore the strengthening of the pro-RE coalition and the ways it has taken advantage of both international and domestic resources to promote RE policy change by policy-oriented learning and argumentative persuasion.

Chapter 3 identifies the dependent variable. It focuses on concrete RE policy change and analyzes the main characteristics of the RE policy system. This chapter unfolds five developing stages of RE policy, from the early stage without a specific RE policy to the tendering policy (concession bidding projects) for wind power beginning in 2003. The issuing of the RE Law in 2005 symbolized the start for establishing a comprehensive RE policy system. In order to overcome grid-connection problems, the RE amendment was issued in 2009. The amendment introduced the Renewable Portfolio Standard (RPS)/quota system combined with the FIT. The amendment set new policies in place aiming to improve the effectiveness of the RE system.

In Chapters 4 and 5, the book explores China's participation in the climate change regime and analyzes how socialization tied to the issue of climate change had a strong influence in terms of the institutional anchoring and resource reallocation needed to support the growth of pro-RE actors at the domestic level. Chapter 4 focuses on the five-stage participation of China in the climate change regime. This is done with a process tracing over 20 years of history of Chinese participation in international climate change activities. This chapter also illustrates the changing interest cognition of China in its interactions with the international level and the implications thereof for domestic policy change. Chapter 5 first gives an overview of the bumpy path towards institutional reform in the energy sector and points out that the institution building of the energy sector is weak and dispersed. This chapter shows that despite the unfavorable context, the pro-RE coalition strengthened its capacity by means of institutional anchoring and resource reallocation as a result of climate change socialization. This chapter explores the two micro-processes involved in the climate change socialization process: role playing and interest calculation.

In Chapters 6 and 7, this book further identifies the pro-RE coalition and then analyzes the role of the strengthened pro-RE coalition in the RE policy change process.

Through specifying key governmental and societal actors in the RE policy-making system, Chapter 6 summarizes characteristics of the pro-RE coalition in China. Chapter 7 aims to investigate how the RE coalition competed with the conventional energy forces in the subsystem through policy-oriented learning and argumentative persuasion. This chapter focuses on RE policy changes made to begin in 2005, attempting to explain how the strengthened pro-RE coalition made efforts starting around 2009 to introduce the RE quota policy into the RE policy system in order to overcome the grid connection bottleneck and improve the current feed-in tariff policy.

Chapter 8 concludes the whole book. This chapter goes back to the research question to answer why China is promoting renewable energy development through integrating RE into energy policy change. It highlights the role of the pro-RE coalition in the RE policy-making system. Then this chapter re-examines the theoretical space for combining the socialization theory with the ACF and makes a summary of the main empirical findings of this book.

Chapter 2
Theoretical Framework

Two main research directions in the study of the interaction of international and domestic politics are the domestic sources of foreign policy-making and the international sources of domestic policy-making. Peter Gourevitch (1978) proposed the concept of "the reversed second image" to describe this process and called for more academic attention to the impact of international factors on the domestic policy-making process. In this chapter, the theoretical analysis is placed on the impact of the international realm and its influence on domestic policy change. Through combining socialization theory and the advocacy coalition framework (ACF), this book aims to explore how international material incentives, knowledge and social influence exert an influence on the ability of advocacy coalitions to strengthen their position by means of institutional anchoring and resource reallocation. It also looks at how advocacy coalitions can take advantage of international sources of material incentives, knowledge and social influence to compete with conventional coalitions and promote policy change in the policy-making system. Since the ACF has mainly been applied to western democratic countries, the last part of this chapter analyzes the general decision-making style of China's bureaucratic system and explores the applicability of this theoretical framework for China. The characteristics of "fragmented authoritarianism" mechanism and the increasing pluralization of China's policy-making process provide a basic political background to investigate the interaction and competition of different stakeholders in the renewable energy policy-making system under the influence of the climate change regime.

2.1 Socialization theory and bidirectional interaction

2.1.1 Definition of socialization and its implications for policy change

Socialization is an interdisciplinary concept that originated from linguistics, sociology and social psychology. It focuses on the interactions of individual and society, such as "in-group identity formation and compliance with group norms" (Johnston 2001: 488-489). Socialization is "the generic term used to refer to the processes by which the newcomer—the infant, rookie, or trainee, for example—becomes incorporated into organized patterns of interaction" (Stryker and Statham 1985). Therefore, at the individual level, the socialization process is regarded as a primary social mechanism that affects personal character and behavior. At the social level, the socialization process refers to the study of how the social actor conciliates/reconciles himself or herself to the collective life (Long and Hadden 1985: 39).

Along with research on international regimes and international institutions, socialization theory has become a main theoretic framework to study the influence of international factors on national behaviors (Bearce and Bondanella 2007; Checkel 2005; Feldman 1997; Flockhart 2004; Flockhart 2006; Goodman 2004; Goodman and Jinks 2004; Hooghe 2005; Ikenberry and Kupchan 1990; Johnston 2003; Li 2010; Qin 2007; Risse and Sikkink 1999; Schimmelfennig 2000; Schimmelfennig 2005; Williams 2010). Krasner provides a comprehensive definition of a regime: regimes "can be defined as sets of implicit or explicit principles, norms, rules, and decision-making procedures around which actors' expectations converge in a given area of international relations" (Krasner 1982: 186). ① During a state's compliance with an international regime, these international principles, rules and norms will find their way to the domestic level. The principles, rules and norms, which are embodied in international regimes, are usually treated as external source of ideas that can have an influence on the interactions of domestic actors.

Based on this, *socialization* refers to a process of "actors internalize[ing] norms, rules and standards of behavior by acting in social structures" (Zürn and Checkel 2005: 1045). Here there is a special interest in international institutions. This concept emphasizes "the socializing effects of international regimes on the individuals who

---

① Principles are beliefs of fact, causation, and rectitude. Norms are standards of behavior defined in terms of rights and obligations. Rules are specific prescriptions or proscriptions for action. Decision-making procedures are prevailing practices for making and implementing collective choice. See Krasner (1982: 186).

participate in them" (Checkel 2005: 808). Johnston (2001) proposes that "the socialization is aimed at creating membership in a society where the inter-subjective understandings of the society become taken for granted" (Johnston 2001: 494) and the internalization of the values, roles and understandings in a normative perspective is the core part of international socialization. As a result, under the social context of international regimes, "wherein member states interact on a regular and sustained basis, the socialization process leads state agents to endorse the expected ways of thinking, feeling and acting" (Li 2010: 351).

Socialization can be defined so as to allow for both sociological and rationalist accounts of norm adoption. In other words, it emphasizes not only the sociological process of regime norm compliance, but also pays attention to the rationalist approach, how the strategic calculation of external constraints as well as incentives promotes the transformation process from the "logic of consequence" (realist rational choice) to the "logic of appropriateness" (constructivist approach). During the socializing process, it is possible for states to reshape their interest preferences and take on new identities, and ultimately "change their behaviors to conform to their new roles and the norms of the system" (Li 2010: 351).

Policy change is a main research field of domestic politics studies. The main aim of policy change theories is to identify the key actors who are involved in the policy-making process and explain the dynamics that influence policy change approaches. Socialization has constructed a bridge to link the domestic and international levels. Due to the internalization of international rules, procedures and norms, an international regime can be gradually integrated into domestic policy operational procedures. Furthermore, along with the rapid development of economic and political globalization, as well as the increasing emergence of trans-boundary problems (such as the climate change and the global financial crisis), international regimes have played an increasingly significant role in multi-level governance. Confronted with trans-boundary problems, international institutional arrangements have advantages in mobilizing global resources (like the role of the World Bank and the GEF in the climate change regime); assisting in the convergence of innovative policies, best practices and know-how from the pioneering countries; and promoting the diffusion of new principles, rules and norms to member states.

Judging the effectiveness of international regimes depends not only on the international agreement-reaching process, but also on implementation at the domestic level. In order to guarantee the domestic implementation of international agreements, the international regimes will provide some incentives or exert some constraints to the member states to accelerate the policy internalization process. Meanwhile, once national leaders have made serious commitments to the international regimes, then the international factors might be integrated into the domestic policy-making consideration to a certain degree. International sources of material incentives and social punishments can aid in solving some domestic problems. Through the two-level interaction policy internalization may become more salient, which might gradually lead to national interest preference reshaping and norm internalization. In short, through the input of international sources (such as material incentives and constraints, as well as non-material principles, rules and norms), the international regime has a potential to influence domestic policy change.

2.1.2 Three micro-processes of socialization

Alastair I. Johnston points out that it is impossible to treat socialization as a homogenization process and that there are several degrees of norm internalization because "not all actors are always exposed to exactly the same configuration of social pressures, nor do they enter into a social interaction with exactly the same prior identifications" (Johnston 2001: 494-496). As a result, there is a "continuous spectrum" in the socialization process, in which two kinds of pro-social behaviors can be treated as two ends of a spectrum. At the first end of the spectrum should be pro-strategy/pro-instrument behavior following the "logic of consequences". In this interest calculation logic, behavioral change is due to the "material rewards and punishments" that are introduced "exogenously by the international regimes" (Johnston 2001: 487). At the opposite end of the spectrum should be pro-norm behavior following the "logic of appropriateness". It relates to endogenously cognitive reconstruction and interest preference reshaping. Therefore, the core questions are how to interlink the two ends and are there any other mechanisms between the rational-choice end and the constructivist end?

Jeffrey T. Checkel (2001, 2005) and Alastair I. Johnston (2003, 2008) have contributed a lot to the micro-processes of socialization studies. They both aim to build a theoretical bridge between the rational-choice approach and the constructivist approach of socialization and to explore the concrete process of socialization—the socialization micro-process (Johnston 2008: 18). ① The three micro-processes which are put forward by Checkel are strategic calculation, role playing and normative suasion (Checkel 2005). In his book *Social States: China in International Institutions, 1980-*

① According to Jeffrey T. Checkel (2001, 2005) and Alastair I. Johnston (2003, 2008), the micro-process means the concrete process of socialization and the linking of the "logic of consequences" and the "logic of appropriateness".

2000, Alastair I. Johnston also identifies three kinds of socialization micro-processes: social influence, mimicking and persuasion. There is a kind of comparability between the two researchers; therefore a table is presented to make the comparison clear (see Table 2.1). However in each comparable micro-process column, the focus is a little different.

Table 2.1 Three micro-processes of socialization

Scholars	Rational-choice/ Instrumental compliance	<——————> The transition process	Constructivist Norm-driven compliance
Checkel (2005)	strategic calculation (material incentives and rewards)	role playing (non-calculative behavior adaptation without reflective internalization)	normative suasion (reflective internalization and new normative understandings)
Johnston (2002, 2008)	social influence (social rewards and punishments; public conformity without private acceptances)	mimicking (copying the behavioral norms of the group to navigate through an uncertain environment)	persuasion (public conformity with private acceptances, reshaping preferences)
Logics	Logic of consequences	<——————>	Logic of appropriateness

Sources: The author compiled the table based on the analysis in Checkel (2005) and Johnston (2002, 2008).

(1) *A comparison of strategic calculation and social influence*

The materialization of international constraints/punishments and incentives/rewards will usually promote the initial behavioral adaptation of states, which could be treated as a stimulus for instrumental pro-social processes. Checkel puts forward the concept of "*strategic calculation*" to describe this level of internationalization (Checkel 2005: 808).① In this paradigm, the dynamics behind the socialization process come from the agent's material calculation (constraints and incentives) and intentions to maximize given interests. Generally speaking, once the nation state joins an international regime, it will be affected to some degree by the institutional structure.

① Checkel (2005) proposes two kinds of internalization: the adoption of new roles (Type I internalization) and changes in values and interests (Type II internalization). See Checkel (2005).

The first-stage/initial compliance degree partially depends on the strength of international pressure (like coercion, sanctions, reputation considering), or the amount of international incentives (international aid, technological support, and training projects).

During theoretical argumentations between rationalists and constructivists, the former also absorb some sociological and psychological factors into the instrumental calculation, such as reputation, honor, belonging, shaming, and uncomforting situations. That is to say, in addition to the pursuit of material incentives in the socialization process, there is also some desire to "improve national status", that is to boost the national profile and build a positive image, enhance national strength and influence; and decrease international pressure, to avoid "face-losing" and diplomatic isolation.

Johnston (2001) titles this micro-process as "*social influence*": "a class of micro-processes that elicit pro-norm behavior through the distribution of social rewards and punishments...[It] is an actor's conformity with the position advocated by a group as a result of real or imagined group pressure" (Johnston 2001: 499-501). Social rewards include "psychological well-being, status, a sense of belonging, and a sense of well-being derived from conformity with role expectations" (Johnston 2001: 499) and social punishments refer to "shaming, shunning, exclusion, and demeaning, or dissonance derived from actions inconsistent with role and identity" (Johnston 2001: 499). Johnston proposes three reasons for social influence. The first occurs when in the absence of material side-payments or threats of sanctions, that is without material incentives or punishments, states still want to "make commitments to participate and join power-constraining institutions" (Johnston 2001: 506). The second is that of a pro-social behavior due to "image benefits, diffuse reputation benefits, and opprobrium costs" (Johnston 2001: 506). The third is when non-commitment behavior leads to a highly international isolating status, where a state is trapped as a distinct minority. This means "being isolated from the cooperating audience or reference group" (Johnston 2001: 506). Under social influence, states may make commitments to international regimes, even without material incentives or coercion, in order to "maximize status, honor, and prestige—diffuse reputation or image—and the desire to avoid a loss of status, shaming, or humiliation and other social sanctions" (Johnston 2001: 506). Here, the national status reflects others' expectations for pro-norm behavior or competent performance (Lovaglia 1995: 402).

In short, based on the interest calculation logic, incentives and rewards can be material (financial assistance, trade opportunities) as well as social (status, shaming), and "one might expect both to play some role in the socialization process"

(Checkel 2005: 809). National interest analysis should not only be constrained to the visible material dimension, but also extended to the social influence dimension, which is also of great importance.

(2) *A comparison of role playing and mimicking*

"*Role playing*" is a concept introduced by Checkel which means non-calculative behavioral adaptation of agents due to bounded rationality, but without a reflective internalization process. (Checkel 2005: 810)

> Agents are viewed as boundedly rational. It is not possible for them to attend to everything simultaneously or to calculate carefully the costs and benefits of alternative courses of action... [It] involves non-calculative behavioral adaptation. (Checkel 2005: 810)

Role playing presupposes "an agent's passive, noncalculative acceptance of new roles evoked by certain environmental triggers" (Checkel 2005: 812). The agent cannot calculate the costs and benefits of everything. As Checkel argues "organizational and group environments provide simplifying shortcuts leading to the enactment of particular role conceptions" (Checkel 2005: 812). In other words, the non-calculative behavioral adaptation of the agent is triggered by "automaticity". "[A]gents adopt certain roles because they are appropriate in that particular setting. However, no process of reflective internalization driven by communicative processes has occurred." (Checkel 2005: 810)

"*Mimicking*" proposed by Alastair I. Johnston is also a transition micro-process linking the two ends of international socialization. It refers to "a pro-group mechanism whereby a novice initially copies the habits, procedural rules—including discursive practices—of the group to navigate through an uncertain environment" (Johnston 2005: 1021-1022). In other words, as novices in an institution, due to bounded rationality, they copy or "borrow models of organizing and talking about issues that are central to the group" in order to enter into the strange environment smoothly (Johnston 2008: 47). However, this public conformity process is without private acceptance and in-depth norm internalization. The hidden logic is "I will do X because everyone seems to be doing X and surviving. So, until I know better, X is what I will do" (Johnston 2008: Preface).

Both "role playing" and "mimicking" emphasize the non-calculative adaptation behavior decoupled from interest calculation. The agent only copies or follows others in order to fit himself or herself quickly into the new environment. This kind of non-calculative behavioral adaptation will lead to institutional, procedural and discursive lock-in effects, which will be analyzed in Section 2.3.1.

(3) *A comparison of normative suasion and persuasion*

Normative suasion means that "agents actively and reflectively internalize new understandings of appropriateness" with the logic that "this is the right thing to do even though I didn't use to think so" (Checkel 2005: 812). In other words, this micro-process emphasizes that due to bounded rationality, the social agents cannot calculate costs and benefits and maximize their interests in any situation. During social communication, it is possible for these agents to "present arguments and try to persuade and convince each other, and meanwhile their interests and preferences are open for redefinition" (Checkel 2005: 811).

Persuasion refers to a "micro-process whereby novices are convinced through a process of cognition that particular norms, values, and causal understandings are correct and ought to be operative in their own behavior" (Johnston 2008: Preface). Different from the instrumental adoption behavior based on cost-benefit calculation, in this stage, "pro-norm behavior... is so deeply internalized as to be unquestioned, taken for granted" (Johnston 2001: 492). Successful persuasion could cut down the gap and distance between actors' basic causal and affective understandings. Persuasion may eventually result in a homogenization process of interests and preferences, which involves agents actively and reflectively internalizing new normative understandings and "changing minds, opinions, and attitudes about causality and affect (identity)" (Johnston 2001: 496).

In sum, both normative suasion put forward by Checkel and persuasion identified by Johnston absorb the essence of communication theory (like Habermasian social theory). "Through social communication, especially presenting argument and persuasive fact, in the absence of overtly material or mental coercion, the agent's perceptions, attitudes, beliefs and motivations are finally convinced to change." (Johnston 2001: 496) Both of them put emphasis on the pro-norm behavior (in the logic of appropriateness). Actors act based on principles of serious deliberative argument (convincing others during their communicative interaction). The socializing agency does not lecture (teaching forcedly) or demand (asking for strongly) but rather uses deliberative argumentation.

2.1.3 Bi-directional interaction and the active role of states in socialization

In the socialization process based on the logics of appropriateness, there is a significant argument about the passive approach (structure-centered) or active approach (agent-centered) of one state internalizing a norm. In the normative suasion research, Checkel makes a distinction between "*manipulative persuasion*" and "*argumentative persuasion*". The former is "asocial and lacking in interaction" under external pressure, while the latter is "a social process of interaction that involves changing attitudes about cause and effect in the absence of overt coercion" (Checkel 2001: 562). Checkel refuses to treat the state as a "passive receiver" in interaction with international institutions. He criticizes the unidirectional-oriented "norm teaching" model put forward by Martha Finnemore (1993). Finnemore emphasizes the "teaching mission" of international organizations as norm principals (rather than agents) in the international system as they try to persuade states to comply with new norms and supply organizational innovations from outside (Finnemore 1993: 592). According to Finnemore's logic, the UNESCO bureaucrats "teach" national civil servants, who then comply with the UNESCO's normative prescriptions (Finnemore 1993). In other words, the international organizations and networks played a "teaching or guiding/supervising" role to generate pressures for compliance by state decision makers. In this process, the "leverage effect of critical mass" is a related and important mechanism. ①

Checkel argues that although the "norm teaching" model also mentions that "learning drives compliance", in the case study of the UNESCO, this "external force driven" learning was devoid of interaction (Checkel 2001: 561). Different from unidirectional "manipulative persuasion", the "argumentative persuasion" process puts an emphasis on "attempts of a communicator to induce a change in the belief, attitude, or behavior of another person... through the transmission of a message in a context in which the persuadee has some degree of free choice" (Checkel 2001: 562). Therefore, during the socialization process, the state is also an active actor and has its choice to accept the international norms. The relation between the persuading agency and the persuadee is a bi-directional oriented interaction.

Johnston (2008) also puts emphasis on the "subjective initiative" of the persuadee in the process of persuasion. Since the persuadee is in a core position to "weigh the evidence, puzzles through counter-attitudinal arguments, and then comes to conclusions different from those he/she began with" (Johnston 2008: 156). He concludes three preconditions for effective persuasion: the actors engage in a high-intensity process of cognition, reflection, and argumentation about the content of new information; the actor is persuaded because of his/her affect relationship to the

---

① Finnemore and Sikkink (1998) put forward the "norm life cycle" model to show three stages of international norm diffusion: the first stage is "norm emergence"; the second stage involves broad norm acceptance (norm cascade), and the third stage is norm internalization. This model puts emphasis on structural influence. Once a critical mass of relevant state actors adopt the norm other countries will follow and accept the norm in order to maintain the legitimate position in the international community. See Finnemore and Sikkink (1998: 888).

persuader (like thinking the persuading agent is authoritative and convincing); the characteristics of the persuadee himself (like the strength of existing attitudes, to what appears to be a deeply internalized desire to avoid appearing inconsistent). In sum, it is the choice of the persuadee to finally accept the arguments from the persuading agent or not. Although the communicative frequency, argumentative skill and the authoritativeness of the persuading agent are the key factors to influence the persuasion effectiveness, the characteristics of the persuadee himself and interest cognition of the persuadee also cannot be underestimated.

Therefore, both Checkel and Johnston put emphasis on the active behavior of the agent in the socialization process (rather than on a passive receiver). In international relations, this can explain why there are such different performances of member states in the same international regime. Why do some member states comply more than others? Following their logic, domestic structures and actors should be included in theorizing about socialization processes. Taking part in international institutions and bargaining to reach an international agreement are only the first steps in the socialization process. The next step is related to domestic policy-making, domestic policy change and policy implementation on certain policy issues. The domestic structure and interaction among different stakeholders are the key factors to deciding the effectiveness of the socialization process. In short, the socialization process is not a unidirectional input process; instead, it is a bi-directional interaction process. The domestic structural context (such as domestic political agenda-setting, interest preference and stakeholders' games) and the domestic salience of the international rule finally decide which international rules or norms will influence state behavior (Cortell and Davis Jr. 1996: 451).

2.2 Interlinking the socialization process with domestic advocacy coalition building

2.2.1 The filtration effect of the domestic structures and policy coalition building

In research on socialization, the filtration effect of domestic structures has gained much attention. The literature has examined why there are different performances of norm internalization in different countries although the situational factors are similar. Many scholars tend to research how different domestic structures may hinder or promote norms reaching agents within a domestic environment or why similar states respond differently to the same international conditions and constraints (Cortell and Davis Jr. 1996; Cortell and Davis Jr. 2000; Katzenstein 1976; Risse-Kappen 1991; Risse-Kappen 1994; Risse-Kappen 1995b). When international rules, norms and principles penetrate a state, the domestic structural context will play a filtering role that influences the internalization process. Therefore, the domestic salience or legitimacy of the norms and rules depends on the domestic political structures and political preference of key governmental actors. Domestic political structures are "important because they condition access to policy-making fora and privilege certain actors in policy debates", so not all international rules and norms will resonate in domestic debates (Cortell and Davis Jr. 1996: 67-69).

Cortell and Davis Jr. refer to domestic structures as "the organization of decision-making authority and to the pattern of state-societal relation" (Cortell and Davis Jr. 1996: 454). Meanwhile, they put emphasis on the concept of "cultural match", which means the consistency degree of international institutions with the domestic discourse, legal system and bureaucratic rules. There are four pathways to interlink the two-level interaction: the national political rhetoric, the material interests of domestic actors, domestic political institutions, and socializing forces (Cortell and Davis Jr. 2000: 73). It is the domestic political structure and domestic interest that decide whether international rules can enter into the domestic political arena or not. For instance, if certain rules can serve for the national political rhetoric, meet the requirements of the material interests of domestic actors and incorporate into the domestic bureaucratic institutions, the salience of certain international rules will be enhanced.

Risse-Kappen elaborates on the concept of domestic structure more systematically. He argues that ideas "do not float freely. Decision makers are always exposed to several and often contradictory policy concepts" (Risse-Kappen 1994: 187), so the filtrating role of the domestic structures cannot be underestimated. He brings forward three components: state structure (centralization versus fragmentation), societal structure (weak versus strong) and policy networks (consensual versus polarized), to construct a framework of six types of domestic structures: corporatist, stalemate, state-dominated, state-controlled, society-dominated and fragile (Risse-Kappen 1995a: 22-23). He specifies that: "To influence policies, transnational actors need, first, channels into the political system of the target state and, second, domestic partners with the ability to form winning coalitions. Ideas promoted by transnational alliances or epistemic communities do not matter much unless those two conditions are met" (Risse-Kappen 1994: 208). He also highlights that "access to the political system as well as the ability to build winning coalitions are determined by the domestic structure of the target state" (Risse-Kappen 1994: 187). The reason why the state-dominated system, like that of China, has an advantage in the socialization process at the domestic level (once the norm filtrates through the domestic structure) is that the coalition-building process within the small group of political elites is often comparatively effective. China is a typical state-dominated state. Although China has refused to make a legally binding GHG emission reduction commitment, the current voluntary carbon intensity reduction target (40%-45% by 2020) has been forcefully pushed at the provincial level. Pro-low-carbon elites in the central government claim that China should take advantage of climate change and use it to promote a domestic economy transformation. Therefore, the domestic coalition building has become a critical precondition for successful norm internalization and domestic policy change. In other words, in the domestic policy change process, new ideas never flow freely but rely on the domestic policy coalition building.

However, Risse-Kappen leaves two questions unsolved: the first one is how to "overcome the hurdle of domestic structure" (Risse-Kappen 1994: 208). Although Risse-Kappen has mentioned that the international actors should pay attention to the domestic structure and cooperate with domestic elites to form "winning coalitions", he fails to elaborate on the concrete process involved in building "winning coalitions". How do domestic actors take advantage of international resources to influence policy-making and policy change? In order to solve this problem, the three micro-processes of socialization put forward by Checkel and Johnston could provide some explanations (this is discussed in the next section). The second one is that Risse-Kappen underestimates the complex situation of different domestic coalitions' competition in certain subsystems. Although Risse-Kappen has mentioned winning coalitions and policy coalition building, he does not mention how the strengthened coalition competes with the conventional or dominant coalition on certain policy issues. In order to answer this question, the advocacy coalition framework put forward by Sabatier could provide some implications and further enrich the policy coalition building theory.

2.2.2 Advocacy coalition framework and the strengthening of advocacy coalitions

The advocacy coalition framework (ACF) which was put forward by Sabatier and Jenkins-Smith (Sabatier 1988; Sabatier 2007; Sabatier and Jenkins-Smith 1993b) provides an effective theoretical approach for exploring how policy change takes place through the interplay of domestic actors in a specific policy domain. They define this specific policy area as a *policy subsystem*, "the set of actors (governmental and social actors) who are involved in dealing with a policy problem" (Sabatier and Jenkins-

Smith 1993b: 24).① According to Sabatier, policy subsystems are treated as the principal unit for understanding policy change, rather than specific governmental institutions. In order to make clear the interaction of different stakeholders in the subsystem, Sabatier and Jenkins-Smith (1993a, 1999) developed the concept of the "*advocacy coalition*". An advocacy coalition is composed of "people from various governmental and private organizations who share a set of same normative and causal values in their belief systems and who often act in concert" (Sabatier and Jenkins-Smith 1993b: 18).

Every advocacy coalition has its *belief system*, which guides its actions. The belief system includes three levels: a *deep normative core* (fundamental normative and ontological axioms), a *near policy core* (fundamental policy positions concerning the basic strategies for achieving normative axioms of the deep core), and *secondary aspects* (the instrumental decisions and information searches necessary to implement the policy core) (Sabatier and Jenkins-Smith 1993a: 31). The deep normative core and near policy core are very hard to change without effective external forces, meaning that major policy change is quite difficult to achieve. By contrast, secondary aspects usually relate with instrumental decisions and the utilization of policy instruments, which are comparatively easy to change.

Table 2.2 Structure of the belief system in the ACF

	Deep (normative) core	Near (policy) core	Secondary aspects
Defining characteristics	Fundamental normative and ontological axioms	Fundamental policy positions concerning the basic strategies for achieving deep core	Instrumental decisions and information searches necessary to implement policy core
Scope	Part of basic personal philosophy. Applies to all policy areas	Applies to policy area of interest (and perhaps a few more)	Specific to policy area/subsystem of interest

① Sabatier and Jenkins-Smith contend "policy subsystems should be broadened from traditional notions of 'iron triangles'—limited to administrative agencies, legislative committees, and interest groups at a single level of government—to include actors at various levels of government active in policy formulation and implementation as well as journalists, researchers, and policy analysts who play important roles in the generation, dissemination, and evaluation of policy ideas". See Sabatier and Jenkins-Smith (1993a: 17).

Susceptibility to change	Very difficult; akin to a religious conversion	Difficult, but can occur if experience reveals serious anomalies	Moderately easy; this is the topic of most administrative and even legislative policy-making
Illustrative components	Nature of man	Scope of governmental vs. market activity	Decisions concerning administrative rules, budgetary allocations
	Ultimate values	Identification of social groups whose welfare is most critical	Information concerning program performance, seriousness of the problems
	Basic criteria of distributive justice	Orientation on substantive policy conflicts, Basic choices concerning policy instruments	

Source: Sabatier and Jenkins-Smith (1993a: 31).

In any policy subsystem, there are at least two coalitions: a "conventional coalition" or "dominant coalition", which supports the status quo from an advantaged and dominant position within the policy subsystem; and a "minority coalition", which proposes changes from a position of disadvantage (Watanabe 2011: 15). There may also be more than two coalitions (Sabatier and Weible 2007; Weible et al. 2009). Advocacy coalitions, with their own value priorities and causal assumptions, always seek to "translate their beliefs into public policies or programs and achieve their objectives, which usually consist of a set of goals and directions, or empowerments, to administrative agencies for implementing those goals" (Sabatier and Jenkins-Smith 1993b: 28). Therefore, this is a *coalition competition process*: different advocacy coalitions compete with each other/or challenge the dominant advocacy coalitions in the subsystem in order to gain sufficient influence to change policy.

Sabatier points out that the *capability of an advocacy coalition* to promote policy change depends upon its *resources*, including such things as "*money*, *expertise*, *number of supporters*, *and legal authority*" (Sabatier and Jenkins-Smith 1993b: 29). It is noteworthy that the resources of various coalitions change over time, since most coalitions seek to "augment their budgets, recruit new members (especially those with legal authority, expertise, or money), and place their members in positions of authority" (Sabatier and Jenkins-Smith 1993b: 29). However, due to the resource-controlling by the dominant coalition, it is quite difficult for the minority coalitions to gain sufficient resources to counter-balance or challenge the dominant coalition. That is why Sabatier and Jenkins-Smith also admit that "although coalitions will seek to increase their resources, the major shifts in the *distribution of political resources* will usually be the product of events external to the subsystem and largely external to activities of subsystem coalitions" (Sabatier and Jenkins-Smith 1993b: 29). If the new/minority coalitions could "successfully exploit and amplify opportunities arising from external events" (Sabatier and Jenkins-Smith 1993b: 29) and take advantage of favorable political opportunity structure from other subsystems, the chance of policy change would be enlarged.

Kingdon's multiple streams approach also suggests that dramatic events or crises can bring problems to the attention of policy-makers and so open a "window of opportunity" for policy change (Kingdon 1995). Because "such changes alter the constraints and opportunities confronting subsystem actors, they constitute the principal dynamic elements affecting policy" (Sabatier and Jenkins-Smith 1993b: 22). They also present a continuous challenge to subsystem actors, who must learn how to anticipate them and respond to them "in a manner consistent with their basic beliefs and interests" (Sabatier and Jenkins-Smith 1993b: 22-23). In sum, the dynamic system events can serve as significant drivers of change. They can shift the allocation of political resources in the subsystem empowering the minority coalition. With more resources the minority coalition finds itself in a better position to influence the policy-making process. Furthermore, the strengthened minority coalition may achieve more authority and use this to promote policy-oriented learning.

2.2.3 Theoretical space to combine the ACF with the socialization theory

The ACF was developed and applied within a disciplinary context that views policy formation as an essentially domestic-level process occurring within states (Litfin 2000: 236). Although Sabatier and Jenkins-Smith put emphasis on the influence of external events and the resources allocated to different advocacy coalitions and mention that policy shifts are the result of changes external to the policy subsystem, including "dynamic system events" at the international level, they do not pay sufficient attention to how international sources (such as international material incentives, social influence and international norms) are linked to domestic sources (such as the domestic political opportunity structure and the institution building of bureaucratic agencies). Although they highlight that political resource reallocation is the key process for building capacity and achieving a power shift among competing coalitions in the subsystem, they fail to explain how the minority coalition can become stronger in the two-level interaction (international and domestic) and how the strengthened minority coalition takes advantage of international resources as well as domestic resources to promote policy change.

Along with the increasing salience of some global public policy issues (such as climate change, the global financial crisis, and transnational water governance), international factors have become significant external factors influencing the interaction of domestic coalitions in certain subsystems. Risse-Kappen (1991, 1994, 1995b) argues that in order to influence policies at the domestic level, transnational/international actors need channels into the political system and domestic partners with the ability to form "winning coalitions" within the political elite (Risse-Kappen 1994: 208). Therefore, "the amount of physical resources and political support that they can mobilize will largely determine the outcome of the actual struggle for power to set the rules" (Tang 2011: 34-35). The concept of "winning coalition" sounds like a kind of expedient tactic to reach a policy target. Sabatier and Jenkins-Smith, in contrast, emphasize the time dimension and that the process of policy change can require a decade or more (Sabatier and Jenkins-Smith 1993b: 16). Therefore, I contend that making a one-decade or two-decade process-tracing of domestic actors' interactions within the subsystem can give a panorama of policy change. It is also one of the key preconditions for studying the influence of international regimes on the domestic structure, to make sure the impact from certain international factors is indeed long lasting.

Some scholars (Dolan 2003; Ellison 1998; Litfin 2000; Meijerink 2005; Princen 2007) have combined international relations theory with ACF research, in order to explore how domestic structures and domestic actors' interactions influence external inputs, or how international factors exert an influence on concrete policy change, especially how advocacy coalitions take advantage of international sources. Karen T. Litfin argues that the "twin phenomena of economic globalization and the internationalization of environmental affairs are blurring the distinction between some policy subsystems and the international arena. Thus advocacy coalitions should be understood as operating increasingly along the domestic-foreign frontier" (Litfin 2000: 236). Litfin uses the ACF framework and multi-governance theory to analyze Canadian climate change policy (Litfin 2000). T. Eimer et al. (2013) propose that the ACF can provide an effective framework to explain why the initial intentions of international norms are substantially reinterpreted at the domestic level. They contend "the ACF allows us to examine whether or not the value priorities, and assumptions concerning the efficacy of specific policy instruments of domestic advocacy coalitions deviate from those enshrined in international agreements, thus paving the way for substantial norm revisions on the domestic level" (Eimer et al. 2013: 2). Ellison combines the intergovernmental theory with the ACF to explore Denver water politics (Ellison 1998). Princen resorts to the ACF model to study the internationalization process of public health policies, and puts emphasis on the domestic structure filtration and advocacy coalitions' interaction (Princen 2007). There is still a large theoretical space for combining the ACF with international relations theory to grapple with the convergence of domestic and international sources to explore policy change.

In this book, I attempt to enrich the ACF by combining it with the socialization theory. The key interlinking knot for these two theories is capacity building or the strengthening of advocacy coalitions. By this it shows how a minority coalition grows stronger through the resource reallocation process. This is a process which can be influenced by external impetus, the ways in which new actors and new institutions emerge out of the socialization process, and how policy-oriented learning and argumentative persuasion (promoted by certain policy coalitions who have been strengthened through the socialization process) take place and impact policy change.

2.3 Strengthening of the advocacy coalition in socialization and its role in policy change

Sabatier and Jenkins-Smith contend that "while belief systems will determine the direction in which an advocacy coalition (or any other political actor) will seek to move governmental programs, its ability to do so will be critically dependent upon its resources" (Sabatier and Jenkins-Smith 1993b: 29). These resources, like money, the number of supporters, expertise, and legal authority determine the action capacity of coalitions. Resource reallocation among different coalitions will lead to policy change in the subsystem. The goal of this book is to interlink the socialization theory with the Advocacy Coalition Framework (ACF) to explore how international sources influence the resource allocation of different domestic coalitions, which subsequently leads to domestic policy change in certain subsystems.

The three micro-processes of socialization put forward by Jeffrey T. Checkel (2001, 2005) and Johnston (2003, 2008) explain how international sources make an impact on domestic actors' behavior and policy choices. However, they do not pay due attention to the capacity building of advocacy coalitions and its role in the domestic policy change process. The capacity building in this book means the strengthening of the capacities (technological, informational, policy-related) of the domestic minority advocacy coalition. This book further develops the concept of "argumentative persuasion" in the socialization process. I contend that "argumentative persuasion" will become more effective at the domestic level when international norms and principles are promoted by certain strengthened advocacy coalition. In other words, if certain domestic policy coalitions become the "spokesperson" for international rules, the function of "argumentative persuasion" will be more obvious in the policy change process.

This book divides the three micro-processes into *two stages* (see Figure 2.2): the first stage explains how certain advocacy coalitions become stronger and gain more resources in the socialization process through role playing and strategic calculation. The second stage explores how the strengthened advocacy coalition can promote domestic policy change through policy-oriented learning and argumentative persuasion. In identifying some micro-logic-chains to enrich the original socialization theory, this book applies the terms "role playing" and "strategic calculation" introduced by Checkel (2001, 2005). These concepts are used to analyze how the climate change regime influences institutional anchoring/lock-in and resource allocation to the domestic pro-RE advocacy coalition. The book then investigates how the pro-RE advocacy coalition has increased its influence in the RE policy making process through policy-oriented learning and argumentative persuasion, making it better able to compete with conventional coalitions in the energy sector to promote RE policy change.

2.3.1 The influence of role playing processes and institutional anchoring on the strengthening of advocacy coalitions

The "role playing" concept forwarded by Checkel (2005: 810) and the idea of "mimicking" proposed by Alastair I. Johnston (2005: 1021-1022) are similar. This book uses in particular the concept of "role playing" although at times it also discusses mimicking. Due to the bounded rationality of novices in contexts of uncertainty, states are involved in non-calculative behavioral adaptation. When states join in the international regimes, they are expected to follow some pro-social behaviors. The state mimics institutional arrangements, procedural and behavioral rules, and discourses embodied in international regimes in a "non-reflective" way. It is an approach for states to smoothly become involved in unfamiliar social contexts by simply following existing institutional arrangements. Mimicking involves borrowing models of organizing and talking about issues that are central to the group (Johnston 2008: 47). Alastair I. Johnston argues mimicking is not "necessarily a response to social pressure. Rather it is, in a sense, a response to safety or appropriate adaptation" (Johnston 2008: 47). It is "a survival strategy for a particular social environment" (Johnston 2008: 47).

Although role playing is not a pro-norm behavior following the "logic of appropriateness", Alastair I. Johnston puts much emphasis on the domestic lock-in effect from role-playing or mimicking processes in international regimes. Johnston points out two basic preconditions for lock-in effect: first, the costs of backing out of an international regime are very high. Costs could include the potential loss of economic incentives and social recognition. Second, procedures, behavior, and language constrain options inside the institution, especially when that state actively makes compliance commitments (Johnston 2008: 46). To a certain degree, this lock-in effect follows the logic of new institutionalism. The theory of new institutionalism argues that organizations arising from certain institutions develop their own interests and try to establish rules that favor an expansion of their own interests and power. The institutions set the rules of the game and determine political, economic and legal outcomes (Cortell and Peterson 2001; Lecours 2005). Although the state follows a kind of non-calculative behavioral adaptation in the international regime at first, this role playing behavior will result in an institutional, procedural and discursive lock-in effect. This in turn promotes a shift from non-calculative-adaptation to reflective norm-driven compliance (Johnston 2008).

2.3.1.1 Institutional lock-in effect in the role playing process

Cortell and Davis Jr. emphasize the role of domestic political institutions in the socialization process: "a common effect of international norm creation is the simultaneous creation of vested interests and bureaucratic routines in a state's institutions" (Cortell and Davis Jr. 2000: 80), since the bureaucratic institutions "provide the rules of the game for citizens and state officials, establish rights and obligations and help national actors define their interests domestically and internationally" (Cortell and Davis Jr. 2000: 79). Once the state joins in the international regime, the participation "may functionally require the creation of specialized domestic organizations and expertise to handle the policy toward the international level" (Johnston 2008: 47). These organizations could be termed as "*window agencies*"; they create a channel for connecting the international and domestic levels. For instance, international funds and international know-how transfer projects need cooperation with window agencies at the domestic level. Current international institutions research mainly focuses on how to design effective and elaborate organizational structures. However, it fails to give due attention to "the effect of promoting these functions on the organization of state-level actors" (Johnston 2008: 47). The *structural cohesion/coherence* requirement from the international regime needs states to develop bureaucratic institutions or organizations at the domestic level that can carry out or oversee international commitments. After bargaining over the rules of coordination at the international level, the next step is to make sure of the coordination of bureaucratic agencies at the domestic level. This coordination requirement may spawn some new organizational structures/new institutions in the national bureaucratic system. This may, in turn, create a standard organizational interest-based commitment to the international institution. Johnston also argues that this does not mean that the organizational structure at the national level needs to be a functionally efficient one at first. The window agencies might be "relatively weak" in their authority or influence. However, along with the salience of certain issues at the domestic level and their entry into the mainstream of the political agenda, newly-established agencies will be given political resources and over time will become authoritative on certain issues. Following a new-functionalist logic, these strengthened agencies will pursue and fight for their own interests. They might become key supporters of the minority coalition and play an authoritative role in solving new problems.

There are mainly *three kinds of institutional lock-in effects* at the domestic level:

First, in the interaction with the international regime, the state needs its own representative team or certain domestic organization to take care of communicating and coordinating with international affairs. Therefore, the state needs to establish a "window agency". Sometimes, the window agency is no more than an irrelevant affiliated organization under a domestic bureaucratic institution. Over time it may gradually be upgraded to an independent, more powerful organization as it gains more resources.

Second, in addition to establishing the "window agency" to communicate with the international regime, some complex issues (such as climate change mitigation), also need institutional coordination among different governmental bureaucracies or agencies. Liu and Diamond (2008) propose that "establishing a new, high-level, authoritative national organization that coordinates all relevant ministries and agencies could reduce conflicts among them" (Liu and Diamond 2008: 2). The coordination among different departments will enhance the regulation effectiveness and strengthen administrative capacity.

Third, due to the principle of the bounded-rationality of policy-makers and the increasing complexity of the issue area, there will be an increasing demand for establishing relevant think tanks or research institutes in order to provide more information and strategies for international negotiations or problem-solving. Bounded rationality is the idea that "in decision-making, rationality of individuals is limited by the information they have, the cognitive limitations of their minds, and the finite amount of time they have to make a decision" (Lacity et al. 2011: 143; Simon 1978: 9). These newly-born research institutes play an authoritative role in providing supportive scientific data for policy-making, as well as making assessments of relevant policies.

2.3.1.2 Procedural lock-in effect in the role playing process

Novices are unlikely to be completely familiar with the rules, procedures, and routines of an international regime. Nor will they have much power in the rule-making field or much weight in discursive processes. If they ignore or violate principles or rules, they still will "not be able to have much impact on the proceedings" (Johnston 2008: 47), and will risk being punished or isolated by the other regime members. Therefore, states establish coordinating organizations and research institutes at the national level to address the issues of the international regime and internalize the regime's rules and procedures into their daily routines. In addition, in order to foster the effective implementation of international agreements as well as to guarantee information transparency, the international regime also requires member states to show compliance with procedural obligations stipulated in the treaty (Dai 2007: 14), submit (sometimes voluntarily) national action programs and assessment reports, and introduce administrative regulations and legislative frameworks to foster policy implementation.

The procedural lock-in effect can be witnessed in three ways: *First*, according to the information transparency requirement, more information and data will become accessible than before. Window agencies will play the role of information transmitter, conveying the international rules and procedures to the domestic level. These may focus on innovative policy instruments, best practices, or scientific knowledge. Interest concerns should be noted here as well. The domestic bureaucracy or agency which actually participates in the international institutions usually actively "adopt[s] certain standard operating procedures in order to articulate their interests, become accepted, or gain the benefits from prestige" (Johnston 2008: 48). *Second*, some new governmental action plans, governmental administrative regulations, even relevant laws will emerge when a "window of opportunity" opens. Although governments do not always take these rules and regulations seriously, the gradually changing political context will let the minority coalition gain more support. For instance, when more and more social actors have access to information, they can make their own judgments about emerging problems and might become the potential supporters of the minority coalition. *Third*, increasingly complex agendas at the international level may require the training of people in the bureaucracy as well as of experts with knowledge about the international rules and procedures for participating effectively in the international regime (Johnston 2008: 48). When certain issues become more salient at the domestic level, personnel training and new standards for measuring political performance may enhance the internalization of related rules and procedures.

2.3.1.3 Discursive lock-in effect in the role playing process

When the domestic bureaucracy or agency, especially the window agency, begins to adopt certain rules, procedures and norms from the international regime, it will also incorporate related discursive practices into its daily routines. The changing discourses of national leaders, due to national reputation concerns, can have considerable impact on the whole bureaucratic system. This process is similar to the "*national political rhetoric*" put forward by Cortell and Davis Jr. (2000: 76). They point out that "the pronouncements of authoritative national leaders illustrate how domestic understandings about the legitimacy of an international norm... repeated declarations by state leaders on the legitimacy of the obligations that an international norm places on states usually raise the norm's salience in the national arena" (Cortell and Davis Jr. 2000: 76). The "original embrace of an international norm may be purely instrumental, indeed cynical, yet still lead to salience" (Cortell and Davis Jr. 2000: 76). If certain kinds of discourses can also serve for some domestic interest concerns, then the discursive lock-in effect will become more salient. Once certain discourses become the "official language" in the political process, and are integrated into political performance assessment, domestic actors will show more compliance to the new discourse. Just as Bourdieu argued one risks becoming marginalized and suffering from "the sanctions of the linguistic market", if one refuses to accept the "official language" (Bourdieu and Thompson 1991: 51; Johnston 2008: 50).

There is also a reinforcing process in the role playing process: First, it is the establishment of domestic institutions (window agency) that must handle international affairs such as dealing with international funds and cooperative projects. Meanwhile, in order to enhance national capacity building in relation to international affairs, relevant national think tanks or academic supporting institutions will be set up to conduct research, collect data and make policy proposals. They gain authority along with the increasing salience of certain issues at the domestic level. Second, in order to "survive as novices in a technically demanding international institution, a state's agents adopt the procedures and work habits used by most other actors in the membership of an institution" (Johnston 2008: 51). These procedures require the creation of an internal policy process that develops a constituency between the international and domestic levels, such as issuing governmental regulations and drafting legislative proposals. Third, the adoption of primary discursive practices from international regimes will constrain how actors talk and think about an institution (Johnston 2008: 52). The national political rhetoric of paramount leaders is also important. If they pick up an issue, possibly due to national reputation concerns, it can play a significant role in developing a discursive lock-in effect.

In this book, I attempt to examine the institutional anchoring of domestic pro-RE actors under the influence of the climate change regime. Through the institutional, procedural and discursive lock-in effects that can occur in role playing, new institutions, administrative procedures and political discourses may emerge in the bureaucratic system. Examples in the case of China are the establishment of the Center for Renewable Energy Development (CRED), the issuing of the Climate Change Law Exposure Draft and the focusing on low-carbon discourses. The pro-RE coalition has taken advantage of these institutional anchoring effects to enhance its own capacity building and promote RE policy change. Based on the analysis above, the first hypothesis of this book is:

H1 *The more institutional, procedural and discursive lock-in effects that occur during the role playing process are related to socialization into the climate change regime, the more supporters of the pro-RE coalition will emerge and the more institutional anchoring will be enhanced. This in turn will mean there will be more possibility for the pro-RE coalition to promote RE policy change.*

2.3.2 The influence of the strategic calculation processes and resource reallocation on the capacity building of advocacy coalitions

Cortell and Davis Jr. (2000) argue that international norms are more likely to become salient if they are perceived to support important domestic material interests, whether about economy or security. The material interest here should be understood in a broad sense (such as interest links to the nation's more general beliefs and durable national priorities), rather than the narrow material interests of different domestic actors (Cortell and Davis Jr. 2000: 77). Invisible national interests, such as national reputation concerns should also be included into the strategic calculation process. Strategic calculation refers to the states consciously complying to some rules of international regimes in order to get more material incentives (international fund, technological transfer, training/know-how projects) and social rewards (national image building, national reputation gaining), while avoiding international social constraints (such as reputational pressures and diplomatic isolation). In other words, it is a pro-group behavior "elicited by exogenous incentives or punishments, and it is characterized by actor's efforts to optimize long-run material well-being" (Johnston 2008: 47).

Although the states make their rational choice calculations based on strategic calculations, international sources exert influence on national agenda-setting processes and send certain signals to domestic society. Economy and Schreurs (1997) argue that "international linkages can influence these cost-benefit analyses by changing resource balances among actors, altering actors' interests or perceptions, or providing means for pushing other policy priorities" (Economy and Schreurs 1997: 10). This chapter identifies two micro-logic-chains to explain how the strategic calculation promotes the domestic political resource reallocation, which provides a "political opportunity structure" for minority or new coalitions to become stronger.

2.3.2.1 Agenda-setting mechanisms and resource reallocation

Agenda-setting refers to the ability of the (certain social context, such as international events, news media) to influence the salience of certain topics on the political agenda of state (Benton and Frazier 1976; Kingdon 1995; McCombs 2005; McCombs and Shaw 1972; Pralle 2009; Rochefort and Cobb 1994). Domestic political coalitions within one state have different policy preferences and interests (Milner 1997: 16), but the dominant/conventional coalition or interest group tries to control political agenda setting. In addition, some policy issues may be ignored for long periods because of the cognitive limitations or bounded rationality of domestic policy actors and institutions, "only to receive disproportionate attention at a later date" (Jones and Baumgartner 2005: 17). Therefore, some topics have been marginalized from the mainstream of agenda-setting. Agenda-setting in socialization process means the ability of the international regimes to influence the salience of certain topics on the political agenda of the state. The "streams" model introduced by John Kingdon (1995) highlights that the problems, policies and politics are three main streams to decide the salience of certain issues in the political agenda (Kingdon 1995). When there is a merging of three streams at a certain time, "windows of opportunity" will open. Pralle (2009) points out that "when a feasible policy solution is attached to what the public and policy-makers perceive as an important public problem, and when political conditions are amenable to change, the policy change will come into being" (Pralle 2009: 19). When a state joins the international regime, some problems which have been ignored (perhaps on purpose) by the conventional coalition may gain greater public concern. They may also be influenced by external knowledge and information input as well as pressure. This occurs in what Kingdon called the problem stream. The international regime also provides some policy solutions and incentives (best practices, international funds, technology transfer and know-how) to encourage pro-group compliance. This is what Kingdon called the policy stream. If an interest win-set between the international level and domestic level forms, the issue may finally enter the mainstream of the domestic political agenda (Kingdon's politics stream). Along with agenda-setting change, a minority advocacy coalition will gain more resources than before: not only from international incentives, but also from domestic resource reallocation due to the salience of the issue.

The question here is how agenda-setting change influences resource reallocation at the domestic level. In the socialization process, some scholars use a "*spiral model*" to explain how domestic resource allocation can be reinforced by international inputs (such as material incentives and social rewards) (Shor 2008; Slater 2007). The "spiral model" proposes a two stage model for understanding how international regimes influence resource reallocation at the domestic level. The first stage can be understood as an "*outside-in oriented approach*". The domestic issue gains more attention on the political agenda due to international supportive resource inputs. In the strategic calculation, the state shows its compliance to the international rules in order to maximize and optimize its long-run material well-being, especially getting more incentives for solving its own problem. The incentives in the form of resources and rewards from the international level can reinforce the minority coalitions' capacity building: for instance, this can occur through technique transfer or training workshops that cultivate expert knowledge in the field in question. They might become key supporters of the minority coalition and increase its authority. International financial aid and support projects at the domestic level need institutions they can cooperate with at the domestic level. These institutions can open up new opportunities for the minority coalition to gain external financial support. During this process, some new institutions might be spawned from the support provided by external actors; these in turn may become new recruiting grounds for the minority coalition. The minority collation might seize these opportunities to promote policy-oriented learning and even play the role of "policy entrepreneur", introducing some innovative policy instruments at the domestic level. International actors often establish preconditions for receiving international aid or funds for target states. They may demand a diagnosing of domestic problems, information transparency, and the timely submission of assessment reports. These processes may promote public attention on the issue in question. When an issue is on the political agenda it in turn will draw more attention from the mass media and stimulate increasing public awareness. In sum, international actors and events can be external drivers of capacity building in a minority coalition. This can be especially significant in the initial stages of a minority coalition's development.

The second stage can be entitled the "*domestic enhancement stage*". This stage emphasizes the domestic resource reallocation process that occurs as a result of the increasing salience of the issue at question at the domestic level. Once the "marginalized" issue has made it onto the political agenda, and is perceived as supporting important domestic material interests, the domestic enhancement stage will begin. If international incentives help the minority coalition to gain some successful experiences (such as in some small-scale demonstration projects), "a reinforcing effect whereby success breeds more success" (Mertha 2009: 1001) can occur. Therefore the government will pay more attention to this issue, and once a certain issue has gained a priority position on the political agenda, the government will accordingly assign more resources to support this new area. This may come in the form of a governmental special fund, a fiscal subsidy, or tax incentives. With the increasing domestic support and resource reallocation, the minority advocacy coalition can become stronger and gain in its ability to counter the resistance coming from the conventional coalition in the subsystem. At this time, the minority coalition can take advantage of resources both from the international and domestic levels. As Dai points out "international factors including international institutions can provide benefits to some domestic actors and thus may shape domestic interest competition... various domestic actors can appeal to international rules and norms to push their domestic agenda" (Dai 2007: 29).

2.3.2.2 Signaling mechanism in the strategic calculation

The main interest of a state in joining an international regime is to maximize interest incentives (including visible incentives and invisible social rewards like credibility and positive national image) and minimize constraints (including visible punishments and invisible social influences like reputation pressure). Through joining international institutions, a state aims to increase its international reputation① and get more recognition in the international community, and send a credible signal to the international audience (Tian 2011). The desire to "establish a trustworthy reputation for future exchanges can be an incentive to engage in norm-conforming, pro-social behavior" (Johnston 2001: 490). Therefore, non-compliance behavior will bring disrepute, and further reduce a state's credibility in the international community. For a state without sufficient credibility, the barriers to joining other favorable international institutions increase. What's worse, it can lead to retaliation from other states. As a result, even though there is no mandatory coercion force or when cooperation works against the national short-term interest, a state may still choose compliance with the international regime due to reputation considerations. Especially when confronted with increasing international pressures, a national leader might make some compromising commitment to international rules and norms, in order to protect its national reputation. Once a commitment has been made the international community and the domestic audience will watch whether the state makes credible their commitment. Behavior thus sends a signal to the international and domestic levels.

The "*domestic audience cost*" is an idea introduced by Fearon (1994a, 1994b). It refers to the ability of domestic actors (political opposition and citizens as voters) to

---

① Reputation refers to a kind of belief or judgment of a state's enduring features or characteristics, from other states in the international system. See Mercer (1996, 2005).

watch governmental leaders and put pressure on them to carry out international commitments and sanction them for "inappropriate" behavior. The audience cost makes backing down in international crises costly to leaders (Fearon 1994a; Fearon 1994b). The traditional idea is that "democracies are better able to signal their foreign policy intentions than non-democracies... and elections and democratic institutions are the way in which domestic groups can coordinate to hold leaders accountable" (Weeks 2008: 35, 37). Weeks points out that the key factor generating domestic audience cost is "whether domestic political groups can and will coordinate to punish the leader for backing down" (Weeks 2008: 35). This theory can also be applied to authoritarian states. Leaders in authoritarian states also require the support of domestic elites who act as audiences in much the same way as voting publics in democracies (Weeks 2008: 36). Authoritarianism in China is not a monolithic block of governmental actors but rather a system that is spilt into different interest elite groups. In China, the main decision making principle is consensus building in the Politburo (Jakobson and Knox 2010: 1). When elites have incentives and ability to coordinate to punish a leader and the potential for punishment is visible to foreign decision makers, domestic audience cost emerges (Weeks 2008: 36). Although an international regime's rules and principles may have quite a difficult time penetrating barriers in authoritarian countries, once they pass through the filtering levels, authoritarian countries may show higher levels of pro-social behavior, making their international commitments credible.

> The more the state dominates the domestic structure, the more difficult it should be for transnational actors to penetrate the social and political systems of the "target" country. Once they overcome this hurdle in state-dominated systems, though, their policy impact might be profound, since coalition-building with rather small groups of governmental actors appears to be comparatively straightforward. (Risse-Kappen 1995a: 6-7)

The critical reason why domestic audiences might impose audience costs on leaders who back down is that failing to make commitments will hurt the national reputation in the international community and influence effective bargaining ability in the future. That is why national leaders are usually cautious about making international commitments, since sending empty signals will threaten their governmental capability and hurt their national reputation. As a result, once the state sends out a signal to the international regime, these commitments will play a role as signposts for domestic actors, or even reflect the general development strategy of the state in the future. This signal effect made at the international level will contribute to the weakening of domestic forces of resistance on certain issues. For instance, the international commitment/signaling effect of the WTO strengthens the force of economic reform-oriented coalitions and weakens conservative forces. Meanwhile, some advocacy coalitions will take advantage of signaling mechanisms to gain more political resources.

This book examines resource reallocation supportive of domestic pro-RE actors in China through the agenda setting and signaling mechanisms of the international climate change regime. The increasing salience of "climate politics" has constructed significant situational factors for domestic policy making. Based on interest calculations, China acts in a pragmatist way in the climate change regime: the international material incentives for RE development, such as the Clean Development Mechanism (CDM), the China Renewable Energy Development Project (REDP), and the China Renewable Energy Scale-up Program (CRESP) have provided external dynamics and resources for the development of domestic pro-RE actors. And through the agenda-setting mechanism, RE development has found its way to the mainstream of the policy agenda. With a stronger position for RE, more and more domestic resources have gone towards pro-RE actors. As a result of the soaring growth of GHG emissions, as the largest GHG emitter, China has been confronted with unprecedented international pressure. In order to save its national reputation and avoid social constraints, Chinese leaders have made some voluntary carbon intensity reduction and RE development commitments. These moves send positive signals to the domestic bureaucratic system and social RE investors. Taking advantage of the resource reallocation, pro-RE actors in China have gained more power and authority to influence RE policy change. Based on the analysis above, the second hypothesis of this book is:

H2 *The more material incentives (financial support and technology transfer) and social influences (especially reputation pressure) from the climate change regime get linked to strategic interest calculations, the more political resources will be re-allocated to the pro-RE coalition. This in turn will provide more possibility for the pro-RE coalition to become stronger in its ability to promote RE policy change.*

2.3.3 The role of a strengthened advocacy coalition in domestic policy change

2.3.3.1 Competition of advocacy coalitions in the subsystem

The ACF analysis has provided a comprehensive theoretical framework that can be used to explore how different advocacy coalitions compete with other coalitions to influence the policy-making process in a subsystem. Every advocacy coalition attempts to translate its own beliefs and policy proposals into governmental programs. Generally speaking, the conventional coalition controls more political resources and takes advantage of its dominant position to limit the resources made accessible to other coalitions. There are two approaches a minority coalition can use to increase its voice in the subsystem: First, it has to become stronger and enhance its capacity by winning more resources. It may be possible to do this by the support of external actors or events. According to Sabatier and Jenkins-Smith, the effects of system-wide events will influence the resources available and constraints facing subsystem actors, such as "changes in socioeconomic conditions, outputs from other subsystems, and changes in the system-wide governing coalition" (Sabatier and Jenkins-Smith 1993b: 34). Second, the strengthened coalition competes with other advocacy coalitions. During this process, policy-oriented learning and argumentative persuasion promoted by a strengthened coalition can play a significant role in domestic policy change. Through combining the socialization theory and ACF, this book aims to explore how the minority coalition can become stronger through institutional anchoring and the resource reallocation process. If the strengthened minority coalition actively takes advantage of domestic resources and international resources in policy-oriented learning and argumentative persuasion process, it will gain more weight in policy-making.

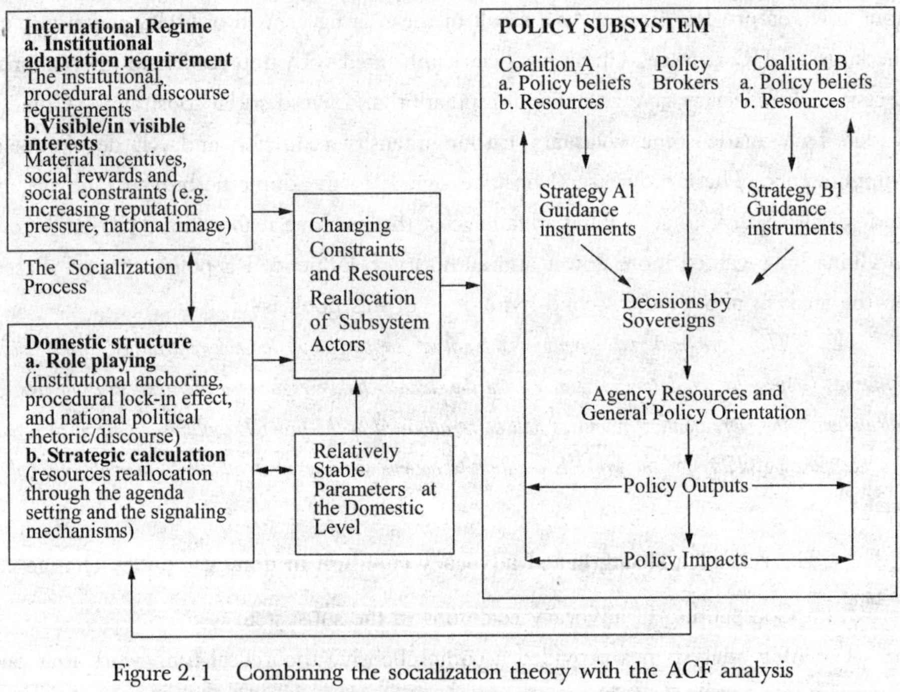

Figure 2.1 Combining the socialization theory with the ACF analysis

Source: The author re-edited Sabatier's ACF figure in order to combine it with socialization theory. See Sabatier and Jenkins-Smith (1993b: 19).

According to Sabatier's ACF, competing advocacy coalitions will make different policy proposals to a third group of actors entitled "policy brokers" (Sabatier and Jenkins-Smith 1993b: 18-19). The main task of "policy brokers" with higher sovereigns is to mediate conflicting strategies from various coalitions and promote consensus-reaching in the policy-making process. The main concern of the "policy brokers" is to "keep the level of political conflict within acceptable limits and in order to reach some reasonable solution to the problem" (Sabatier 1988: 141). However, there is a "double-identity" problem for policy brokers—these brokers are "usually elected officials or high civil servants who might, in other circumstances, themselves be advocates rather than brokers" (Bennett and Howlett 1992: 280). Therefore, policy brokers are not always value-neutral. Policy brokers may also be influenced by new knowledge and ideas. What they learn can have great impact on the consensus-reaching process.

2.3.3.2 Policy-oriented learning promoted by a strengthened advocacy coalition

Policy-oriented learning means "relatively enduring alterations of thought or behavioral intentions that result from experience and which are concerned with the attainment or revision of the precepts of the belief system of individuals or of collectivities (such as advocacy coalitions)" (Sabatier and Jenkins-Smith 1993b: 42).① Policy-oriented learning occurs in the context of a political process "where advocacy coalitions compete over the authoritative allocation of values and over the ability to use the instruments of government in their behalf" (Sabatier and Jenkins-Smith 1993b: 45).

Policy-oriented learning includes learning within a coalition's belief system and learning across the belief systems of different coalitions. The former learning model specifically refers to the learning efforts by the minority coalition. This book focuses on policy-oriented learning promoted by the minority coalition. A minority coalition has incentives to conduct policy-oriented learning in order to challenge conventional coalitions in the subsystem. Through new knowledge inputs, lesson drawing and problem investigation, the minority coalition seeks to "improve their understanding of variable states and causal relationships consistent with their policy core" (Sabatier and Jenkins-Smith 1993b: 48).② In sum, the minority coalition attempts to increase the feasibility and scientific basis of their policy guidance. This is done in order to realize

---

① Changes in the distribution of beliefs within a coalition generally will start with individual learning or turnover, be resisted by group dynamics, and then get diffused throughout the group. See Sabatier and Jenkins-Smith (1993b: 42).

② There is a rich literature explaining policy change and policy convergence across various boundaries, such as lesson-drawing (Bennett 1997; James and Lodge 2003; Rose 1993), policy transfer (Dolowitz and Marsh 1996, 2000; James and Lodge 2003; Stone 1999, 2004), policy diffusion/policy convergence (Bach and Newman 2010; Bennett 1991; Busch et al. 2006; Busch and Jörgens 2005; Carrapatoso 2011; Howlett and Joshi-Koop 2011; Karch 2007; Marsh and Sharman 2009), and epistemic community (Haas, E. B. 1990, 2004; Haas, P. M. 1989, 1990).

their policy core beliefs. Policy-oriented learning normally "entails experimenting with a variety of guidance instruments and other implementing mechanisms over time in an effort to achieve one's policy goals" (Sabatier and Jenkins-Smith 1993b: 44).

To obtain more resources is of great importance for policy-oriented learning: new supporters, especially experts and research institutes may help a minority coalition to gain more convincing information and authority to be better able to design policy proposals. Alternatively, the minority coalition can seek financial support and investment from the international level.

There are three stages involved in interlinking policy-oriented learning and policy change: the first stage is for the minority coalition to identify problems in the current system, and then seek sufficient resources to identify their causes and obtain political support (Sabatier and Jenkins-Smith 1993b: 46). In the second stage, the minority coalition exposes policy loopholes in policy implementation to the public and documents performance gaps in existing governmental programs. Third, to improve their understanding of the causal reasons for such gaps, the minority coalition can propose policies to deal with the problem and prepare for *an analytical debate* with the conventional coalition. Sabatier identifies this analytical debate as a "persuasion" process, in which "each side attempts to persuade or convince the others—as well as neutral parties, particularly potential policy brokers—of the validity of its claims" (Sabatier and Jenkins-Smith 1993b: 55). Promoting the analytical debate in a professionalized forum might lead to learning across coalitions; however, it depends on the level of interest conflict.

2.3.3.3 Argumentative persuasion promoted by a strengthened advocacy coalition

Sabatier argues that the analytical debate is a persuasion process. I use the concept of "argumentative persuasion" to further explore the role of a strengthened minority coalition in influencing policy change. Argumentative persuasion refers to the strengthened minority coalition's ability to challenge the validity and causal assumptions of the conventional coalition's policy initiatives and to stimulate the inner reflection process by criticizing the defects and limitations of former policy strategies. It attempts to do this by providing convincing and sound policy strategy alternatives. There are some overlapping parts between the last stage of policy-oriented learning and argumentative persuasion. In this book, I put more emphasis on learning within the non-dominant but strengthened coalition, and this paves the way for argumentative persuasion to be used in competition with conventional actors.

The strengthened non-dominant coalition can take advantage of international and domestic resources, to enhance their persuasive power in the collective argumentation with the conventional coalition. The first step is to take full advantage of *international resources* to challenge the causal assumptions of the policies promoted by the dominant coalition. International sources of influence can include knowledge, information, and widely accepted norms supported by the international regime. Other sources of influence can be international success experiences, best practices and innovative policy regulations. These can be introduced at the domestic level as innovative policy instruments by the strengthened coalition or the newly empowered coalition (positive argumentative power). Furthermore, national reputational pressure from the international regime (negative argumentative power) can also be used by the new coalition to point out domestic problems and enhance persuasion power in collective arguments. Argumentative analysis usually is stimulated by either threats to core values or perceived opportunities for realizing core values (Jenkins-Smith 1988).

Second, with the gradual strengthening of the formerly marginalized coalition, the minority coalition may *gain more authority and political resources* that can be used to challenge the dominant coalition's views. Research institutes and think tanks working with the non-dominant coalition might challenge the validity of data presented by the dominant coalition concerning the seriousness of the problem. They can do this based on their own comprehensive research and investigation. The crucial role of technical information is to alert people about the extent to which a given situation affects their interests and values. New institutional arrangements may strengthen information transparency and the influence of related discussions. During this process, the newly strengthened coalition can provide more policy alternatives in the problem solving process. They may attempt to mobilize the political opposition to support their proposal by pointing out the costs of inaction or of the existing system. In other words, by informing themselves and others they may attempt to create or enlarge an existing coalition (Sabatier and Jenkins-Smith 1993b: 45). Through successful changes brought about by minor policy change in the early stage of policy, such as with the adoption and implementation of innovative policy instruments, a new or newly empowered non-dominant coalition may be able to use this success as persuasive proof of the benefits of change. They may be able to present others with believable expectations linked to a better vision that may even win over their opponents to their argument. This may especially be the case if achievements have received international recognition.

Based on the analysis above, the third hypothesis of this book is:

H3 *The more effective the policy-oriented learning and argumentative persuasion promoted by the pro-RE coalition are, the more possibility the pro-RE coalition will have to influence RE policy change.*

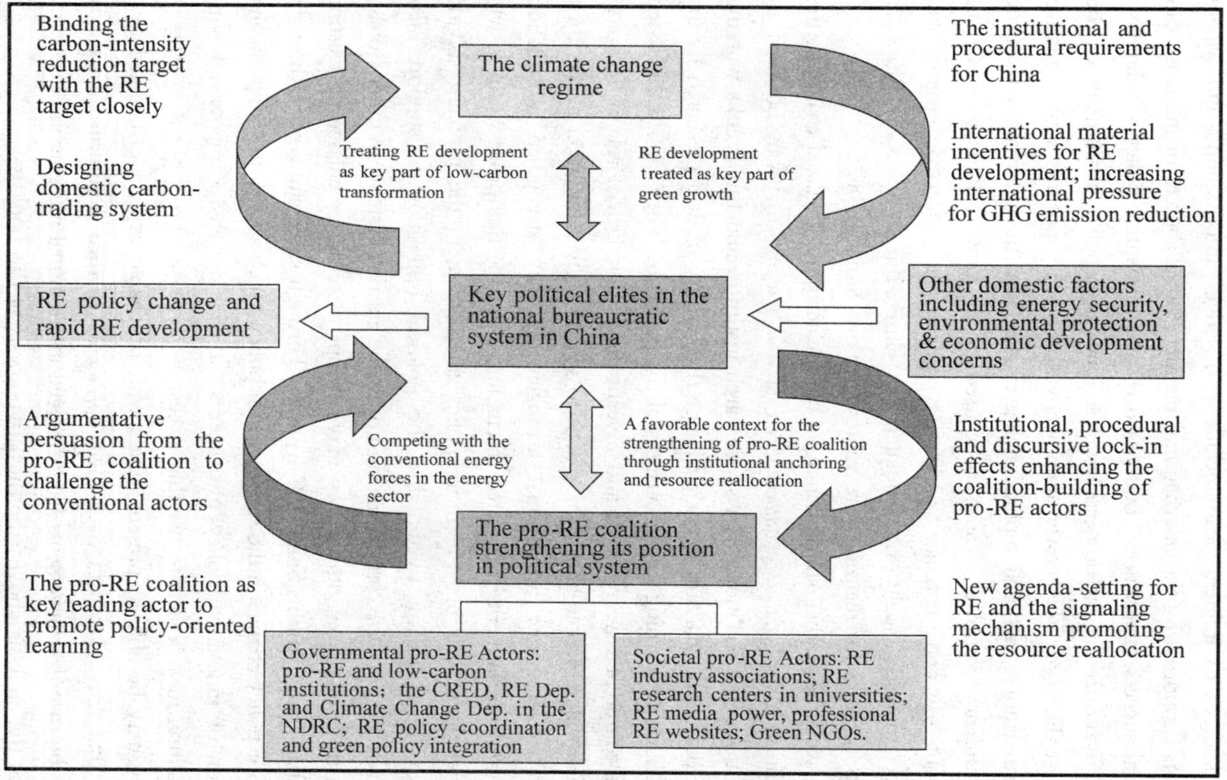

Figure 2.2 Strengthening of the pro–RE coalition in the process of climate change socialization and its role in RE policy change

Source: Drawn by the author

The main argument of this book is that the socialization processes tied to climate change, including institutional anchoring and resource reallocation, helped strengthen the pro-RE coalition in its competition with the conventional energy forces in the policy-making process. It is these dynamics that have promoted RE policy change and rapid RE development in China. Based on this argument and the three hypotheses above, Figure 2.2 illustrates the theoretical framework used in this book.

2.4 Applicability of the theoretical framework in China

2.4.1 General decision-making style of China's bureaucratic system

In the authoritarian Chinese system, although there is no clear party electoral competition, competition/contention between different advocacy coalitions on certain policy issues is still observable. Even within the most powerful governmental institution, the National Development and Reform Commission (NDRC), sometimes there are different positions on certain agenda items. China is not a homogeneous authoritarian entity, so the framework of "*fragmented authoritarianism*", first proposed in 1988, has "remained the most durable heuristic through which to study Chinese politics" (Lieberthal and Oksenberg 1988: 4; Mertha 2009: 996).

> Policy made at the central government becomes increasingly malleable to the parochial organizational and political goals of various vertical agencies and spatial regions charged with enforcing that policy. (Mertha 2009: 996)

In China's "fragmented authoritarianism", although the "top-down" approach is still an obvious characteristic of the policy-making and policy implementation process, the decision-making process is not controlled by one or two paramount leaders. The Politburo standing committee, as the most powerful decision-making agency led by the Communist Party of China, has seven to nine standing committee members. These paramount leaders represent the interests of different factions. The policy-making process in their executive meetings is usually based on the "consensus building" principle (Jakobson and Knox 2010: 1). Although concrete decision-making occurs in a "black box", from the policy output, it can be seen that the policy-making process is a bargaining and compromising process among different stakeholders. "Outcomes are shaped by the incorporation of interests of the implementation agencies into the policy itself." (Mertha 2009: 996) In the bureaucratic bargaining process, key ministries in the central government, high-level think tanks, powerful state-owned enterprises, provincial actors and other stakeholders all attempt to translate their own interests into policy outcomes.

Heberer (2009) proposes three main features of "fragmented authoritarianism": First, different actors affect political output: the central state, state-owned enterprises, different ministries, newly strengthened institutions, provinces and local actors, new social strata, new social organizations, and public opinion. The influence of different actors on domestic and foreign policies varies a lot (Heberer 2009: 4). Second, the Chinese party-state is not a homogeneous entity but a diverse entity. Although compared with western democratic countries, China is a "state-over-society" model, the state does not exist without society and it is based on an interaction between both state and society. Moreover, the state is subdivided into vertical and horizontal levels and organizations. Therefore, the state has to be conceived of as an ensemble of various organizations interacting with society at various levels and shaped by inner tensions and conflicts (Heberer 2009: 4). Finally, a growing public sphere is emerging. This is occurring via the Internet and in research institutions, think tanks, industry associations and NGOs. Public opinion is also increasingly influencing domestic as well as foreign policies (Heberer 2009: 4).

In addition, Heberer (2009) mentions that "*political pragmatism*" is a salient pattern of Chinese development and political culture (Heberer 2009: 6). It means the government tends to tackle and solve concrete problems and issues in a pragmatic way. Deng Xiaoping theory has had a far-reaching impact on China's developing ideology: "It doesn't matter whether a cat is white or black, as long as it catches mice."① Economically speaking, China is in a period of transition from a planned to a market economy. There is also an *economization of politics* underway. The latter means that economic development dominates politics and the activities of the central and local governments. Economic results and economic development successes are decisive for the assessment of an official and his career. Politically speaking, *regime legitimacy* is of great importance. It is no longer based on ideology, but rather functionally defined: by the promises of modernization and development; of gaining national strength; of preserving political, economic and social stability; and by establishing both a "socialist democracy" and a "rule of law" (Heberer 2009: 6). Bruce Gilly points out that China's political leadership attains legitimacy by means of continuous institutional change and performance (Gilly 2009). For instance, confronted with great pressure due to its high levels of energy consumption, climate change and deteriorating environmental conditions, economic growth dominated model has undergone a transition. The green growth and low-carbon economy models have been emphasized

---

① This famous sentence is a summarization of the pragmatism logic of Deng Xiaoping's theory. Deng did not worry too much about whether a policy was capitalist or socialist as long as it improved the economy.

more by national leaders. Nevertheless, GDP-ism still dominates many policy areas. At the international level, China also behaves in a pragmatic way. Take the climate change negotiations as an example. China refuses to adopt a mandatory GHG emission reduction commitment, at least before 2030 (in the 2011 Durban conference, China did show its willingness to consider 2020) (Chinafaqs 2011). China is afraid a legally binding target will hamper its economic growth rate. Still, China has shown its commitment to the climate change regime by initiating voluntary low-carbon initiatives. This also reduces international pressure on China. China has also tried to get incentives (financial support, clean technology, know-how, and best practice ideas) to deal with its own domestic problems.

2.4.2 Increasing pluralization in China's policy-making process

Mertha (2009) highlights *the increasing pluralization of the policy-making process* in China. Although there is a need for great improvement in democratization, there has been an increasing influence of new actors in the policy-making process, such as once marginalized officials, newly emerging institutions, scholars and scientists from research institutes and think tanks, social associations, non-governmental organizations, media powers like the Internet, TV and newspaper. These actors have successfully entered the political process by adopting strategies necessary to "work within the structural and procedural constraints of the fragmented authoritarianism framework" (Mertha 2009: 996). The point of entry is "through the agency slack that results from the inability of institutions to adapt sufficiently to rapid socioeconomic change" (Mertha 2009: 996). In other words, along with changes in the social-economical context and increasing international influence, the central government has realized its limited capability to handle the increasing range of domestic problems. Therefore, it has provided a chance for other and new institutions to act. Put in another way, "latent" actors are being activated. Sabatier and Jenkins-Smith also point out that "one must also be willing to identify potential ('latent') actors who would become active if they had the appropriate information" and "activating latent constituencies is often one of the strategies of coalitions" (Sabatier and Jenkins-Smith 1993b: 24).

Along with the increasing pluralization of the policy-making process in the "fragmented authoritarianism" framework, the minority coalition or newly strengthened coalition has more channels to integrate itself into the policy-making process. Mertha (2009) puts forward three points to explore newly strengthened actors in the consensus building mechanism.

First, problems which governmental bureaucracies face are arguably more fast-moving and complex than before (Mertha 2009). Take RE development for example. As a later comer, China did not have much experience in developing large-scale RE, so learning the innovative policy-instruments from other pioneering countries, such as the U. K. and Germany, is a rational choice. After the State Development Planning Commission (SDPC-former agency of NDRC) took up the main responsibility for the climate change negotiations in 1998, it established the Center for Climate Change as well as the Center for RE Development (CRED) under the Energy Research Institute. It did this in order to cultivate its own think tanks dealing with the climate change negotiations and renewable energy development. Later, CRED became the key agency responsible for drafting the RE Law and RE Law Amendment. In 2012, this institute was upgraded to the China National Renewable Energy Center (CNREC), which is responsible directly to the State Council.

Second, there seems to be "a gradual recognition by state actors that as information becomes more accessible in China as a whole, experts who are versed or literate in such information are useful, and the state actors (who do not possess the same skills) therefore seek out such expertise" (Mertha 2009: 1001). In other words, the channel between "science/knowledge and policy" has attracted more attention than before. China has attached more importance to the role of research institutes, think tanks, experts, and scholars in policy consultation than before. The typical case is the *Politburo Collective Study Sessions* held three or four times every month beginning in 2003 in the highest-level policy-making agency of China. The scholars or experts have a direct chance to share their professional knowledge as well as provide policy proposals to national leaders.

Third, Mertha also points out there is "a reinforcing effect whereby success breeds more success" (Mertha 2009: 1001). Once active actors in the pro-RE coalition are allowed to participate more in renewable energy policy making, and their efforts contribute to a RE policy outcome deemed successful, more similar efforts are likely to ensue. These could include introducing innovative policy instruments, like tendering policy and feed-in tariff policy. These have contributed greatly to the dynamic growth in RE in China. This in turn encourages policy makers to learn more from pioneering countries while exploring China's own policy systemization and innovation.

In sum, it can be said that the policy-making process in China is not solely shaped by the central leadership but by a broad variety of actors. The increasing pluralization of the bureaucratic system has provided more chances for new actors to be involved in the policy-making process. The advocacy coalition framework can be applied to a coalition analysis of China's policy subsystem. Here this is done in relation to RE policy making and RE policy change.

Chapter 3
Background of Renewable Energy Development and the Renewable Energy Policy Change Process in China

The aim of this chapter is to provide an overview of the RE development in China and identify the dependant variable—the RE policy change in the past decades. The chapter includes four sections. The first section provides an overview of the coal-dominated energy supply mix and the country's rapidly growing oil dependency. It has shown that the vested interest groups in coal and oil sectors are deep-rooted, which results in there being a great difficulty of institutional reform and structural optimization in energy sector. However, China has made remarkable progress in RE development in the past decade, and the issuing of the RE Law in 2005 has provided a great impetus to promote rapid growth of RE in the 11th FYP period (2006-2010). The second section focuses on the development of wind, solar and biomass power, and exposes the emerging problems of RE development at the domestic and international levels in recent years. The third section is the main part of this chapter and analyzes RE policy change through the process tracing. RE policy change is identified as the dependent variable in this book. The last section specifies the three levels of the RE policy system and summarizes characteristics of the RE policy system.

3.1 The fossil fuel-dominated energy supply mix

Driven by the rapid economic growth, especially in the fields of industrialization, urbanization and motorization, China's energy consumption climbed from 1.46 billion tce in 2000 to 3.25 billion tce in 2010 with an annual growth of approximately 8.3%

(Zhang et al. 2012: 1).① According to the IEA statistics, the country's energy consumption could grow to 4 billion tce in 2015 and 4.5 billion tce in 2020 (IEA 2011b). The main characteristic of the energy mix is that over 90% of China's energy supply comes from fossil fuels.② The coal-dominated energy structure has changed little during the past decade; there is a heavy path dependency on "black energy". And due to the strong growth of the transportation sector, especially in the private automobile consumption field, China's oil dependency has increased to over 57% in 2012 (IEA 2012b).

3.1.1 The stable coal-dominated energy structure

China relies on coal for more than two-thirds of its energy needs (around 70%), including 80% of its electricity needs. China is the largest coal producer, coal importer and coal consumer in the world. According to the IEA statistics, over the last decade, more than 80% of the global increase in coal demand came from China alone (IEA 2011b). Its share of global coal demand rose from 27% in 2000 to 47% by 2010 (IEA 2011b). In 2011, coal consumption further increased by 9.7% to reach 3.578 billion tons, accounting for 49% of global coal use and representing more than three quarters of global consumption growth in 2011 (IEA 2011b). Coal imports in 2011 increased by 10% to 182.4 million tons, which marks China's overtaking of Japan to be the largest coal importer in the world.③ This increase in fuel consumption in 2011 was mainly driven by "the increase in power production, building construction and expansion of infrastructure, as indicated by the growth in the cement and steel production" (Olivier et al. 2012: 20). Coal is expected to remain the dominant fuel source for the coming two or three decades.

The coal-dominated structure has been extremely stable for almost two decades; coal has remained the cornerstone of the electricity supply. This carbon lock-in structure is quite hard to break. There are mainly two reasons explaining the path dependence of coal. *First*, China's coal reserves rank second place in the world after the U.S. and the price of coal has stayed relatively low. Since the 1980s, China's economy started to grow rapidly, which led to higher levels of energy consumption,

---

① The global energy consumption growth rate was approximately 2.5% over the same period. See Zhang et al. (2012: 1).

② Coal, oil and natural gas accounted for 68%, 19% and 4.4% of China's energy supply respectively in 2010. See Zhang et al. (2012: 1).

③ In 2011, China overtook Japan as the world's largest coal importer. According to end 2011 statistics, China's coal imports were coming from: Indonesia, Australia, Vietnam, Mongolia, North Korea, Russia, South Africa, and the United States. See IEA (2011b).

especially in the coal sector. ① Due to the market economy reforms as well as the deregulation in the coal sector, the number of township mines grew surprisingly. This further reduced the coal price as there was competition with state-owned mines. In the late 1990s, the country tried to reduce its dependence on coal. The Chinese government initiated a policy campaign in 1998 to shut down small coal mines, most of which were township mines. Those small mines had caused serious problems, such as resource degradation, environmental damage and surprisingly many fatal accidents. As a result, in the late 1990s to 2002, the ratio of coal in primary energy consumption started to decline. However, since 2003, energy demand grew more rapidly due to a booming economy. Only coal could satisfy this energy demand since the coal price was more competitive than any other energy (Horii 2012: 84). *Second*, beyond energy cost reasons, the Chinese government's strategic goal to reduce the dependence on expensive imported natural gas and petroleum has been a major factor driving reliance on coal. This strategy has been central to China's economic growth, energy security and macroeconomic stability (Morse et al. 2009). For instance, to compete with township mines, the price of state-owned mines also remained at a lower level, and to cover their deficit, the government delivered a large amount of subsidies until the mid-2000s (Horii 2012: 83). Furthermore, in the electrical power sector (the largest coal consumer accounting for 54.8% in 2011), the government set two different prices for its coal supply, in order to guarantee the coal-fired power plants get sufficient coal with the favorable price lower than the market. Therefore, coal-based electricity has occupied the dominant position in the electricity mix. ② This coal-biased strategy enhanced the carbon lock-in and made it harder to shift away from coal dependence. It is, however, projected that the demand for coal in both industry and power will stabilize after 2030 (IEA 2012a). According to *Strategic Action Plan for Energy Development* issued by State Council in 2014, the proportion of coal consumption will be controlled within 62%.

3.1.2 Increasing oil dependency and supply-oriented energy security

Although coal consumption occupies the dominant place in the energy structure, the role of oil is also significant and cannot be easily replaced. Whereas domestic oil production increased slowly climbing from 138.3 Mt in 1990 to 198.8 Mt in 2009, China's oil consumption grew rapidly from 114.9 Mt in 1990 to 408.3 Mt in 2009,

---

① From 1979 to 2010, China's economy grew by 9.9% and energy consumption grew by 5.6% annually. See Wang, Z. et al. (2012).

② 78.7% of China's electricity was produced from coal in the power sector in 2009 and over 82% of its electricity in 2011. See Wang, Z. et al. (2012).

with an average annual growth rate of 7.0% (Leung 2011: 1330). ① Therefore in 2009, the ratio of China's dependency on foreign oil exceeded 50% for the first time in its history to reach 53.7% (IEA 2010). ② According to the statistics of the IEA, its dependency on imported oil will reach 60.5%, 76.9% and 82% by 2015, 2020 and 2030, respectively (Cheng 2008: 301). According to Goldman Sachs' statistics, China surpassed the U. S. to be the biggest oil importer around October 2013 (REUTERS 2013). As a result, the rapid growing reliance on imported oil has led to increasingly serious concerns about the supply-dimension of energy security (Kennedy 2010: 139).

Behind the rapid growth of oil consumption, the transport sector has gradually become the actual driver of China's oil demand since 2001. The share of the industrial sector in total oil consumption declined from 59.2% in 1990 to 42.1% in 2007 whereas that of the transport sector increased from 17.6% to 35.9%, meaning that the oil demand of transport has grown faster than that of industry (Leung 2011). Since 2001, China's vehicle production and sales have experienced a sharp growth and the increased vehicle population comes overwhelmingly from private vehicles (PVs) since 2000. It was remarkable that since 2007, the growth rate accelerated, achieving a growth rate of nearly 10%-15% 2007 to 2012 (Leung 2011: 1333). In 2010 China's domestic vehicle production and sales reached 18.26 million and 18.06 million respectively, which made China become the largest automotive market in the world (Zhang et al. 2012: 3). The heavy reliance of the transportation sector on oil highlights that it is irreplaceable so far in China's growing economy. According to 2012 statistics from the China Automotive Energy Research Center (CAERC), more than 80% of China's automotive energy supply would have to rely on the international market in 2030 (Zhang et al. 2012: 3).

Supply-biased energy security orientation and concerns about increasing external dependency remain prevalent, therefore "it is predictable that heavy dependency on oil importation will not decrease in the long run" (Aden and Sinton 2006: 253). With the 10th Five-Year Plan (2001-2005), the central government began to put priority to establish a national strategic oil reserve in order to enhance the national energy security. This was described as "expanding the existing and establishing a new national petroleum reserve bases" in the 11th Five-Year Plan (2006-2010). It is reinforced in

---

① The stagnation in oil supplies stems from the aging of China's oil fields, particularly those in the northeast, such as Daqing oil field. See Downs (2006: 10).

② China's crude oil supply comes from 24 countries, with Saudi Arabia (19.6%), Angola (12.1%) and Iran (10.9%) being the top three. The nation's net natural gas import in 2011 was 28.18 billion cubic meters, with a foreign dependency ratio of 21.56%, 9.4 percentage points higher than in 2010. See IEA (2011b).

the 12th Five-Year Plan (2011-2015): "China will improve the oil reserve system; strengthen natural gas and coal reserve and develop an emergency response system" (Yuan and Zuo 2011: 3856). In order to guarantee sufficient oil supply in the long run, China has attached much importance to oil diplomacy with oil-exporting countries (tending to sign long-term oil supply contracts and setting up more oil pipelines to mitigate the "Malacca Dilemma"①) and to its "go-out" strategy to encourage its state-owned oil enterprises to invest overseas. It reflects a belief that oil produced by Chinese oil companies abroad is a more secure source than that purchased on international markets. Beyond, conventional actors in the energy sector like the state-owned oil enterprises have strong vested interests in the oil business. There is strong resistance to energy structure optimization and industrial upgrading when those reforms might influence their interests. This kind of resistance was seen when state-owned oil enterprises refused to purchase and sell bio-fuels according to the RE Law. Although promoting RE development is regarded as a kind of national energy strategy to guarantee the long-term energy security, the strong resistance from conventional interest groups in the energy sector cannot be ignored.

3.2 Rapid RE development and emerging problems

Against the backdrop of coal-dominated energy supply mix and the emphasis on national strategic oil reserves, China nevertheless has made remarkable progress in RE development in the past decade. Since 2010, China has become the world leader in wind power installation capacity, solar hot water utilization, solar PV panels manufacturing and RE investment capacity (Zhang et al. 2012: 1). Renewable energies contributed approximately 9.1% of the country's primary energy supply in 2010 (Zhang et al. 2012: 1). However, most of this RE supply is from hydropower (about 78%); the proportion of wind power, solar power and biomass energy only accounts for less than 3%. Although hydro power currently dominates China's RE supply, its growth has been much lower than that of non-hydro RE over the past seven years (2006-2012). Furthermore, hydro power is already a well commercialized technology, so hydro power is no longer as much a focus of RE policy discussions as wind, biomass or solar power (Zhang et al. 2012: 1). In addition, the development

① Malacca Dilemma: Over 80% of these imports are likely to come from Africa and the Middle East, crossing the Indian Ocean and passing through the narrow Malacca Strait. At the same time, renewed tensions with the United States over Taiwan from the mid-1990s highlighted the possibility of conflict with a state that seemed well positioned to exploit China's growing reliance on oil imports. See Zha (2005).

of new energy/hybrid vehicles (electricity or bio-diesel driven automobiles) has also gained increasing attention. Therefore, the author mainly focuses on the non-hydro RE development.

3.2.1 Wind power

3.2.1.1 Wind power as the fastest growing RE

Compared with other forms of RE, wind power has been the fastest growing RE and contributed a lot to rapid RE development in the past decade. The average annual growth rate of wind turbine installations has kept as high as around 100% from 2005 to 2010. China's installed capacity of wind turbines has grown from 1.267 GW in 2005, to 12.02 GW in 2008, and 44.73 GW in 2010. Based on this rapid development, China has become the nation with the largest wind turbine installation since 2010. The accumulative installed capacity of wind turbines has reached 62.36 GW in 2011 (CREIA et al. 2012). This rapid development could not be achieved without great amount of wind power investment. According to the statistics of the PEW research center, over 80% investment in China's RE sector in 2010 is for wind power (PEW 2010).

In addition, the technological development and the degree of localization of wind turbine manufacturing are more mature than other renewable energies. The growth of turbine size serves as an important indicator for China's progress in the wind technology capability (Zhang et al. 2012: 5). According to the 2012 statistics of Chinese Wind Energy Association (CWEA), the average size of wind turbines installed has increased from 618.32 kW per unit in 2000 to 1466.8 kW per unit in 2010 (Zhang et al. 2012: 5). Now the main-stream wind turbines are 1.5 MW and 2 MW turbines. The localization rate of wind turbine production and its technological innovation level have been significantly improved than before. Approximately 25% of the added wind turbines installations in 2004 were supplied by Chinese manufactures, but the number was over 80% in 2010.

The mid-long term development target of wind power is the most ambitious one compared with other renewable energies. In the 12th FYP for RE Development, the 2015 target for the on-shore wind energy is set as 100 GW (even 150 GW in unofficial data). For the off-shore wind energy it is set as 5 GW by 2015 and 30 GW by 2020. According to the China Wind Power Outlook 2012 issued by Greenpeace, the Chinese Renewable Energy Industries Association (CREIA), and the Global Wind Energy Council (GWEC), China's installed capacity of on-shore wind power can reach 200-300 GW by 2020 and more than 400 GW by 2030 (CREIA et al. 2012). According to the Strategic Action Plan for Energy Development (2014-2020) issued by State

Council in 2014, the wind power installed capacity will reach at least 200 GW; wind power electricity price equals to the coal electricity price (State Council 11/2014). However, the realization of these ambitious targets relies on further RE policy changes, especially to improve the grid connection situation.

3.2.1.2 Emerging problems in wind power sector

Wind power curtailment worsening the grid-connection problem

The curtailment of wind power did not get due attention until the China Wind Power Outlook 2012. Now the high percentage of off-grid wind power (around 20% - 30%) has received more attention than before, although the obvious grid curtailment phenomenon since about 2010 has not received sufficient attention. The grid curtailment refers to a reduction of grid companies in the scheduled capacity of RE power delivery (GWEC 2012). In other words, the amount of full-load hours of on-grid RE power has been decreased by grid SOEs.

> Solving the issues linked to grid curtailment is challenging: the grid system was designed for a coal dominated power system and the lack of flexibility makes it difficult to integrate more wind in the system. This is especially the case in areas with rich wind resource in the northwestern and northeastern China—some large wind bases are planned to be built in this area. The fact that the grid companies are the biggest monopolies in China makes discussion of improving grid services difficult. (GWEC 2012)

In 2010, the accumulated wind turbine installation capacity was 44.73 GW, while on-grid wind power was only 31 GW. The off-grid wind power was 13.66 GW, accounting for 31% of the total wind power installation. Even the on-grid wind farms in the northeastern and northwestern China were frequently forced to limit their power generation by grid enterprises, which resulted in serious wind power curtailment. By the end of 2011, total installed capacity of wind power had reached 62.36 GW and the on-grid power had reached 47.84 GW (76.7%). There was an increase in the grid-connection rate in 2011 compared with the rate of 69.9% in 2010 (CREIA et al. 2012). These statistics show that the grid connectivity situation of the newly installed wind power has improved. However, the curtailment of on-grid wind power at this time has reached an unprecedented scale. Especially in northeastern and northwestern China, the curtailment has become more frequent. The grid enterprises shut down wind power casually according to their own will. According to the statistics of CWEA, the top 10 provinces for wind generation lost a total of 6 TW · h of wind power due to curtailments in 2011, accounting for 17% of projected generation. Wind curtailment was most serious in eastern Inner Mongolia and Jilin, and the curtailment rate was over 20%.①

Wind turbine grid disconnection accidents

Until 2010, wind turbines had operated for around 4 or 5 years before their operating stability was tested. Since the second half of 2010, there has been obviously an increase of nation-wide wind turbine accidents, especially grid disconnection accidents. There were 80 grid disconnection accidents of wind farms in 2010. From January to August 2011, the accident number even increased to 193 (2.4 times than that of 2010) (Xinhua News 2011b). On 17 April 2011 there were two massive grid disconnection accidents within one day. The accident in the large-scale wind farm of Gansu Guzhou caused 702 wind turbines to disconnect from the grid. Another grid disconnection accident on the same day took place in the large-scale Hebei Zhangjiakou wind project, which had a negative impact on the operation of 644 wind turbines (Xinhua News 2011b). There were also some other accidents, such as wind turbine nacelle fire accident, turbine falling-down accidents in wind farms of Liaoning, Inner Mongolia, and Gansu.

Wind turbine disconnection accidents had serious impacts on grid stability. With the rapid development of wind power installation, the impact of wind power on the grid has gradually increased from the local grid to the regional main grid. A small defect of a wind turbine can trigger fluctuations in the grid voltage, leading potentially to a large-scale wind turbine grid disconnection. It might further cause the disintegration of the regional grid and result in power blackout accidents. Bai Jianhua, the Deputy Chief Economist of China State Grid Energy Research Institute said the main reason for many wind turbine grid disconnection accidents is that most of wind power turbines do not have low voltage ride through (LVRT) capability (CNB Daily 2011).② However, from the side of wind turbine producers, the grid enterprises and wind farm managers also have inescapable responsibilities: the grid enterprises fail to improve the grid deployment and the management of wind farms needs a better coordination among different stakeholders.

① The top five wind power curtailment provinces are Gansu, Inner Mongolia, Jilin, Heilongjiang and Liaoning. Their curtailment rates are 25%, 23%, 21%, 14% and 11% respectively. See CREIA et al. (2012) and Schuman and Lin (2012: 94).

② Low voltage ride through capability allows wind turbines to continue to operate during or after voltage dips and temporary faults. This maintains an uninterrupted grid connection. With this technology, the grid can adjust more quickly, which improves entire power grid safety and stability. See CNB Daily (2011).

3.2.2 Solar power

3.2.2.1 Imbalanced development of solar power

Solar power can be divided into two main uses: solar heating (solar water heating—SWH/solar cooker) and solar PV power (solar panel manufacturing and solar PV power generation). The SWH has been used as a commercialized RE technology for more than a decade. The major reason for the widespread diffusion of SWH systems is that SWH can provide hot water more cost effective than natural gas or electricity-powered water heaters (Zhang et al. 2012: 3).① The energy supply from SWH systems reached approximately 20.7 Mtce in 2010, accounting for more than 95% of China's total solar energy supply (Zhang et al. 2012: 3).

China's accumulated installation of SWH grew from 26 million square meters in 2000 to 169 million square meters in 2010 with an annual growth rate of 20.6% (Zhang et al. 2012: 3). Since 2007 China kept being the most important SWH manufacturing and SWH installation nation in the world. According to the 12th FYP for RE Development, the installations of SWH systems will reach 400 million square meters by 2015, and 800 million square meters by 2020 (NEA 8/2012). Therefore, the SWH development in China is a successful story.

However, solar PV power utilization has a rather imbalanced development pattern: on the one hand, the PV panel/cell production has achieved an exponential expansion in the past decade, and 90% of the output are exported to the overseas market, especially to the EU market (Germany, Spain, Italy being the leading countries); on the other hand, due to stricter technological requirements, higher investment and insufficient governmental support, the PV power generation has developed rather slowly.

The output of Chinese solar cell manufacturers climbed from 50 MWp in 2004 to 8,000 MWp in 2010 with an annual growth rate of over 40%. Solar PV manufactures supplied approximately 50% of the global demands for solar cells in 2011 (Zhang et al. 2012: 4). Compared with the strong growth of solar PV panel production, the installed capacity of solar PV systems grew slowly, from 70 MWp in 2005 to 860 MWp in 2010. The contribution from solar PV systems to China's RE supply is rather limited in absolute terms.

The Chinese government now begins to pay more attention to the industrial

---

① The cost effectiveness of SWH systems results largely from the application of the all-glass vacuum tube (AGVT) technology in SWH systems. The application of AGVT technology increases the utilization efficiency of solar energy resource in SWH systems to a large extent, leading to marked improvement in SWH system's performance. See Zhang et al. (2012: 3).

upgrading of solar power. It means that RE development priority will shift partly from wind to solar power. According to the 12th FYP for RE Development, the installations of solar PV power systems will reach 21 GW by 2015 and 50 GW by 2020 (NEA 8/2012; Wang, Z. et al. 2012). Later in the Strategic Action Plan for Energy Development (2014-2020) issued by State Council in 2014, this target was further improved to 100 GW by 2020 (State Council 11/2014). By then, the photovoltaic power price will equal to general sales price of national grids (State Council 11/2014). If the policy implementation of this target can be fostered effectively, China will become the leading country of solar PV generation and provide a promising domestic market for solving the overcapacity problem of solar panels products.

3.2.2.2 Emerging problems of solar power

Anti-dumping duty and anti-subsidy tariff from the U.S. and the EU

The increasing import demand for PV equipment in the EU and the U.S. spurred the rapid development of solar panel production in China in the past five years. Solar panel industry relies overly on the export market. According to statistics from the China Solar Energy Society, solar panel production in 2010 was 10.67 GW, in 2011 this number jumped to 21.17 GW. Nevertheless, the domestic PV installation was only 3.6 GW in 2011, and most of solar panels rely on the overseas market. ① However, the over-reliance on the overseas market has been challenged seriously by the anti-dumping duty and anti-subsidy tariff from the U.S. and the EU under the influence of global financial crisis. ②

In October 2011, Solar World and six other solar panel manufacturers in the U.S. initiated an anti-dumping proceeding against Chinese solar panel importers (Leone 2012). According to this charge, the Department of Commerce (DOC) of U.S. launched an investigation and imposed tariffs of 31% to 250% on Chinese solar imports in May 2012. In October 2012, the DOC set final anti-dumping duties ranging from 18.32% to 249.96% on solar-energy cells imported from China together with anti-subsidy tariffs from 14.78% to 15.97% (Wingfield 2012). Combining the anti-dumping duties and anti-subsidy tariffs and subtracting the double-counting part, the tariff for the entire solar panel industry ranges as high as 23.75% to 254.66%. The cost of solar panels produced in China's main solar-power enterprises is about

① As much as 70%-80% of China's PV solar modules have been exported to Europe and about 10% to the U.S.

② The PV power industry has been seriously affected by the financial crisis. The rate of PV installation in many western countries slowed down due to the reduction of governmental financial support and subsidies. Solar panel industries in the EU and the U.S. are also confronted with overcapacity. The world-wide financial crisis could trigger the tendency of trade protectionism in the RE industry.

\$0.75, while the average price of a solar panel in the U.S. is \$0.97 (Leone 2012). Adding the 30% tariff to the imported solar panel means that Chinese solar panels will become less competitive and lose their market in the U.S. ①

Following the initiative of the U.S., the EU also has launched an anti-dumping investigation into the imports of China's solar panels since September 2012 (EC 2012). ② Compared with the U.S., the EU anti-dumping investigation has much greater influence on China's solar panel industry, since the EU is the largest PV export market for China (accounting for 70%-80%) (Zhang et al. 2012: 4). The cost of solar cells supplied by Chinese manufactures is often 20%-30% lower than that by European manufacturers (Zhang et al. 2012: 4). In June 2013, the European Commission made a decision to impose 11.8% provisional anti-dumping tariffs on Chinese solar panels and it would rise to an average 47.6% in August (European Commission 2013). A high anti-dumping duty would be undoubtedly a disaster to the Chinese solar industry. Although the price commitment agreement of the EU-China PV trade disputes which was approved by the European Commission entered into force officially since August 2014, the validity period of this agreement only lasts to the end of 2015. Then how EU determines the price of PV panel from China will once again become the focus of attention. As a result, many Chinese solar panel enterprises might have no choice but withdraw from the European market and turn to explore new markets, such as Africa, Southeast Asia and Australia. At the same time, China has begun to pay more attention to promoting its industrial upgrading and enlarging the domestic market by supporting the PV power generation strongly.

Overcapacity and vicious competition

In addition to the great pressure from the anti-dumping duty and anti-subsidy tariff at the international level, the disorderly development of solar PV equipment industries together with a lack of professional market analysis is among the main reasons for the overcapacity and vicious competition. For instance, in 2011, major Chinese PV panel producers expanded their production capacity rapidly: Sun-tech Power expanded its annual production capacity by 33% to 2.4 GW, and Trina Solar

---

① The Coalition for Affordable Solar Energy (CASE) held opposite stances on the anti-dumping duty and claimed that "low-cost Chinese panels have made solar energy more competitive with fossil fuels and spurred an installation boom". The DOC believes that China's great amount of solar panel imports are detrimental to the innovation capacity and job-position of the green industry of the U.S.

② As early as 25 July 2012, EU Pro Sun, an ad hoc association representing more than 20 European companies producing solar panels and their key components, launched an anti-dumping complaint to the European Commission that solar panels and their key components imported from China enter the European market at prices below market value (EC 2012).

expanded by 90% to 1.9 GW (CGI 2012: 78). In 2012, the biggest 150 Chinese PV panel makers have the capacity to produce 40 GW solar panels products. However, the worldwide demand has only shown from 20 GW to 40 GW between 2012 and 2013. This means that the exponential growth of the solar panels production in China has even exceeded the global PV market demand. Meng Xiangan, the secretary-general of the China Solar Energy Society, has pointed out that more than half of solar panels production in China is overcapacity (CRES 2012).

According to Han Qinming, the chief analyst of Solarbuzz, the anti-dumping duty from the U.S. and the EU has further increased the domestic overcapacity, which leads to low operating rates in solar equipment industries (Solarbuzz 2012). The average operating rate of solar panel producers was only 60%-70% at the beginning of 2012 (BJX 2012). In the middle of 2012, the number has dropped down to less than 50%. The poly-silicon producers have been confronted with the most dismal situation: their operating rate is only 20% due to the sharp decline in poly-silicon orders (BJX 2012). According to the analysis of Solarbuzz, solar equipment manufacturing industries will undergo a "major reshuffle": the number of solar cell firms will decrease from around 400 (in 2011) to less than 100 within the next five years (Solarbuzz 2012). The "major reshuffle" can eliminate the overcapacity and promote a more rational development of solar industry. However, if the government fails to play an active guiding role for the domestic solar industry in the most critical moment, there will be the risk of a sharp shrinking, threatening the entire solar industry.

3.2.3 Biomass energy

3.2.3.1 A comparatively slow development of biomass energy

Different from wind power and solar power, "biomass energy" is a wider concept encompassing various utilization approaches. Biogas, briquette, biomass power and bio-fuels (non-grain bio-ethanol and bio-diesel) are the four major energy carriers from biomass used in China (Zhou et al. 2012: 16). The utilization of biogas and briquette could be traced back to the late 1980s, and they were treated as one of the main supplement sources for energy utilization in rural areas. Especially small-scale dispersed biogas utilization has gained great promotion. Therefore, biogas and briquette can be titled as "old generation biomass". By comparison, biomass power and bio-fuels are the representatives of "new generation biomasses" with more promising development prospect.

To be more specific, electricity supply and liquid fuel for automobiles (especially oil) are the two main types of bio-energy. Biomass power can be treated as a significant alternative supply for electricity consumption. It could decrease China's heavy reliance on coal thermal plants. The utilization of hybrid automobiles, electricity automobiles and bio-fuel automobiles is a new trend for the green transformation in the traffic sector. Especially the utilization of bio-fuels is often regarded as a promising substitute for the gasoline and diesel in the transport sector globally.

The energy supply from the four biomass carriers increased by 2.39 times from 8.84 Mtce in 2005 to 29.99 Mtce in 2010 (Chang et al. 2012). Biogas and briquette, as the old generation of biomass, have also achieved great progress. The remarkable growth of biogas installations is largely attributed to government support. The Chinese government has provided more than 31 billion *yuan* of capital subsidies for the biogas development from 1996 to 2012 (Chang et al. 2012). For the new generation of biomass, there is a fast growth of installations of biomass power due to the introduction of the feed-in tariff for biomass power generation: the feed-in tariff for biomass power was 0.25 *yuan*/(kW · h) higher than that of the electricity from the coal-fired power plants equipped with desulfurization facilities from January 2006 to June 2010. Then biomass power has a fixed feed-in tariff of 0.75 *yuan*/(kW · h) (Zhou et al. 2012: 16). Compared with the other three biomass carriers, the development of bio-fuels is rather slow due to the insufficient support and a non-grain bio-fuel policy. On the whole, biogas (as the old generation of biomass) and biomass power (as the new generation of biomass) are the top two biomass utilization, accounting for around 55% and 36.1% of biomass supply respectively in 2010 (Zhou et al. 2012: 16).

Compared with the ambitious targets of wind power and solar power in the 12th FYP for RE Development, the target for biomass power is rather moderate: the installed capacity of biomass power will reach 13 GW by 2015 and annual biomass energy utilization will be equivalent to 50 million tons of standard coal by 2015 (NEA 8/2012). This target includes the annual biogas utilization will be 22 billion cubic meters: 10 million tons of biomass briquettes will be used, 350 million to 400 million tons of biomass alcohol, and 1 million tons of bio-diesel and aviation bio-fuel will be used (NEA 8/2012). Yan points out that traditional biomass energy sources, such as briquettes and biogas, can potentially go along towards helping the country to meet its biomass targets, while the new generation of biomass energy, like biomass power and bio-fuel, still need stronger support (Yan 2012): for instance, the target for bio-diesel and aviation bio-fuel is only 1 million tons by 2015.

3.2.3.2 "Two-end domestic constraints" for biomass development

Contrary to wind and solar power, the biomass development has been confronted with "two-end domestic constraints". There is a constraint of raw materials supply of transportation and the sales system.

Biomass development is firstly confronted with problems of the collection and transportation of cheap non-grain raw materials. Since China is a densely populated country (1.3 billion people) with a great amount of grain consumption, the government has put much emphasis on the "non-grain policy" for biomass generation. ① Therefore, crop straw has become the main source of biomass power and biomass-fuel generation (Newenergy Net 2012). However, the Chinese agriculture is still mainly based on small household farms without large-scale mechanized production②, which results in the collection, transportation and storage problems of crop straws for biomass industry. In addition, the insufficient crop straws supply and the competition of biomass companies within one region lead to increasing prices of raw materials (Newenergy Net 2012). Most of biomass companies have been in a dismal situation with very small profitable space, due to the difficulty in getting sufficient raw materials at a low price. ③ Ma (2011) contends that local governments should establish professional supportive institutions for biomass development, especially those assisting raw materials collection and coordinating the transportation for crop straws. Another solution is to enhance R&D on new alternative materials for biomass generation, such as seaweed.

Similar to the grid-connection problem of wind and solar power, biomass has two kinds of "grid connection" problems: one is the transmission of biomass power in the grid, and the other one is to connect the bio-fuels to the fuel transportation and sales channels. The former one can be solved by the feed-in tariff and RE mandatory quota, while the latter one has failed to get sufficient attention. It is hard for bio-fuels to enter the fuel transportation and fuel sales system like oil, mainly due to the strong resistance from the vested interests in the oil industry. How to open sales channels for bio-fuels and make them be accepted by people have become a critical issue for the bio-fuels industry (Wang, H. 2012). The RE Law issued in 2005, has established the legal status of bio-fuel and explicitly stipulated that the oil sales companies have responsibility to integrate the bio-fuels into their fuel sales system. However, there have been no special administrative regulations to further foster the implementation of this law. Therefore, many bio-fuel companies, especially bio-diesel producers, are

---

① In order to guarantee a food supply for China's large population, the government issued the non-grain policy to biomass industry, which means the raw materials for biomass production can not come from grain.

② Different from the large farms operating in the U.S., the land resources in China are decentralized in different small households, which leads to difficulties in using large-scale mechanized operations to harvest crops.

③ Even though some biomass companies have their own land for crop growing, the crop harvested from the limited land resources are far less than the demand.

confronted with a limited development prospect, due to the high cost of raw materials, narrow sales channels and a marginalized status in the market.

3.2.4 RE power generation receiving more attention

RE power generation contributes to the diversification of China's coal-dominated electricity supply mix and can improve the electricity supply in the rural areas which suffer from the electricity shortage. According to the 12th FYP for Energy Development issued in 2013, the coal consumption rate will be decreased from 70% to 65%. The proportion of non-fossil energy consumption will increase to 11.4% and the non-fossil energy power capacity will account for 30% by 2015 (State Council 1/2013). Therefore, increasing the proportion of RE power in the electricity supply mix began to gain much more priority in the national energy strategy. The electricity generation from renewable sources would account for more than 20% of total electricity generation by 2015 (NEA and CNREC 2012). If adding the non-fossil power generation from nuclear power, the cumulative non-fossil electricity generation will reach around 420 GW by 2015 and reach around 700 GW by 2020.

The remarkable cost reduction of RE installation costs has also created a favorable context for increasing the competitiveness of the RE power. Due to the technology innovation and large-scale localization of manufacturing, the generation cost of wind turbines installed in Chinese wind farms has decreased from 6,000 *yuan*/kW in 2007 to 4,000 *yuan*/kW in 2010. The price of solar PV panels installed has declined from 27 *yuan*/Wp in 2007 to 8 *yuan*/Wp in 2010 (Wang, Q. et al. 2010; Wang, Z. et al. 2012). Nevertheless, the green transformation of the electricity market still has a long way to go, since the coal thermal plants so far take account for over 80% in the electricity supply mix and there is still strong resistance from vested interest groups in the energy sector.

3.3 Process tracing of RE policy change in China

China was a late-comer in RE development compared with pioneering countries, such as Denmark or Germany. However, within one decade, China has achieved significant progress in RE development. It has been driven strongly by the change of energy policy, increasingly supporting RE. RE policy progress resulted strongly from a "learning by doing" process. As described above, it was a change from almost no RE policy to a RE policy burgeoning stage, followed by the introduction of the tendering system in 2003 (the former U.K. model), the use of a feed-in tariff system (FIT) starting in 2005 (based on the German model) and finally the efforts made to combine a quota system (based on the U. S. model) with FIT beginning in 2009. The main aim of introducing the new policy instrument by the pro-RE actors was to solve the emerging problems in RE development and constrain the resistance from conventional energy and grid companies in the energy sector.

3.3.1 The first stage (1978-1993): RE policy almost in a vacant situation

Since the beginning of what could be called the Deng Xiaoping's Era in 1978, developing RE (especially small-scale biogas, solar stove and solar water heating) was regarded as a supplementary measure to promote energy construction in rural areas. The Ministry of Agriculture (MOA) played a critical role in promoting the demonstration of dispersed RE utilization in rural areas. For instance, in 1979, the Fourth Plenary Session of the 11th Central Committee of the CPC issued the Decision of the CPC Central Committee on Issues of Accelerating Agricultural Development and put emphasis on a vigorous promotion of biogas in rural areas in order to solve energy problems. In 1986, the former National Economic Commission issued the Opinions on Strengthening Rural Energy Construction: all provinces and autonomous regions should compile their own long term plan for rural energy development, which included "promoting the utilization of firewood-saving cooker, methane, forest energy, small hydroelectric power, small thermal power, straw utilization, solar energy cooker, wind energy, geothermal energy in rural areas" (Li and Cao 2012: 826-827). In addition, during this early stage, the funds which were put into the field of RE development, were mainly used to promote traditional small-scale RE in rural areas. For instance, in the 7th FYP period, the Ministry of Finance provided a 3 million RMB loan to support energy development in the countryside, including a fund for small-scale biogas and solar stove development. However, there were basically no special policies or laws concerning RE development during this stage. Developing RE mainly served as a rural energy supplement, rather than being a significant alternative to conventional energy.

Still, significantly, in this early stage, societal actors such as RE associations and communities gradually emerged. In October 1980, the China Biogas Association was founded and held its first National Rural Energy Symposium in Beijing. And in 1983, the National Standard for Household Biogas Stove was promulgated by this association. In June 1992, the China Rural Energy Industry Association was established and played an active role in promoting the demonstration and popularization of biogas in rural areas. Small-scale wind power projects (most of them were off-grid) were launched in the 1980s for the primary purpose of supplying power in remote areas (IPCC 2012: 913). In 1984, the Wind Energy Professional

Committee was established by the Chinese Society of Electrical Engineering. Then in 1989, the National Standard for Small-scale Wind Generators was promulgated and implemented.

From 1978 to 1992, the SWH industry achieved comparatively rapid development (REN21 2009a: 31-32). In 1979, the Chinese Solar Energy Society was founded and R&D of SWH gained more attention than before. ① In the 6th FYP (1981-1985), the RE technology was for the first time included into the National R&D program, although the program was allocated only 3 million *yuan*. In the 7th FYP (1986-1990), the State Science and Technology Commission (SSTC) and the Ministry of Agriculture (MOA) promoted the technology commercialization and utilization of solar energy in rural areas. In 1987, the Beijing Solar Energy Research Institute introduced a copper and aluminum composite plate production line from Canada and succeeded in developing more efficient solar heating plates to promote large-scale SWH promotion (REN21 2009a: 31-32). ②

In summary, the RE development in this period still stayed at a dispersed and small-scale level. Its main purpose was to promote rural energy construction under the supervision of MOA. There were no special policies or laws issued related to RE, and no large-scale RE projects were promoted. The highlight in this stage was the comparatively rapid development and diffusion in the utilization of SWH promoted by societal actors. During this process, pro-RE actors (such as RE industrial associations, research institutes and universities) played an active role in promoting SWH commercialization (even without a national funding or credit support). There was not much large-scale RE development as the government did not provide a more favorable policy context or strong support.

3.3.2 The second stage (1993-1998): RE policy development in the initial stage

In this phase, the influence of domestic factors and the impact of international factors gradually began to converge in the direction of supporting RE development. At the domestic level, China has turned from a net exporter of oil products to a net importer in 1993, which symbolizes the end of energy self-sufficiency era. Since then, the dependence on oil imports grew dramatically. The large-scale RE development has

---

① In 1979, Tsinghua University, Shanghai Institute of Ceramics under Chinese Academy of Sciences, and the Second Glass Factory in Shenyang started to undertake research on an all-glass evacuated tube collector prototype.

② In the beginning of the 1990s, a series of high grade technologies and products, such as all-glass evacuated heat collecting tubes and heat collectors with evacuated tubes, were developed successfully, laying a sound foundation for the commercialization of SWH in China. See REN21 (2009a: 28).

begun to gain more attention, although the supply-biased energy security concern stayed in a dominant position. In 1993, the Law of Science and Technology Progress was issued, and R&D on RE technology development obtained more support from this legislative framework.

At the international level, with the increasing interaction with the international environmental regimes in the early 1990s (especially since China joined the Montreal Protocol as well as the UNFCCC), the increasing concerns on sustainable development and energy-saving have also provided a benign context for RE development. After the UN Rio-summit on environment and development in 1992, China issued its own action agenda in 1994—China's Agenda 21—to promote sustainable development and a rational use of resources. In the same year, the State Council passed the White Paper on Population, Environment and Development and pointed out that "China should develop new energy and RE according to the local conditions" (Li and Cao 2012: 829-830).

In January 1995, the former National Planning Commission, the former National Science Commission, and the former Economic and Trade Commission put forward the Guidelines for the Development of New Energy and Renewable Energy in China (1996-2010), which was a key document to guide the development of RE industries (Li and Cao 2012: 829-830). The Electricity Law was issued in 1995 and it was the first Chinese law starting to discuss the energy policy. Within this law, it declared that the "Chinese government will encourage the development and utilization of new and RE resources" (Han 2009: 31). This principle was reaffirmed in the China Energy Conservation Law in 1998.

Therefore, since the beginning of the 1990s, the RE development has undergone a gradual transition, from only focusing on dispersed small-scale RE utilization for rural energy supplement, to introducing integrated middle or large-scale modern RE projects. Moreover, China has begun to take full advantage of international resources to conduct bilateral or multilateral renewable cooperation (such as the trial of large-scale wind power project) and promote the SWH products to step to the international market. In this stage, both mid- and large-scale wind power and solar power projects have achieved some progress, especially promoted by the international RE cooperative projects. For instance, in December 1993, China and Germany signed an agreement to co-product 250 kW large-scale grid-connected wind turbine. And in the same year, the Xinjiang Electricity Generating Authority used the grant from Denmark and domestic investment to install 4 sets of 450 kW wind turbines in Chaiguobu wind farm. From 1990 to 1998, the average annual growth rate of wind power plants surpassed 60% and the installed gross capacity in 1998 amounted to 224,000 kW. In the field of solar power development, the 10kW PV power plant in Geji, Tibet was installed in October 1993. It was the first large-scale PV power plant in Tibet. In addition, the SWH industry has made great progress and entered the stage of large-scale industrialization. In 1998, the number of SWH enterprises exceeded 2,000 and the total installed capacity of solar water heaters amounted to 15,000,000 cubic meters, which ranked first in the world (Li and Cao 2012: 829-830).

However, the RE industry development still did not gain sufficient political attention in the 1990s compared with the western pioneering countries. There was still a lack of a systematic RE policy (concrete RE policy instrument and relevant administrative regulations) to promote large-scale RE projects. For instance, the development of large-scale wind power was still constrained in a sporadic stage. Solar energy merely focused on the low-tech SWH, rather than R&D for solar PV power. Furthermore, the supply-biased energy security orientation still dominated. China treated guaranteeing sufficient oil imports at reasonable price as the core task of energy security. During the 9th FYP (1996-2000) and the 10th FYP (2001-2005) period, priority was given to "reinforce oceanic exploration, explore overseas energy resources, establish overseas petroleum and natural gas supply base and diversify oil supplies" (Yuan and Zuo 2011: 3856). Especially in the 10th FYP, China clearly put much emphasis on the creation of a "strategic petroleum reserve system in order to enhance the national energy security". Therefore, RE development could not achieve great progress.

3.3.3 The third stage (1998-2005): launching of the tendering system policy

The reason why treating 1998 as the key beginning year for the third stage is that the most powerful department in macro-economic planning and energy regulation—the State Development Planning Commission (SDPC)① formally took the full charge of the climate change negotiations in 1998 and signed the Kyoto Protocol. This institutional change has reflected that China has realized the serious influence of the climate change regime on the domestic economic development and energy regulation. Furthermore, in order to support the climate change negotiations and further consideration on flexible mechanisms of the Kyoto Protocol, the SDPC established the Center for Climate Change and the Center for Renewable Energy Development under the Energy Research Institute of the SDPC.② In 2002, China ratified the Kyoto

① The SDPC was the former organization of the National Development and Reform Committee (NDRC) before 2003.

② Interview with Ren Dongming, Director and Professor in Center for Renewable Energy Development (CRED), Energy Research Institute, NDRC (6 August 2010, in Beijing).

Protocol, which sent a signal of China becoming more deeply involved in the climate change regime. The most remarkable turning in this period was that China changed its suspicious attitude towards flexible mechanisms embodied in Kyoto Protocol, especially showed its interest to CDM projects around 2002. The CDM has played a significant role in stimulating the large-scale RE development (especially the large-scale wind projects) and accelerating the modernization process of RE industry in the early stage. ① At the domestic level, the new government led by President Hu Jintao and Premier Wen Jiabao has showed its political commitment to optimize the national development approach since 2003. Former president Hu Jintao introduced the concept of "scientific outlook on development", which highlights the balanced and sustainable society building, as well as energy saving and resources conservation.

Against this backdrop, more environmental and clean energy laws and policies have come into being, such as the Environmental Impact Assessment Law issued in 2002, the Cleaner Production Promoting Law issued in 2003. In this period, China began to design its own nationwide RE policy and to pay more attention to the large-scale RE modernization process. The first indication of this new focus was that the value-added tax (VAT) on electricity generated from wind farms was reduced from 17% to less than 8% in 2002 (Lema and Ruby 2007: 3884). ② This VAT reduction was primarily an incentive for developers to engage in wind power. However, the NDRC has realized that the VAT reduction was far less to create a pro-RE market in short run (Lema and Ruby 2007: 3884). Therefore, following the former UK model, the NDRC introduced the tendering policy to China in 2002 and effectuated this policy since 2003. ③ *The tendering policy* is "using competitive bidding process to select projects that offer the best price" (Wiser et al. 2002: 7). During this process, "different renewable developers submit proposals to build new renewable generation facilities and indicate the price they would accept for their output, and the lowest priced RE project will be selected then" (Wiser et al. 2002: 7). The main goal of tendering policy is to promote the large-scale RE development by the concession bidding projects.

---

① Since 2001, the Longyuan Wind Energy Development Co., Ltd. began to develop the Huitengxile wind farm project in order to bid for the CERUPT emission reduction purchase plan of the government of the Netherlands. In the second half of 2002, the Dutch government and the Chinese government signed a contract on China's first CDM project. The Chinese enterprise received about 2.77 million Euros revenue within one decade (the emission reduction crediting period), accounting for 13% of its total investment.

② The common VAT-level in China is 17%.

③ The U.K. Non-Fossil Fuel Obligation (NFFO) is the most widely cited example of a tendering policy. Through the NFFO, the U.K. government placed five successive competitive orders for RE between 1990 and 1999. See Mitchell (2000).

In 2003, the NDRC issued the Wind Power Concession Program (NDRC 2003) in order to create further incentives for international and domestic investors to develop large-scale wind farms through bidding procedures, and to encourage a reduction in the price of wind power through government-overseen competitive processes and make clear the production cost for wind power (Xia and Song 2009). Domestic and international companies were all invited to bid for relatively large-scale potential projects (100-200 MW). Successful bidders were selected according to the price per kWh of wind electricity proposed and the share of domestic components utilized in the wind farm (IPCC 2012: 913).① From 2003 to 2008, the NDRC has continuously organized five rounds of wind concession projects, putting a higher priority to the localization of wind power turbine manufacturing (Xia and Song 2009).

Although concession bidding projects aim to find a reasonable price for the feed-in tariff (FIT), the shortcomings of this policy is the emerging vicious price competition. For instance, some bidding prices were far below the reasonable price range [even as low as coal-fired electricity 0.382 *yuan*/(kW · h)]. Furthermore, the state-owned energy enterprises with much stronger fiscal strength usually win the bidding with very low prices even though there is not enough profitable space. Small- and middle-sized private companies are gradually being marginalized in this green market. Since the tendering policy cannot guarantee a reasonable price for RE development, it was gradually substituted by the feed-in-tariff policy (FIT) after the issuing of the RE Law in 2005. Since 2009, the tendering policy is only applied to off-shore wind park construction and large-scale solar PV projects, whose generation prices are comparatively high. For example, in March 2009, the National Energy Administration (NEA) organized the Dunhuang large-scale solar PV concession bidding in Gansu Province. The tariff set after the bidding was 1.09 *yuan*/(kW · h). The accumulation of basic data related to solar PV power generation, provided the foundation for designing the feed-in tariff for the grid-connected solar PV power.

This stage served as a significant prelude to the introduction of specific RE policies. The launching of CDM projects and the implementation of tendering policy and concession bidding projects have played an important role in promoting large-scale RE development in the early stage, especially for stimulating large-scale wind power projects. Through bidding procedures, the government has an opportunity to investigate a reasonable supportive price for RE generation and based on this to design the FIT later. In a word, the successful experience from the tendering policy has paved

① According to the tendering policy, wind concession projects will last for 25 years and the bid price is guaranteed as a feed-in tariff for the first 30,000 full load hours achieved.

the way for introducing FIT policy which is embodied in the RE Law.

3.3.4 The fourth stage (2005-2009): introducing the feed-in tariff (FIT) by issuing the Renewable Energy Law

In 2005, former Premier Wen introduced the idea of creating a two-direction oriented society: an energy and resources-saving society and an environment-friendly society. In order to realize this target, the NDRC initiated ten major nationwide energy-conservation projects beginning in May 2005 (Cheng 2008: 302). At the international level, the Kyoto Protocol came into effect in the same year, and the Chinese government began to show more interest in capability building through CDM projects. For instance, in August 2006, the State Council approved the establishment of the CDM Fund and its management centre. In November 2007, MOF and NDRC jointly launched the operation of the CDM Fund.

Against this background, RE policy change has been promoted greatly by dynamics from the domestic and international levels. After two years of efforts, the RE Law was approved by the National People's Congress Standing Committee in February 2005 and enacted on 1 January 2006. The issuing of the RE Law symbolized the formation of the relatively complete RE policy system: from scattered supportive policy measures to an integrative RE policy system. It provides a basic legislative framework for promoting RE development by stipulating the national RE development targets, and designing central and local RE utilization planning (NPC 2/2005; Schuman and Lin 2012: 91).

In this stage, the main focus of the RE policy system was to develop the feed-in tariff policy following the German model. The *feed-in tariff (FIT)* refers to "a price-based policy which offers RE developers a guaranteed power sales price, coupled with a purchase obligation (a guaranteed market) by electric utilities in a relatively long time (such as 20 years)" (Mendonça et al. 2010; Wiser et al. 2002). In addition, feed-in tariff policy often includes the "tariff degression" mechanism: the RE feed-in tariff goes down over time as RE technologies develop, in order to spur RE production cost reduction (Mendonça and Jacobs 2009; Mendonça et al. 2010; Wiser et al. 2002). The main aim of the tariff degression is to track and encourage technological innovation and improve RE competitiveness (Couture and Gagnon 2010). The RE Law issued in 2005 stipulated three key principles to promote the implementation of the feed-in tariff policy:

(1) A *mandatory connection and purchase policy*. According to this policy, the grid companies are required to sign an agreement with renewable electricity generators in their jurisdiction to purchase all of the electricity generated from the generators, and

provide grid connection services. The guaranteed price and mandatory grid connection were enshrined in Articles 13, 14 and 19 (NPC 2/2005) of the RE Law: "the government encourages and supports various types of grid-connected renewable power generation...grid enterprises shall enter into grid connection agreements with renewable power generations enterprises that have legally obtained administrative license, and buy all the grid-connected power produced with RE within the coverage of their power grid, and provide grid-connection service for the generation of power with RE..." (NPC 2/2005).

(2) *Formulating fixed feed-in electricity prices* for different renewable electricity generators. This system provides an additional payment for each kilo-watt hour of RE generated electricity, which is above the whole sale electricity price for the coal-fired power (Schuman and Lin 2012: 91). The feed-in tariff depends on the types of RE resources available in a particular region and their production cost (Wiser et al. 2002: 2).

(3) The *cost-sharing mechanism* is funded by a surcharge on electricity sales in order to support the RE feed-in tariff, grid connection projects, and independent/public RE grids. In order to foster the effective implementation of the cost-sharing mechanism, it is better to establish a Special Fund of RE development to cover activities such as science and technology research for RE, standard setting, pilot projects demonstration, RE utilization in rural areas, and RE resource assessments (Schuman and Lin 2012: 91).

However, the RE law is basically a general legislative framework, which is not sufficient to provide detailed rules and procedures to foster the effective implementation of the three key FIT principles above. For instance, it does not stipulate the concrete feed-in tariffs for wind power, solar power and biomass; it does not make clear the punishment for the grid-enterprises if they fail to purchase the RE electricity. Therefore, China has issued several administrative regulations to enrich the general rules of the RE Law, such as the Interim Management Measure for Renewable Power Tariff and Cost Allocation issued by the NDRC in 2006, the Regulatory Measure on Off-Take Purchase of Electricity from RE Sources by Grid Companies issued by the State Electricity Regulation Commission (SERC) in 2007, the Interim Measure on Allocation of Income from Surcharges on Renewable Power Prices issued by the NDRC in 2007 (REN21 2009b). The State Council released the Mid- and Long-Term Development Plan for RE in September 2007. It set the mid- and long-term targets for meeting 10% of China's primary energy consumption from RE sources by 2010 and 15% by 2020, including hydropower, wind, solar and biomass energy (NDRC 7/2009; Schuman and Lin 2012: 92). In 2008, RE development Planning during the 11th FYP Period was issued, in order to guide the government at all levels and all sections of society to develop RE (Wang, Z. et al. 2010: 119). Although these administrative regulations have paved the way for the rapid development of RE, the final feed-in tariffs for different RE have not been stipulated clearly in the special regulations.

Three key principles of the RE Law (fixed price, grid connection and cost sharing) are interrelated with each other: the fixed on-grid price firstly guarantees the profitable space for the RE generators, nevertheless, the precondition for the guaranteed purchase is the RE power transmission through national grids. The cost sharing mechanism will make sure that the excess between the expenses incurred in the purchase of average power price generated with conventional energy shall be shared in the selling price of the whole of society. In this stage, RE development was still confronted with two problems:

The first is the unclear fixed price for different RE in different regions. For instance, from January 2006 to June 2010, the feed-in tariff for biomass was 0.25 *yuan*/(kW · h) higher than that of electricity from coal-fired power plants, which proved to be insufficient to promote biomass development. The large-scale wind power projects were mainly supported by the tendering policy from 2005 to 2009, and there was no clear nationwide fixed price for wind power (although some wind-rich provinces have their own FIT policy). This is a main reason for the rather slow development of solar PV power. There was no FIT for solar PV power until 2011.

Second, the grid-connection problem has emerged as a factor seriously constraining RE electricity generation. Until 2009, the installed capacity of wind power has accounted for 1.85% of the total installed capacity of electric power, while the on-grid wind power only accounts for 0.75% of total electricity consumption. The grid-connection problem leads to the imbalance development of RE. Take wind power for example, the "upstream" industry such as wind turbines manufacturing and wind farms construction develops rapidly due to the favorable fiscal subsidy. By comparison, the "downstream" support for RE power transmission is still insufficient, especially the state-owned grid enterprises are unwilling to purchase the "unstable and low-quality" RE power.

In summary, the issuing of the RE Law in 2005 has symbolized the formation of relatively comprehensive RE policy system. In this framework, the feed-in tariff policy has gained its official position to promote RE development with emphasis on three mechanisms: the fixed price mechanism, the grid connection mechanism and the cost-sharing mechanism. This legislative framework has provided great dynamics for the rapid RE development, which leads China to rise as a world leader in wind power installation capacity, solar panel manufacturing, and the RE investment. Nevertheless, behind the great achievement of RE development, there are some problems, such as grid-connection problem, beginning to obtain increasing attention. The policy loopholes in the RE Law need to be improved in order to foster the effective implementation of the feed-in tariff and guarantee healthy and orderly RE development. Therefore, there has been increasing voices for amending the RE Law.

3.3.5 The fifth stage (2009 to the present): combining the quota system with the FIT

High global expectations were tied to the Copenhagen Conference at the end of 2009 because the international community hoped that a new legal agreement addressing climate change could be reached (Li and Cao 2012). Confronted with unprecedented levels of international pressure, China made a voluntary carbon intensity reduction commitment and a non-fossil energy development commitment before the Copenhagen Conference: reducing the amount of CO_2 emitted per unit GDP by 40%-45% by 2020 compared to 2005 levels and obtaining 15% non-fossil energy in the energy supply mix by 2020 (Carraro and Tavoni 2010). Although this voluntary commitment has encountered critiques from the international community (which questions whether it is ambitious enough or not), Carraro and Tavoni, through their in-depth study, have proposed that the 40%-45% carbon-intensity reduction commitment could not be met simply and "China's recent experience of a lower income elasticity of carbon intensity suggests additional efforts and leadership could be required" (Carraro and Tavoni 2010). This commitment has sent a strong signal to the domestic level and has stimulated steps being taken towards the promotion of a low-carbon transition and RE development.

> ...assessing the challenge of the carbon intensity target proposed by China is not an easy task. If China were to continue on its long-term historical trend, then the 40%-45% objective would essentially yield nothing more than the baseline. No additional effort. No leadership to fight climate change. The Copenhagen Accords would be even emptier than what is now perceived. This is what energy scenarios seem to predict to be the most likely case. Yet, the significant variations over time and across countries suggest that the proposal could turn into a serious mitigation policy, and possibly a very challenging task, even for somewhat lower rates of decarbonisation of the Chinese economy. (Carraro and Tavoni 2010)

Furthermore, since China surpassed the U. S. to become the largest energy consumer in the world in 2010 and must deal with very high energy dependence levels, China has taken the carbon-intensity reduction target more seriously in order to spur domestic economic structural transformation. In the 13th meeting of the 11th NPC Standing Committee in 2010, the NDRC issued a report to officially involve the carbon intensity reduction and RE development as significant compulsory binding indicators into the 12th Five-Year Plan. In the 12th Five-Year Plan, it clearly mentions that China strives to establish a competitive RE industry system and make a reduction of 16% energy intensity and 17% carbon intensity by 2015 compared with 2010 levels. Furthermore, the NDRC issued the 12th FYP for RE Development (NEA and CNREC 2012): it stipulates that the annual RE consumption will reach 478 million tons of standard coal equivalents (tce) by 2015, including 400 million tce coming from commercialized RE, representing more than 9.5% in overall energy mix (NEA and CNREC 2012).

These national commitments and the strategic emphasis on the low-carbon approach have provided more dynamics for RE policy change, especially to improve the RE Law and realize the three key principles. The FIT prices for wind energy, solar energy and biomass were eventually fixed by key administrative regulations. The NDRC has officially set the feed-in tariff for wind power through issuing the Notice on Policy to Improve Grid-Connected Power Pricing for Wind Power in 2009 [0.51 *yuan*/(kW · h), 0.54 *yuan*/(kW · h), 0.58 *yuan*/(kW · h), 0.61 *yuan*/(kW · h) for four different wind-resources regions respectively]; set the feed-in tariff for biomass [0.75 *yuan*/(kW · h)] through issuing the Standard for Feed-in Policy of National Unified Agricultural and Forestry Biomass in 2010, and set feed-in tariff for solar PV power through issuing the Notice on Feed-in Policy of Solar Photovoltaic in 2011 [1 *yuan*/(kW · h), 1.15 *yuan*/(kW · h)].

Even though the feed-in prices for different RE were fixed gradually, the implementation of feed-in tariff policy has still encountered strong resistance from conventional energy forces. In order to "bring more teeth" to the RE Law, the National People's Congress passed amendments to the RE Law in December 2009, which took effect in April 2010. Three main achievements of the RE Law Amendment are:

First, the *RE quota system* was introduced in order to improve the implementation of the mandatory RE connection and purchase policy. The mandatory RE quotas were enshrined in the RE Law Amendment. Article 14 was amended to govern the grid purchase of RE, to establish a priority dispatch system which favors RE electricity transmission, and to set technical standards for grid connection (NPC 12/2009). It also stipulates that the quota system will design RE targets based on RE electricity generation rather than the installed capacity (Schuman and Lin 2012: 91). It symbolizes that the main focus on RE development has shifted from the quantity of the installation capacity to the quality of the RE power generation. However, this amendment fails to clarify the concrete RE quotas for different stakeholders, like the state-owned grid enterprises (NPC 12/2009).

Second, a *RE fund* was established in order to improve the cost sharing system for implementation among provincial and local levels, and especially to speed up payments for RE incentives. It also stipulates the access cost and other relevant costs that cannot be recovered from the selling price of electricity, and allows the power grid enterprises to apply to the RE development fund for subsidies (Li and Cao 2012).

Third, the amendment highlighted the significance of *improving the planning procedures and enhancing the coherence of national and local planning.* In the years following the promulgation of the RE Law, problems in RE development and utilization planning started to become visible, such as inconsistencies between national and regional planning, and unmatched generation and grid construction planning (Li and Cao 2012). Therefore, to enhance the planning coordination among different levels is of great importance.

In these amendments, the most profound achievement is to introduce the quota system to combine with the FIT in the RE legislative framework. The *Renewable Portfolio Standard (RPS)/the quota system* is defined as a market-based mechanism that "generally places an obligation on electricity supply companies to produce a specified fraction of their electricity from RE sources" (Jaccard 2004; Wiser et al. 2002). ① The main aim of introducing the quota system and combining it with FIT is to set mandatory RE quotas for the state-owned grid enterprises and state-owned power enterprises and to coordinate the RE planning between the central government and the provincial governments.

In 2010 after the RE Law Amendment came into effect, the State Council issued the Decision on Accelerating the Cultivation and Development of Strategic Emerging Industries. The decision stipulates that RE ranks as a significant strategic industry and emphasizes RE grid transmission by implementing a quota system. The government has sought to address grid-connection problems by setting out more specific generation-based RE quotas (Schuman and Lin 2012: 92). In May 2012, the Regulation for Management of Renewable Power Quotas (Exposure Draft) was issued by the NEA, in order to allocate concrete mandatory RE quotas on the big power enterprises, state-owned grid enterprises and provincial level actors. It symbolizes that the nationwide mandatory RE quota allocations have been launched. As a result, conventional energy actors will be under greater pressure to realize their RE quotas.

---

① The RPS has been adopted in order to promote green market development by the U. K. and 30 of 51 States in the U. S.

3.4 Framework of the RE policy system and its characteristics

3.4.1 General framework of the RE policy system in China

Based on the process-tracing of the evolution of RE policy, it can be seen that China has gradually established its RE policy system and this system has been in the process of improvement. Any policy system in China includes three levels: basic laws issued by the National People's Congress (NPC), key administrative regulations like Five-Year Plans (FYP) issued by the State Council, and supportive administrative regulations by ministries and local governments.

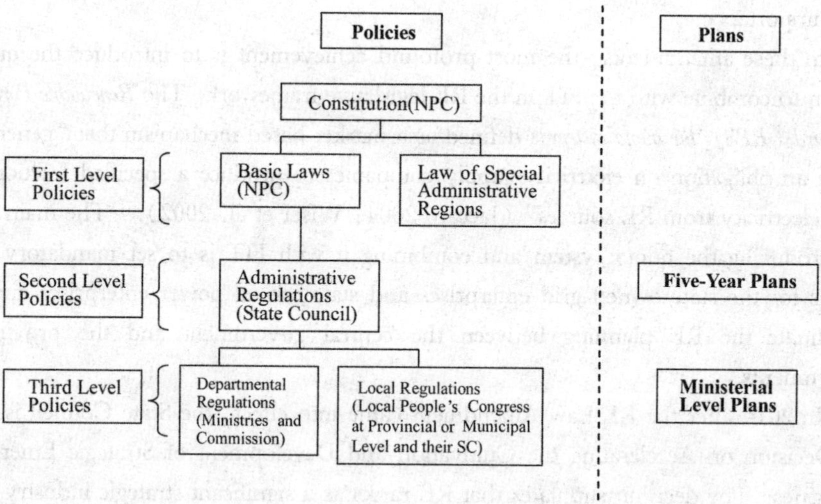

Figure 3.1 Hierarchical structure of the policy framework in China

Source: Lee (2012: 25).

The RE policy system framework also includes the following three policy levels:

The *first policy level* is represented by the key RE laws, such as the RE Law issued in 2005 and the RE Law Amendment in 2009. Basic laws provide "significant direction and guidance for the entire country by consolidating and disseminating important social and economic policy goals to lower levels in the governmental hierarchy system" (Lee 2012: 17-18). This level provides a basic framework to guarantee the legislative position of RE, especially laying the foundation for the FIT policy framework in the RE Law and introducing the quota system by issuing the RE Law Amendment. However, the basic laws like the RE law are usually "considered vague and abstract, and leave much room for interpretation when it comes to policy implementation" (Lee 2012: 15). Therefore, the effective implementation of the basic laws depends on the support of administrative regulations from the State Council and the ministries. During this process, different interest groups and advocacy coalitions attempt to influence the law's interpretation and translate their own willingness into the policy implementation stage. In addition, the other relevant laws, like the Climate Change Law and the Circular Economy Promotion Law also play a supportive role in fostering the policy implementation (see Appendix I).

The *second policy level* relates with key administrative regulations issued by the State Council, such as the 12th FYP issued in 2011, the 12th FYP for RE development in 2012 and the 12th FYP for the energy development in 2013. The FYPs is "a series of roadmaps that lay down the central government's objectives and goals for the next five years" (Lee 2012: 15) and set "key indicators of the directions and changes in development philosophy" (Casey and Koleski 2011; Lee 2012). The FYP are usually drafted by ministries and other organizations under the purview of the central government. After they are accepted by the State Council they are implemented as a form of strategic guidance and provide more specification on the legislative framework (Lee 2012: 15). Governmental research institutes under different ministries and national think tanks have played an increasingly significant role in providing the policy proposals and taking the basic policy drafting job. In the RE policy system, the FYP has played a fundamental role in reiterating or clarifying the government's standpoint on RE development and has formulated quantitative targets for future RE development direction. The strategic targets for RE development are also embodied in key national climate change plans (see Appendix I).

The *third policy level* contains RE-supportive administrative regulations issued by ministries and local regulations. This book focuses more on the ministerial level, since the regulations-making at the local level usually has to follow the main direction of the ministerial regulations. Since the RE law and quantitative targets embodied in the FYP only provide a general development guidance framework, the implementation of RE policy needs more concrete supportive regulations. The main aim of issuing these RE-supportive administrative regulations is to foster the effective implementation of the RE law as well as the national strategic RE targets. In the RE policy-making system, the National Development and Reform Commission (NDRC), the National Energy Administration (NEA) under the

NDRC, the Ministry of Finance (MOF), the Ministry of Science and Technology (MOST) and the State Electricity Regulatory Commission (SERC) are the key actors issuing RE administrative regulations.

These administrative regulations can be divided into three groups: the first group focuses on the three key principles of the FIT system and relevant RPS considerations, including the fixed RE tariffs, grid-connection and cost sharing mechanisms; the second group is the fiscal subsidy for RE development, which consists of the special fund, low-interest credit loans and favorable tax rates; the third group is related to RE generation and development standards. The requirements of standardization production are of great importance to prevent disorderly development and to unify RE grid-connection standards (see Appendix I).

In the RE policy system, the administrative regulations related to the FIT and the quota system provide more concrete specifications and operative procedures to foster the policy implementation of the RE Law and FYP for RE development. The RE Law Amendment issued in 2009 introduced the quota system combining it with the FIT. Concrete mandatory RE quotas for state-owned grid enterprises have been finally stipulated in the Regulation for Management of Renewable Power Quota (Exposure Draft) after three years in 2012. As a fiscal supplement to the FIT and the quota system, the role of fiscal subsidy to promote RE development cannot be underestimated. The main fiscal subsidies for RE development include:

(1) The *special fund*. The special fund policy is the most effective way to overcome the barrier of financial resources for the promotion of RE development (Han 2009: 36). The RE Law and the Mid- and Long-Term Development Plan for RE require that the national fiscal system launch special funds. The local fiscal system shall allocate a budget for supporting RE development. Furthermore, the Interim Measure on Special Fund Management of RE Development set detailed regulations for the subsidy standards. The recipients of these funds should provide self-complementary funds at least equal in size to the special funds (Han 2009: 36). The special funds have played an indispensable role in encouraging the development of wind power before fixing the feed-in tariff for wind power (like the Interim Measure on Management of the Special-Project Funds for Industrialization of Wind Power Generation Equipment in 2008) and solar PV (like the Interim Measure on the Management of Public Subsidies for Golden Sun Demonstration Projects). The Golden Sun Project was launched in March 2009 and received the most subsidies from the government of any renewable energy

project until now. The central government has allocated 10 billion RMB annually to provide subsidies for the construction of solar PV roof and solar PV architectures (Wang, Z. et al. 2012: 184-185).①

(2) *Favorable tax rates.* According to Article 26 of the RE Law, "the government grants tax benefiting to projects listed in the National RE Industrial Development Guidance Catalogue and specific methods are to be prepared by the State Council" (NPC 2/2005). In the Mid- and Long-Term Development Plan for RE issued in 2007, it mentions that "the government grants a favorable tax rate to renewable technology R&D and equipment manufacture". There are three significant favorable tax rate regulations. The first one is a favorable value-added tax (VAT) rate on several renewable energies. In China, the normal VAT rate for enterprises is 17%, while it is 13% for methane, 6% for small hydro and 8.5% for wind power (Han 2009: 38). Second is the refund of custom tariffs. According to the Notice on Import Tariff Adjustment for Large Wind Turbines, Key Components and Raw Materials in 2008, although China has cancelled the duty-free policy on imported wind turbines, it still keeps tariff incentives on the import of key components and shortage materials of wind turbines in order to encourage domestic R&D on wind turbines (Han 2009: 38). Third is the reduction of the income tax rate or business tax rate. For example, for power plants using RE resources, the income tax is exempted during the first 5 years of operation. For all RE generating enterprises, the income tax rate is 15%, which is lower than the income tax rate of normal enterprises (33%) (Han 2009: 38).②

(3) *Low-interest loans.* In 1999, the NDRC and the MOST issued the Notice on Several Problems for Promoting RE Development, in which certain favorable policies for RE power generation were set forward, including back loans with 2% interest subsidy (Han 2009: 38). Article 25 of the RE Law states that "national government and financial institutions may offer preferential loan with interest subsidy (low-interest loans) to RE development and utilization projects that are listed in the National RE Industrial Development Guidance Catalogue and qualified for the credit conditions" (NPC 2/2005). There are two main factors

① The standards are RMB 9 *yuan*/W for demonstration projects using crystal silicon module and RMB 8 *yuan*/W for those using non-crystal silicon membrane module. Along with the decreasing costs for PV modules, the subsidy will be reduced year by year.

② According to the Energy-saving and New Energy Automotive Industry Development Plan in 2012, the energy-saving and new energy automotive industry and their key components production enterprises can enjoy a business tax exemption policy.

that can explain the mushrooming development of RE at the local level (especially for wind power and solar panel manufacturing): the first reason is that the provincial authority has the wind power project approval rights (under 5 MW) according to the RE Law, and second that local renewable projects have been financially stimulated by low-interest loans from state banks (Andrews-Speed 2012: 216).①

3.4.2 The main characteristics of China's RE policy system

Based on the above analysis, the main characteristics of China's RE policy system are:

First, the legislative framework of RE Law is not yet sound enough; its effective implementation will need to be supported by many subsequent administrative regulations. The law only sets out abstract guidance and a general framework of legislation on RE. It introduces three key principles: fixed price, grid connection and cost sharing, following the German feed-in tariff model. However, it fails to provide detailed rules and procedures to foster the effective implementation of the three key principles. As a result, the FIT policy cannot get enough drive without specific governmental regulations to back it up. There are altogether more than ten administrative regulations that were formulated from 2006 to 2012 in order to enrich and substantiate the abstract articles of the RE law. For instance, the fixed prices of the main renewable energies (on-shore wind power, solar PV and biomass) were not clearly formulated in the RE Law, but through three key administrative regulations: the Notice on the Policy to Improve Grid-Connected Power Pricing for Wind Power in 2009, the Standard for Feed-in Policy of National Unified Agricultural and the Forestry Biomass in 2010, and the Notice on Feed-in Policy of Solar Photovoltaic issued in 2011. The bottleneck of grid connection has not been solved yet. Although SERC issued the Regulatory Measure on Off-take Purchase of Electricity from RE Sources by Grid Companies in 2007 after the RE law, the effectiveness of the implementation was limited. The central government considered to introduce the quota system into the FIT system, in order to enforce grid-connection.

In 2010, the Decision on Accelerating the Cultivation and Development of Strategic Emerging Industries clearly defined the strategic position of RE and put emphasis on the role of the quota system in strengthening the grid connection of

① Beginning in 2011, the NEA planned to withdraw wind power project approval rights (for wind farms under 5MW) from the provincial level, in order to enhance RE supervision and avoid disorderly development.

RE power. How to best introduce the quota system (the allocation of a quota index) and how to combine the quota system with FIT have generated a heated dispute among different stakeholders. The issuing of the Regulation for Management of Renewable Power Quota (Exposure Draft) in 2012 symbolized that the official position was now supporting a quota system policy. In order to enforce the ratification and execution of the Regulation for Management of Renewable Power Quota, NDRC issued The Assessment Measure for Renewable Power Quota (Trial Implementation) in 2014 was published, which marked that the central government would take great efforts to overcome the grid-connection bottleneck in the nearby future. However, the combination of the FIT and the quota system, as well as the implementation of the three key principles still has a bumpy path to go, since solving these issues will require an entire structural reform of the energy system, especially the market reform of the electricity system. The more renewable administrative regulations related to the RE Law are issued, the more intensive the interest game will be among stakeholders in the energy sector. More administrative regulations also reflect a greater interest among policy makers in pushing green reform.

Second, national strategic targets in the Five-Year Plan play a significant role in RE policy change. The Five-Year Plan in China refers to a series of social and economic development initiatives to map the strategies for economic development. It sets the targets for economic growth and launches structural reforms, which provide a significant blueprint for the immediate future (Yuan and Zuo 2011). Since China launched its 1st FYP in 1953, five year plans have played a pivotal role in guiding general economical and social development. It is said that the past decade (2003-2012) has witnessed that rapid growth of RE development. During this period, the strategic guidance role of the FYP cannot be underestimated. Since the 10th FYP (2001-2005), some environmental targets have been embodied in the national plan, which was reflected in the government's increasing concern in the environmental costs of the economic development (China dialogue 2012: 5). Since the 11th FYP (2006-2010), the government began to reflect seriously on the heavy-energy-dependence development model, and the energy security concept has been transformed from an energy supply-biased orientation to an energy-use security approach together with concerns about environmental acceptance (State Council 3/2006). The great achievement in the FYP was to set an energy intensity reduction target, reducing energy consumption by 20% per unit of GDP within five years (State Council 3/2006). If saying "the 11th FYP still held growth and development as its primary goal, the 12th FYP (2011-2015) has demonstrated a much more robust ambition that makes the difficult transition towards a more sustainable model" (China dialogue 2012: 5-6). It was the first time that both a carbon intensity reduction target and a RE development target appeared in a national strategic plan (State Council 3/2011).① In the 12th FYP, RE is highlighted as "strategic emerging pillar industry" in the macro-economy development (State Council 3/2011). Furthermore, under the general framework of the 12th FYP, the government also issued a special plan—12th FYP for Renewable Energy Development to foster the effective implementation of RE. Examples are the plan to launch a green energy demonstration projects in 108 counties and pilot projects of a large-scale use of RE in buildings in 35 cities and 97 counties. At present, the 13th FYP (2016-2020) regarding new energy is being formulated, and renewable energy especially wind-power is possible to see its status change from the currently widely-known "alternative energy" to one that will play a significant role in the country's energy structure. The clean-tech sector will get a boost with ambitious targets under the 13th FYP: a steady increase in the importance of RE in the primary energy make-up, reaching 15% in 2020; under energy industry plans to deal with atmospheric pollution, that figure needs to reach 13% in 2017(Deng 2014). As a significant foundation laid for 13th FYP, Strategic Action Plan for Energy Development (2014-2020) was issued by the State Council in November 2014. It showed that by 2020, non fossil energy accounts for 15% proportion of primary energy consumption; the proportion of coal consumption will be controlled within 62%. By 2020, wind power electricity price equals to the coal electricity price and the photovoltaic power price equals to general sales price of national grids. In summary, the focus of current and future energy policies of China is placed on increasing energy efficiency, developing new and renewable energy, reducing carbon dioxide emissions and improving the capability of dealing with climate change. China is on a transition to a more sustainable development (Yuan and Zuo 2011: 3858).

① Carbon dioxide emissions per-unit GDP would be reduced by 17% compared with that in 2010 and non-fossil energy as a share in the consumption of primary energy would be increased to 11.4% by 2015. See State Council (3/2011).

Chapter 4
Process-tracing of China's Participation in the Climate Regime

Many scholars (Chan 2006; Deng 2008; Johnston 2008; Kent 2007; Ross 1998) have analyzed China's tendency as a large rising power to comply with international economic, security, cultural, and environmental regimes. Su argues that the attitude of China towards international institutions has undergone a gradual change, from that of a "system revolutionist" to a "system-reformer" and increasingly that of a "system participator and maintainer" (Su 2002, 2005, 2007). Phrases like "peaceful rising" and "harmonious world" which were introduced by the central government show China's willingness to keep to the current international order rather than break it. As Hu Angang, a key government advisor, points out, the rapid development of China owes to the peaceful international environment of the last 30 years (Hu and Hilton 2010). In addition, China's active participation in international institutions and its active compliance with their principles and rules show that China has begun to pay much more attention to positive international image and reputation building. Since the 1990s, climate change in particular has gained increasing salience at the international level and has become a kind of major green political issue. The achievement of each stage in the climate change negotiations is no doubt a compromise result between the political and economical trade-offs of different countries. Due to the soaring growth of GHG emissions, China has been confronted with increasing pressure from the international community. The climate change negotiations are far beyond China's foreign policy and they have profound political, economic and normative influence on China's domestic policy change. This chapter first introduces the climate change regime and then traces China's participation therein over the past two decades. Treating climate change as a significant social context, the last section of this chapter summarizes China's interests in the climate change regime and analyzes the influence of carbon reduction pressures on its domestic policies.

4.1 The climate change regime

4.1.1 A brief history

In 1972, the UN Conference on the Human Environment in Stockholm was the first major UN conference on international environmental issues. As a milestone event, it served as a prelude to other international environmental politics developments. Climate change has gradually drawn increasing attention from the academic community since the 1970; the First World Climate Conference was held by the World Meteorological Organization (WMO) in 1979 (Harris 2011a: 2). Along with the discovery of a severe thinning of the ozone layer, the successful adoption of the Montreal Protocol on Substances That Deplete the Ozone Layer in 1987 further simulated international concern in atmospheric problems. The Intergovernmental Panel on Climate Change (IPCC) created by the WMO and the UNEP in 1988 began intergovernmental efforts to study the problem (Harris 2011a: 2). The IPCC's creation symbolized that climate change was not just an academic issue, but also being upgraded to the governmental practice level. These factors contributed to climate change emerging on the international political stage, especially "when the UN General Assembly took up the issue for the first time and adopted resolution 43/53 in 1988, declaring climate change to be 'a common concern of mankind'" (Yamin and Depledge 2004: 22). In 1990, the IPCC issued its First Assessment Report (FAR) on the state of climate change, which paved the way for the issuing of the Ministerial Declaration of the Second World Climate Conference in 1990.

The UN Framework Convention on Climate Change (UNFCCC), which set the foundation of the climate change regime, was signed at the 1992 UN Conference on Development and the Environment (Earth Summit) (Chen 2009: 104). The UNFCCC defines the main principles countries agreed upon, such as the "common but differentiated responsibility" of nations. Although the treaty itself set no binding limits on greenhouse gas emissions for individual countries and contained no enforcement mechanisms, it constructed a significant mechanism, the Conferences of the Parties (COP), to discuss, assess and set targets on climate change on an annual basis. The COP has taken place since the UNFCCC entered into force in 1994.

The key milestone during the early intergovernmental negotiating process was the adoption of the Kyoto Protocol by COP-3 in 1997, which set binding obligations for industrialized countries to reduce their emissions of greenhouse gases.① Although it was a product of compromise and bargaining, it has represented a significant step in the course of international efforts to "build effective global governance on the climate change as it marked the first time Annex I countries agreed to a binding commitment" (Liang 2010: 64-65). The Kyoto Protocol included three flexibility mechanisms: the joint implementation (JI), the clean development mechanism (CDM) and the emission trading mechanism. The CDM allows industrialized countries to buy Certified Emission Reduction units (CERs) from emission reduction projects in developing countries, which provides an institutional channel for financial exchanges, project cooperation, technology transfer and expertise training. The Kyoto Protocol came into force in 2005 and formally constructed the main structure for the rolling emission reduction commitment periods.

Since the Kyoto Protocol's first period of emission reduction commitments was to expire at the end of 2012, negotiations to establish emission reduction commitments for a second commitment period started in 2006, right after the Kyoto Protocol came into force in 2005. The Bali Road Map, which was introduced in the COP 13 in the Bali Conference in 2007, was the first step on the bumpy journey to a Post-Kyoto Protocol agreement. The aim of the Bali Conference was to reach an agreement on the approach for arriving at a new Post-Kyoto regime at COP 15 in Copenhagen in 2009 and "brought new urgency to the governments to identify their national interest and frame their negotiating position in the coming round of international bargaining" (Liang 2010: 64-65). Negotiations resulted in the adoption of the Bali Action Plan, reiterating the "common but differentiated responsibilities" of countries to address climate change. This plan defined four pillars as the foundation for a new agreement: mitigation, adaptation, technology transfer, and financing.② The Bali Roadmap "has launched a process that at least in theory could replace the Kyoto Protocol with an agreement involving all countries" (Clémençon 2008: 73), especially involving the U.S., which retreated from the Kyoto Protocol in 2001, in a Post-2012 cooperative framework.

The opening of the Copenhagen Conference in 2009 was remarkable for its unprecedented international participation, involving 192 countries (including 119 heads of state and government) and tens of thousands of non-governmental delegates and activists. It symbolized that the response to the climate change has been

① The U.S. signed the Kyoto Protocol, but did not ratify it.

② The adaptation pillar reflects the growing recognition of the necessity to act in this area. The pillar's technology and financing both relate to the divergent economic capacities of countries and link mitigation and adaptation activities by developing countries with commitments of developed countries to support them.

unprecedented and truly "global" in scope (Harris 2011a: 2). There was a great expectation that this conference would reach a consensus on designing a legally binding framework for Post-Kyoto era. However, the Copenhagen Accord that was formulated, was neither legally binding nor contained any legally binding commitments for reducing CO_2 emissions, due to many countries' opposition. Nevertheless, as of 2010, 138 countries had either formally signed onto the agreement or signaled they would sign. Tony Tujan suggests "the perceived failure of Copenhagen may prove useful, if it allows people to unravel some of the underlying misconceptions and work towards a new, more holistic view of things" (Tujan 2010). Zhang also argues that "although failed to reach a legally binding global agreement, the Accord reflects a political consensus on the main elements of the future framework among the major emitters and representatives of the main negotiating groups" (Zhang 2010b: 239).

The 2011 Durban Conference's greatest achievement was bringing all of the world's major greenhouse gas emitters (including the U. S. and important developing economies like China, India and Brazil) into a new international legal framework for carbon reduction. The establishment of the Ad Hoc Working Group on the Durban Platform for Enhanced Action (ADP) symbolized the emerging tendency to use a two-track negotiation. ① The ADP aims to develop a protocol (instrument or an agreed outcome) with legal force under the Convention applicable to all Parties. Based on the work of the ADP, this new legally binding framework will be signed by 2015 and come into effect by 2020 (DCCEE 2011). ② The 2012 Doha Climate Change Conference was the last conference before the ending of the first commitment period of the Kyoto Protocol. It was a decisive moment for the survival of the Kyoto Protocol, whether to start the second commitment period or not. Finally member countries have taken many efforts to launch a second commitment period extending to 2020 under the Kyoto Protocol framework (from 2013 to 2020), and avoid the appearance of a possible "global carbon emission reduction gap" between the first and subsequent commitment period. That the Kyoto Protocol was amended so that it will continue to 2020 had symbolic value as it is the only existing and binding agreement under which

① The "two-track negotiation" refers to negotiations occurring under the "Kyoto Protocol" framework linked to developed countries' emission reduction obligations and to those tied to the "United Nations Framework Convention on Climate Change", where both developed and developing countries have responsibilities.

② Other progress should include: "to develop new market mechanisms to drive opportunities for low cost greenhouse gas abatement; set up an adaptation committee to help developing countries adapt to the impacts of climate change; set the Rules for Climate Technology Centre and Network to speed up technology transfer, facilitate deployment of low carbon technologies, build national and international capacity, and support R&D of new clean technologies". See DCCEE (2011).

developed countries commit to cutting greenhouse gases. The "2012 doom day anticipation" for CDM projects has proven to be wrong as they will continue to exist until 2020, although it is true that they have been confronted by many difficulties during the global carbon market downturn. One of the key achievements was to determine the future focus of Post-Kyoto negotiations: to move toward a universal legally binding climate change agreement covering all countries to be adopted by 2015 (UNEP 2012). The one-track negotiation mechanism will replace the two-track negotiation mechanism. By 2020, this new universal climate agreement will come into effect to formally take the place of the Kyoto Protocol and open the gate of the Post-Kyoto era. Although the Kyoto Protocol was extended in the Doha Conference, Canada, Japan, Russia and New Zealand's decision to resist new commitments (the U.S. abandoned the protocol already in 2001) in the second commitment period has brought more challenges for the effectiveness of global emission reduction efforts and added more uncertainties into the future Post-Kyoto mechanism building process (IISD 2012). After the 2013 Warsaw Climate Change Conference and the 2014 Lima Conference, although financing remains contentious within the UNFCCC process, developments outside the formal negotiations signal a growing awareness that investing in low carbon growth makes long term sense for governments, businesses and financial institutions (Hilton 2014).

4.1.2 Definition of the climate change regime and its four interactive levels

There are two ways to understand the connotation of the climate change regime. In a narrow sense, Danish (2007) proposes the current international climate change regime refers to a network of agreements and mechanisms. The UNFCCC, the Kyoto Protocol and agreements reached in Post-Kyoto negotiations, having direct impacts on tackling climate change, form the basic framework for the global climate cooperation. In a broad sense, the international rules, institutions and procedures related to climate change mitigation and adaptation as well as embodied norms and common cultural cognition all can be treated as a general climate change regime (Krasner 1982; Yamin and Depledge 2004). Starting from the latter definition, it can be said that the climate change regime has been built with three main dimensions:

First, *is the institutional dimension*, which includes the UNFCCC (1992), Kyoto Protocol (1997), and subsequent significant agreements: the Bali Road Map, Copenhagen Accord, Cancun Accord, and the Durban Accord. Some scholars also mention that the Montreal Protocol (1987) has had great impact on cutting some of the specialized industrial gases that are linked to the ozone layer and contribute a lot to climate change (Keohane and Victor 2010: 7).

Second, is the core organizational dimension: The Conference of the Parties (COP) serves as the "supreme body" of the regime; the Subsidiary Body for Scientific and Technological Advice (SBSTA) and the Subsidiary Body for Implementation (SBI) assist the COP; there is a permanent Secretariat; and, there are rules of procedure to govern the negotiations (Yamin and Depledge 2004: 23). Thanks to the stable organizational framework of the annual COP, the climate change negotiations have continuity and are relatively stable, which is favorable for reaching consensus. The stable organizational framework guarantees a feed-back and evaluation process that can facilitate the implementation of national emission reduction targets.

Third, is the key supporting organizational dimension: the Global Environmental Facility (GEF), the IPCC, and some Specialized UN Agencies (the UNEP, the UNDP, and the WMO). The GEF plays a central role in providing formal financial mechanisms for both the UNFCCC and the Kyoto Protocol. As the crosscutting financial instrument for major international environmental conventions, the GEF mainly cooperates with the World Bank, the UNEP and the UNDP (Michonski and Levi 2010: 6). For instance, the World Bank, through the GEF, sponsored the Prototype Carbon Fund (PCF) in the late 1990s to channel early investment into the Kyoto Protocol's CDM, in order to encourage investment in clean energy technologies and practices in developing countries. The successful experience of PCF projects further contributed to the quality-raising of subsequent CDM projects (Keohane and Victor 2010: 8). The IPCC, as a scientific intergovernmental organization, plays an authoritative role in providing comprehensive scientific assessments of the risk of climate change caused by human activity and offering possible options for adapting to these potential environmental and socio-economic consequences or mitigating their effects. The IPCC has issued five assessment reports in 1990, 1995, 2002, 2007 and 2014. The Fifth Assessment Report (AR 5) has stood as the authoritative theoretical foundation for current political actions to fight against global warming.

In sum, the international climate change regime has developed a comprehensive structure to promote interaction with member states. The three dimensions above can be translated into *four interactive levels*: the interest incentives interactive level, the institutional interactive level, the knowledge interactive level and the normative interactive level. These four interactive levels can be treated as the basic line to study the two-level interplay between the international climate change regime and domestic policy change. The *interest incentives interactive level* refers to the visible or invisible incentives provided by the climate change regime for developing countries: the material incentives include a supportive fund, technology transfer, CDM projects, CCS cooperation, and know-how training projects; the non material incentives mainly refer to the promising green prospects of the global carbon market, which was stimulated by the flexible mechanisms in the Kyoto Protocol and supported by the emission reduction commitments of member states, such as the EU carbon trading system and CDM projects in developing countries. The invisible incentives give a predictable future for a low-carbon economy and global green market development. Simulated by this low-carbon prospect, more developing countries are designing their own domestic carbon trading markets, such as China, Mexico, South Korea and Brazil. The *institutional interactive level* means the functional communication and institutional maintenance in the principal-agent structure of the climate change regime, involving the requirements for institutional and procedural link-up in the member states, such as compliance to the procedures, rules and principles of the climate change regime, establishment of a "window agency" responsible for dealing with climate change and promoting the governmental green policy integration, and submitting the national plans, reports and assessments of climate change mitigation measures. The *knowledge interactive level* refers to the special knowledge provided by the climate change regime concerning the climate change statistical data, climate change mitigation and adaptation measures, best practices and innovative policy instruments from policy entrepreneurs. In terms of climate change knowledge diffusion, the IPCC has played an authoritative role in influencing climate change research. The knowledge at this level also includes technological knowledge and normative knowledge, partly overlapping with interest and normative interactive levels. The *normative interactive level* includes the normative rules embodied in the UNFCCC, the Kyoto Protocol and other agreements signed in the climate change negotiations; and the widely accepted common rules in environmental governance, such as sustainable development and green growth; and normative power (social power of climate change) supported by the climate change regime, such as different kinds of normative social influence, like international reputational pressure, shaming punishment and imposed cognitive dissonance for the member states. The four interactive levels are illustrated more clearly in Figure 4.1.

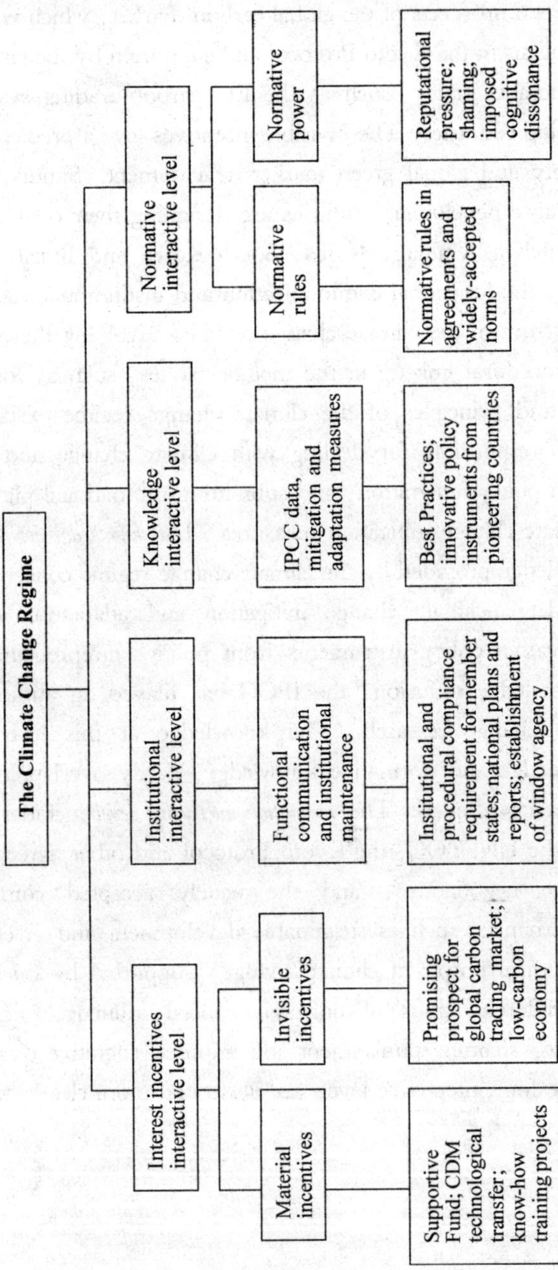

Figure 4.1 Four interactive levels in the climate change regime

4.1.3 Climate change diffusion and the climate change regime complex

Along with the intensification of the international climate negotiations, climate change awareness has grown and diffused internationally. Michonski and Levi emphasize that " climate change has become a top-tier subject for international negotiation and debate, not only for environment specialists but also for people and institutions focused on economics, development, energy, technology, and other pressing international issues" (Michonski and Levi 2010: 1). Therefore, the topic of climate change has gradually entered the agenda of various international institutions or conferences, such as the G-8 Summit, the G-20 Summit, the Davos Forum, the Asia Pacific Economic Cooperation (APEC), and the WTO discussions. Therefore, in order to treat the climate change regime as part of a broader social context, it is essential to understand the "much broader complex of multilateral institutions whose rules, decisions, and activities can be expected to have important consequences for international efforts to confront climate change" (Michonski and Levi 2010: 1).

Keohane and Victor introduce a new concept, the " climate change regime complex" (Keohane and Victor 2010: 5) to describe the current clustered institutional management of climate change. They make a continuum of nested international regulatory institutions to explore the different level of regime complexes: at one end of the spectrum are fully integrated institutions that impose regulation through comprehensive, hierarchical rules; while at the other end are highly fragmented institutional arrangements with no identifiable core and weak or nonexistent linkages. And between the two ends are regime complexes, which are loosely coupled sets of specific regimes (Keohane and Victor 2010: 2-4). In the climate change-area, due to the diffusion of climate change management to other institutions, this issue-area is "governed by a regime complex rather than a comprehensive regime or a fully fragmented, dispersed set of institutions" (Keohane and Victor 2010: 5). The climate change regime complex can be defined as a "loosely coupled system of institutions, without clear hierarchy or core, are linked by the climate change issue in complementary ways" (Keohane and Victor 2010: 4).

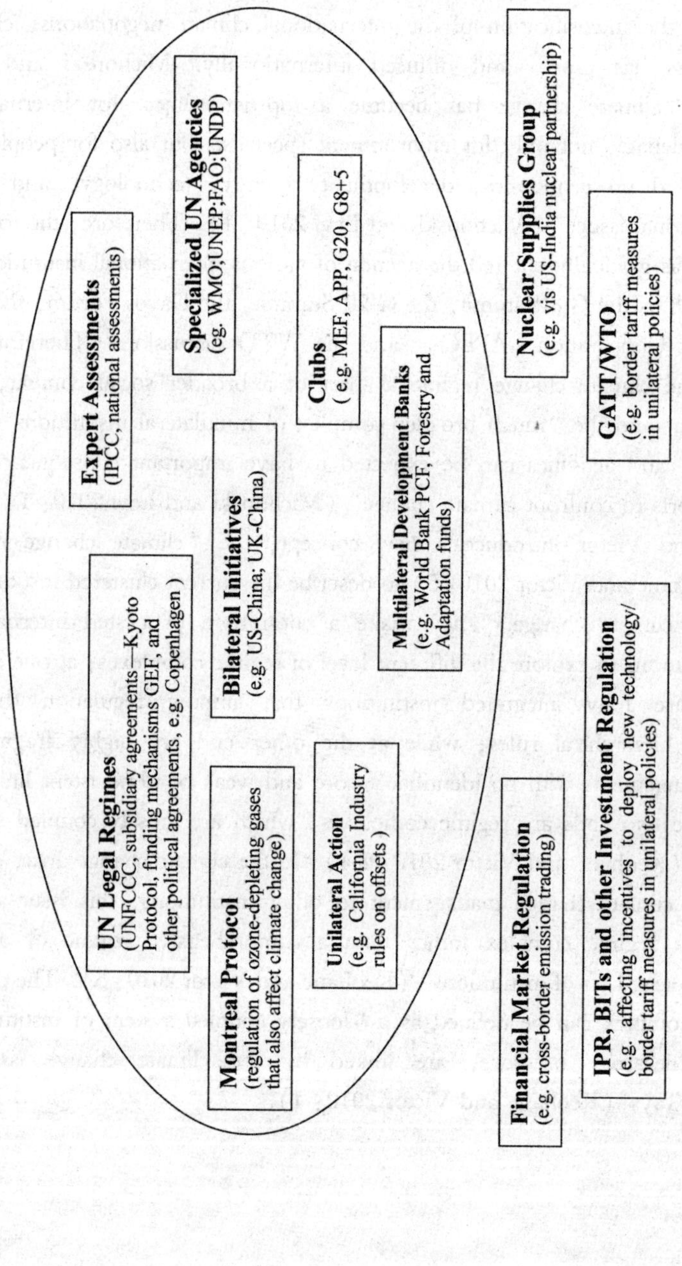

Figure 4.2 The regime complex for climate change

Source: Keohane and Victor (2010:5)

In addition to the climate change regime based on the UNFCCC and the Kyoto Protocol which has been mentioned before, there are three other main institutional forums addressing climate change in the climate change complex: *first*, various institutions have adopted climate change in their political agendas. Climate change has infiltrated into some established economic, political, energy or scientific institutions, such as the G-8, the G-20, the Major Economies Forum (MEF), the International Maritime Organization (IMO), the World Trade Organization (WTO), and the International Energy Agency (IEA). These institutions "provide governance for areas that intersect with potential climate change policies, and will thus inevitably take actions or make decisions that affect global responses to climate change" (Michonski and Levi 2010: 2).① *Second*, there are newly established international institutions concerning climate change. Due to dissatisfaction with the current binding system of the UNFCCC and the Kyoto Protocol (out-of the current two-track negotiation arrangement), or tending to enhance the regional cooperative level on climate change, or boosting the national profile to a certain degree, some states have promoted the establishment of new institutions or fora mainly for dealing with climate change. For instance, the Bush Administration established the Asia Pacific Partnership on Clean Development and Climate (APP) in 2005.② *Third* is bilateral cooperation concerning climate change. In addition to the multilateral institutions outside the UNFCCC, bilateral initiatives on climate change are also significant institutional channels. China is attentive to cooperative programs on clean energy and energy conservation with industrialized countries. For instance, one of the most important achievements of EU-China cooperation has been the establishment of the EU-China Partnership on Climate Change, which was declared at the 8th EU-China summit meeting in September 2005 (European Commission 2005). The EC-China Energy Dialogue resulted in a whole range of concrete cooperative projects, such as the establishment of the EU-China

① The WTO could play a significant role in regulating trade in low-carbon technologies and setting standards for low-carbon products; the IEA, as a main energy regulatory institution, promotes clean energy and energy efficiency development by providing positive information in frequent reports and consultations with governments; the G-8 and the G-20 are forums for cooperation on economic issues at the head of state and ministerial levels, every G-8 meeting during the last five years included a prominent statement on climate change. See Keohane and Victor (2010: 6).

② This six-member regional club aimed to create a voluntary, non-legally binding framework for international cooperation to facilitate the development, diffusion, and deployment of low-carbon and energy efficient technologies and practices among the partners through concrete and substantial cooperation.

Institute for Clean and Renewable Energy (ICARE) in 2009① and the Europe-China Clean Energy Centre (EC2) in 2010 (European Commission 2005-2012).② In addition, the U.S. has also created a variety of partnerships with China; salient ones are the China-US Energy Policy Dialogue (EPD) and the China-US Strategic and Economic Dialogue (S & ED). Issues of climate change and clean energy have gained more attention in these high-level dialogues.

4.2 Process-tracing of China's participation in the climate change regime

Having joined the international climate change regime since the early 1990s, China has been confronted with great challenges and opportunities. The country has been identified as a key actor in global climate talks especially since becoming the largest emitter of GHGs in 2007 (Liang 2010: 61). China has undergone increasing international reputational pressure to make a legally binding commitment for GHG emission reductions. Along with the diffusion of climate change in other international institutions and bilateral/multilateral cooperation, the constraining power of the climate change regime complex has increased. The unprecedented reputational pressure has made Chinese leaders treat their voluntary climate mitigation commitments more seriously. The climate change regime has provided some material incentives for developing countries to combine climate mitigation and adaptation with green economic development, like the international fund for RE cooperative projects, technological transfer support, advanced knowledge and best practices diffusion. These external impetuses have stimulated the growth of pro-RE and climate mitigation actors at the domestic level. Influenced by the "stick and carrot" policy in the climate change regime, the stance of China on climate change has undergone gradual change. China

---

① The ICARE is a Five-Year project which was set up in 2009 in order to foster scientific cooperation between leading European and Chinese researchers by creating a research platform on RE under the cooperation framework of "Sino-EU Clean Energy Center Joint Declaration". It was signed in the 11th EU-China summit in May 2009. This institute aims to provide education and training to those working in the RE sector and produce qualified graduates to fill the gap between growing industry demands for RE experts and the skills currently available in the Chinese job market. See ICARE (2009).

② The EC2, a Five-Year cooperation project, was launched by the European Commission, the Chinese NEA and the Ministry of Commerce of China in April 2010 with the support of the Italian Ministry for the Environment, Land and Sea. It aims to promote the exchange of knowledge on cleaner energy technologies, support the improvement of energy conservation and efficiency and provide a platform for capacity building of China's energy planning and energy reform, thus assisting China in its transition to a low-carbon economy. See EC2 (2010).

joined the negotiations for the United Nations Framework Convention on Climate Change (UNFCCC) in 1991, signed the Kyoto Protocol in 1997, ratified the Kyoto Protocol in 2002 and made a carbon-intensity reduction commitment in 2009; this section divides the diachronic process of China's participation in the climate change regime into five stages.

4.2.1 The first stage (1972-1991): joining the Montreal Protocol as a prelude

In the early 1970s, the People's Republic of China was restored as the official representative of China in the UN, and began to pay more attention to its national status in the international community (Chan 2006; Kent 2007). In 1972, China sent its delegation to take part in the UN Conference on the Human Environment in Stockholm, which symbolized a starting point to involve itself in international environmental governance. The Reform and Opening-up policy of China promoted by Deng Xiaoping in 1978 accelerated the pace of China's integration into the world. China has gradually shifted from "the insular and autarkic state" (Economy 2001b: 230) to involve itself more deeply in international regimes in order to gain more international legitimacy and acceptance.

The negotiations on the Montreal Protocol on Substances That Deplete the Ozone Layer in 1987 served as the prelude to the international concerns on atmospheric problems. Although China participated in the Montreal Protocol negotiations, it only presented itself as an observer during the negotiation process and did not play a major role in shaping the treaty (Hodgson 2011: 32-35). The government did not pay enough attention to the atmospheric problem, which led to the shortage of research investment, weak technological support as well as insufficient monitoring data supply. China did not sign this protocol at first since some developing countries proposed that "the Montreal Protocol does not reflect that the developed countries are primarily responsible for emissions of CFCs which causes ozone depletion" (Kent 2007: 169). Therefore, the protocol underwent an amendment at the 2nd meeting of Parties and China officially joined the Montreal Protocol Amendment at the 3rd meeting of the Parties in 1991.

Influenced by the foreign policy thoughts of Deng, China has become more integrated into the international community than previously, but still has maintained a "lay low" approach. It has been suspicious of international norms (Economy 2001b: 232).① Nevertheless, China's ratification of the Montreal Protocol paved the way for its participation in the climate change negotiations.

4.2.2 The second stage (1991-1997): joining the climate change regime without enough preparation

In 1990, the IPCC released its first assessment report pointing out that anthropogenic greenhouse gas emissions were likely leading to climate change. The UN multilateral international climate negotiations began in 1991, aiming to reach consensus on the Climate Change Framework Convention. Different from its marginal role in the Montreal Protocol, China showed a more active attitude towards the climate change regime. Since China felt diplomatically isolated in the early 1990s and tried to reduce western countries' hostility toward the country, China's participation in the climate change regime served as an ideal channel for the country to regain its international position (Chen 2009: 106-107).

Due to the lack of a comprehensive and in-depth understanding of the climate change regime, China treated the convention as a basic international environmental agreement. It conducted only limited research on the cost estimation of GHG emission reductions, the feasibility of current technology and the exact influence on the national energy structure and economic development. This limited cognition on climate change was reflected in the institutional composition of the climate negotiation delegation. In September 1990, the National Group of Coordination on Climate Change was established in order to coordinate diplomatic negotiations (Yan and Xiao 2010: 83). The members of this delegation were from the China Meteorological Administration (CMA) as the main leading institution, the Ministry of Foreign Affairs (MOF), the State Science and Technology Commission (SSTC) and the State Environmental Protection Administration (SEPA). However, this coordinating group did not include officials in charge of the economic development department (Yan and Xiao 2010: 83). China was among the top ten countries to ratify the Convention in 1992 and formulated its domestic "Agenda 21" in 1994. It then passed the Air Pollution Law in 1996 according to the provisions in the UNFCCC. However Lü and Liu (2004) also

---

① In the early 1990s, former paramount leader Deng Xiaoping gave guidance to China's foreign and security policy apparatus that, collectively, has come to be known as the 24 character strategy: "observe calmly; secure our position; cope with affairs calmly; hide our capacities and bide our time; be good at maintaining a low profile; and never claim leadership." Later, the phrase, "make some contributions" was added. See Special Section: China in the World—A Foreign Policy Overview. Available HTTP: <http://worldsavvy.org/monitor/index.php? option=com_content&view=article&id=126&Itemid=184> (accessed on 12 July 2012).

point out "climate policies have not been high on the agenda of government decision makers, and no explicit climate mitigation or adaptation policies are in place by then" (Lü and Liu 2004: 20). The Agenda 21 at that time was no more than an abstract framework without concrete supportive regulations. Nevertheless, it symbolized that China began to show its compliance with international norms of environmental protection in the following Conferences of Parties (COPs), which paved the way for the approval of the Kyoto Protocol in 1997 (Chen 2009: 106-107).

Although China did not realize the real influence of climate change on its energy regulation and economic development in the early stage of its participation in the climate change regime, the country treated the climate change regime as a significant forum to reinforce its diplomatic relations with other developing countries. As the largest developing country in the world and a permanent member of the UN Security Council, China paid more attention to playing a pivotal role in coordinating and representing the interests and positions of the developing world. These efforts promoted the formation of the "bloc of G-77 plus China". Since June 1991, China aligned itself closely with India and strongly opposed legally binding emission reduction targets for developing countries and insisted on industrialized countries providing technology and financial aid to developing countries (Chen 2009: 104). Especially in the 1992 UN Conference on Environment and Development (Rio Earth Summit), China and India, on behalf of other developing countries, insisted that based on historical equity grounds, developed countries should take on more responsibility. Developing countries, they argued, have the right to develop (Chen 2009: 106). The consistent stances from the "bloc of G-77 plus China" finally led to the embodiment of basic principle of "common but differentiated responsibility" into the UNFCCC framework, which was reflected in the three classifications of countries: Annex I, Annex II and non-Annex I. Although insisting on maintaining a non-commital position in terms of climate change, China and other G-77 developing countries eventually accepted some provisions under the UNFCCC: to establish national emissions inventories, submit reports on national programs, and promote sustainable development and relevant information exchange (Chen 2009: 106).

4.2.3 The third stage (1997-2002): participating more cautiously in the climate change regime

When the UNFCCC came into force in 1994, the requirement for a legally binding protocol drove the COP 1 and the COP 2 negotiations, which eventually spawned the formation of the Kyoto Protocol (COP 3) in 1997. As a result of the efforts of all parties, the Kyoto Protocol became the first international treaty to set detailed legally-binding obligations for industrialized nations to reduce their greenhouse gas emissions; China signed the Kyoto Protocol in May 1998. China's increased involvement in international environmental policy negotiations represents "a clear increase over China's passive observer status during the Montreal Protocol negotiations where it was largely inactive" (Hodgson 2011: 32-35).

However, compared with the negotiation and ratification of the Convention, the attitude of China became more conservative and cautious than before. This was because China's leaders had come to appreciate the potential influence of climate change on its energy regulation and economic development. For instance, the ratification time of the Convention was only one year (1991-1992), while the ratification for the Kyoto Protocol took China five years (1997-2002). Benjamin Gilman, Chairman of the U. S. House of Representatives' Committee on International Relations, criticized the hardline position of China and summarized China's position at the Kyoto Conference as "a policy of Three NOs: no obligations on China, no voluntary commitments by China, no future negotiations to bind China" (Liang 2010: 68). China as a leader among the Group of 77, reiterated the principle of "common but differentiated responsibility" of states for climate change, which was formed under the UNFCCC framework. This basic principle laid the foundation for the two-track negotiation mechanism: developed countries (Annex I) being most responsible for climate change would take the lead in reducing GHG emissions and helping developing countries' climate mitigation and adaptation through technology transfer and financial support (Harris 2011a: 8); while developing countries (non-Annex I), would not be legally required to limit their GHG emissions in any way (Liang 2010). Furthermore, climate change had a spillover effect on other issue fields. The Clinton administration explicitly proposed linking the climate negotiations with China's accession to the WTO. No doubt, these kind of diplomatic pressures increased the sensitivity and vigilance of China on climate change. That was why China showed a more cautious and hardline position to the climate change negotiations at this time.

In the meantime, China has gradually realized that the national communication mechanisms, national capacity building expectations, and the technology transfer which are embodied in the Kyoto Protocol not only relate to environmental concerns, but also have great influence on economic growth, national strategic development, and energy system transformation. In the ratification process of the Kyoto Protocol, China began to show its proactive attitude to climate change cooperative projects. This tendency was further enhanced by the promise of developed countries in the Bonn Conference (COP 6) in 2000 to increase the GEF funding to assist developing countries to reduce their greenhouse gas emissions (Kent 2007: 170-171). In the UN World Summit on Sustainable Development (WSSD) in 2002 Johannesburg, China announced its decision to ratify the Kyoto Protocol to address the challenge of global climate change and appealed to other reluctant parties to ratify the protocol as soon as possible (Chen 2009: 107). ①

In this context, climate change began to gain more attention at the domestic level, which led to institutional changes in the bureaucratic system. Along with its increasing political awareness and economic sensitivity on climate change in the late 1990s especially when the Kyoto Protocol was adopted in 1997, the main responsible role for the climate change negotiations shifted to the most powerful agency in economic planning and energy regulation—the State Development and Planning Commission (SDPC, former agency of the NDRC). This occurred in 1998. In the same year, the SDPC representatives from China signed the Kyoto Protocol and the former National Climate Change Coordination Group was re-titled as the National Climate Change Policy Coordination Group, which was led by Zeng Yanpei, the director of the SDPC. This new bureaucratic arrangement symbolized climate change entering the policy mainstream.

Since the SDPC is the authoritative agency in general economic planning and energy sector regulation, rising concerns about climate change in the SDPC will have a penetrating effect on economic development and energy consumption patterns. This institutional change has promoted an attitudinal change in relation to the three flexible mechanisms embodied in the Kyoto Protocol, since the SDPC put emphasis on technology transfer rather than merely focusing on sovereignty concerns like the Ministry of Foreign Affairs (MOFA). To be more detailed, China once held a high degree of vigilance and skepticism about the three flexibility mechanisms and emphasized strict defining of the using range of flexible mechanisms as well as its specific operating rules, in order to prevent potential deviation from the basic principles of the UNFCCC, especially shifting the reduction responsibility to developing countries (Yan and Xiao 2010: 83). However, China gradually changed its attitude

---

① Although many countries have signed the Kyoto Protocol after 1997, the protocol's coming into force was subject to the domestic ratification process. It proved to be a bumpy path. The Bush Administration retreated from the Kyoto Protocol in 2001, with the excuse that developing countries did not share the legally binding commitment to GHG emission reduction, and the GHG reduction would affect the economic development of the U. S. This retreat hindered the entry process of the protocol into force. In the Marrakech Conference (COP 7), the vast majority of countries agreed to make a non-principled compromise with Canada, Australia, Japan and Russia in the Marrakesh Agreement in order to accelerate the Kyoto Protocol into force. In October 2004, Russia finally switched its originally skeptical and hesitant position and ratified the Kyoto Protocol, which essentially saved the Kyoto Protocol.

towards the CDM around 2001; this external impetus has stimulated the initial development of large-scale renewable energy (Hatch 2003; Heggelund 2007).① China has signed the most CDM projects in the world and nearly half of all CDM projects are operated in China, which results in a great amount of GHG emission reductions. Therefore, it is said that "the Kyoto Protocol saw a major increase in the level of Chinese participation and assertiveness" (Hodgson 2011: 32-35).

4.2.4 The fourth stage (2002-2009): becoming more deeply involved in the climate change regime

After 2002, China's participation in the international climate negotiations became more active, and played a positive role in promoting the ratification of the Kyoto Protocol. It was noteworthy that China began to combine international regime compliance with finding a solution for domestic environmental problems. Chinese leaders started to put climate change concerns into the national sustainable development strategic framework as well as socio-economic planning. At China's first Conference on Climate Change in April 2002, Hu Qili, the Vice-Chairman of the National Committee of the Chinese People's Political Consultative Conference, admitted that "China's progress was now hindered by three problems—a rapidly expanding population, shortage of resources, and environmental deterioration—the settlement of which all depended on the resolution of climate problems" (Kent 2007: 170-171). Moreover, China began to pay attention to the enactment, implementation and improvement of relevant legal documents on climate issues, such as enacting and revising the Energy Conservation Law, the RE Law, the Circular Economy Promotion Law, the Clean Production Promote Law and other related laws as well as regulations to promote economic and industrial structural adjustment and optimize the industrial energy structure, especially enhancing RE development and improving energy efficiency.

In 2005, the Kyoto Protocol came into force, which indicated that the international community had taken a solid step forward for global warming mitigation, and it served as a prelude for the Post-Kyoto negotiations. Although as a developing country, China is not legally required to limit its GHG emissions, China has been confronted by increasingly great pressure after it surpassed the U. S. to become the largest GHGs emitter beginning in 2007. And the U. S. expressed that the key

① China's reaction to the range of flexibility mechanisms—from joint implementation (JI) under the UNFCCC to activities implemented jointly (AIJ) authorized at COP 1 to the CDM under the Kyoto Protocol adopted at COP 3—can be characterized by a gradual shift from flat rejection to cautious acceptance to enthusiastic support. See Zhang (2003).

precondition for pulling it back into a Post-Kyoto regime would be China's making a legally binding commitment to climate change mitigation. The Bali Conference in December 2007 symbolized the formal beginning of the designing of a Post-Kyoto regime framework; especially the emerging of the "Bali Road Map" paved the way for the Post-Kyoto negotiations. The watershed in the Bali Conference was that developing countries came to the table and showed a willingness to discuss emissions reductions of their own (voluntary reduction commitment) for the first time. China has further softened its hardliner position since 1997 and turned to a more proactive, engaged, and flexible approach in the UN Bali climate negotiations (Liang 2010: 68). China and other developing countries for the first time agreed to "discuss nationally appropriate voluntary mitigation actions in the context of sustainable development, supported and enabled by technology, financing and capacity-building, in a measurable, reportable and verifiable manner" (Liang 2010: 69). For instance, although China still has adhered to the principle of "common but differentiated responsibilities" and objected to any legal responsibility on quantifiable reductions, the national leaders considered using voluntary targets instead of absolute emission obligations to show a degree of national compliance to the climate change regime and ease external pressure. The NDRC, as the leading actor in the climate change negotiations, issued China's National Climate Change Program in response to climate change in June 2007. This national program was China's first global warming policy initiative and includes guidelines, principles and objectives to address climate change, and sets out China's positions on international cooperation.

4.2.5 The fifth Stage (2009 to the present): making a carbon-intensity reduction commitment

The biggest changes between the Copenhagen Conference in 2009 and prior climate change negotiations was the challenge that emerged to the two-track negotiation pattern and the greater pressure placed on big developing countries. It was unprecedented that all the major economies at Copenhagen pledged to take specific individual responsibilities and especially developing countries agreed to submit their intended mitigation actions (Zhang 2010b: 239-240). China's participation obtained special attention in the Copenhagen Conference. Just like Hodgson mentions, "if say China was an observer at the Montreal Protocol negotiations and a participant in the Kyoto Protocol negotiations then it was a major player in the Copenhagen Accord" (Hodgson 2011: 32-35). In the conference, China for the first time announced its voluntary national climate mitigation action targets, and pledged to cut carbon dioxide emissions by 40% to 45% per unit of gross domestic product by 2020 compared with levels in 2005 (carbon intensity reduction), and aim for 15% energy from non-fossil fuels by 2020. However, this voluntary climate mitigation action target did not meet the high expectation of the Copenhagen Conference. Also for the first time, China, instead of the U. S., was blamed for dragging its feet on international climate negotiations and leading to the conference's "disappointed outcome" (Zhang 2010b: 239-240). ① Oberheitmann and Sternfeld point out that while the Chinese government has adopted policies to decrease energy intensity, economic growth rates near 10% mean continued growth in emissions. This growth "will more than offset the 116 million metric tons of carbon emission reductions achieved under the Kyoto Protocol" (Oberheitmann and Sternfeld 2011).

Beginning in 2009, climate politics related to the role of China have become much more heated. The so-called G-2 model raised by economist C. Fred Bergsten in 2005 emphasized the influential roles of the U. S. and China in global affairs. ② Although China was cautious about the G-2 model, it was labeled as being one of the "two key players" along with the U. S. in the negotiations (Brzezinski 2009). At the same time, China still insisted on treating itself as the leader in the bloc of developing countries and put emphasis on economic development rights and differentiated responsibilities for emissions reductions. China took an initiative to ally with India, Brazil, and South Africa to form the group of BRICs, in order to hold their ground on the two-track negotiation framework. However, China's efforts could not stop the split within the G-77 in the climate change regime. In the 2009 Copenhagen Conference, Brazil took steps in making voluntary quantified emission reduction targets of 36.1%-38.9% below business as usual emission levels despite the absence of commitments (Johnston 2001: 192). ③ Brazil's quantitative emission reduction targets trapped China and India in their relatively passive positions.

Following frustrations at the Copenhagen Conference in 2009 and struggles to

---

① Such blame was previously always targeted at the U. S. Then several international leaders, including then British Prime Minister Gordon Brown, accused China of obstructing the negotiations process. British Energy and Climate Change Secretary Ed Miliband (2009) even wrote in *The Guardian* that China had led a group of countries that had "hijacked" the climate negotiations and had at times presented "a farcical picture to the public".

② As the two most influential and powerful countries in the world, there have been increasingly strong suggestions within American political circles of creating a G-2 relationship where the U. S. and China would work out solutions to global problems together.

③ If Brazil can achieve this goal, then its greenhouse gas emissions in 2020 will be close to its 1994 level, equivalent to a decrease of 20% based on 2005 levels. The main GHG emissions in Brazil are from rainforest deforestation, so the reduction cost will not be very high if the commitment is taken seriously. Furthermore, Brazil has pursued climate mitigation in order to boost its international profile and establish a good reputation.

save the multilateral climate regime in the 2010 Cancun Conference, the Durban Conference in 2011 was an important turning point that helped resuscitate the Kyoto Protocol and paved the way for the Post-Kyoto framework (IISD 2011). Due to increasing international pressure, China yielded on the issues of transparency and carbon intensity targets, but upheld the principle of "common but differentiated responsibilities" and insisted on not considering legally binding cuts until becoming a middle-leveled developed country in 2030. However in the Durban Conference, Xie Zhenhua, the vice chairman of the NDRC and the leader of the Chinese delegation to the UN Climate Change Conference, declared that China should also negotiate a legally binding document after 2020 and China would accept a legally binding arrangement with conditions (Chinafaqs 2011).① It was the first time that China showed its willingness to bear the obligations of a legally binding commitment matched with China's economic development and capabilities. This declaration was interpreted as "China taking a proactive stance in global negotiations by promising to put in place legally binding carbon reduction plans" (IISD 2011). Furthermore, the establishment of the Ad Hoc Working Group on the Durban Platform for Enhanced Action (ADP) showed the strong pressure for merging the climate negotiations into a single track. In the 2012 Doha Conference, one of the main tasks set for the second commitment period of the Kyoto Protocol was the design of a legally binding framework to cover all the member countries by 2015. The engagement of China and the U. S. has been a major breakthrough in international climate change negotiations and has set the stage for a successful outcome at talks in 2015 Paris Conference. Presidents Xi Jinping and Barack Obama demonstrated game-changing political will by pledging to tackle emissions at the Asia Pacific Economic Cooperation (APEC) Summit in Beijing in 2014. Especially after the 2014 Lima climate change conference, China is becoming "less defensive and more inviting, trying to take on a leadership role" (Soutar 2015). The world's largest emitter of GHG "will work hard" to peak its CO_2 emissions before 2030, Premier Li Keqiang said at a summit meeting with the French government in Paris ahead of the climate plan's publication in Beijing. Then China submitted its Intended Nationally Determined Contribution (INDC) document to UN's climate team, that is, China planned to reduce the carbon intensity of its economy 60%-65% per unit of GDP by 2030, compared with 2005 levels, and reiterated a previously-announced aim that RE

① The conditions include: new carbon-cutting pledges by rich nations in the second commitment period under the Kyoto Protocol; fast launch of the Green Climate Fund agreed on in Cancun under a supervisory regime; implementing the consensus on adaptation; technology transfer, transparency, capacity building and other points agreed upon in former conferences as well as appraising developed countries' commitment during the first period of the Kyoto Protocol. See Chinafaqs (2011).

should make up 20% of its primary energy supply by the same date (China dialogue 2015).

4.3 China's interest cognition in the climate change regime and its implications for domestic policy change

Based on the analysis of five-stage participation of China in the climate change regime, it can be said that its stance on climate change has undergone continuous change. Along with heightened cognition of climate change's influence and increased experience in the negotiations, China has become more active, engaged and flexible in the climate change regime. The aim of this section is to summarize China's changing stance and interest cognition in the climate change regime based on a five-stage participation evolution analysis. It will also illustrate the increasing international pressure on China to take carbon reduction measures and what this has meant for domestic policy change (People Net 2010a).

4.3.1 China's changing stance and interest cognition in the climate change regime

China's climate change and energy policy is not only a domestic issue, but has significant repercussions for the rest of the world. How to understand China's position and its interest in the climate change regime is a hot research topic (Chan 2006; Harris 2003; Harris 2006; Harris 2007; Harris 2009; Harris 2011a; Harris 2011b; Lewis 2008; Lewis 2009; Lewis 2011; Li and Xu 2010; Liang 2010; Ojekunle et al. 2009; Richerzhagen and Scholz 2008; Teng and Gu 2007; Vandenbergh 2007; Wiener 2007; Ye et al. 2007; Yu 2004a; Yu 2004b; Zhang 2006; Zhang 2007; Zhang 2010a; Zhuang 2009). At the core of this literature is the question whether China's climate change policy has remained constant or undergone a gradual change.

Some scholars point out that whether (when) China should make a legally binding commitment to GHG emission reductions under the climate change regime, is the core question for national climate change policy research. The stance of China in the climate change regime has been constant. China has refused to set a carbon cap for total emission reductions until China reaches the moderate level of a developed country by 2030. Although China has taken some voluntary energy intensity and carbon intensity reduction initiatives, the climate change mitigation target (to limit the increase in global temperature to a maximum of 2 degrees) will not be achievable without further efforts (Harris 2009; Harris 2011a; Harris 2011b; Liang 2010; Moore 2011). Like Harris (2011b) argues, politically speaking, "China's role in climate change diplomacy is crucial to so-far failed efforts by states to reach consensus on robust efforts to reduce GHGs pollution and to respond to the inevitable consequences of climate change" (Harris 2011b: 141-142). China's priority for economic development (domestic driven factor) has been treated as the main reason to explain China's constant stance in the climate change negotiations (Liang 2010: 70-71). Economic development, the core interest of the Chinese Communist Party, is regarded as the reason behind China making a non-legally binding commitment for GHG reduction (Moore 2011: 147). Economic development remains the dominant discourse and top agenda goal, and "although the attention to climate change has recently increased among China's leadership, it has not surpassed economic development as a policy priority" (Lewis 2008: 154).

It is true that economic growth is essential to regime survival and social stability (Harris 2011a: 8) and China still refuses to make a legally-binding commitment, however, some scholars put more emphasis on the gradual change of China's stance in the climate change negotiations: although China continues to be cautious about quantified emissions cuts, it "does not mean that China's original stance on climate change remains unchanged" (Chen 2009: 116). In contrast to its previous skepticism about global warming, climate change has gradually become involved in a green transformation, a strategic target in the 12th FYP and 13th FYP. Through observing China's historical positions in the climate change regime since the 1990s, Zhang proposes that there are both continuities and changes (Zhang 2006, 2007). There is a clear tendency that, with its increasing involvement in the regime, China's stance on climate change has shifted from conservative and suspicious to proactive, more flexible and open. Based on a five-stage analysis, Table 4.1 diachronically illustrates China's stance in the climate change regime.

Table 4.1 Diachronic comparison of China's stance in the climate change regime

Issues	1991	1997	2001	2005	2007	2009	2011	2012	2013	2014
Whether asks for financial and technology assistance from developed countries?	Yes	Yes	Yes	Yes	Yes	Yes	Yes	Yes	Yes	Yes
Whether mentions to promote RE development?	No	Unclear	Yes	Yes	Yes	Yes	Yes	Yes	Yes	Yes
Whether supports the CDM?	No	Hesitated	Yes	Yes①	Yes	Yes	Yes	Yes	Yes	Yes
Whether makes a (voluntary) commitment to GHG emission reductions?	No	No	No	No	Yes②	Yes	Yes	Yes	Yes	Yes
Whether has a national climate change plan?	No	No	No	Planning	Yes	Yes	Yes	Yes	Yes	Yes
Whether has quantitative indicator for carbon-intensity reduction?	No	No	No	No	No	Yes	Yes	Yes	Yes	Yes (further targets)
Whether has the climate change legislative framework at the domestic level?	No	No	No	No	No	Planning	Preparing	Yes	Yes	Yes

Whether is prepared to accept a legally binding commitment?	No	No	No	No	No	No	Planning	Yes	Yes	Yes
Whether shows a softened stance on the shift of the two-track negotiation to a one-track negotiation?	No	No	No	No	Unclear	Yes	Yes	Yes	Yes	Yes
Whether agrees to adopt the carbon tax or/and carbon trading system?	No	No	No	No	No	Discussion	Designing	Yes	Yes	Yes
Whether officially sets a deadline to reach the GHG emission peak (2030 or even earlier)?	No	No	No	No	No	No	No	Unclear	Ambiguous	Yes

①China has become more flexible and practical. It began to put more emphasis on mutually beneficial technological cooperation between developed and developing countries and established a technological transfer mechanism for climate change mitigation based on market economy principles. It also supported the climate fund, and explored new approaches to expand the carbon financing scale.

②The watershed development in Bali was that developing countries came to the table willing to discuss emissions reductions of their own for the first time.

Sources: Own data from 2007-2014, 1991-2005 data partly adapted from Zhang (2006, 2007).

Based on Table 4.1, China's changing attitude on climate change, from suspicious and ambivalent to active and assertive, has reflected a kind of national preference shifting. In the beginning of the 1990s, China took part in the climate change regime mainly as a foreign policy requirement, so as to break its diplomatic isolation. It allied with developing countries in dealing with international issues. China has evolved from an observer in the Montreal Protocol, a participant in the UNFCCC, an active leader of G-77 in the Kyoto Protocol, to a key player in the Bali Conference and a critical player in the Copenhagen Conference. Along with the rising position of climate change on the policy agenda, related domestic environmental issues, such as environmental pollution as well as water management also gained much more attention. Especially the frequency of extreme environmental events in recent years, such as the large-scale PM2.5 smog pollution in the northern parts of China, further enhanced the convergence of domestic environmental problems with international climate governance. The Chinese government has recognized that involving climate change into national sustainable development strategy and overall socio-economic development planning is conducive to the establishment of a resource-saving and environment-friendly society. Around 2009, China also changed its ambivalent attitude towards a domestic carbon trading system, launching several carbon trading trials beginning in 2011. Therefore, the interest of China's participation in the climate change can be understood along three dimensions as discussed below.

4.3.1.1 More green factors become embodied in the core interest area of the economic development

Protecting China's economic interest and promoting economic development are the first and foremost considerations of Chinese policy-makers in the climate change negotiations. Moore mentions that the climate policy "must be weighed against the grand strategic objectives of stability, security, and prosperity laid out over the past thirty years of reform and opening" (Moore 2011: 147). Any climate change initiative that harms the economy or hampers economic growth is likely to be vigorously resisted by China (Zhang 2003: 82). Even though the deeply-rooted "development first" mindset is hard to be changed and plays a significant role in shaping the national position in the climate change negotiations (Chen 2009: 115). The growing awareness of climate change constraints on economic growth in general, and the potential damages of dangerous climate change in particular, has gradually prompted green policy integration as well as a green transformation of the governmental policy making process. This also has led to "stronger official rhetoric in favor of green development" (Boyd 2012a: 1).

China still emphasizes its identity as a large "developing country" and insists on its economic development right to eliminate poverty. Moore criticizes that China's policy on climate change is best understood as "a collection of policies calculated to pursue its economic interests and avoid the cost of the economic development, but which have co-benefits for the reduction of greenhouse gas emissions" (Moore 2011: 148). At the same time, China's interest preference and understanding of economic development have undergone a gradual transformation. The new interests behind a transformation of economic growth model to that of a low-carbon economy have also been a main locomotive for climate change policy making (Kang 2010: 66). Boyd points out that "the appearance of targets and policies that specifically target carbon emissions reductions in the 12th FYP for the first time suggests that the climate change mitigation is becoming a motivation for policy action in its own right, rather than simply a co-benefit of policies enacted for other purposes" (Boyd 2012b: 1). From Table 4.1, it can be seen that China changed its conservative attitude to the carbon tax and carbon trading system after the 2009 Copenhagen Conference. The NDRC issued the Notice on Carbon Trading Trials Scheme in October 2011 and initiated a group of municipal and provincial-level carbon-trading trials (Wang, T. 2012). During the lifetime of the 12th Five-Year Plan, that is by 2015, cap-and-trade mechanism is to be introduced nationwide. China has tended to rely on market-oriented measures that combine green growth with climate change mitigation and take advantage of climate change to promote its economic structural transformation. A global low-carbon technology competition is also behind the climate change negotiations. This has been stimulated by the global carbon market, including the EU emission trading system (ETS) and CDM projects. Boyd points out that "the idea of low-carbon leadership has reframed China's global role and supported China's emergence at the forefront of low-carbon markets" and that the Chinese government has "strong interests in seeing China successfully compete and lead in global low-carbon energy markets" (Boyd 2012a: 2).

4.3.1.2 A more pragmatic role in achieving material incentives from the climate change regime

China's principled position on climate change has consistently revolved around the themes of "common but differentiated responsibilities" and transfer of technology and financial resources from developed to developing countries (Zhang 2003: 82). Specific to the climate change regime, China's involvement has been motivated by the availability of external financial and technical assistance, transfer of advanced, environmentally friendly technologies, foreign investments, and management know-how (Zhang 2003: 73). China's move to a less carbon-intensive economy has also been bolstered by its active participation in international climate change cooperation

(Zhang 2003: 73). Rapid economic development in the past three decades has caused serious environmental pollution problems due to the country's low energy efficiency, energy-intensive development pattern, and shortage of clean energy technology. Through participating in bilateral and multilateral climate projects, China can obtain more financial and technological support for sustainable development, and learn about low-carbon development from western pioneers. This can aid in China's bid to transform its domestic economic development mode. Through international climate change cooperation, China can also boost its image as an environmentally responsible nation and use climate change to further its foreign policy goals. Now China is a major recipient of environmental funds from the World Bank, the Asian Development Bank, and other donor agencies (Zhang 2003: 73).

Especially the funding from such sources as the Global Environment Facility (GEF) and the prospect of technology transfer and provision of financial assistance promised by the CDM are significant for the capacity building of climate mitigation and adaptation (Zhang 2003: 73). The GEF, which was launched in 1991, is perhaps the most important multilateral funding mechanism that has a climate change focus. About 77% of the GEF projects in China in the climate change area are for energy efficiency and RE development (Zhang 2003: 73).① For instance, the China Renewable Energy Development Project (REDP), and the China Renewable Energy Scale-up Program (CRESP) supported by the GEF and World Bank have provided a significant impetus for RE development. As shown in Table 4.1, China was at first very cautious about the Kyoto flexible mechanisms and maintained a hardline position representing the interests of the G-77. The key turning point was when China accepted the CDM mechanism beginning in 2001 (Zhang 2003: 73). The CDM is intended to assist developed countries in achieving compliance with their obligations under the Kyoto Protocol and developing countries in acquiring environmentally sound technologies and financial assistance for sustainable development. The initial CDM incentives played a significant role in RE development, promoting a green transformation of energy security in the long run.

4.3.1.3 A more flexible attitude in boosting the national image under increasing pressure

Enhancing China's international image and elevating its international prestige in the international community are important goals of Chinese foreign policy (Zhang 2003: 78). Alastair I. Johnston points out that compared with most countries, China

① The grants earmarked for China represent about 9% of the total GEF grants approved during the 1991-2002 period and more than 17% of the total funding for climate change. See Zhang (2003).

is particularly sensitive to external criticisms of its policy and behavior in international regimes, and would go out of its way to avoid diplomatic isolation and international censure (Johnston 1998). He argues that international image plays an important role in China's decision to participate in arms control negations and environmental cooperation because Chinese leaders "are concerned to project an image of an responsible major power" (Johnston 1998: 560). The image effect—for fear of opprobrium—can lead to more cooperative behavior. One of the significant reasons why China joined the climate change regime in the early stage was to break its diplomatic isolation in the early 1990s. By taking part in the climate change regime, China gained an opportunity to boost its prestige and shore up support from developing countries (Zhang 2003: 78). For instance, China played an active role in promoting the formation of "bloc of G-77 plus China" and aligned itself closely with India to oppose legally binding emission reduction targets for developing countries and lead the drive to embody the basic principle of "common but differentiated responsibility" in the UNFCCC framework. Through participating in the climate change regime, China also attempted to improve its relations with western developed countries through showing its willingness to engage in environmental protection and climate mitigation, such as issuing China's 21 Century Agenda in 1994 and the National Climate Change Program in 2007.

According to Johnston, China's concerns on preserving a favorable international image as a responsible major power is a critical variable determining the cost-benefit analysis behind international cooperation: the more international criticism China is likely to meet on some issue of international cooperation, the more likely it will be to try to find ways to minimize this criticism through incrementally substantive cooperative commitments (Johnston 1998: 559; Zhang 2003: 78). When China surpassed the U. S. to become the largest GHGs emitter in 2007, China was confronted by increasing pressure and critique from the international community. The rapid growth of China's GHG emissions stimulated heated arguments about the country's responsibility in the Post-Kyoto framework's design in Copenhagen that have continued. In order to save its national reputation and minimize external pressure, China has made three main changes in its stance: before the 2009 Copenhagen Conference, national leaders for the first time agreed to set quantitative indicators for carbon intensity reduction and non-fossil fuel consumption targets (Carraro and Tavoni 2010); in the 2011 Durban Conference, China showed its willingness to make a legally binding GHG emission reduction commitment beginning in 2020, rather than insisting on discussing this issue after 2030 (Chinafaqs 2011); and, in the 2012 Doha Conference, China accepted the shift from the two-track negotiation mechanism to a one-track negotiation mechanism, which means designing a legally binding framework to cover all developed and developing countries by 2015 (IISD 2012). After the APEC Summit in Beijing in 2014, China submitted its Intended Nationally Determined Contribution (INDC) document to UN's climate team for preparation of Paris Conference in 2015. INDC released a more ambitious target than that of Copenhagen Conference, to reduce the carbon intensity of its economy 60%-65% per unit of GDP by 2030 (China dialogue 2015). Meanwhile, it is the first time for China to undertake to peak its emissions of climate-changing gases or even before. According to the 2015 newly published report of LSE's Grantham Institute, which was authored by climate economists Nicolas Stern and Fergus Green, "based on current policies and new measures aimed at shrinking the country's carbon footprint and cutting the use of coal, China's output of greenhouse gases could peak in 2025, five years earlier than it has promised, meaning that the world's largest emitter may be able to quicken the pace of cuts in coming decades" (McGarrity 2015).

4.3.2 Pressure to reduce carbon emissions as a driving force for domestic policy change

Although China is a top GHGs emitter, China usually uses two facts to defend its position on the CBDR principle: first is its low historical GHG emissions compared with developed countries; second are its low per capita emissions and the link between its enormous emissions and its large population. However, these two basic facts have met with greater challenges in the Post-Kyoto negotiations.

First, although China's historical emissions are low, China was responsible for almost 50% of new CO_2 emissions between 1997 and 2007 (Oberheitmann and Sternfeld 2011: 205). According to data from PBL Netherlands Environmental Assessment Agency, China's emission share in 2011 is 29%, which is much higher than the U.S. (16%) and the EU (11%) (Olivier et al. 2012: 6). The IEA (2009) estimates that about half of the growth of global energy-related CO_2 emissions until 2030 will come from China (Zhang 2010b: 251). Furthermore Oberheitmann and Sternfeld put forward that assuming different growth paths for the Chinese economy, by 2050 this share might increase to 45% in the "high" scenario of the model described above (Oberheitmann and Sternfeld 2011: 205). Second, although China's per capita emissions are relatively low, its carbon emissions are expected to increase at a rate of 2.5% to 5% annually (Oberheitmann and Sternfeld 2011). Especially in big cities like Beijing, Shanghai, and Guangzhou, the per capita emissions level has already approached or even surpassed the level of cities in developed countries. According to the World Bank report, the per capita carbon emissions in major Chinese cities have been higher than those in many of the world's large cities since 2010. Large Chinese cities like Beijing, Tianjin and Shanghai, have six times higher carbon intensity and energy intensity than New York, London, or Tokyo. ① According to the PBL report, China's average per capita CO_2 emissions increased by 9% to 7.2 tonnes CO_2 in 2011. This number is well within the 6 to 19 tonnes/person range spanned by the major industrialised countries; it is similar to the per capita emissions in the European Union of 7.5 tonnes in 2011 (Olivier et al. 2012: 6). Due to these statistics, China will be confronted with greater pressure from the international society in the climate change negotiations in the future. Its former approach to defending itself will not be effective any more.

As a developing country, China has a long way to go in its industrialization, urbanization, and modernization. Its coal-dominated energy mix cannot be substantially changed in the near future, which makes controlling GHG emissions rather difficult. However, the climate change regime has created a *carbon reduction pressure* to promote China to accelerate its steps for a green transformation. The carbon reduction pressure mechanism means that social influence from the climate change regime, especially climate change commitments made by a state, have constrained the behavior of the state and spurred it to head for a low-carbon development approach. This external dynamic is conducive to breaking China's carbon lock-in dependence and vested interest patterns in the energy sectors. Even if China had not issued an absolute cap on GHG emissions for domestic climate mitigation, the general national compliance tendency and national leaders' voluntary climate action commitment would have a carbon reduction pressure: to transmit the international pressure to the domestic level and devolve the national climate targets to the provincial level. Therefore, it definitely is leading to a profound wave of domestic policy changes in the energy sectors. The expert Li Shuo, from Climate & Energy Campaign at Greenpeace China, summarizes the role of the climate change regime in China's domestic policy change as follows:

> Top-down, rule-based structure of UN climate negotiations is crucial in pushing

---

① According to the statistics of the 2010 World Bank report, Beijing, Tianjin, and Shanghai's per capita carbon dioxide emissions were respectively 10.1, 11.1, and 11.7 tons, closing in on or even exceeding the New York level of 10.5 tons per capita, the London level of 9.6 tons per capita, the Singapore level of 7.9 tons per capita, and the Tokyo level of 4.9 tons per capita. From the perspective of carbon dioxide intensity and energy intensity, the Chinese large cities are higher. For instance, the carbon dioxide intensity of Beijing, Tianjin and Shanghai in 2010 were 1,063, 2,316, and 1,107 tons/million U.S. dollars respectively, six times more than that in New York, London and Tokyo. See website: http://money.163.com/12/0504/01/80KHNDE800253B0H.html (accessed on 21 March 2012).

China to make progress on cutting carbon emissions (...) although China has long had its own energy intensity targets, without the 2009 Copenhagen deal it might have waited even longer to make commitments on energy intensity, carbon intensity and non-fossil fuel ratios, and those commitments may have been smaller and less legally binding—than the 2005-2020 energy and emissions targets. (Li 2013)

According to the World Bank report, if China introduces a carbon pricing mechanism, "whether achieved via carbon trading or taxation, would impact such variables as the cost of emissions reduction and structural shifts in the economy" (World Bank 2011: 280). As described in the three scenarios in the figure: if China follows the "business as usual (BAU)" scenario, there will be a continued strong growth in CO_2 emissions to 2030 and it will be hard to introduce a CO_2 emission cap; while the implementation of a carbon price policy would help push China to reach its carbon emission peak around 2020-2025 (World Bank 2011: 280).

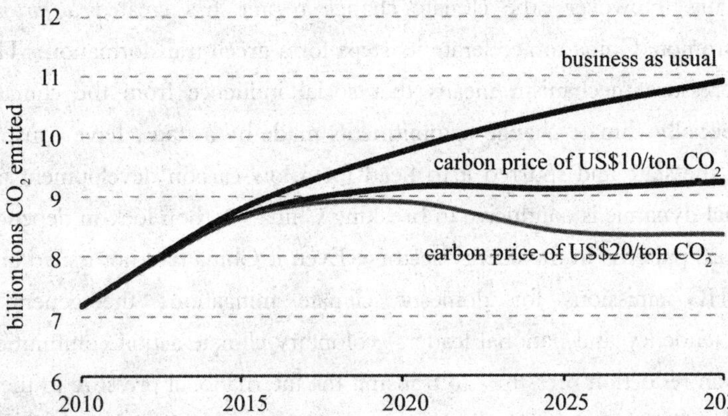

Figure 4.3 China's annual CO_2 emissions under three scenarios (2010-2030)

Source: World Bank (2011: 281).

However, it is usually rather difficult for carbon taxation or carbon trading proposals to enter the mainstream of the political agenda, due to strong resistance from the coal coalition and heavy-energy-consumption industries. From the diachronic comparison of China's stance in the climate change regime, it can be seen that even in 2007, China still held an absolutely negative position on carbon taxation and carbon trading. However, along with the increasing pressure from the climate change negotiations, especially the harsh critiques after the 2009 Copenhagen Climate Change Conference, China began to lose its hard-line attitude to carbon pricing even putting carbon pricing policy onto the political agenda (Carraro and Tavoni 2010). The quantitative carbon-intensity reduction target is now a national strategic target in the 12th FYP. Pushed by these carbon reduction pressure events, the NDRC finally issued the Notice on Carbon Trading Trials Scheme to launch a group of municipal and provincial-level carbon-trading pilots. This marked a milestone in that China has changed its stance on the carbon pricing mechanism and shown its determination to promote a green transformation.

Since the climate change regime has provided a significant external social context for China, the carbon reduction pressure mechanism has played an increasingly salient role in the energy policy-making process. Take RE development for another example. The carbon intensity target (reducing 40%-45% by 2020) and non-fossil fuel development target (to 15% by 2020), which were issued by the Chinese State Council before the 2009 Copenhagen Conference, were tied together. This linkage has reflected in the total energy consumption controlling mechanism embodied in the 12th FYP. The carbon reduction pressure will strongly continue to promote RE development in the future. Since the NDRC has strong local institutional branches, the general target will be broken down into provincial level targets in order to foster implementation. The central government has introduced a more "green index" to the assessment system of local official political performance, which will provide more dynamics to foster the implementation of low-carbon development policies, such as RE development and energy efficiency improvement at the local level.

Chapter 5
Capacity Building of the Pro-RE Coalition Through Climate Change Socialization

The main aim of this chapter is to focus on the building of capacity in the pro-RE coalition through climate change socialization. There are three sections in this chapter. The first section gives an overview of the bumpy path of institutional reform in the energy sector and summarizes characteristics of the energy policy-making system. It is hard for pro-RE actors to gain more political resources in the coal-dominated energy mix, unless there is an external impetus that breaks open existing interest structures. The second and third sections analyze the influence of role playing and interest calculation processes on domestic RE policy change, especially how pro-RE actors strengthen their position in the policy-making system. Through institutional, procedural and discursive lock-in effects and political resource reallocation at the domestic level, the pro-RE coalition has gained a more favorable "political opportunity structure" to obtain more legal authority, financial support, expertise and supporters to promote further RE policy change. Without the climate change regime, it would have been hard for the pro-RE coalition to obtain sufficient political resources to spur rapid RE development.

5.1 Institutional reforms in the energy sector and characteristics of the energy policy-making system in China

"The relative institutional chaos characterizes China's energy sector" (Betz 2013: 18), since there is no well-staffed and authoritative agency to formulate and implement energy policy, no Ministry of Energy, and no general Energy Law. Along with the increasing demand for energy supply since the late 1990s, institutional reform in the energy sector has gained more attention. The reform process in the energy sector, however, has been rather challenging and the efforts to establish a Ministry of Energy have been confronted with great resistance. This is because the energy sector involves many stakeholders and conventional interest groups.

5.1.1 The bumpy path of institutional reforms in the energy sector

In the 1950s, there were separate ministries for coal, electricity and oil. In 1970, a new Ministry of Fuel and Chemical Industries was established to combine the functions of those three ministries, but it was dissolved five years later due to its ineffective governance. Because of the emerging energy shortage in the early 1980s, Chinese leaders set up the State Energy Commission (SEC) (1980-1982) which subsequently developed into the Ministry of Energy (MOE) in 1988. The jurisdiction of the MOE had overlapping authority with the State Planning Committee (SPC) (Tsang and Kolk 2010: 6), and during the same period, the management and production functions of the previous industrial ministries were taken over by state-owned enterprises, which further weakened the position of the MOE. ① The influence of the MOE was confined to the electric power sector, due to the refusal of other industries to coordinate their planning and investment with it (Betz 2013: 18). Therefore, the MOE failed to carry out its mandate and was abolished in 1993 (Tsang and Kolk 2010: 6). As a result, China has been short of a ministerial-level agency devoted to the country's energy-development policies since then, and this absence has greatly reduced the central government's power to formulate and implement its strategic energy plans (Zha 2006: 186). In 1998, there was a new round of institutional reforms in the energy sector. The Ministries for Coal and Electrical Power were abolished, and replaced by provincial level coal companies and a State Power Corporation respectively (Andrews-Speed 2012: 146-147). During this process, state-owned enterprises (SOEs) in the energy sector gained more power. The State Development and Planning Commission (SDPC) "retained authority over medium and long-term plans, pricing and energy efficiency, and the degree of coherence in energy policy-making deteriorated rather than increased due to the bureaucratic competition" (Andrews-Speed 2012: 146-147).

In 2003, the SDPC was upgraded to the National Development and Reform Commission (NDRC), in order to deal with the energy crisis which the new government led by President Hu Jintao faced within the same year (Downs 2006). The State Council established the National Energy Bureau (NEB) under the NDRC,

---

① The State Planning Commission (SPC) was founded in 1952, and in 1998 the SPC was upgraded to the State Development Planning Commission (SDPC), then beginning in 2003 the SDPC was upgraded to the National Development and Reform Commission (NDRC).

making it responsible for the coordination of the energy plans, policies and projects of other ministries involved in energy policy-making and of energy companies (Betz 2013: 18). The NDRC as the macroeconomic management agency is the most powerful ministerial department formulating policies for economic and energy development and guiding overall economic system restructuring. It has exclusive authority for energy regulation. The reforms in the energy sector after the abolishment of the MOE were all carried out under the framework of the NDRC. However, the NEB was only a bureau-level agency without sufficient authority to control the behavior of state-owned enterprises. ①

Due to the rapid growth of energy demand and the increasing demand for effective energy regulation, in May 2005, the State Council established a State Energy Leadership Group headed by former Premier Wen Jiabao, with Vice-Premiers Huang Ju and Zeng Peiyuan as deputy heads. The membership of the Leadership Group included leaders from 13 central ministries and commissions. In early June 2005, the State Energy Leadership Office was set up as the executive organ of the Leadership Group (Cheng 2008: 302). The establishment of this institution indicates that the central government began to attach strategic importance to energy governance. ② On 27 June 2005, the CPC Political Bureau held its collective study session on energy regulation. Former President Hu put emphasis on encouraging the development of nuclear energy and renewable energies, optimizing the energy structure, and promoting the development of a recycling economy (CPC People 2010). In 2008, the NEB was upgraded to the National Energy Administration (NEA) under the NDRC framework, from a bureau-level to a vice-ministerial level agency. In the hierarchical orientation of governance, ranks are significant because a governmental unit with the same rank cannot issue binding orders to other units. Although promoted, the NEA is still only equal to or even lower than many state-owned energy enterprises, which are ranked at the ministerial or vice-ministerial levels.

As a transitional solution instead of establishing a Ministry of Energy, the State Council set up the National Energy Commission (NEC) headed by former Premier Wen Jiabao in 2010 (as a coexisting organization with the NEA). The NEC, parallel with the NDRC, is a high-level coordination body with a ministerial rank, which is responsible for drafting national energy development plans, reviewing the national

① According to the hierarchical level arrangement in the bureaucratic system of China, the bureau level is lower than the vice-ministerial level.

② The main tasks of this team, as a high-level coordinated agency, are to research on national energy development strategy and major energy policy planning, to explore energy developments and energy conservation, to discuss energy security and emergency response, and to promote international energy cooperation.

energy strategy and fostering the implementation of a unified energy policy and the coordination of international cooperation. ① The NEC is to be composed of 21 ministers and directors from different departments, including the NEA and the Central Bank (Betz 2013: 18). However, since conventional interest groups in the current energy sector have controlled most of the political resources, such as through the monopolization of SOEs in the energy sector, reform of the energy sector and energy market liberalization are rather difficult.

5.1.2 Characteristics of the energy policy system in China

This section summarizes three main characteristics of the energy policy system.

5.1.2.1 Weak institution building of the energy sector

Although China has become a top energy consumer in the world due to its rapid economic growth, institutional building in the energy sector (efforts to build an authoritative and effective Ministry of Energy) is still disproportionately weak and dispersed. After several rounds of institutional reforms, the efforts to establish an authoritative agency (an Energy Ministry) to enhance energy regulation and foster energy policy coordination among different stakeholders have proven to be a failure. Along with soaring growth in energy demand, institution building in the energy sector has become a significant issue on the political agenda. An example is the establishment of the high-level coordinating agency—the NEC to replace the former State Energy Leadership Group in 2010 and act in parallel with the NEA in the energy regulation field. The establishment of the NEC is a transition or compromise to deal with the increasing demands to reestablish an Energy Ministry.

The absence of an authoritative agency in the energy sector has left a power vacuum in relation to energy regulation. Therefore, other stakeholders, like powerful state-owned enterprises in the coal, oil and electricity sectors can exert more influence on the energy policy-making process. SOEs became actively involved in the "drafting of the country's energy laws and began to occupy key posts in the state's supervisory bodies" (Betz 2013: 17). Figure 5.1 shows key actors in the energy policy system. The State Electricity Regulatory Commission (SERC) and the State-owned Asset Supervision and Administration Commission (SASAC) are vice-ministerial level agencies that regulate the behavior of SOEs. However, the interests of SOEs are not

① Instead of re-establishing a Ministry of Energy, China's leaders have created two inadequate entities: the National Energy Commission and the National Energy Administration. The former is tasked with overall policy guidance and coordination, while the latter provides the manpower and expertise for day-to-day work. The NEC committee was composed of 21 members from various government agencies. It is said that the NEC will have a strong voice in price-setting of electric power, which is an important authority of NDRC. See Kennedy (2010).

always aligned with these ministries and as they pursue their own interests, they are sometimes beyond governmental control (Jakobson and Knox 2010). Illustrated by Figure 5.1, other ministerial organizations have the authority to issue regulations relating to their sphere of activity (Andrews-Speed 2012: 152). The Ministry of Land and Resources (MOLAR) manages resource extraction and exploitation; the Ministry for Environmental Protection (MEP) is responsible for environmental assessments of energy infrastructure; the Ministry of Science and Technology (MOST) takes charge of technological investments in the energy sector. Therefore, the issuing and implementation of certain energy policy regulation needs to be coordinated among different actors. The dispersed structure and nature of China's energy sector has "granted considerable bargaining and veto power to individual ministries and state enterprises" (Andrews-Speed 2012: 152). The weak institution building in the energy sector has resulted in more bargaining and compromising among different stakeholders. The result of this competition depends on the resources controlled by different actors.

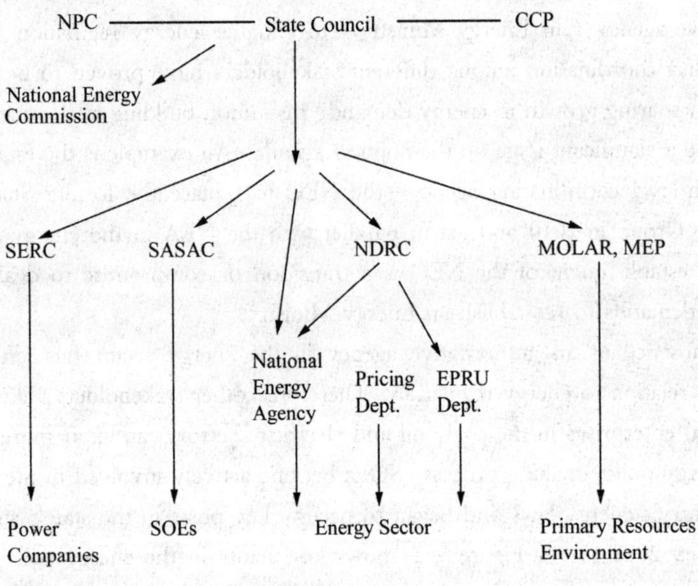

Figure 5.1 Key actors in the energy policy-making system of China

Abbreviations: NPC—National People's Congress; CCP—Chinese Communist Party; NDRC—National Development and Reform Commission; SERC—State Electricity Regulatory Commission; SASAC—State-owned Asset Supervision and Administration Commission; MOLAR—Ministry of Land and Resources; MEP—Ministry for Environmental Protection; EPRU Dept.—Environment Protection and Resource Utilization Department; SOEs—state-owned enterprises.

Source: Andrews-Speed (2012: 147).

Apart from the long-time lack of a Ministry of Energy, another highlight of the weak institutional setup in the energy sector is the long-time absence of an *Energy Law*. Until the present, the main laws in the energy sector are the Electricity Law which was issued in December 1995 (came into effect in April 1996), the Coal Law in August 1996 (effective in December 1996), the RE Law in 2005, the Energy Conservation Law in 2007 and the RE Law Amendment in 2009. However, there are some contradictory elements between the newly issued laws (the RE Law, the Energy Conservation Law) and the "old" Electricity Law. For example, although the RE Law claims that grid enterprises shall buy all the grid-connected RE power within the coverage of their power grid, the grid-connection responsibility is not embodied in the Electricity Law and there is no provision concerning punishments for violations. Therefore, pro-RE actors call for the amendment of the "out-dated" Electricity Law and require more attention to RE development in the drafting of an Energy Law. The Energy Law could provide a general legislative frame for regulating social relations in energy development, utilization and management. However, the development of an Energy Law has encountered much resistance. Although in December 2007 and in July 2010 the government issued draft versions of an Energy Law for social discussion there was little progress towards final ratification due to the strong resistance from the state-owned energy enterprises and vest interest groups in coal sector. Moreover, the draft itself is so "ambiguous and self-contradictory on some key points, such as ownership, pricing and access to infrastructure, that it has little value for charting the future development of the energy sector" (Andrews-Speed 2012: 152).

5.1.2.2 The central position of the NDRC in the energy policy system

The NDRC, as the most powerful bureaucratic agency for macro-economic planning and energy regulation, plays a central role in making and implementing energy policy. Since 2003, major institutional reforms in the energy sector have been undertaken within the NDRC framework in order to coordinate and centralize energy regulation: the State Council established the NEB under the NDRC in 2003, and then set up the State Energy Leadership Office as the executive organ of the State Energy Leadership Group (Cheng 2008: 302) within the NDRC in 2005, and the NEB was upgraded to the NEA in 2008. Although these efforts have not lead to the emergence of an authoritative agency in the energy sector, the NDRC has gained much more power in energy regulation through these institutional changes.

There are more than 30 departments (bureaus or administrations) in the NDRC framework, taking charge of designing the general plan of economic and social development, and responsible for energy policy formulation. In regard to administrative implementation and supervision, the NDRC dominates the implementation of energy policies and the departments in charge of finance, science and technology and technical supervision (Wang, Z. et al. 2010:124). According to Figure 5.1, an important aspect of energy policy—the right to fix prices—still rests with the NDRC (Betz 2013: 18). The Pricing Department of the NDRC controls the energy pricing right, which is treated as the most significant lever in steering the economy (Downs 2008). Another important organization within the NDRC is the Environment Protection and Resource Utilization Department, which oversees energy efficiency policies (Andrews-Speed 2012: 146-147), especially when energy intensity reduction has gained much importance in recent years.

The NEA within the NDRC plays a direct role in the national energy policy-making system and cooperates closely with the high-level NEC, which was set up in 2010. Within the NEA, the Energy Research Institute (ERI), as a governmental research institution, provides a strategic vision for China's energy problems and knowledge support. The ERI has the authority to draft energy policy initiatives and provides energy policy proposals directly to the NDRC. The Center for Renewable Energy Development (CRED) within the ERI is the leading research center in the RE governance and takes the responsibility for drafting many legislative and administrative RE policies. Apart from the ERI, the State Council's Development Research Institute (DRI) plays a significant role in influencing energy policy-making (Andrews-Speed 2012: 147), especially the designing of energy regulations in national Five-Year Plans.

5.1.2.3 The special role of state-owned enterprises in the energy policy-making system

Although the Chinese government since 1978 has shown a tendency to push market-oriented liberalization of the energy sector, there has been "the ongoing reliance on strong state involvement in the energy sector" (Andrews-Speed 2012: 149).① The most obvious characteristic of this state involvement in the energy market is the existence of state-owned energy enterprises (SOEs). In the mid- and late-1990s, the restructuring of the energy industry empowered state-owned enterprises with more autonomy and power. Along with the power expansion of these newly commercialized state-owned enterprises in the coal, oil, and electricity sectors, these powerful stakeholders have sufficient capacity to influence governmental energy policy in order to guarantee their vested interests. Especially the lack of an authoritative energy agency creates an ideal environment for state-owned energy enterprises to influence policy to

① Deng Xiaoping introduced reform and opening-up policy to encourage market-based reform and intensify international communication.

their own advantage (Andrews-Speed 2012: 151).①

The most important state-owned energy enterprises—the oil companies, power companies and grid companies—hold ministerial rank, "giving them direct access to the state's political leaders and their chief executives all hold the rank of vice minister" (Lee 2012: 88). In other words, the chief executives of SOEs have a "double-identity" as the leader of a company and as a kind of high-level governmental official. As mentioned above, even when the NEB was upgraded to the NEA under the NDRC framework in 2008, the hierarchical level of the NEA is only vice-ministerial. Therefore, SOEs have a higher hierarchical standing than ministries and this enables them to get away with disobeying ministerial policies (Lee 2012: 88). It is difficult for the NEA to regulate and coordinate the behavior of SOEs as it does not have sufficient authority to do so.

SOEs have an additional advantage in their embedded *guanxi* (personalized networks of influence) with paramount leaders in the energy sectors.② To a certain degree, SOEs in the energy sector are able to "directly act upon the motivations of the Politburo Standing Committee and paramount leaders, which are to ensure economic growth and social stability" (Lee 2012: 87). These SOEs also previously "loaned employees to the government's understaffed energy bodies and they thereby became involved in the drafting of the country's energy policies" (Betz 2013: 18). So the SOEs would take advantage of these personal channels and the current power vacuum in domestic energy governance to affect energy policy making and pursue their own economic interest. Relying on their high hierarchical level and special *guanxi* resources with paramount leaders in the energy sectors, to some extent SOEs even can challenge the authority of the NDRC and refuse to implement related energy policies. For instance, it is hard for the NEA to require the two national grid enterprises (the State Grid and the China Southern Power Grid) to purchase all the RE power according to

① In the 1990s, different from that in the oil sector, both state-owned large mines and township and village coal mines coexisted. Demand for coal exceeded supply and the smaller mines with their lower operational standards and lower costs in the late 1990s were able to undercut the larger mines in the market. In order to protect their own interests, large state-owned coal enterprises lobbied high-level governmental official to launch a campaign to close the township and village mines. See Andrews-Speed (2012: 151).

② *Guanxi* describes the basic dynamic in personalized networks of influence, and is a central idea in Chinese society. In Western media, the pinyin romanization of this Chinese word is becoming more widely used instead of the two common translations—"connections" and "relationships"—as neither of those terms sufficiently reflects the wide cultural implications that *guanxi* describes. See Gold and Guthrie (2002).

the feed-in tariff policy embodied in the RE Law.① In the oil sector, the state-owned oil enterprises were not only able to "maintain their effective duopoly over China's oil and gas markets after the structural reforms of 1998, but they have been allowed to squeeze out smaller players in the domestic market" (Andrews-Speed 2012: 151). Since they have great vested interests in the current oil and natural gas business, they have shown their strong reluctance to obey the RE Law, which required them to purchase bio-fuels and integrate bio-fuels to current oil transportation and sales systems.

5.2 Institutional anchoring in the role playing process and the strengthening of the pro-RE coalition

As shown in the process-tracing of China's participation in the climate change regime found in Chapter 4, China has shown an increasingly proactive and flexible attitude in the climate change negotiations. This was done in order to smooth interactions in this social context through the adoption of the institutional and procedural requirements of climate change regime (Johnston 2008: 47). The changing discourses of authoritative national leaders on climate change also exerted an influence on the "national political rhetoric" in the domestic bureaucratic system (Cortell and Davis Jr. 2000: 76). This micro-process of socialization can be called a role playing process in the climate change regime. Elizabeth Economy (2001a) argues that the requirements of the regime result in "new domestic actors, new bureaucratic arrangements, or the new bureaucratic linkages that influence policy outcome and international regimes spur the emergence of new domestic institutions to manage China's involvement in the regimes and encourage the introduction of new actors" (Economy 2001a; Yu 2008: 113). Although compliance behavior might not originate from reflection, the "role playing" efforts can break the dependence on the old approach and result in a new pattern of institutional anchoring. This can occur in three ways: an institutional lock-in effect, procedural lock-in effect and discursive lock-in effect (Johnston 2008). Through role playing in the climate change socialization process, the institutional anchoring of RE governance is fostered: new RE bureaucratic arrangements are established and new RE actors and supporters emerge. RE

① The NEA, like its predecessors, was equipped with a broad mandate—to manage energy-related industries, draft energy plans and approve foreign energy investments. The NEA did not, however, have sufficient clout either to mitigate the fighting among different agencies or to impose its will on the heads of state energy enterprises. See Betz (2013: 18).

development became one of the key targets in the National Climate Change Programs and the Climate Change Law. Terms like "low-carbon economy", "carbon-intensity reduction" and "green growth" have been promoted by national leaders. On the whole, the role playing process in the climate change socialization phase provided a strong impetus for capacity building of the pro-RE coalition.

5.2.1 The institutional lock-in effect in the climate change role playing process

After China joined the climate change regime, the structural cohesion and coherence requirements made by the international level required that the country establish institutions to implement its international commitments and incorporate climate change into the established institutions, especially since China signed the Kyoto Protocol in 1998 and ratified it in 2002. The implementation of the international agreement relies on bureaucratic institution building at the domestic level. These newly emerging bureaucratic institutions have created channels to link the international and domestic levels, therefore, they could be called "window agencies" (Yu 2008). With the development of new bureaucratic institutional embedding in the domestic political system, the back-out cost will gradually be increased, which leads to an institutional lock-in effect.

In addition to the establishment of "window agencies" at the domestic level, there is also a requirement for institutional coordination and green policy integration, since the complex issue of climate change needs the cooperation and coordination of many ministries. Along with the salience of climate change at the domestic level, green "window agencies" have gained more authority and power to promote green policy integration and institutional coordination in the bureaucratic system. There will be increasing demand for establishing related think tanks and research institutes to provide knowledge support and policy initiatives to policy makers. The influence of the climate change regime has created an advantageous situation for the growth of RE bureaucratic supporters, expertise and societal promoters at the domestic level. Moreover, the pro-RE coalition has gained increasing access to political resources and thus can better defend its own interests.

5.2.1.1 Institutional anchoring and its implications for pro-RE coalition building

China joined the UNFCCC in order to improve the diplomatic relations with western countries and looked for more diplomatic support from the third world. The National Group of Co-ordination on Climate Change, which was established in 1990, worked mainly on meteorological science and climate change's impact on China. However, it was no more than a loosely organized "window agency", since its lead agencies, the China Meteorological Administration (CMA) and the National

Environmental Protection Agency (NEPA) lacked sufficient authority (hierarchal level) and capability to coordinate different bureaucracies in terms of their climate change actions (Yu 2008: 118). Moreover, the economic regulation agencies were not included in this national coordination group. This institutional defect became more obvious when China became involved more deeply in the climate change negotiations. ① Along with the increasing political awareness of and economic sensitivity on climate change in the late 1990s especially when the Kyoto Protocol was adopted in 1997, the main responsible role for the climate change negotiations shifted to the most powerful agency in economic planning and energy regulation—the SDPC in 1998. And in the same year, the SDPC representatives on behalf of China signed the Kyoto Protocol. The former National Climate Change Coordination Group was re-titled as the National Climate Change Policy Coordination Group, which was located in the SDPC.

This new bureaucratic arrangement symbolized that climate change achieved much more political attention. The SDPC/NDRC became the key institution responsible for the climate change negotiations. ② This institutional linkage between energy regulation and climate change created an advantageous chance for translating voluntary climate change commitments into the economic development pattern. The stance of the SDPC/NDRC was similar to that of the MOFA and the MOST: presenting a pragmatic attitude towards material incentives such as development funds, technology transfer and international cooperative projects. The National Climate Change Policy Coordination Group under the leadership of the SDPC/NDRC has gradually played a more proactive and flexible role in the climate change negotiations, such as showing a cooperative attitude towards CDM projects and behaving actively in the China Renewable Energy Development Project (REDP) since 2001 and the China Renewable Energy Scale-up Program (CRESP) since 2006. More "window agencies" to deal with climate change and RE development have been established within the SDPC/NDRC, such as the Center for Renewable Energy Development (CRED), the Research Center for Energy Environment and Climate Change (RCEECC) and the

① The position of the CMA was gradually marginalized and the spilt between different bureaucracies grew wider: the NEPA promoted active involvement in climate change activities also to pursue sustainable development; the SETC and the SSTC showed a relatively active stance on climate change and treated climate change action as a great opportunity to catch up in advanced technologies through technology transfer; while the MOFA focused more on traditional sovereignty integrity and remained conservative about the climate change mitigation commitment. Interviews with Duncan Freeman, Senior Research Fellow in Brussels Institute of Contemporary China Studies, Vrije Universiteit Brussel (4 May 2010, in Brussels).

② The State Environmental Protection Administration was established in 1998 and was upgraded to Ministry of Environmental Protection (MEP) in 2008.

CDM Project Management Center in the Energy Research Institute (ERI), the Department of Climate Change within the NDRC, the Department of New Energy and Renewable Energy under the NEA.

The establishment of these new bureaucratic agencies has laid an institutional foundation for pro-RE coalition building. For example, the CRED, which was established in 1998 after the NDRC took full charge of the climate change negotiations, has gradually played a pivotal role in leading research on the feasibility of different RE policy instruments and drafting policy proposals for the NDRC, like drafting the RE Law and RE Law Amendment for the NPC's legislative ratification. The Department of New Energy and Renewable Energy (DNERE) set up in the NEA has played a significant role in RE policy coordination and implementation at the national and local levels, and taking responsibility for RE fund management with cooperative support from Ministry of Finance (MOF). Since the NDRC has a nation-wide branch structure (provincial NDRC), these new bureaucratic arrangements, which are representative of the interest of RE development, will have profound influence on the local level. In sum, in the role playing that occurred in relation to the climate change negotiations, new bureaucratic arrangements for RE development have come into being and the pro-RE actors' position has been greatly enhanced.

Furthermore, the institutional anchoring process cannot only be seen in the rising number of new bureaucracies concerning climate change and RE development, but also in their higher level in the bureaucratic hierarchy. 2007 was a significant year for institutional change. In January 2007, China's National Climate Change Assessment Report was released. It emphasized the devastating impacts of climate change on China. In June 2007, along with the announcement of China's National Climate Change Program, the Climate Change Coordination Group under the NDRC was elevated to the National Leading Group on Climate Change (NLGCC) directly under the State Council and was led by former Premier Wen Jiabao (Hallding et al. 2009: 125-126).① At the same time, the State Council Energy Conservation and Emissions Reduction Leading Group was established to set national guidelines and strategies for energy saving and RE development. The high-level bureaucratic arrangements of the National Leading Group on Climate Change and Energy Conservation and Emissions Reduction Leading Group are the same institutions with two different names, which shows that climate change is tied closely with energy, and especially RE development. Under the State Energy Leadership Group, an advisory committee including 40 experts

① The "Leading Group" is a super-ministerial mechanism created to largely coordinate the complex decision-making process in some policy fields where there are probably more than 10 ministries involved.

and consultants was established; their aim is to improve the level of scientific policy-making. The Energy Conservation Committee and the Renewable Energy Development Committee are two important specialized committees in the research group. ① Before the 2009 Copenhagen Conference, China made a significant carbon intensity reduction, which formed a carbon reduction pressure mechanism to strongly promote climate change mitigation and RE development at the domestic level. In November 2011 before the Durban Climate Change Conference, the NDRC established the National Strategic Research and International Cooperation Center for Climate Change (NCSC), the first national-level think tank focused on strategic research and international cooperation for climate change (China News 2011) (for more detailed information on the pro-RE institutions see section 7.2).

5.2.1.2 Governmental institutional coordination and green policy integration

Apart from the establishment of new bureaucratic agencies in order to support the participation in the climate change regime, the institutional lock-in effect has also been reflected in the governmental institutional coordination and green policy integration. Due to the increasing complexity of climate change, it necessarily needs inter-bureaucratically mutual efforts to deal with the climate mitigation issue. Yu (2008) argues that the climate change regime is "a determinant variable in inducing China to make a responsible, comprehensive and coordinative policy against climate change through the related coordination institutions" (Yu 2008: 114). To be more specific, climate change itself is a comprehensive framework, which involves many perspectives: regarding the dimension of energy regulation, it includes the control of fossil fuel consumption, RE development and energy conservation; regarding the dimension of economy development, it includes a transformation towards green growth, green market regulation, carbon tax implementation, the low-carbon finance and the carbon trading design; regarding the technological dimension, it includes the clean technology innovation capacity, national R&D investment, green intellectual property rights protection, clean technology diffusion and utilization. In this comprehensive framework, it definitely needs mutual efforts from different ministries. Many Chinese bureaucracies "have to get involved in institutional coordination toward achieving the objectives of the UNFCCC and their work policies through inter-ministerial coordination, and in the context of a national plan" (Yu 2008: 115). Therefore, along with China becoming involved more deeply in the climate change

---

① Under the Advisory Committee, there are six specialized committees. They are the Specialized Committee of Coal, Electricity and Nuclear Energy Committee, Oil and Gas Committee, RE Committee, Energy Conservation Committee and Energy Economics Committee.

regime, any further climate mitigation commitment making and negotiation stance changing require greater domestic inter-ministerial coordination efforts.

China built the National Group of Coordination on Climate Change composed of 13 bureaucracies in 1991. The CMA and the NEPA were in charge of climate policy coordination. However, due to the limited institutional capacity of the CMA and the NEPA and increasing complexity of climate change issue, the main responsibility for climate change negotiations was transferred to the SDPC in 1998 and the National Climate Change Policy Coordination Group was re-established in the same year. This inter-agency organization included representatives from the SDPC/NDRC, the MOFA, the MOST, the SEPA, the CMA and other 10 ministerial-level departments (Chen 2009: 117; Yu 2008), and the SDPC/NDRC took main responsibility to organize the inter-ministerial conference (which all together involve 14 ministries to join in climate change discussion). ① As an authoritative agency in the economic development and energy regulation, the SDPC/NDRC has larger competence to be a pivotal representative of China in the climate change negotiations and promote the inter-ministerial coordination.

There are four coordination groups under the National Climate Change Policy Coordination Group relating to: scientific assessment, impact assessment, economic implication and matters related to the Convention. And different ministries have their own tasks as listed in Table 5.1.

① The Committee chaired by the State Development and Planning Committee (the SDPC was upgraded to the NDRC in 2003), included 14 participating departments: the Committee of Development and Planning, the Ministry of Foreign Affairs, the Ministry of Science and Technology, the State Economic and Trade Commission, the China Meteorological Administration, the Ministry of Finance, the State Environmental Protection Administration, the Ministry of Agriculture, the Ministry of Communications, the Ministry of Water Resources, the Ministry of Construction, the State Forestry Administration, the State Oceanic Administration and the Chinese Academy of Sciences. The Ministry of Foreign Affairs, the Ministry of Science and Technology, the China Meteorological Administration, the Ministry of Finance, the State Environmental Protection Administration, and the Ministry of Agriculture were the vice heads of this committee. The other bureaucracies (i. e., State Economic and Trade Commission, Ministry of Communications, Ministry of Water Resources, Ministry of Construction, State Forestry Administration, State Oceanic Administration and Chinese Academy of Sciences) did not play an important role in this committee. See Yu (2008).

Table 5.1 Four coordination groups under the National Climate Change Policy Coordination

Working Groups	Main Responsible Agencies (co-chaired by)
WG I: Scientific assessment	China Meteorological Administration (CMA) and Chinese Academy of Sciences (CAS)
WG II: Impact assessment and response strategies	Ministry of Science and Technology (MOST) and the State Environmental Protection Agency (SEPA—upgraded to Ministry of Environmental Protection—MEP in 2008)
WG III: Economic implications	State Development Planning Commission (SDPC) and the State Economic and Trade Commission (SETC) and Ministry of Finance (MOF)
WG IV: The matters related to the Convention	Ministry of Foreign Affairs (MOFA) and the Ministry of Science and Technology (MOST)

Source: Yu (2008: 120).

Stimulated by this inter-ministerial coordination, climate change and RE development have entered the political agenda of different governmental bureaucracies. Relevant climate change and RE research institutions as well as special climate change and RE departments have come into being within different ministries. The enhancement of governmental coordination has resulted in the accelerated pace of green policy integration in various governmental agencies. According to Yu's research (2008), it is climate change that "involves so many ministries to the large-scale governmental coordination process for the first time in the history" (2008: 120). With the increasing international pressure from the climate change regime, the coordination efforts have been enhanced. One milestone event in 2007 was that the coordination group was further upgraded to the National Leading Group on Climate Change (NLGCC), which now is the national-level coordinating agency to promote inter-ministerial coordination and green policy integration. The former Premier Wen took on the role of group leader and delivered important speeches in every group meeting. Within the NLGCC, the concrete tasks have still been carried out by the NDRC. This inter-ministerial coordination also has significant implications for RE development, because RE policy implementation needs the supportive coordination from many ministries, such as the clean technological transfer and international RE cooperation support from the MOST and the MOF; technological innovation support from the MOST and the MOF; CDM projects supervised by the China CDM Fund and the CDM Management Center; ecological assessment from the MEP. Since the NDRC takes full responsibility of the climate change negotiations and energy regulation, this institutional coordination advantage has brought great dynamics for RE policy implementation and RE development.

There are four main functions of inter-ministerial coordination and green policy integration regarding climate change. They have significant implications for the pro-RE coalition building:

First, it provides a forum for information communication and idea exchange, and it stimulates the inter-ministerial policy learning. The Briefing on Climate Change COP Negotiation Process is distributed to relevant ministries on time. Apart from the informative data from the climate change regime, such as from the IPCC, China has launched its own inter-ministerial comprehensive research on scientific climate assessment, impact assessment and economic adaptive approach studies. The institutional coordination is beneficial for different institutions to share research information, exchange views with each other and broaden their horizons in an interdisciplinary way (Yu 2008: 119). The institutional coordination process is also a learning process from knowledge accumulation. The institutional coordination enhances mutual learning process among different ministries. Since climate change is a very complex issue, the institutional coordination improves the capability of officials in different ministries to learn from each other. For instance, different departments have gained knowledge about CDM and RE development during the inter-ministerial coordination. Therefore, the RE issue has gained a higher priority in the climate change mitigation, and the RE policy implementation as well as the policy assessment has been enhanced among the governmental coordination.

Second, it improves consensus building on climate change and low-carbon development. The Chinese political system is known for its heavy reliance on meetings and official documents to build policy consensus and to ensure policy coordination (Lu 1997). The China National Coordination Committee always holds a conference twice a year just before and after the COP (Lu 1997; Yu 2008: 120). Different departments have their own understanding about the climate change influence on their jurisdiction areas and pursue different interests in climate change mitigation actions. Therefore, the institutional coordination has played an active role in coordinating ministerial interests and accelerating common understanding in climate change. The policy consensus will contribute a lot to improve China's capability in implementing the required procedures/rules of the climate change regime. Without consensus-building among different stakeholders, the climate change mitigation action as well as RE development, which involves many actors in the policy implementation process, cannot achieve great progress.

Third, inter-ministerial coordination accelerates institutional green policy integration. With the growing salience of climate change and low-carbon development on the policy agendas, many bureaucratic actors have begun to pay more attention to their own institution building on climate change and RE development. The inter-ministerial coordination itself requires different bureaucratic agencies to establish their own climate change research groups, set up special institutional arrangements for climate change, and be prepared well for the inter-ministerial coordination conference. These institutional changes have further enhanced green policy integration of different sectors: many bureaucracies have set up their own climate change or low-carbon departments within their institutional framework. This green policy integration expansion among different ministries has paved the way for low-carbon pattern designing as well as RE development. In the process of drafting the 12th FYP, energy intensity reduction and carbon intensity reduction are the two main binding targets for economic development. Against this backdrop, the government has set the ambitious RE targets in the 12th FYP (11.4% by 2015 and 15% by 2020), which promote incremental RE policy change. During this process, the capacity of pro-RE actors has been greatly fostered.

5.2.1.3 The strengthening of the pro-RE societal actors in the institutional anchoring

The multi-country poll which was organized by the World Public Opinion. org and commissioned by the World Bank in December 2009 (WPO 2009)①, has revealed that public concern on climate change is generally higher in developing countries, and China ranks top (68%) willing to bear higher prices for energy and other goods to fight climate change (WPO 2009). Due to the increasing salience of climate change at the domestic level, the role of the institutional lock-in effect in the social research institutions and societal associations in the fields of climate change, low-carbon pattern and RE development cannot be overlooked.

Two decades ago, China had only a very small scientific community specializing in the climate change and relevant issues (Economy 2001b: 249-250). With its deeper involvement in the climate change regime, there has been an increasing need for knowledge support and policy consultations from research institutes and universities. According to the recent investigation, over 70% universities in China have constructed relevant institutes or research centers focusing on climate change mitigation, low-

① The poll questioned 13,518 respondents in 15 nations—Bangladesh, China, Egypt, France, India, Indonesia, Iran, Japan, Kenya, Mexico, Russia, Senegal, Turkey, the United States, and Vietnam. See WPO (2009).

carbon development and RE development. In addition, the multilateral and bilateral climate change and clean energy cooperation have promoted the establishment of climate change and RE research institutions. For instance, the Europe-China Clean Energy Centre (EC2), which was founded in Tsinghua University in April 2010, is a Five-Year cooperation project funded by the EU under the EU-China Climate Strategic Partnership framework. The EC2's main tasks are "to promote an increased use of clean energy in China and to support the Chinese government's efforts to shape a more sustainable, environmental friendly and efficient energy sector" (EC2 2010). ① These kinds of institutional lock-in effects in social research institutes have provided more supportive knowledge and introduced more policy proposals for policy makers. Moreover, the salience of climate change and low-carbon development in research institutes and universities have increased the public awareness for green growth and enhanced the social acceptance for RE utilization.

The cooperative projects from the climate change regime have also promoted the development of domestic RE industry associations and societies. For instance, the Chinese Renewable Energy Industries Association (CREIA) was established in 2000 with the support of the UNDP, the GEF and the SETC. The CREIA obtained legal registration as the Renewable Energy Professional Division of the China Comprehensive Resource Utilization Association from the Ministry of Civil Affairs in 2002. Another example is the China Renewable Energy Development Project (REDP). The REDP is an eight-year international program for promoting on-grid wind power and off-grid solar PV power development in China, which is supported by the World Bank and the GEF. This program has certain cooperative relations with RE industry societies. Even though the REDP was ended in June 2008, the China Photovoltaic Industry Association within the China Renewable Energy Society (CRES) is being established to continue the work (Luo and Wang 2008).

In the pro-RE coalition, societal actors (including societal research institutes, universities, RE industry associations, environmental NGOs) are significant components to promote RE development. Under the influence of climate change, more societal actors concerning climate change and RE development have emerged, which has greatly enhanced the capacity building of the pro-RE coalition. With a pluralization tendency in the "fragmented authoritarianism" pattern, societal actors have played an increasingly important role in promoting RE policy change. For

① EC2 network of excellence acts as an intelligent hub to provide advice to players in the energy sector, including Chinese and European institutions, companies and researchers, as well as training to policy makers, in both China and Europe. See EC2 (2010).

instance, the CREIA aimed to expose the inappropriateness in the current RE policy implementation and promote further RE policy change through issuing wind power curtailment reports.

5.2.2 The procedural lock-in effect in the climate change role playing process

Apart from the emergence of new bureaucratic agencies and the increasing institutional coordination regarding climate change in the role playing process, the acceptance and the internalization of rules, procedures of international climate regime in the daily routine are indispensable to enhance the procedural lock-in behavior. During the international socialization process, the climate change regime as social context exerts influence on domestic bureaucratic actors through procedural obligations, such as to make compliance with substantive obligations stipulated in the treaty and foster effective implementation as well as guarantee information transparency (Dai 2007: 14), like requiring their member states to issue relevant administrative regulations, to submit (sometimes voluntarily) the national or local climate change mitigation action program reports, national action assessment, and constructing e-governmental websites to release the up-to-date information. When climate change enters the mainstream of political agenda, the procedural lock-in effect does not only show up on the governmental document level (issuing relevant laws, administrative regulations and submitting implementation and assessment reports), it is also embodied in the official performance evaluation standards system. In other words, the performance of GHG emission reductions/carbon intensity reduction, low-carbon development, and RE development has been gradually evolved into the local officials' performance assessment. This procedural lock-in effect has empowered pro-RE actors with more legal authority and power to increase their voice in RE policy-making process.

5.2.2.1 Procedural lock-in effect and its implications for the pro-RE coalition building

China has participated in the climate change regime since 1992. The UNFCCC framework clearly stipulates that each party has the obligation to submit its National Communication on Climate Change, including "the national inventories of emissions by sources and removals by sinks, the overall description of the measures taken or envisaged for the implementation of the Convention as well as other information that the party considers suitable to submit" (NCOCC 2007). And "every state should design the national climate change program, national climate mitigation and adaptation plan, and promote the relevant training and education" (NCOCC 2007).

When China signed the Kyoto Protocol, the Chinese government began to attach more importance to the international obligation and pressure, especially when the SDPC took the full responsibility for the climate change negotiations and enhanced the inter-ministerial coordination in 1998. In order to provide scientific and technological support for China's participation in the climate change negotiations, and to construct a scientific basis for sustainable development policy-making, the central government organized an inter-ministerial research team (including 12 governmental ministries) to compile its first National Communication on Climate Change since China ratified the Kyoto Protocol in 2002. In October 2004, China released and submitted the Initial National Communication on Climate Change to the UNFCCC. Enabling China to Prepare Its Second National Communication Project was started up in March 2007 as a preparatory project for China's Second National Communication Project (NCOCC 2007).① In March 2009, the subproject for Enabling China to Prepare Its Second National Communication to the UNFCCC was launched (NCOCC 2009). Su Wei, the director of the Department of Climate Change within the NDRC, a special representative of the UNDP and relevant officials and experts from the MOFA, the MOST, the MEP, the CMA, the ERI participated in the meeting where the report was presented. In April 2011, the draft Second National Communication on Climate Change of China was released in the NCOCC conference (NCOCC 2011).

In addition to the role of the National Communication on Climate Change in establishing procedural requirements for the climate change regime, the central government also set up the research group on the National Assessment Report on Climate Change looking at China's performance since ratifying the Kyoto Protocol in 2002. After a four-year joint effort of 88 experts from 17 ministries and research institutes, the First National Assessment Report on Climate Change was issued in 2006. The compilation of such a comprehensive national assessment regarding climate change marked a milestone for China. In 2008, the second national assessment task was launched and in November 2011 China published its Second National Assessment Report on Climate Change. Compared with the first report, this report "causes more sobering thoughts about the consequences and costs of global warming for China"

① More than 20 leaders and experts from National Climate Change Leading Group member units, the project steering committee, United Nations Development Program (UNDP), Global Environment Fund (GEF), the project implementation and supporting units, and relevant research institutions attended the meeting. See NCOCC (2007).

(Buckley 2012).① The second report began to put emphasis on low-carbon development approaches to respond to climate change and gave special attention to RE development. In August 2012, the first conference for compiling the Third National Assessment Report on Climate Change was held in Beijing. Over 16 ministries and institutes took part in this conference, showing that the work of making a national climate change assessment report has been institutionalized.

Since the 2007 Bali Climate Change Conference, China has become more active and flexible in the climate change negotiations, and the effects of procedural lock-in have been enhanced through several significant governmental documents. In 2007, China's National Climate Change Program and China's Scientific & Technological Actions on Climate Change were issued. It was the first time for China to upgrade climate change to a national strategic level and to release its own national climate change plan. Beginning in 2001, the NDRC has annually issued China's Policies and Actions for Addressing Climate Change (the White Paper on Climate Change) just before the annual climate change negotiations begin. The white paper has served as a road map for national climate mitigation and adaptation efforts. In the 2012 document, China's Policies and Actions for Addressing Climate Change, the central government attached priority to low-carbon development and RE development, including continuing the promotion of Low-carbon Pilot Projects, initiating Pilot Programs for Carbon Emissions Trading, strengthening RE development, and gradually establishing statistical and accounting systems for GHG emissions (NDRC 11/2012).②

---

① Over the last 50 years China's average surface temperature has risen by an average of 1.38°C. China has confronted extremely grim ecological and environmental conditions under the impact of continued global warming and changes, including intensified floods, droughts and storm surges; aggravated forest fires; shrunken wetlands; and changed rain, heat and disease patterns. See Buckley (2012).

② In 2009, the China Research Society of Urban Development (CRSUD) of the Chinese Academy of Social Science (CASS) cooperated with the China Meteorological Administration (CMA) and the Chinese Academy of Science (CAS), issued the first *Green Paper on Climate Change Actions: Addressing the Climate Change(2009): Leading to Copenhagen*. Since then, green papers have been issued annually along with the white paper on climate change. Green papers include: *Addressing Climate Change (2010): The Challenge from Cancun and China's Action*; *Addressing Climate Change (2011): The Dilemma of Durban and China's Strategic Choice* and *Addressing the Climate Change (2012): Climate Financing and Low-Carbon Development*. It is interesting that the white paper, *2012 China's Policies and Actions for Addressing Climate Change*, and the green paper, *Addressing the Climate Change (2012): Climate Financing and Low-Carbon Development*, were issued on the same day, 21 November 2012. The former focuses more on the governmental stance and climate policy, while the latter is more academic and makes policy recommendations. Both emphasize that climate change should be treated as an opportunity for China to accelerate its low-carbon transformation according to the Scientific Outlook on Development. Furthermore, the rules and thoughts from these climate change documents have gradually found their way into the national Five-Year strategic plan. In the 12th FYP, the carbon intensity reduction target and RE development target are tied closely with national economic structural transformation.

The 2009 Copenhagen Climate Conference was treated as a landmark event for China's participation in the climate change regime. China announced for the first time its index targets on carbon intensity reduction and RE development. Yet, China also was confronted with unprecedented pressure to take more responsibility for a climate commitment. The procedural lock-in effect is not solely constrained to governmental regulations and reports; it has also penetrated the legislative framework. China has already issued numerous laws and regulations related to climate change and environmental protection, such as the Energy Saving Law, the RE Law, and the Circular Economy Promotion Law, but there is no special legislative framework on climate change giving the ministries more legal power to fight against global warming (ICTSD 2012). ① Therefore beginning in 2009, the Law Institute of the Chinese Academy of Social Sciences (CASS) was empowered by the NDRC to draft the first climate change legislation in order to enhance emissions mandates and spur China to realize its carbon intensity reduction target. Wang Guangtao, the director of the NPC's Environment and Resource Protection Committee, has pointed out that "China tends to draw up new laws and regulations to provide a stronger legal basis for combating climate change" (China Daily 2009). After a three-year effort, China issued the Climate Change Law (Exposure Draft) in May 2012. It is China's first law to tackle climate change, and sets out tasks and obligations for both governmental institutions and corporations (Point Carbon 2012). Li Liyan, the deputy director of the NDRC's Climate Change Department, said that "this draft has covered a wide range of climate-related issues, and is the most comprehensive climate law draft hammered out so far" (Point Carbon 2012).

This draft law stipulated five important systems: the climate change planning system; the governmental responsibility system; a coal consumption cap and a domestic carbon trading system; a carbon tax and its implementation system; and an information disclosure system (China News 2012a; China News 2012c). Take the governmental responsibility system for example, it will introduce the target-reaching accountability and performance evaluation regulations for the governmental officials taking charge of climate change mitigation actions. The regional emission reduction

---

① China has issued several laws to promote energy conservation, clean production and RE development, gradually creating a green legislative support system. Relevant laws include the Atmospheric Pollution Prevention Law issued in 2000, the Clean Production Promotion Law of 2002 (came into force in January 2003 and was amended in February 2012 to meet a low-carbon requirement), the RE Law of 2005 (came into force in 2006 and was amended in 2009 in order to solve the grid-connection problem), the Energy Conservation Law of 2007 (came into force in January 2008), and the Circular Economy Promotion Law issued in 2008 (came into force in January 2009).

performance (carbon intensity reduction), energy efficiency per unit of GDP (energy intensity reduction) will become the key standards in the political performance evaluation system for local officials. In the past, China adopted total amount control mechanisms to set a cap for major air pollutants. And in the field of climate change mitigation, China aims to control the sources of GHG emissions, that is to say, to cap coal consumption as well as to start an emission quota system to reduce GHG emissions (China News 2012c). Obviously, the implementation of a coal consumption cap can spur rapid RE growth, especially when a RE quota is coupled with the carbon trading system.

The issuing of the Climate Change Law (Exposure Draft) has brought more political resources and confidence for the actors in the pro-RE coalition, since RE development is treated as a main measure to realize the targets in the Climate Change Law. When a RE development target is tied up with a carbon intensity reduction target in the performance evaluation system for local officials, RE development has attracted more attention. If a legally binding agreement covering all the member countries is reached by 2015 in the single-track negotiation pattern of the second commitment period of the Kyoto Protocol, China will be further embedded in the climate change legislative framework, both at the international and domestic levels.

5.2.2.2 Greening the standards of official performance assessment

Since the early 1990s, local GDP growth figures have been treated as the main indicator to measure local officials' performances and determine their future political promotions. Local officials are "incentivized to promote pure economic growth, as it is the source of the local fiscal revenue increase" (Chen 2009: 148). For those provincial governments which are evaluated as failing to meet those targets, the leading officials will not "be eligible to take part in the annual award competition, or to receive any honorary title" (Chen 2009: 148). This GDP-first assessment system leads to a "GDPism worship" culture among China's officialdom, which emphasizes economic growth even when it is at the expense of environmental protection. For instance, when local governments try to attract external or foreign investment to stimulate local economic development, environmental assessments for new projects are not taken seriously enough and the potential for ecological degradation is ignored. In addition, key local industries sometimes have especially close relations with bureaucratic officials since they are the main fiscal revenue sources for local governments.

With China's deeper involvement in the climate change regime and the emergence of institutional and procedural lock-in effects in the governmental bureaucracy, the GDP-biased assessment standards for official performance have undergone gradual change, although this change has encountered great resistance. To be more specific, pressured by the international community to reduce its GHG emission reductions, China has worked on "realizing its voluntary climate mitigation commitment, providing national emissions inventories, submitting reports on national green programs, and promoting information exchange and information transparency" (Chen 2009: 115). These national-level commitments that aim to promote a real green transformation of China require that national-level green targets are broken down to the local level. An effective way to stimulate enthusiasm of local officials for climate change mitigation, low-carbon development and RE development is to adjust the former "Black GDPism" standards and embrace green indices when evaluating officials' performances.①

However, the transformation of performance assessment standards for local officials has proven to be a bumpy path. The notable example here is the strong resistance from local governments to publicize results of "comprehensive environmental and economic accounting" (Green GDP) (Liang 2010: 76). In 2003, former President Hu Jintao put forward the Scientific Outlook on Development with the new idea of "Green GDP". State environmental agencies attempted to implement a green national accounting (Green GDP) exercise to "publicize the extent to which environment-related costs of economic activity reduce actual GDP" (Li and Lang 2010). After a two-year effort, the first Green GDP report—the *China Green National Economy Accounting Report 2004* was released in 2006. According to this report, in 2004, environmental pollution cost over 3% of the GDP②, and in some provinces the pollution-adjusted growth rates were reduced almost to zero or negative numbers (Liang 2010: 76). This report sent a strong warning signal to the central government. The second Green GDP report was originally scheduled for release in March 2007; however "the Green GDP report for 2005 was blocked from release by the NBS in 2007 and it has no chance to be materialized due to strong local-level resistance" (Cary 2011). It was said that this report would be exposing even higher losses and reductions in GDP than the 2004 report, including figures on economic losses from pollution of each province. Although this event stimulated heated social debate, the Green GDP index was a short-lived idea, becoming rather marginalized before ever making itself into high-level key vocabulary (Cary 2011). In the second half of 2007, the issuing of

① Performance evaluations of government officials "determine whether officials are rewarded or penalized based on their performance in meeting economic, social, and environmental targets—have proven to be one of the most effective tools for implementing China's centrally determined targets at the provincial and local level." See Schuman and Lin (2012).

② The Chinese Green GDP report in 2006 showed that the financial loss caused by pollution in China was 511.8 billion *yuan* ($66.3 billion), which was 3.05 percent of the nation's economy. See Liang (2010: 76).

the National Climate Change Program has shed light on the rebirth of the Green GDP. In November 2007, State Council released a regulation tending to use green figures of per-unit GDP energy consumption and major pollutants reduction to assess the performances of provincial officials and top-1000 state-owned enterprises (Sina News 2010). Instead of pure GDP figures, the Chinese government is trying to "measure local officials' achievement through a much more complicated system which also includes environmental indexes" (Chen 2009: 148). However, "the quantified scoring methodology of this assessment system has been greatly questioned and did not reach a serious implementation at the local level" (Chen 2009: 148).

The Copenhagen Climate Change Conference created an advantageous chance for the green assessment index to gain attention. Different from the lead up to previous COPs, China made carbon intensity reduction and RE development commitments before the Copenhagen Conference (Carraro and Tavoni 2010). China had undergone unprecedented international pressures and critiques. As the largest GHGs emitter in the world, China was treated as a vital stakeholder in the climate change regime and was expected to take more international responsibility for climate mitigation. Therefore China has made serious efforts to foster the realization of its commitments. To a certain degree, the climate change regime has created a carbon reduction pressure on China to introduce a stronger green index for the performance assessment of local officials (People Net 2010a).

Since the beginning of 2010, the voices for introducing the suspended Green GDP index to the official performance evaluation system again got increasingly louder. In the National People's Congress (NPC) and Chinese People's Political Consultative Conference (CPPCC) in March 2010, low-carbon economy and energy conservation have become heated discussion topics and many members proposed to link the carbon emission reduction index with the official performance assessment system. In 2010, the draft of the *Index System of China's Resources and Environment Statistics*, which was an upgraded version of a Green GDP, came into being and entered the stage of inter-ministerial coordination discussions. The new index system covered the core indicators in four areas: resources, environment, ecology and climate change (Feng 2010). ① According to the requirement of sustainable development, the research group working on this green index system conducted in-depth research on the transformation of the economic development pattern. The comprehensive index system includes an energy

① Although the Green GDP report was suspended in 2007, then Vice Premier Li Keqiang held a multi-sectoral conference to find a way to Green GDP in the future. This was done at the time of the Olympic Games in Beijing in 2008. Due to this concern, the research for an Index System for China's Resources and Environment Statistics was launched in the same year.

consumption indicator, GHG emissions indicator, resources stock indicator, environmental indicator, and ecological quality indicator. It paved the way for the new binding indicators found in the 12th FYP (Feng 2010). It is said that the 12th FYP (2011-2015) is a significant stage for the green transformation. Former President Hu Jintao's talk of achieving ecological progress at the 18th Party Congress in 2012 elevated environmental issues and climate change to higher places on the agenda than ever before: "Resource consumption, environmental damage and ecological efficiency shall be included in systems for evaluating economic and social development, in order to establish a system of targets, evaluation and rewards and punishments that reflects the requirements of an ecological civilization" (Meng 2012).

In the 18th Party Congress, the unprecedented emphasis on the ecological process further "shaked up the existing mechanisms for evaluating official performance, and more green indicators will be evolved into the promotion incentive system" (Boyd 2012c), such as a low-carbon index, carbon emission reduction index, energy consumption cap index and RE development index. ① China aims to establish a unified nationwide index system for energy consumption by 2015; the system is to be included in the performance assessments of local governments (Xinhua News 2012a). This energy consumption cap, which is coupled by the carbon intensity reduction target, has constructed favorable context for rapid growth of RE. In addition, a RE development target and index for official performance evaluation were formally embodied in the 12th FYP for RE Development. Through making clear the concrete RE development target and RE quota index at the local level, the RE index has become one of new incentives for local officials, who are promoted on the basis of how well they do in developing a RE and low carbon growth pattern. Furthermore, the Regulation for Management of Renewable Power Quota (Exposure Draft), which was issued in 2012, also mentions the evaluation mechanism for RE development. It requires power generators and grid companies to report their progress in meeting RE targets to the local branch of the NEA on a monthly basis. The local NEAs submit the progress evaluation in provincial/municipal level to the NEA directly. ②

---

① An energy consumption cap was finally embodied in the 12th FYP for Energy Development which was issued in the beginning of 2013: the total primary energy consumption and electricity consumption will be controlled within 4 billion tons of coal equivalent (tce) by 2015 and the coal consumption rate will decrease to 65%.

② "After a six-month evaluation period, the NEA will publish a report on the performance in meeting the quota targets. No penalty for non-compliance has been set in the regulations, but progress in meeting the renewable power quota targets will be used by the central government in their performance evaluations of state-owned generators, grid companies and provincial/municipal governments." See Schuman and Lin (2012: 93).

In September 2015, the State Council issued the Overall Plan for the Reform of the Ecological Civilization System, and put forward 8 main reform directions. This is the most authoritative reform program introduced since Chinese President Xi Jinping promoted the concept of "ecological civilization" in recent years. This latest blueprint for "ecological civilization" proposes to try out ways to grade officials on environmental protection. Proposals cover protection of natural resource rights; establishment of a national parks system; better and stricter systems for protection of arable land and water resources management; establishment of a green financing system; and improvement of environmental compensation mechanisms. A following pilot scheme will be carried out in five different locations, including Hulunbuir in Inner Mongolia. It is the first time such a trial has been proposed by central government. It will take place in three stages: a launch in 2015, expansion in 2016, then in 2017 full audits in the trial locations, with regular audits starting from 2018. The aim is to get local officials to give greater priority to the environment, compared to the economy (Zhang 2015).

5.2.3 The discursive lock-in effect in the climate change role playing process

The institutional lock-in effect and the procedural lock-in effect in the role playing process, have laid the foundation for the salience of climate change and low carbon discourses in the political system; due to the requirement of the "national political rhetoric", national leaders make repeated announcements or declarations to show their compliance with the climate change regime for instrumental political purposes, even without normative internalization. However, the frequent emergence of climate change discourses from paramount leaders will promote the discursive lock-in effect in the entire bureaucratic system (Cortell and Davis Jr. 2000: 76). Once the climate change and low-carbon development discourses become the "official language" on the political agenda, or are even being integrated to the political performance assessment system, the domestic actors will show more compliance for the new discourses. Just as Bourdieu mentioned one would become marginalized and take the risk of suffering from "the sanctions of the linguistic market" if one refuses to accept the "official language" (Bourdieu and Thompson 1991: 51; Johnston 2008: 50). This section mainly focuses on changes in governmental discourses since 2002 through analyzing key official documents, such as FYPs and annual government work reports, as well as the significant speeches of paramount leaders. Through the process-tracing of green discourses, this section aims to explore the implications of discursive lock-in effect in the climate change socialization for the pro-RE coalition building.

Table 5.2 Diachronic comparison of governmental discourses in the CPC Congresses

Leaders	Time	Political discourses	Key words
Jiang Zemin	The 15th National Congress of CPC (1997)	Huge environmental and resource pressures caused by population growth and economic development (The first appearance of the word "environment" in a CPC national congress report)	Resources & environment pressure
Jiang Zemin	1992-2000	Sustainable development New industrialization path (2002)	Sustainable development
Jiang Zemin	The 16th National Congress of CPC (2003)	The contradiction among ecological environment, natural resources as well as economic and social development has become increasingly prominent.	Green contradiction
Hu Jintao	2003	The Scientific Outlook on Development, means putting people at the first place and aiming at comprehensive, coordinated and sustainable development.	Scientific Outlook on Development
Wen Jiabao	The 5th Plenum of 16th Central Committee of CPC (2005)	To construct two-oriented society: energy and resources-saving society as well as environment friendly society; Harmonious Society including man and nature relationship; Innovation-oriented country	Two-oriented society

Hu Jintao	The 17th National Congress of CPC (2007)	Promote ecological process by basically forming energy-efficient and environment-friendly structure of industries, pattern of growth and mode of consumption. We should establish a large-scale circular economy and considerably increase the proportion of RE sources in total energy consumption.	Ecological process Circular economy
Hu Jintao	The 5th Plenum of 17th Central Committee of CPC (2010)	Green and low-carbon development (2009) Green growth, low-carbon economy	Low-carbon economy
Xi Jinping Li Keqiang	The 18th National Congress of CPC (2012)	On ecological civilization: we must give high priority to making ecological progress and incorporate it into all aspects and the whole process of advancing economic, political, cultural, and social progress, work hard to build a beautiful country, and achieve lasting and sustainable development.	Ecological civilization Beautiful China

Source: The discourse analysis is based on the author's analysis of CPC national congress reports, and also relies on Meng (2012).

5.2.3.1 Process-tracing of green discourses of national leaders: from "Scientific Outlook on Development" to "Ecological Civilization"

The government's first environmental discourse appeared at China's first environmental protection conference in 1973, just after China took part in the UN Conference on the Human Environment in Stockholm in 1972. It showed some hints that China began to involve itself in the international environmental regulation arrangement and started taking care of its own domestic pollution problems. When China sent its delegation to the UN Conference on Environment and Development (UNCED) in 1992 in Rio de Janeiro, the key discourse of "sustainable development" embodied in this summit was accepted by most countries in the world. After China ratified the UNFCCC, the country also issued its own 21st Century Agenda in 1994 to show its concern on sustainable development. In 1997, the National Sustainable Development Report was published. According to Meng (2012), the first time the word environment appeared in a CPC national congress report was in 1997, at the 15th National Congress of CPC.

However, the discourse of "sustainable development" was too abstract and vague to be implemented at the central and local levels. Basically speaking, the materialization of the "sustainable development" concept needed to develop a green discursive system to support a national green transformation in order to gain attention. When the government was led by President Jiang Zemin, although the government realized the great pressure on resources and environment caused by population growth and economic development, sustainable development and its implications for the welfare of the environment and society did not get sufficient attention.

When the President Hu Jintao and Premier Wen Jiabao came to power in late 2002, they were confronted with an "increasingly divided society with devastating environmental conditions, mounting resource scarcities, alarming social and regional disparities resulted from China's market economic reforms, and increasing international fears about the global implications of China's rise" (Hallding et al. 2009: 123). In order to reverse the adverse situation, they seriously reconsidered China's development pattern and introduced a new discourse focused on *the Scientific Outlook on Development* in July 2003. This discourse was formally endorsed by the National People's Congress in March 2004 and became the official guiding socio-economic ideology of the CCP. The Scientific Outlook on Development means putting people first and aims at comprehensive, coordinated and sustainable development in order to promote comprehensive economic, social and human development. The main feature of this ideology is "to incorporate sustainable development, social welfare, a humanistic society to a comprehensive development approach, so as to reduce the social inequities, prove the environment protection and improve the national innovation capability" (Constantin 2007: 7).

In October 2007 the 16th National Congress of the CPC, the Scientific Outlook on Development was enshrined into the Constitution of the CCP, and became one of the CCP's significant guiding ideologies. It was listed as a successor to and extension of past ideologies analogous with ideologies such as Marxism-Leninism, Mao Zedong's Thought, Deng Xiaoping's Theory and the Three Represents Theory of Jiang Zemin.① Since the 11th National People's Congress in March 2008, the Scientific Outlook on Development is used as a guiding principal for China's socioeconomic development. The Scientific Outlook on Development introduced a new environmental dimension to the debate on climate change. China's climate policy highlights the delicate balance between economic growth, energy security, environment, and climate change mitigation (Andrew-Speed 2012). It was not until 2005/06 that climate change mitigation began appearing as a serious issue on the Chinese leadership's agenda. The IPCC reports and domestic research about the severe climate events affecting China, such as food and water crises, attracted leaders' attention to China's role in climate change. Climate change was rapidly upgraded to the top of the agenda, and by June 2007 China issued its National Climate Change Program (Hallding et al. 2009: 125-126). In March 2008, climate change became one of the key issues during the 11th National People's Congress in response to energy security and ecological concerns. This shows that China became aware of the severity of the burden of pollution and energy consumption amid its economic miracles over the past decades. The strong focus on GDPism had shown its defects and drawbacks for long-term development, that is "why China treats the ecological civilization as a priority by incorporating it into the country's overall development plan, together with economic, political, cultural and social progress" (Xu 2012).

In January 2013, President Xi Jinping and Prime Minister Li Keqiang came into power. Compared with the former government, this government, has shown its determination to take advantage of the climate change pressure as an opportunity to spur domestic economic structural transformation (Su 2012). Since coming to power, Xi has repeatedly stated the importance of environmental protection and further refined his idea of an "ecological civilization", saying that "environmental quality is key if that society is to be well-off" (Liu 2015). Before 2013, when Li Keqiang was still vice

① The Three Represents Theory was introduced by former President Jiang Zemin. Its main content includes to represent the requirements of the development of China's advanced productive forces; to represent the orientation of the development of China's advanced culture; to represent the fundamental interest of the overwhelming majority of people in China. See Jiang (2008).

premier minister, he had already shown some political aspirations in pushing climate change mitigation and RE development. During his state visit to foreign countries, climate change mitigation and RE cooperation issues were top priorities. He is also the chair of the China Council for International Cooperation on Environment and Development (CCICED), which is a high-level research institute to promote the exchange and dissemination of international successful experiences in the field of environment and development (CCICED 2010). In December 2012, when speaking at the CCICED annual conference, Li said China needed to change its development model in order to build an "ecological civilisation" (Lin 2013). For instance, Li pushed for better disclosure of data on China's air quality, as well as promoting transparency in environmental governance. It was thanks to Li's advocacy to call for the monitoring and release of PM2.5 (air-borne fine particles measuring 2.5 microns or less in diameter) data to be conducted nationwide, that Chinese cities started reporting levels of air pollutant PM2.5 in 2014 (Lin 2013). So Li is treated as "a strong figure" in the politburo promoting the green transformation of China, especially in RE development. He heavily promoted distributed power generation systems as a means of solving the grid-connection bottleneck (BJX 2013).

In his opening statement at the 18th National Congress of the CPC, the former President Hu Jintao said "we must give high priority to making ecological progress, work hard to build a beautiful country, and achieve lasting and sustainable development of the Chinese nation" (Xinhua News 2012b). The subsequent administration has emphasized the significance of ecological civilization and called for building a "*Beautiful China*" in the country's overall development plan. Zhou Shengxian, the minister of environmental protection, further explained that a "Beautiful China" means a resource-conserving and environmental-friendly economy and society (Xu 2012).① The 18th CPC National Congress in 2013 formally integrated the ecological civilization construction into the constitution of the CPC for the first time. It symbolizes that ecological progress is elevated to a higher strategic level and the ecological civilization is put on an equal footing with the areas of politics, economy, society and culture (China Daily 2012).

---

① At the 17th CPC National Congress in 2007, Hu advocated ecological progress for the first time and called for the establishment of "the ecological civilization" in many official documents (Xinhua News 2012b). However, Jiang Dahe, a professor at the College of Environmental Science and Engineering of Shanghai-based Tongji University, has pointed out that "although the concept of ecological civilization appeared five years ago, there are not many measures [that] can be seen. Just like the Green GDP concept which was introduced in 2004, however, the statistical indicators of Green GDP have not [been] carried out yet." See China Daily (2012).

5.2.3.2 The salience of climate change and the discourse shift to carbon intensity reduction

Although China joined the UNFCCC as early as 1992, the discourses of "climate change", "energy conservation", "GHG emission reductions", "low-carbon economy" were not taken seriously and stayed rather marginalized. The situation did not improve until China realized the great economic and political influence of the climate change regime and finally ratified the Kyoto Protocol in 2002. Then, "climate change" gradually became a kind of salient "national political rhetoric" which was and still is frequently used by paramount leaders at both international and domestic levels. In addition, the requirement of GHG emission reductions has been coupled with increasing domestic demands for environmental protection, energy efficiency improvement and economic structural transformation. A green discourse has gradually been established in the government enriching the connotation of sustainable development, although there is still a bumpy path ahead before some of these discourses will be transposed in practice. The discourse shift and political agenda change have contributed a lot to the reformation of the energy sector. The conservation society and low-carbon economy are two main discourses, which have great implications for energy regulations:

Conservation society and circular economy

The concept of "conservation society" has two connotations: *first*, to reduce the waste of resources consumption in the economic operation; *second*, to improve energy efficiency and to create more wealth by consuming less resources and energy. It aims at "putting an end to the bottlenecks hindering development and to support the transformation of the current conception of economic development toward a more sustainable concept of development" (Constantin 2007: 14). Later, this concept was enriched further by the concept of the circular economy. It refers to changes in the traditional linear growth economy which heavily depends on resource consumption, to an economy based on resource recycling and eco-development.

Conservation society first appeared in the 10th FYP (2001-2006), but was "only recently exposed in greater details by Ma Kai, the head of the NDRC" (Constantin 2007: 14). In 2004, the issuing of the Short and Long Term Strategy of Energy Development (2004-2020) has offered a general framework for a strategic energy development. The most important parts of the conservation society is to reduce energy consumption, and to adjust and optimize the energy structure based on technological innovation (Constantin 2007: 15). At the fifth plenary session of the 16th Party Congress in 2005, former Premier Wen Jiabao proposed the "two-oriented" society: a conservation society and circular society. The former emphasizes promoting the coordination of economic development with population, resources and environment through improving resources conservation and energy efficiency. The latter focuses on reducing resource consumption and waste generation, and improving the re-utilization rate of resources. The conservation society and circular economy concepts both put emphasis on the reduction of energy intensity and improvements in energy efficiency, which is closely related to a green transformation of energy security and climate change mitigation. On August 29, 2008, the Circular Economy Promotion Law was ratified and came into force on January 1, 2009. This means that energy conservation and the circular economic pattern were given a legislative position in the national strategy. In September 2011, the 12th FYP's Comprehensive Work Plan for Energy Conservation and Emission Reduction was issued by the State Council, which symbolized that the energy conservation and GHG emission reductions have been tied together to guide climate change mitigation. Since then, carbon intensity reduction has gained more and more attention coupled with the emphasis on energy intensity reduction.

Low-carbon economy

The systematic discussion of "low-carbon economy" can be traced back to the 1992 UNFCCC framework and the 1997 Kyoto Protocol. It refers to an economy that has a minimal output of greenhouse gas (GHG) emissions into the environment because of the application of clean technology innovations as well as the promotion of green policy integration in different sectors (manufacturing, agriculture, transportation, and power-generation). In order to promote the transition to a low-carbon economy and spur the internalization of external environmental cost, some policy supportive instruments are necessary, such as emissions trading and/or a carbon tax. Different from the conservation society and circular economy, which mainly focuses on the energy intensity reduction, the low-carbon economy idea puts much more emphasis on decreasing carbon intensity and CO_2 emissions and has greater implications for climate change mitigation and RE development.

After China issued its own National Climate Change Program in 2007, the "low-carbon economy" discourse found its way into national strategic planning. On September 8, 2007 at the 15th APEC Summit, former President Hu Jintao raised four proposals to explicitly advocate the development of low-carbon economy for the first time (Sina News 2007). In this important speech, he mentioned the word "carbon" four times: developing low-carbon economy, promoting the research and diffusion of low-carbon energy technologies, increasing carbon sinks and promoting the development of carbon absorption technology/carbon capture and storage technology (CCS) (Sina News 2007). In December 2007, the State Council Information Office issued a White Paper on China's Energy Conditions and Policies, highlighting the development of energy diversification and listing RE development as an important part of the national energy development strategy (State Council 2007). In 2008 in the annual sessions of the National People's Congress and the Chinese People's Political Consultative Conference, a member of the national committee of the CPPCC, Wu Xiaoqing raised the low-carbon economy issue onto the conference agenda (China News 2008). He argued that whether China would come to the forefront of world development in the coming decades and actively take actions to respond to serious challenges such as climate change largely depended on China's ability to cope with low-carbon economy adjustment, such as embarking on the technology research and pilot studies of RE development (China News 2008).

In 2009, the international community at the Copenhagen Conference exerted unprecedented pressure on China and urged China to take on greater international responsibility to control its GHG emissions. In this context, the political discourses of paramount leaders have undergone an obvious "low-carbon" shift. Former President Hu pledged at the UN Climate Change Summit in 2009 to further integrate the climate change concern into China's economic and social development plan and continue to take effective measures towards implementation (Xinhua News 2009a).① In the 2009 State Council meeting shortly before the Copenhagen negotiations, former Premier Wen Jiabao proposed the low-carbon economy as a key characteristic of a new, sustainable economic growth model (Moore 2011: 153). After 2009, the "low-carbon" discourse became mainstream in the political agenda, which further promoted a resource shift towards low-carbon initiatives and RE development. The discourse lock-in effect has translated into a carbon-intensity reduction target and low-carbon pilot projects. For instance, in August 2010, the NDRC launched Low-Carbon Pilot Cities and Provinces Project, five provinces (Guangdong, Liaoning, Hubei, Shaanxi, Yunnan) and eight cities (Tianjin, Chongqing, Shenzhen, Xiamen, Hangzhou, Nanchang, Guiyang, Baoding) have acted as low-carbon pilots to demonstrate low-carbon development plan and RE utilization. Subsequently in 2011, the NDRC issued the Notice on Carbon Trading Trials Scheme to initiate carbon-trading trials (Wang, T. 2012), which created advantageous change for RE policy change. Rapid growth

---

① Hu mentioned four points: first, enhance the work of energy conservation and improve energy efficiency, aiming to significantly decrease the carbon dioxide emissions of per unit GDP by 2020 based on the 2005 level. Second to develop RE and nuclear energy, realize the non-fossil energy share of total primary energy consumption of 15% by 2020; third, increase forest carbon sinks through enlarging the 40 million hectares forest by 2020 compared with 2005, and increase forest stock volume by 1.3 billion cubic meters compared with 2005; and, fourth, develop a low-carbon economy and circular economy, promoting the research and diffusion of climate-friendly technologies. See Xinhua News (2009a).

and strong momentum in RE sectors, such as wind and solar power as well as green technologies, clearly indicate that "China's political ambition and determination is strongly in favor of alternative and more sustainable development paths" (McKinsey and Company 2012).

5.3 Resource reallocation in the strategic calculation and the pro-RE coalition building

There are two kinds of interest calculation consideration for states in the climate change regime: material incentives (visible financial support, cooperative projects and technology transfer) and social influence (invisible international reputational pressure, national credibility, shaming). Since China joined the climate change regime in the early 1990s, these interest considerations have played a significant role in influencing China's climate change stance and its RE development concerns. In the past two decades of climate change negotiations, China has become more and more deeply involved in the international regime and has shown an increasingly positive attitude towards the international climate cooperation. The RE issue has entered the mainstream of the policy agenda due to international impetus and the good performance of RE development in low-carbon economy transformation and carbon intensity reduction. The agenda-setting mechanism has provided dynamics for a political resource reallocation by combining the international impetus and domestic resources. In addition, the national leaders' commitments in the climate change conferences have become positive signals for domestic actors to promote RE development, which leads to further national resource reallocation in the direction of the pro-RE actors. During this process, the national interest calculation has endowed the pro-RE coalition with more power and bigger voice in the policy making and policy reform, which paves the way for further energy policy change towards RE.

5.3.1 Agenda-setting and resource reallocation in the climate change socialization

The "spiral model" explained earlier shows how the international regime influences the resource reallocation at the domestic level. In its strategic calculations, the state shows its compliance to the international rules in order to maximize and optimize its long-run material well-being, especially getting more material incentives for solving its own problems and minimizing international constraints. Therefore, in the outside-in oriented stage, certain issues gain more political attention due to an external impetus, which in turn can strengthen minority coalitions. In the climate change regime, the international promotion of various incentives to participate in the regime and the successful experience of RE development have pushed the RE issue onto the mainstream of the political agenda. In the domestic enhancement stage, the domestic resource reallocation process will be reinforced due to the increasing salience of certain issue at the domestic level, and the government will accordingly assign more resources to support this new area, such as favorable policies, governmental special fund, fiscal subsidy, and tax incentives. The agenda-setting change and the strengthening of the pro-RE coalition provide great dynamics for RE policy change.

The Clean Development Mechanism (CDM) and the Global Environment Facility (GEF) are the principal financial mechanisms of the Climate Convention. The GEF is the largest dedicated financing source for the commercialization of new low-carbon energy technologies in developing countries (Miriam 2008). The GEF's resources have been strategically allocated for near-term and long-term mitigation technologies, policies, projects and capacity-building activities (Lazarus and Polycarp 2011: 319).① Furthermore, the GEF, together with the World Bank, also invested more than $ 200 million in support of development and implementation of the RE Promotion Law, such as the China Renewable Energy Scale-up Program (CRESP). In addition to this kind of multilateral international incentive for RE development, the role of bilateral RE cooperation projects within the climate change regime complex also cannot be overlooked. An example is the Sino-Danish Renewable Energy Development Program (RED). In sum, these international incentives have promoted the large-scale RE development and leveraged RE policy change (Lazarus and Polycarp 2011: 319).

5.3.1.1 CDM projects and carbon market development as the most significant incentives to promote RE development

The CDM is the most significant incentive mechanism under the climate change regime used to promote RE development in developing countries. ② The World Bank is the largest Certified Emission Reductions (CERs) buyer, managing a number of carbon funds, including the Prototype Carbon Fund and the Umbrella Carbon Facility, and is acting as a trustee of governmental carbon funds in some European countries. When the Kyoto Protocol was signed in COP 3 in 1997, China still held a

① For example, the GEF's 2003-2006 budget included nearly $ 300 million each for energy efficiency and RE, over $ 100 million for the development of long-term mitigation technologies. See Lazarus and Polycarp (2011: 319).

② CDM, as one pillar of the three flexible mechanisms, allows developed countries to invest in GHG emission reduction projects in developing countries and to claim the resulting Certified Emission Reductions (CERs) to assist them in compliance with their binding GHG emission reduction commitments under the Protocol.

cautious and suspicious attitude towards the Flexible Mechanisms of the Kyoto Protocol (Hatch 2003; Heggelund 2007). Since the SDPC has become the main responsible agency for the climate change negotiations in 1998, it has gradually shown a relatively open stance to the CDM and technology transfer (Hatch 2003; Heggelund 2007). ① In the COP-7 Marrakech Conference in 2001, a package of high-level political decisions related to the Kyoto Protocol was adopted in the Marrakech Accord. This accord elaborated the detailed modalities and procedures for the CDM, including institutional, methodological, technical, and procedural aspects, aiming to start the CDM project implementation promptly even before the Kyoto Protocol entered into force (Lü and Liu 2004: 20). When China ratified the Kyoto Protocol in August 2002, it became eligible to compete for CDM projects.

The first CDM project in China was the Huitengxile wind farm project in the Inner Mongolia Autonomous Region, which could be traced back to 2001. Participants in the project are the project organizers (Inner Mongolian Wind Power Corporation, together with Chinese Renewable Energy Industries Association) and the investor (CERUPT, the Dutch Government's CDM credit procurement program) (Lü and Liu 2004: 23). ② In the second half of 2002, the Dutch government and the Chinese government signed a contract for China's first CDM project. ③ This kind of CDM contract, which was signed even before the Kyoto Protocol came into effect, hastened the improvement of detailed CDM implementation procedures/regulations at the international and domestic levels (Chen 2009: 130). The Chinese government enacted a draft regulation on the management of CDM projects in June 2004, 7 months before the implementation of the Kyoto Protocol. Then in October 2005, led by the NDRC, the MOST, the MOFA, and the MOF jointly issued the Measure on Operation and Management of Clean Development Mechanism Projects, in order to guarantee the orderly implementation of the CDM (Chen 2009: 130). As the main target of CDM projects, RE development gained more importance on the political agenda. According to the 2011 NDRC data, the new and RE projects alone accounted for over 70% of the projects and over 50% of the CERs (Hong et al. 2011: 1699).

The CDM market in China developed rapidly within a short period of time. Its trade volume increased 62% between 2005 and 2007 and its trade turnover tripled

---

① The stance of the SDPC was close to the SSTC and the SETC, which was open for international incentives and technological transfer, rather than being too conservative or constrained by sovereignty concerns.

② Nine turbines of 600 kW each of Huitengxile wind farm were installed in 2001 and another ten 600 kW turbines were installed in 2002. See Ditan360 (2012).

③ The Chinese enterprise could receive about 2.77 million euros revenue within one decade, accounting for 13% of its total investment. See Ditan360 (2012).

(Hong et al. 2011: 1697; Schroeder 2009). In 2006, the world share of China's CDM projects accounted for only 8% and this proportion increased to 45% in 2011. The world share of average annual CERs grew from 44% in 2006 to 63% in 2011 (Hong et al. 2011: 1697; Schroeder 2009). China has become the largest market for CDM projects in the world, ranking top in both numbers of registered projects and annual certified emissions reduction (CER). It created a good opportunity for China to break the carbon lock-in structure and transform to a low-carbon economy. The effective implementation of capacity building projects enhanced China's domestic capacity of engaging in CDM activities. As of the end of August 2012, China had approved 4,540 CDM projects, focusing on new energy and RE, energy conservation and the enhancement of energy efficiency and relevant areas (NDRC 11/2012). Their estimated annual certified emissions reduction (CER) reached 730 million tons of CO_2 equivalents. A total of 2,364 of the projects have been registered with the UN CDM Executive Board, accounting for 50.41% of the world's total registered programs (NDRC 11/2012). Until the present, 880 of the registered Chinese projects have been approved, and the total issuance volume has reached 590 million tons of CO_2 equivalent, which is a major contribution to the implementation of the Kyoto Protocol (NDRC 11/2012).

Next to the CDM, the rapid development of the carbon market has provided a promising prospect for RE development. ① Spawned by the binding emission limits of the Kyoto Protocol, global carbon trading has grown "from an estimated market value of about $15 billion in 2005 to reach a record value of close to $144 billion in 2009" (ClimateWire 2011). During only five years, the practice of trading in GHG allowances and carbon emission offsets credits has enjoyed rapid growth with more than a tenfold explosion (ClimateWire 2011). The Global Carbon Market was still growing in 2011, but not exponentially like it did from 2005 to 2009 and reached $176 billion in 2011 (ClimateWire 2011). It is estimated that the global carbon market will grow to $3.5 trillion by 2020, and become equal to the oil trading business (Wang, Z. et al. 2012). In terms of carbon trading, investment is closely associated with RE electricity projects. For instance, "in November 2008, projects in the CDM pipeline—those officially applying or approved for CERs—represented over $125 billion in new project investment, and two-thirds ($83 billion) is associated with renewable electricity projects (hydro, wind, biomass and other)" (Lazarus and Polycarp 2011: 322-323).

---

① The ETS and the CDM are two main parts of the global carbon market. Most industrialized countries plan to use emissions trading systems to regulate domestic emissions through the ETS. These industrialized countries also meet their emissions obligations by purchasing certified emission reductions (CERs) from project-based activities in developing countries through the CDM. See Hong et al. (2011).

Beyond carbon trading, the increasing voice for climate change mitigation has stimulated green market development, especially in the fields of clean technology innovation and low-carbon products trading. For instance, there has been rapid growth of global green trade in wind turbines, solar panels as well as RE technology. The promising green market has drawn more and more carbon finance and RE investment over the last few years. Stuart Bernstein, the Global Head of Clean Technology and Renewables Group in Goldman Sachs, mentions: "When it comes to clean technology and renewables, we're truly at a transformational moment in time" (Bernstein 2012). According to Bloomberg New Energy Finance analysis, "global investment in RE projects will rise from $195 billion in 2010 to $395 billion in 2020 and to $460 billion by 2030" (BNEF 2011: 1). The BNEF has provided an optimistic and promising vision for RE development in the mid-long term:

> After 2020 more ambitious energy policies coupled with much lower unit costs of renewable technologies will drive further deployment of RE technologies. The benefits of cost reductions over time will mostly affect the solar sector, where unit costs are expected to fall by 60% over the next 20 years. The wind sector will broadly match solar and grow from $71 bn in 2010 to $140 bn in 2020 and $82 bn in 2030. The bio-energy sector will see renewed activity with the commercialization of second-generation technologies and global supply chains developing in the movement of biomass fuels. Investment in bio-fuels, biomass and waste-to-energy is projected to increase from $14 bn in 2010 to $80 bn in 2020. (BNEF 2011: 2)

Furthermore, with the diffusion of climate change to the agenda of many other international institutions, such as the WTO, the IEA, the WB, the G8, and the G20, "low-carbon economy" and "clean energy" have gradually become new key standards in the climate regime complex. They exert an important influence on the global economy and social activities. For instance, in June 2009, the House of Representatives of the U. S. passed the American Clean Energy and Security Act, in which it stated that the U. S. has the right to impose a "carbon tariff" on imported products after 2020 if industrial GHG emissions in the country of origin of imported products is higher than that in the US (Chinastakes 2009). Beginning in 2011, the EU planned to impose new carbon tariffs on flights to or from destinations outside Europe and called that opponents should work with the EU to create a global scheme to cut aviation pollution (CBC News 2011).① China, as the largest GHGs emitter in the

① Although China, India, Russia and the U. S. were among the countries opposed to the EU flight carbon tax, the European Court of Justice ruled that the EU tax on CO_2 pollution from aircraft was legal. See CBC News (2011).

world, has been confronted with greater pressure since the 2009 Copenhagen Conference, because it is since forced to pay "carbon tariff" for exporting commodities according to their carbon emissions intensity.

Therefore, much importance has been attached to the green market and "carbon standards". China can get incentives from the global carbon market through CDM projects and has an economic interest in a thriving green market, such as its strong solar cell/panel export. In the meantime, China has been confronted with the challenges of demands for a "carbon tariff" on its exported products. In this context, the Chinese leaders have realized that with formation and enlargement of carbon market, which is based on the clean technology innovation and RE development, the only way to enhance national capacity building and improve national green competition is to learn from the pioneering countries and readjust its own economic structure. Adopting the innovative policy instruments to promote RE development, considering the carbon tax or even launching a domestic carbon trading system have formally and officially entered the political agenda. China as a novice in innovative green regulation (RE policy and carbon tax), has to emulate the best practices of the pioneering countries proactively and accumulate experience for its own green innovation, in order to escape its current passive position regarding the "carbon standard" and gain more developing opportunities in the green market.

5.3.1.2 REDP and CRESP as significant RE promotion projects in the climate change regime

In addition to the CDM program, the World Bank and the GEF, as main financial supporters in the climate change regime, also promote RE growth in developing countries through special funding projects, such as the REDP and the CRESP.

The *China Renewable Energy Development Project* (*REDP*) was set up in 2001 with international grant financing provided by the WB and the GEF with £ 2.5 million. The SDPC was the key cooperative agency in this eight-year project (2001-2008) (Luo and Wang 2008). The REDP aims to establish sustainable markets for off-grid solar and on-grid wind sectors in China to increase electricity access in rural areas in an environmentally sustainable way. The long-term objectives of the project will seek to reduce the barriers to commercial RE development in China through mobilizing resources, catalyzing investments and enhancing project demonstration to create a favorable pro-RE policy environment (World Bank 2010). The project consists of the installation and operation of 20 MW of grid-connected wind farms in Shanghai; PV market development, including the supply of about 10 MW of photovoltaic (PV) systems to solar home systems (SHS) and institutions in remote areas of six

Northwestern provinces of Gansu, Inner Mongolia, Qinghai, Sichuan, Xinjiang and Xizang; and technology improvement, including support for technology upgrading to improve the performance and reduce the costs of solar PV technologies in China (World Bank 2010).①

The *China Renewable Energy Scale-up Program* (*CRESP*), which was launched in 2006 after China issued the RE Law, is the largest comprehensive international cooperation program with the Chinese government in the field of RE development (10 to 12 year program) (CRESP 2010). The main aims of the CRESP are to "enhance the RE policy system establishment and improvement, foster the implement RE scale-up development (especially promote the technology transfer and innovation) and achieve the scale-up development of renewable energies (improve RE industrial system)" (CRESP 2010). Although the CRESP is managed by the MOF in principle, the main "window agencies" handling its organization and implementation are the NEA and the CRED, which are the key actors responsible for drafting the RE regulations.

The program implementation cycle has been divided into three different implementation phases. In the first phase (2006-2011), China received altogether $40.22 million grants and $200 million loans from the WB and the GEF to promote establishment of policies about RE system, foster the organization and implement of three types of activities on both national and regional levels, including policy study and development, technical program and provincial demonstration (support the provincial demonstration projects) (CRESP 2011). Regarding the technological progress, wind and biomass power generation were given a higher priority. In the project application process, the CRESP organized international and domestic experts to make assessments on the applicants from various aspects and put emphasis on the technology transfer and technology innovation. The CRESP supported 5 wind power enterprises, which owned the technological capacity to develop MW-scale wind turbines, with $4.5 million to promote their further R&D. Moreover, the research of the 3MW off-shore wind turbine generator system (WTGS) was also one of the sub-grant projects on the Wind Turbine Technology Transfer. With the CRESP support, the Shanghai Donghai Bridge 100MW off-shore wind farm became the first off-shore Demonstration

① Solar-home-systems (SHS) are stand-alone electrical systems which use a PV module to provide power. REDP operated with approved suppliers (about 80) and participating wholesale companies (32), which had to meet increasingly strict standards of product quality, service and management, in order to be approved by the program. Participating companies were paid a subsidy for each system sold, provided that they passed the regular checks of REDP. As the quality standards were increased, the subsidy was increased from $1.50/Wp to $2.00/Wp (about 25% of the final sale price). See World Bank (2010).

Wind Farm Project (CRESP 2011).

In the technological support progress of biomass, the CRESP provided R&D guidance and financial support for biomass direct combustion, gasification and briquette equipments, which promotes the rapid development of biomass industry in China (CRESP 2011). For province-level demonstrative projects, the program supported the implementation of 24 RE demonstrative projects in 4 pilot provinces, including Jiangsu, Zhejiang, Fujian and Inner Mongolia, laying a solid foundation of the large-scale promotion of RE technology (CRESP 2011). ① In the second phase (beginning in 2012), the fund support will be reduced to $30 million, since China's RE development results in the first phase surpassed the expectations when the program was designed. The second phase focuses on promoting the commercial renewable electricity suppliers to provide energy to the electricity market, and enlarging the 4 pilot provinces into 10 (CRESP 2011). And in the third stage, it aims to promote the provincial pilot projects to the national level and realize the large-scale commercial renewable electricity supply throughout China in a cost-effective way (CRESP 2011).

In sum, the REDP and the CRESP have played a positive role in stimulating the technological transfer and technological innovation in the RE industry. Although the number of supported projects is quite limited, these projects have performed well. They have been technology innovators and have survived financially in the market. They have played an exemplary role and have led large-scale RE development.

5.3.1.3 Other bilateral or multilateral incentives

In addition to the CDM, the REDP and the CRESP, there are still other bilateral and multilateral incentives from the climate change regime in a broad sense. Although these incentives might not be directly from the UN climate framework, the main objective of them is usually to enhance the national capacity for GHG emission reductions through RE cooperation and RE technological innovation. Therefore, these incentives belong to the climate change regime in a broad sense or regime complex of climate change, such as the RED and the REEEP.

The *Sino-Danish Renewable Energy Development Program* (*RED*) is a Five-Year program (2009-2013) operated by the Chinese and Danish governments (RED 2009). The Danish government has provided 100 million Danish Kroner (equivalent to about 130 million RMB) to China to promote its RE development. The main

① For example, the following projects have successively become China's RE scale-up demonstrative projects, including the 30MW Intertidal Zone Pilot Wind Farm in Rudong, Jiangsu Province; 5MW Biomass Gasification Thermal, Power and Steam Project in Gaoyou, Jiangsu Province; 205KW Low-fold Concentrating Photovoltaic Power Plant in Pingtan, Fujian Province; 20MW Tidal Power Station in Jiantiao, Zhejiang Province. See CRESP (2011).

development objective of RED is to reduce the future GHG through increased use of RE and the immediate objective puts emphasis on enhancing national institutional and technical capacity to develop the RE sector (RED 2009). The DNERE and the CRED are main implementing agencies. The Energy Research Institute hosts the Program Task Force (PTF) and the Program Management Office (PMO) for technical activities and daily management and works closely with all stakeholders (RED 2009). In the perspective of enhancing the governmental agencies' capacity in managing the RE sectors, there are several significant RE institutions that have been proposed by the RED, such as the CNREC, the RE Analysis and Information Centre created in 2012 and sector strategies implemented for wind, biomass and solar power. In the perspective of supporting RE technology innovation, development and transfer, the innovation support facility has funded the bilateral cooperation on RE development, like studying the Chinese RE market, and identifying particular rewarding Sino-Danish cooperation opportunities; as well as promoting cooperation projects in RE research, development or demonstration (RED 2009). For instance, the Tsinghua University and Aalborg University have taken the responsibility to initiate an analysis of the potential areas for Danish-Chinese R&D cooperation within innovative RE technologies from April to June 2011.

The *Renewable Energy and Energy Efficiency Partnership* (*REEEP*) is an international network for accelerating the global market for sustainable energy with a primary focus on developing countries and emerging markets (REEEP 2009b). It was initially launched by the U. K. in August 2002 alongside the 2002 World Summit on Sustainable Development (WSSD) in Johannesburg. In 2004, the REEEP was formally established in Vienna and within a decade, it has grown to comprise 385 partner organizations including 45 governments as well as a range of private companies and international organizations (REEEP 2009b). ① As an information provider and connector, the REEEP supports RE development and energy conservation via sub-networks such as the Sustainable Energy Regulation Network (SERN), which compiles overviews of energy policy in 163 countries; and RE and International Law (REIL), a forum providing high-level, off-the-record policy discussions (REEEP

① The REEEP has been supported primarily by governments (Australia, Austria, Canada, the European Union, Germany, Ireland, Italy, Netherlands, New Zealand, Norway, Spain, Switzerland, the US and the United Kingdom), by institutions such as the OPEC Fund for International Development, and by contributions from the private sector. In general, REEEP has played an active role in up-scaling clean energy business models. As a founder, REEEP has supported more than 180 clean energy projects in 58 countries—often as a risk-taking cornerstone investor—disbursing €18.4 million and leveraging an additional €35.1 million in co-funding. See REEEP (2009b).

2009b). At the same time, it provides public search engine platform in clean energy field (www.reegle.info).

The REEEP's Secretariat in East Asia is located in the *China Renewable Energy Industries Association* (*CREIA*). The projects conducted in East Asia have amounted to more than 30, and China is one of the key countries supported by the REEEP. The REEEP activities in China include three main dimensions: *First*, the REEEP aims to implement the National Action Plan for Rural Biomass RE Development (REEEP 2009a). In this field, it involves identifying the technological, political and financial barriers to the development and use of biomass in rural China. It aims to develop a National Action Plan for rural biomass development and enable China to meet its national biomass development target (Ebert 2012). *Second*, the REEEP has promoted Sustainable Finance for RE and Energy Efficiency Project. The main aim of this project is to develop a transparent and competitive financial market available for RE development, including a wide range of financial tools and risk mitigation instruments (REEEP 2009a). *Third*, the REEEP has cooperated with the Chinese Academy of Sciences, to study the national policy, strategy and draw up a roadmap for China's wind power industry development (REEEP 2009a).

Apart from the RED and the REEEP, China has shown an increasing interest in the RE global governance and attempted to join more bilateral and multilateral RE institutions, such as the *International Renewable Energy Agency* (*IRENA*). The IRENA, which was founded in 2009, is an intergovernmental organization "to promote widespread and increased adoption and sustainable use of all forms of RE" (IRENA 2011). It serves as "the principal platform for international cooperation, a repository of policy, technology, resource and financial knowledge on renewable energy" (IRENA 2011).① China announced to join the IRENA on 14 January 2013 (IRENA 2013). Along with a deep involvement in the global RE governance, the domestic pro-RE actors will have more channels to get the international incentives and domestic support to promote the energy policy change through integrating RE.

5.3.1.4 Stimulated domestic subsidy and investment for RE development

The international incentives, such as the CDM, the REDP, the CRESP, the RED, the REEEP and the IRENA have played a significantly leveraging role in

① In line with these aims, IRENA provides a range of products and services, including: RE Readiness Assessments, conducted in partnership with governments and regional organizations, to provide policy guidance and facilitate the sharing of case studies and best practices; the Global Renewable Energy Atlas, hosted on the IRENA website; the IRENA Renewable Energy Learning Partnership (IRELP), an online learning network; Handbooks for RE policy development; Technology briefs and cost studies to strengthen evidence-based policy-making and investment; Facilitation of renewable energy planning at regional levels. See IRENA (2011).

stimulating the large-scale RE projects (especially demonstration projects) with direct financial support as well as indirect carbon finance. They have promoted the technology transfer and know-how diffusion, and provided RE policy suggestion and RE development strategy proposals. During this process, although the international incentives for RE development projects are limited, the successful performance of large-scale RE projects has attracted the attention of national leaders. They have learned the significant role of RE development to break the carbon lock-in pattern in China and to reduce the international GHG emission reductions pressure in an effective way. Along with the salience of the RE issue on the political agenda, the "domestic enhancement" stage of the "spiral model" has been launched. This shows that the central government has begun to reallocate more resources and invest more financial subsidy as well as R&D research fund to the field of RE development.

Take the CDM for instance, the CDM projects have played a catalytic role in inducing national leaders to learn about the new national interests embodied in RE development. After the Kyoto Protocol came into effect in 2005, the Chinese government began to show more concerns on the capability building of CDM projects. In August 2006, the State Council approved the establishment of CDM Fund and its management centre. In November 2007, the MOF and the NDRC jointly launched the operation of CDM Fund.① Upon approval of the State Council, the MOF, the NDRC and other ministries jointly promulgated Regulation of China CDM Fund in September 2010. The China CDM Fund is governed by the Board of China CDM Fund and managed by China CDM Fund Management Centre (inter-ministerial deliberative agency), which is favorable for further ministerial coordination of different departments (the NDRC, the MOF, the MOFA, the MOST, the MEP, the MOA and the CMA) on the CDM development (CDMFUND 2012).② In 2010, the Measure on the Operation and Management of Clean Development Mechanism Projects was amended to increase the efficiency of CDM program development and validation and verification. With the establishment of the China CDM fund, the RE projects have obtained a higher priority in the national development planning. The actors in the pro-RE coalition, especially the RE investors and enterprises have become

① The funds mainly come from: (1) national revenue from CDM projects; (2) operating revenue; (3) donations from domestic and international institutions, organizations and individuals; and (4) other sources.

② The main function of the CDM Fund Management Centre is not only the collection, management and use of the funds to promote the domestic CDM projects development, but also policy research on the implementation of China's National Climate Change Program and international climate cooperation, climate change financing, low carbon development and Carbon Market Development. See CDMFUND (2012).

direct beneficiaries from the CDM projects. The good expectation for the global carbon trading market has further stimulated RE investment. The RE industry associations and societies have also grown stronger during this period. Due to the development requirements for participating in the CDM, some governmental institutions (such as the CDM Fund Management Centre) and research institutes came into being.

In addition to the CDM fund, RE development has obtained more resources, including the feed-in tariff support, fiscal subsidies, and technology R&D investment since the RE Law was issued in 2005 and the Mid- and Long-Term Development Plan for RE was issued in 2007. In the perspective of fiscal subsidies, the central government provides a favorable feed-in price, tax rates and low-interest loans for the entire RE industry; and at the same time, the government pays more attention to supporting the significant plans and demonstration projects through special funds. Some demonstration projects have received more financial support so as to play an exemplary role in RE strategic development, such as the "Golden Sun" Projects launched in March 2009, which is the driving force to promote the large-scale PV power development with 10 billion RMB investments annually. The "Golden Sun" initiative will grant up to 50% of the installation cost of photovoltaic power plants.

In the perspective of renewable R&D investment and technological innovation, the MOST supports the research, development and demonstration of RE technologies through the National High-tech R&D program (863 Program), the National Basic Research Program (973 Program), the Key Technology R&D program and the Fund for Technology Based Firms (Zhang et al. 2012: 5). The NDRC operates the National High-tech Industry Development Program, which aims at facilitating R&D and demonstration of the advanced technologies with RE technology being targeted. The National Nature Science Foundation of China (NSFC) increased its funding budget for the basic RE researches (Zhang et al. 2012: 5). The government carries out the intellectual property right strategy and technological standard strategy to promote the technological innovation (Wang, Z. et al. 2012: 188-189). All other activities seeking funding are required to submit applications to the local government, but final decisions are made by the Ministry of Finance (MOF) at the central level (Schuman and Lin 2012: 97).

Apart from the fiscal subsidies and R&D investment from the government, the social and private investments in the RE sector have also been stimulated by the general green growth tendency. In other words, with the government's RE targets acting as a driver in China, domestic sources have dominated RE investment. According to the Pew Charitable Trusts, China's efforts have rapidly increased investment in RE from less than a \$0.2 billion in 2004 to over \$12 billion in 2007 (Lazarus and Polycarp

2011: 316). Ambitious, mandatory targets for wind and solar power and the ample availability of credit have been the primary engines of that nation's clean energy growth. Beginning in 2009, China has invested $ 34.6 billion into the RE sector, installing substantial new clean energy-generating capacity to meet ambitious RE targets (Lazarus and Polycarp 2011: 316). From 2004 to 2009, the growth rate was over 148% and it was the first time that China surpassed the U.S. to take the leading place for overall clean energy finance and investment (PEW 2010: 19). In 2010, China invested over $ 47.31 billion in various RE sources projects. According to a UN report, global investment in RE reached a record $257 billion in 2011, a 17% increase from the amount invested in 2010 (Tanquintic-Misa 2011). China was responsible for almost one-fifth of total global investment, spending $ 52 billion on RE in 2011 (Tanquintic-Misa 2011).

According to China's 12th FYP (2011-2015), during these five years, the newly installed capacity of wind power will reach 70 million kilowatts, which will require a total investment of about 530 billion RMB (State Council 3/2011). Solar PV power capacity will reach 20 million kilowatts, with a total investment demand of about 250 billion RMB (State Council 3/2011). The various types of biomass energy will need an investment of about 140 billion RMB (State Council 3/2011). Adding the development of solar water heaters, shallow geothermal energy utilization, the total investment demand for RE during the 12th FYP period will reach around 1.8 trillion RMB (State Council 3/2011). Xie Zhenhua, the deputy director of the NDRC, pointed out that in order to complete the energy-saving emission reduction targets of the 12th FYP, the government will invest around 2 trillion RMB, which will also stimulate more social investments through encouraging economic policies (Xinhua News 2012d). It is estimated that there will be over 4 trillion RMB spend on green investments from the government and society in total by 2015, which is unprecedented in scale for green growth in the world (Xinhua News 2012d).

5.3.2 Signaling mechanism and resource reallocation in the climate change socialization

In addition to the material incentives pursuit in the socialization process, there are also some "maximizing national status" concerns for China: to boost the national profile and create a positive image, keep national reputation and credibility, enhance national soft power and avoid negative social influences such as shaming, exclusion, reputation punishments. In the reputation building process, the international community will exert significant influence on the domestic policy through the "signaling mechanism"—if the national leaders made commitments to international regime, these commitments will be publicized in the international community in order to raise the national reputation and send positive signals to the domestic level. Once China joined the climate change regime, along with China's rapid economic growth and great amount of GHG emissions, it required China to enhance its compliance degree according to its capability. Especially when China became the largest emitter in 2007, confronted with increasing international pressure, the country has been forced to make carbon reduction commitments, even if just a compromised/transitional one, to the international community in order to save its national credibility and national reputation. Once the positive signals have been released, the national behavior will be watched by the international as well as the domestic audience.

In authoritarian states like China, national leaders require the support of domestic elites who act as an audience, and the main decision making should be based on the consensus building within the Politburo (Weeks 2008: 36).① Once the paramount leaders make (voluntary) commitments to the climate change regime in order to reduce the international pressure, they will take efforts to force the policy implementation at the domestic level. Based on this, the signaling mechanism in the climate change regime will foster the implementation of international carbon intensity reduction and RE development commitments. It results in the political resource reallocation among different stakeholders in the RE subsystem.② As analyzed in Chapter 4, the carbon reduction pressure from the climate change regime has significant influence on the domestic energy policy change. In this process, the pro-RE actors can get access to more political resources and enhance their capacity building under the influence of the signaling mechanism. The strengthened pro-RE coalition becomes the driving forces to spur RE policy change.

5.3.2.1 Resource reallocation of the signaling mechanism for RE development

Due to the heavily coal-dominated energy structure as well as the national priority being placed on supply-biased energy security, which has led to efforts to guarantee fossil energy imports since the late 1990s, promotion of a green transformation has not been easy. Nevertheless, the gradual change in the stance of China in the climate

---

① The precondition for this kind of audience cost is that elites might have incentives and ability to coordinate to punish the leader, and secondly the potential for punishment is visible to decision makers. See Weeks (2008).

② In authoritarian countries, the state has access to powerful measures to hasten policy implementation in a top-down way. It can adjust or change relevant supportive policies in accordance with the national commitment target.

change regime and with its national commitments to climate mitigation has sent strong signals to domestic actors. Although the international community has criticized the climate mitigation efforts of China as not being enough and expects China to take more ambitious steps, China's current commitments have had a significant influence on domestic policy making. China has taken efforts to involve the climate change concerns into the national sustainable development strategic framework as well as socio-economic overall planning. Since a great amount of GHG emissions comes mainly from the rising energy consumption as a result of the rapid economic development, the green transformation of the energy sector has been given more importance, and special priority has been placed on the development of RE and improvement of energy efficiency. The signaling mechanism from the climate change regime, as an external impetus, spurred the political and economic resource reallocation at the domestic level. China's state-over-society/state-dominated domestic structure enhanced the effect of signaling mechanisms, especially after national elites reached a general consensus on the introduction and implementation of a national climate mitigation commitment.

In terms of RE governance, these signals from the climate change regime increased positive expectations for the RE investment market and became an affirmative signpost for pro-RE actors. Taking advantage of these signaling mechanisms, the pro-RE coalition has gained much more legal authority, financial support, and expertise support to enhance its own capacity. Once the signaling mechanism transferring the international commitment to the domestic level, the pro-RE coalition will take full use of this signaling effect to make a breakthrough in coal-dominated energy supply mix, challenge the national veto players for RE development and prove the feasibility to design more ambitious RE targets. To be more specific, the pro-RE actors (both governmental and societal) have achieved a favorable context to enhance their influence on policy making. They have done this in providing RE policy proposals, exploring the feasibility of innovative RE policy instruments in China, making assessments of current RE policy implementation, giving scientific evaluation for mid-long term RE targets and taking efforts to overcome the main bottlenecks in RE development—grid-connection and RE power curtailment.

The year 2007 witnessed the great progress of China's stance in the climate change negotiations. China began to make a commitment to the voluntary action of emission reduction and officially issued the National Climate Change Program, within which RE development was attached much importance. In the same year, several administrative regulations to guarantee the feed-in tariff implementation were issued, such as the Mid-

and Long-Term Development Plan for RE (2007-2020), which was the first generally strategic plan for RE development. In 2009 before the Copenhagen Climate Change Conference, China announced its voluntary carbon intensity reduction target as well as the RE consumption target. It symbolized that China for the first time was officially binding the carbon reduction and RE development targets together and sending a positive signal to the domestic stakeholders in the RE governance. In this process, the pro-RE actors have obtained more expertise, financial support and policy procedural support, such as treating RE development as one of the green indexes used to assess the local officials' political performance.

In addition, it is remarkable that the signal mechanism exerts great influence on the strategic FYP. During the 11th FYP period (2006-2010), although China for the first time adopted reducing energy consumption (energy intensity reduction) and cut the total discharge of major pollutants, there were no clear targets for carbon intensity reduction as well as RE development. While in the 12th FYP which was issued in March 2011, it clearly stated the following compulsive objectives to address climate change: by 2015, carbon dioxide emission per-unit GDP would be reduced by 17% and energy consumption per-unit GDP by 16% as compared with that in 2010; the proportion of consumption of non-fossil energy to the consumption of primary energy is to be increased to 11.4% (NDRC 11/2012). Soon in September 2011, the State Council issued the Comprehensive Work Plan for Energy Conservation and Emission Reduction during the 12th FYP Period. The plan is a programmatic document promoting the energy conservation and emission reduction tasks of the 12th FYP. It clearly sets forth the overall emission reduction requirements, main targets, key tasks and policy measures of the 12th FYP.① In sum, it showed that China has taken climate change mitigation tasks seriously in its economic and social development. China "fosters the concept of green and low-carbon development, and takes addressing climate change as an important strategy for its economic and social development as well as an important opportunity for economic restructuring and the transformation of its economic development pattern" (NDRC 11/2012).

5.3.2.2 Decomposition of national commitment targets into local RE development

China has a top-down approach to designing and implementing RE policies, such

---

① Under this guideline, China issued the 12th FYP for RE Development in 2012. Annual RE consumption is to reach 478 million tons of standard coal equivalents (TCE), including 400 million TCE coming from commercialized RE, representing more than 9.5% in overall energy mix by 2015 (NDRC 11/2012).

as setting long-term, consistent targets (such as in the FYPs) and sending positive feed-in price signals to encourage sustained investment in RE projects (Schuman and Lin 2012: 102). When the carbon intensity reduction target was tied together with RE development targets in 2009, the signal effect of the climate change commitment on RE policy making and policy change was also reflected at the local level, through the way of target devolution. In the RE Law, it stipulates "energy authorities of the State Council set middle and long-term target of the total volume for the development and utilization of RE at the national level... and based on this, all provinces, autonomous regions and municipalities should cooperate with national level to promote RE development" (NPC 2/2005). However, there are few specific regulations about the targets to be set at the local level in this law. It simply "required the provincial-level energy department to formulate the RE plan for its own jurisdiction without referring to seeking direction or oversight at the national level" (Schuman and Lin 2012:94). This general and abstract legislative framework is insufficient for promoting the in-depth coordination between central and provincial levels.

With the increasing pressure from the climate change regime as well as the increasing difficulty of energy intensity and carbon intensity reduction in the rapidly growing economy of China, in order to realize the national commitments, the central government decided to enhance the coordination between central and provincial level through further RE policy change. In other words, although the central government has established national mid- and long-term targets for RE development and utilization, policy implementation still needs cooperation from provincial-level governments to set corresponding mid- and long-term RE targets and plans. The RE Law Amendment which was issued in 2009 has strengthened the central government's oversight over provincial-level RE planning. Under the amendments, "provincial-level governments are now required to formulate their own RE plans based on the national RE development and utilization plan and targets for their jurisdiction, and submit the proposal of their RE development plans as well as the sequence implementation report to the NEA and the SERC" (Schuman and Lin 2012:94). ① In sum, due to the break down of the national target onto the provincial level, the local pro-RE actors have gained more legal authority, financial support, institutional support and expertise to

---

① The 2009 amendments also specify that RE development plans are to take into account local conditions, and cover development targets, major tasks, regional distribution, key projects, implementation progress, matching grid construction, service systems, and guarantee measures, among other elements. See the RE Law Amendment.

grow stronger. In addition, local RE investment actors have been stimulated further by the promising expectation for green market, and the local RE governmental agencies and research institutes could obtain more political resources and financial support.

In order to realize the national voluntary carbon-intensity reduction and RE development targets by 2020 which were committed to before the 2009 Copenhagen Conference, the State Council issued the Energy Conservation and Emissions Reduction Comprehensive Work Plan for the 12th FYP (2011-2015). The plan decomposes the national green target onto the provincial level, through the rational index allocation of energy conservation and emission reduction targets (NDRC 9/2011). As a key guiding document for realizing China's energy and environment goals—such as the target that energy intensity should fall by 16% and carbon intensity by 17% as detailed in the 12th FYP—the plan sets mandatory energy intensity and major pollutant emissions targets for provinces and highlights a number of key policies to achieve them (NDRC 9/2011). The provincial level energy intensity targets for 2015 are varied due to the whole level of economic development, industrial structure, energy-saving potential, environmental capacity, national deployment of industries and other factors (NDRC 9/2011).

Table 5.3 Energy intensity reduction targets in China's 12th FYP (2011-2015)

10% Reduction	15% Reduction	16% Reduction	17% Reduction	18% Reduction
Hainan	Gansu	Anhui	Beijing	Guangdong
Qinghai	Guangxi	Chongqing	Hebei	Jiangsu
Tibet	Guizhou	Fujian	Liaoning	Shanghai
Xinjiang	Inner Mongolia	Heilongjiang	Shandong	Tianjin
	Ningxia	Henan		Zhejiang
	Yunnan	Hubei		
		Hunan		
		Jiangxi		
		Jilin		
		Shaanxi		
		Shanxi		
		Sichuan		

Source: NDRC (9/2011).

In addition, an *energy consumption cap* was embodied in the 12th FYP for Energy Development which was issued in the beginning of 2013: the total primary energy consumption and electricity consumption is to be controlled at a level of 4 billion tons of coal equivalent (tce) by 2015 and the coal consumption rate is to decrease to 65% (NDRC 1/2013). It is said that the energy consumption cap has paved the way for the cap on GHG emissions, and this energy consumption cap target also has been broken down to the provincial level. The decomposition of national energy and environment-related targets has shown the Chinese government's determination to rebalance its economic structure towards more energy-efficient growth. In order to realize the targets embodied in the carbon intensity index allocation and quota setting, the provincial levels have begun to pay more attention to regulating their own specific policies/regulations for energy conservation, RE development as well as pollutant control (sulfur dioxide, nitrogen oxide, chemical oxygen demand and ammonium nitrogen). The signal mechanism has become a strong dynamic to push the improvement of local RE policy systems and policy implementation coordination between the central and local levels. For instance, promoted by the pro-RE coalition, the NEA issued the Regulation for Management of Renewable Power Quota (Exposure Draft) in May 2012. It includes *a decomposition mechanism for the RE quota* at the provincial level (for more detailed information on the RE quota decomposition see section 8.4).

As mentioned above in the discussion about the procedural lock-in effect, making commitments to the climate change regime has promoted the greening of standards in the local official performance assessment system. To be more specific, the State Council will construct a complete evaluation and assessment mechanism for energy production, distribution and consumption as well as RE development at the local level annually. Once emissions reduction and RE development requirements become key standards to measure local officials' political performance, their performance in terms of climate change mitigation and RE development will also be taken into account. Within this evaluation system, the assessment results will form an important component in the comprehensive appraisal and evaluation of leading bodies and leading officials, and will be incorporated into governmental and state-owned enterprise management performance evaluations. The State Council will also implement an accountability system, and commend and award areas, organizations and individuals that have achieved outstanding success. Therefore, it is significant to design a better set of standards to evaluate the performance of local officials, such as through the combination of the enforcement of Five-Year targets with the completion of annual target assessments, and foster the assessment of annual targets with progress tracking.

Chapter 6
The Renewable Energy Policy System and Characteristics of the Pro-RE Coalition in China

Climate change socialization provides an external impetus to influence institutional anchoring and resource reallocation in the subsystem and promotes capability building of the pro-RE coalition. Based on the analysis in Chapter 5, the first section of this chapter focuses on a comprehensive understanding of the pro-RE coalition in China's RE subsystem. The second section specifies the key governmental and societal actors and conventional interest groups in the RE policy system. The last section summarizes characteristics of the pro-RE coalition in China.

6.1 The pro-RE coalition in the RE policy system of China

6.1.1 Understanding the pro-RE coalition

In Sabatier's ACF framework, the advocacy coalition refers to "people from various governmental and private organizations who share a set of same normative and causal values in their belief systems and who often act in concert" (Sabatier and Jenkins-Smith 1993b: 18). Therefore, the advocacy coalition is a set of governmental and social actors who share causal values and form a coalition in order to translate their beliefs into the policy-making system and to promote policy change. Based on this definition of an advocacy coalition, the *pro-RE coalition* in this book is defined as a set of actors from various governmental and societal organizations who share a set of normative and causal values pertaining to sustainable development, green growth, climate protection and RE development. They often act in concert to promote energy policy change towards RE. To be more specific, the pro-RE coalition in China is a set of governmental and social actors including: bureaucratic agencies and paramount leaders supporting RE development, particularly the newly established governmental institutions responsible for RE regulation, RE research institutions and think tanks, RE research scholars and experts, RE policy research centers in the universities, RE industry associations, environmental NGOs and relevant media power, such as professional RE websites.

Risse-Kappen emphasizes that the influence of international actors on domestic policy change depends on the formation of "winning coalitions". He states, "transnational actors needed channels into the political system and domestic partners with the ability to form 'winning coalitions' within the political elite" (Flockhart 2006: 98; Risse-Kappen 1994: 208). However, Risse-Kappen does not make clear how international sources provide the external impetus to create a new domestic policy coalition. According to Sabatier, a certain subsystem usually contains two or more advocacy coalitions and the dominant coalition usually has more and stronger supporters and controls more political resources. It is hard for the new/minor advocacy coalition to change the current interest patterns, unless there is an external impetus leading to a breakthrough to a new institutional structure and resource allocation pattern. Sabatier mentions that the capability building of the advocacy coalition to promote policy change depends upon its access to political resources, which include "money, expertise, number of supporters, and legal authority" (Sabatier and Jenkins-Smith 1993b: 29).

In this book, I treat the "capability building" of the pro-RE coalition in China as a key bridge between socialization theory and the ACF framework. Through exploring micro-processes of role playing and strategic calculation in the socialization process, this book contends that the governmental and societal actors in the pro-RE coalition both become stronger by means of institutional anchoring and resource reallocation in the climate change socialization process. The growth of the pro-RE coalition is reflected along three dimensions: *first*, increasing membership (e.g., newly established governmental institutions, emerging governmental RE research agencies and social academic institutions for RE development, and RE industry associations); *second*, the ability to gain more resources through resource reallocation in a favorable policy opportunity structure; and, *third*, the degree of their involvement and their ability to wield authority in the policy-making process.

6.1.2 The belief system of the pro-RE coalition

According to Sabatier's ACF framework, similar causal values and beliefs are the basic "glue" that hold together governmental and societal actors in the same advocacy coalition (Sabatier 1988; Sabatier 2007; Sabatier and Jenkins-Smith 1993a). The belief system is a kind of cognitive structure which includes three levels: normative core belief, policy core belief and instrumental policy belief (Sabatier and Jenkins-Smith 1993a: 31). ① In the field of RE development in China, there are three main streams of belief systems or cognitive structures: the sustainable development stream, the green growth stream and the pro-GDPism stream.

The sustainable development stream puts emphasis on ecological values, arguing they should be on par with economic growth values and the desire for economic growth needs to be rationally controlled. The supporters in this stream claim that there needs to be a major policy shift in the energy sector and RE development can be treated as a significant energy source to replace fossil fuels through technological innovation in order to reach the goal of environmental protection and a harmonious relationship between nature and humans. Some believe that even technological innovation can not solve all problems, unless people learn to control their greed. On the contrary, the pro-GDP/economic growth stream focuses on the priority of economic development and even tends to promote rapid economic growth at the cost of environmental protection. They amplify the technological difficulties in developing RE and contend that RE is rather unstable and expensive compared with fuel fossil. They hold a suspicious attitude towards climate change and refuse to invest too much in RE technology innovation. Pro-GDPism supporters refuse any RE policy change that will hurt conventional vested interests in the energy sector. The green growth stream is a stream in transition that interlinks the sustainable development and pro-GDPism streams and emphasizes the compatibility of environmental protection and economic growth. Although they are cautious about the systemic shift in the energy sector, they promote RE technologic innovation and low-carbon economy development through introducing innovative policy instruments.

Considering the complexity of the real world, the pro-RE coalition in China consists of a sustainable development stream and a green growth stream. Both are supporters of RE development. For instance, some RE research institutes, RE industry associations and environmental NGOs are strong supporters of the sustainable development stream of RE development and lobby governmental leaders in order to prove the feasibility of ambitious RE targets and a deep green transformation. Although some governmental institutions, such as the Department of New Energy and Renewable Energy (DNERE) within the National Energy Administration, are

① According to Sabatier, the belief system includes three levels: a deep normative core (fundamental normative and ontological axioms), a near policy core (fundamental policy positions concerning the basic strategies for achieving normative axioms of deep core), and secondary aspects (instrumental decisions and information searches necessary to implement the policy core). See Sabatier and Jenkins-Smith (1993a: 31).

supporters of RE development, they belong to the green growth stream and put emphasis on the compatibility of "green" and "growth". Although these RE development supporters aim at realizing green growth through promoting the application of innovative RE policy instruments, they are still cautious about any systematic reform of the energy sector. In the current pro-RE coalition in China, the green growth stream is the mainstream. It advocates a transition period from pro-GDPism to the ideas supported by the sustainable development stream.

The "green growth" supporters still put more emphasis on the "economic growth" dimension than the "green" dimension, and argue there is still no clear definition of a "low-carbon economy". The imbalanced development, overcapacity and vicious competition in RE development, which was mentioned in Chapter 3, has shown the "lingering shadow" of the "economy growing worship" of the RE industry and RE market. Many local officials launched regional RE industries not for the "win-win" of environmental protection and economic growth, but simply to get more subsidies from the central government and improve their personal political performance evaluation through "Green GDP" growth. The "enclosure movement"① pursued by state-owned power enterprises in wind farm construction projects also shows this "pro-economic growth" tendency. During an interview with a staff member of a wind power enterprise, it became clear that state-owned power enterprises were "enclosing" many wind farms. They were not really attempting to develop RE, but rather were trying to get more proportion approval to develop coal-power plants (more details see section 6. 2. 3). If the quota system is effectively carried out from 2015 on, the proportion of all forms of energy—both RE and coal will be set for the state-owned power enterprises. Even within the pro-RE coalition, different actors have different preferences related to RE development with some focusing more on sustainable development and others emphasizing green economic growth. Although China has achieved incremental change in RE policy instruments and even has begun to launch a strategic transition of its energy sector②, a systematic shift from a coal-dominated energy supply mix to real sustainable development still has a rather long way to go.

---

① The "wind power enclosure movement" refers to the rapid expansion in wind power investment and wind farm construction by power SOEs. Large power SOEs offer a "bottom price" even lower than production costs in concession bidding in order to seize more wind-rich renewable energy projects.

② The 12th FYP for Energy Development which was issued in January 2013, proposed an energy consumption cap strategy in order to constrain coal consumption and promote RE development.

Table 6.1 Comparison of belief systems concerning RE development

	The pro-RE coalition: the green growth is the mainstream		Conventional energy coalition
Belief Category	Sustainable development	Green growth	Pro-economic growth
Normative Core Belief			
Nature of man	Man is part of nature, not superior to it.	Man belongs to nature and develops in nature.	Man has dominion over nature.
Values priority	Priority is placed on ecological values and economic growth should be on par with ecological concerns.	Ecological values should be on par with economic growth values.	Priority is placed on economic growth values, rather than ecological values. Economic growth should be guaranteed even at the cost of ecological values.
Policy Core Belief			
Attitude towards climate change mitigation	Climate change mitigation is related to long-term development and human survival; the utilization of RE is indispensable for sustainable development.	Takes climate change mitigation as an opportunity to spur a green transformation. Developing RE is an effective and pragmatic way to promote climate change mitigation.	Be suspicious of climate change. Climate change mitigation is too costly to constrain economic development. Hesitates or even refuses the introduction of RE.
Attitude towards energy security	The supply of fossil fuels is limited in the long run and environmental acceptability should be emphasized. Energy consumption patterns should be transformed and RE should be accepted by society in order to replace fossil fuels.	Combines supply-biased and environmental acceptability dimensions. RE could be a significant supplement to a coal-dominated energy mix, but now is still not competitive compared with fossil fuels.	Guarantees the steady traditional energy supply at a reasonable price. The inadequate supply of fossil fuels is the biggest threat. Guarantees a profitable space for fossil fuels in the market. RE power is too unstable and expensive.

Attitude towards environmental protection and RE technological innovation	Priority is placed on environmental protection. Economic growth desire should be controlled rationally, since technological innovations can not solve all problems. Protests against pollution are tied to RE generation, such as what occurs in poly-silicon production.	Integrates ecological concerns into economic growth. Ecological modernization and technological innovation will result in a win-win situation. Green growth and low carbon concerns can be integrated into economic growth.	Poverty is the largest pollution. Environmental protection cannot hinder economic growth. Economic growth targets should be realized although this may require sacrificing of environmental protection. RE technological innovation costs too much, hinders economic development and challenges vested interests.
Instrumental Policy Belief			
Necessity for institutional and structural reforms	Political, economic, institutional and structural reforms are significant for a green transformation and harmonization between human activities and nature protection.	Institutional reforms could provide a political opportunity to break the old interest pattern and strengthen the position of pro-RE actors in the political system.	Resistant attitude. Institutional and structural reforms will hurt vested interests of conventional energy forces.
The degree of RE policy change	There should be major RE policy changes, such as a structural change in the energy sector and electricity market and changes in policy strategies and policy goals.	Fosters implementation of RE instrument policies, and promotes major new policies, such as the introduction of a quota system.	Resistant to energy structure reform since coal supplies are cheap and stable; has a suspicious attitude towards RE policy change.
Attitude towards RE development problems (such as grid connection and curtailment problems)	High efficacy expectations for RE development. Emphasizes that hidden interests and interest conflicts, rather than technological problems hinder RE development. Refuses to make compromises with conventional actors.	Puts an emphasis on technological innovation and fosters the implementation of new RE policy rather than shirking responsibility by pointing to technical gaps. Accepts compromising with conventional actors.	Emphasizes the technical difficulties and economic cost in RE development. Focuses on the negative impact of unstable RE power on the national grid. Aims to reduce the position of RE in the national strategy and to guarantee the position of fuel fossils and nuclear power.

Source: Compiled by the author.

6.2 Key actors in the RE policy system of China

The main characteristic of China's policy making is under the model of "fragmented authoritarianism" (Lieberthal and Oksenberg 1988: 4; Mertha 2009: 996), in which elites' interests do not always align and policies are shaped by a multiplicity of actors (Downs 2004). Jakobson and Knox (2010) also mention the fractured tendency of the policy making system since "many of these official actors have narrow perceptions of China's national interests and even rival motives as a result of their varying domestic portfolios and international outreach activities" (Jakobson and Knox 2010: 1). Since there are many stakeholders involved in the energy sector and institution building in China is weak, the authority over RE policy making is also fractured, and multiple agencies should be taken into account. The NDRC, as the most significant agency in micro-economic planning, energy regulation and climate change negotiations, exerts considerable influence on RE policy regulation. The state-owned enterprises (SOEs) in the energy sector also play an important role in influencing the RE policy making and policy implementation. Apart from the NDRC and SOEs, other administrative stakeholders in finance, technology, commerce fields all have different interests and preferences related to RE, and different levels of authority. Due to their now stronger institutional anchoring and greater access to resources in the bureaucratic system, more pro-RE institutions and actors are coming into being. Thus, RE supporters are gradually gaining more power in relation to the RE policy-making process. Emerging new actors, like RE research institutes and social RE industrial associations, also have increasing influence on RE policy change. Therefore, it is of great importance to identify key actors in the RE policy system and specify the characteristics of the pro-RE coalition as will be done in the following sections.

6.2.1 Governmental actors in the RE policy making system

This section puts emphasis on the governmental stakeholders in the RE policy making system along three perspectives: key actors in the NDRC, key governmental RE policy research agencies and key RE policy supportive actors in the bureaucratic system (see Appendix II).

6.2.1.1 Key governmental actors in the NDRC

As mentioned in Chapter 5, the energy sector with its weak institutions has undergone a bumpy path of institutional reform. As there is no Ministry of Energy, the NDRC plays a significant role in macro-economic planning and energy regulation.

Beginning in 2003, institutional restructuring focused on the NDRC. Even though the high-level energy coordinating agency—the National Energy Commission (NEC) was established in 2010, leaders from the NDRC still have considerably more weight in energy policy making compared with other ministries. In the RE policy making system, the NDRC also plays a central role in RE policy design and formulation. There are four departments with a close relationship with RE policy making: the Pricing Department, the National Energy Administration (NEA), the Department of the Resource Conservation and Environmental Protection (DRCEP), and the Department of Climate Change (DCC) in the NDRC. Of these four departments, the Pricing Department and the NEA play a direct role in the RE policy formulation.

The *Pricing Department of the NDRC* is mainly responsible for setting prices for economic goods, including for fossil fuel as well as renewable energies. In the feed-in tariff policy, guaranteeing the favorable fixed feed-in price for wind, biomass, and solar PV power has played a significant role in RE promotion.

The *National Energy Administration (NEA)* is the direct department responsible for formulating and implementing energy development plans and industrial policies; promoting institutional reform in the energy sector, including planning for RE development, and is in charge of collecting funds from the RE surcharge and distributing them to grid companies. In the NEA, there are two significant agencies in charge of RE policy formulation and implementation: the *Center for Renewable Energy Development (CRED)* within the Energy Research Institute (ERI) and the *Department of New Energy and Renewable Energy (DNERE)*. When the main responsibility and authority of climate change negotiations was shifted to the more powerful governmental agency—the State Development and Planning Commission (SDPC) in 1998, the SDPC established the CRED, along with the *Research Center for Energy Environment and Climate Change (RCEECC)* in the ERI, in order to obtain more knowledge and policy proposals for the climate change negotiations and CDM project implementation. The *CDM Project Management Center* was set up within the ERI in 2001 in order to guide the development of CDM projects in China. Based on the international experience of RE legislation, the CRED began to explore the feasibility of the RE Law formulation in China, study innovative policy instruments for the development of the RE industry, and offer annual reports and policy proposals for the ERI and the NDRC. Since the CRED is only a research institute, the DNERE was established in 2001 in order to supervise RE development, set up the industrial standards for RE, promote the electricity system reform, and coordinate the implementation of RE projects.

With the pressure emanating from the international climate change negotiations and the increasing role of RE development in GHG emission reductions, the CRED was upgraded to a national level research institution—the *China National Renewable Energy Center* (*CNREC*) in February 2012. The CNREC is a high level governmental think tank responsible for drafting RE policies and providing proposals for relevant administrable regulations. With its growing authority and capacity in RE policy making, the CNREC directly assists the State Council as well as the main energy sectors with the promotion of RE policy research, coordination of the management of the RE industry, the establishment of a RE industry system, and the carrying out of national demonstration projects as well as international cooperation (CNREC 2012).

Within the NDRC, the establishment of the *Department of Resource Conservation and Environmental Protection* (*DRCEP*) and the *Department of Climate Change* (*DCC*) enhanced institution building for RE governance. Although many scholars criticize that Chinese climate change stance is controlled by the "super pro-economic development" agency (the NDRC) and the climate change policy seems more like an energy policy (Harris 2009; Harris 2011a; Harris 2011b; Liang 2010; Moore 2011), it is undeniable that RE development has benefited a lot from stronger institutional coordination and green policy integration, since the NDRC has the highest regulative authority for climate change as well as energy sector decisions. After China issued the National Climate Change Program in 2007, the *National Leading Group on Climate Change* (*NLGCC*) headed by former Premier Wen Jiabao was established (replacing the former National Climate Change Policy Coordination Group) to show the increased seriousness and emphasize the importance of the decisions of the Chinese leadership related to climate change mitigation. Its office was also located within the NDRC. It also has another name—the *State Council Energy Conservation and Emissions Reduction Leading Group* (one institution, two names). The national leading group is "the informal body of members in the State Council that generate information to advise the State Council on policy, and later aid in coordinating the implementation of policy decisions made by the top leaders with the relevant bureaucracies" (Lee 2012: 36). This new supra-ministerial policy making organization on climate change and low-carbon development is supposed to guarantee more effective coordination among ministries and other government agencies than the previous inter-ministerial one could; it is also responsible for closely coordinating between climate change and clean energy issues. The establishment of the State Council Energy Conservation and Emissions Reduction Leading Group strongly promoted the issuing of the Mid- and Long-Term Development Plan for RE Development in September 2007. In November 2007, the NDRC and the MOF jointly launched the operation of the CDM Fund and upon approval of the State Council, the MOF, the NDRC and other ministries jointly promulgated the Regulation of China CDM Fund in September 2010. The Measure on the Operation and Management of Clean Development Mechanism Projects was amended in the same year to increase the efficiency of CDM program development and verification.

The current head of the Chinese government delegation in the climate change negotiations, Xie Zhenhua, is also the deputy director of the NDRC. Before he became the deputy director in the NDRC, he was the director of the State Environmental Protection Administration (SEPA). The Department of Climate Change was established in 2008 and its director, Su Wei, is also the Deputy Head of Chinese climate delegation. The institutional arrangement of the Department of the Climate Change within the NDRC has symbolized that climate change has entered the political mainstream. The relevant RE development and energy conservation sectors now have more channels to obtain political recourses. The voluntary carbon intensity target, which was issued before the 2009 Copenhagen Conference, linked the carbon intensity reduction target with the RE development target. This linkage was reflected in the total energy consumption controlling mechanism in the 12th FYP for Energy Development (NDRC 1/2013; State Council 3/2011).① No doubt, this carbon reduction pressure will strongly promote RE development.

In November 2011, the NDRC established the *National Center for Climate Change Strategy and International Cooperation* (*NCSC*) before the Durban Climate Change Conference, which is the first national-level think tank on climate change to focus on strategic research and international cooperation. Based on research findings, the NCSC provides policy proposals and policy consulting directly to the State Council and paramount leaders. Li Junfeng, the deputy director of the Energy Research Institute (ERI) of the NDRC was appointed as the director of the NCSC (Green Dialogue 2011). He has rich experience in RE development and climate change mitigation. Li participated in the first CDM project in China, which once played a leading role in promoting the drafting work of the RE Law and the Mid- and Long-Term Plan for RE Development (Green Dialogue 2011). The NCSC became a key high-level "window agency" to enhance international low-carbon cooperation, encourage the exchange of foreign experts, and promote national strategic research on climate change, especially the launching of comprehensive research initiatives on a carbon trading design (China News 2011). The design of a domestic carbon trading market will have significant implications for RE development, since RE projects are the main sources for carbon

① The total primary energy consumption and electricity consumption are to be controlled at levels of 4 billion tons of coal equivalent (tce) and 6.15 trillion, respectively, and the proportion of RE consumption in total primary energy consumption is to be increased to 11.4% (NDRC 1/2013; State Council 3/2011).

emission reduction credits. They thus closely interlink climate change mitigation efforts and RE development targets (see Appendix II).

6.2.1.2 Key governmental policy research institutes

Problems with which governmental bureaucracies are faced are "arguably more fast-moving and complex than before" (Mertha 2009). In response, there has been increasing pluralization of policy research agencies and think tanks, which now also have a louder voice in the policy-making process. Since China is a late-comer in RE development without much experience, key governmental research agencies have had to play a central role in learning from the experiences of other countries and providing RE policy proposals to paramount leaders. Apart from the key RE research agency, the CRED, and the key climate change strategy research agency, the NCSC in the NDRC, there are several other key central governmental research agencies addressing climate change and RE development:

The *Development Research Center of the State Council* (*DRC*), established in 1981, is a high-level comprehensive policy research and consulting institution directly under the State Council. The DRC has a team of prominent economists and qualified experts and researchers in the fields of macroeconomic policy, development strategy and regional economic policy, industrial economy and industrial policy (DRC 2011). Its main aim is to conduct advanced study on the overall, comprehensive, strategic and long-term issues related to national economic and social development so as to provide policy recommendations and consulting advice to the CPC Central Committee and the State Council. It is also responsible for the drafting of policy proposals for mid- and long-term development plans and regional development policies (DRC 2011). The DRC also launches international collaborative research and exchanges information with relevant international organizations and research institutions. It further provides information and foreign-related policy recommendations to the CPC Central Committee (DRC 2011). Energy policy and RE policy research have gained much priority in the DRC research since China ratified the Kyoto Protocol in 2002. In 2005, the *Center for Climate Change and Energy Regulation* was established in order to gain expertise in low-carbon development and RE development fields (DRC 2011). With the rising salience of climate change and RE development at the domestic level, the DRC began to cooperate with the CRED to draft RE policy proposals for the FYP. It submits them to the State Council for discussion. This was the case with the 12th FYP for RE Development, which was issued in August 2012.

The *China Council for International Cooperation on Environment and Development* (*CCICED*), established in 1992, has also played a significant role in promoting China's policy innovation in low-carbon development and green economy strategy. Its main task is exchanging and disseminating international successful experiences in the field of environment and development; studying key environment and development issues, and putting forward policy recommendations to national leaders and policy makers (CCICED 2010). Premier Li Keqiang is also the Chair of the CCICED. The CCICED holds the Annual General Meeting at which Council Members present their comments and finalize their policy recommendations to paramount leaders of the State Council (CCICED 2010). As a high-level think tank, the CCICED has increasing influence on the ecological process of the national Five-Year Plan. For instance, the task force group focuses on designing a mid- and long-term roadmap for improving environmental quality and environmental targets for the 12th FYP. Among the environmental targets, implementation of total emission control at the sectoral and regional levels has been treated as a key task, and RE development has gained much importance (CCICED 2012b).①

The *State Expert Advisory Committee* (*SEAC*) was established in 2007 under the National Energy Leading Group. In 2005, the State Council established the National Energy Leading Group within the NDRC as a high-level coordinating agency for energy management. The main tasks of the National Energy Leading Group are to study the national energy development strategy and plan; to research energy conservation, energy security and emergency responses; and, to promote international energy cooperation. In order to enhance professional research and improve the level of policy consulting, the State Expert Advisory Committee was established in 2007 (NEA 2007). The committee consists of 40 prestigious Chinese experts, providing services for the nation's policy-makers by making suggestions on energy strategy and offering solutions for major problems in energy development (NEA 2007). The committee has six branches: coal, power, nuclear energy, oil, gas, RE and energy conservation. The number of experts in RE research branches was 10, reflecting the significant position of RE development research at the national level (NEA 2007). The RE research branch gathers expertise from RE industry associations and climate change mitigation institutions, like the committee members Shi Dinghuan, who is the chairman of China Renewable Energy Society (CRES) and the committee member, Li Junfeng, who is the director of the high-level climate change think tank—the NCSC.

The most authoritative general academic institutions in China are the *Chinese Academy of Science* (*CAS*) and the *Chinese Academy of Social Science* (*CASS*). These two academic think tanks have taken the lead in clean energy research. In 2006, the

---

① As discussed in Chapter 4, RE FYP belongs to the second level of the RE policy system, so the RE targets design is usually tied closely with the carbon emission control in the FYP.

Institute of Policy and Management of the CAS cooperated with the Research Institute of Economics and Technology (RIET) to establish the *Center for Energy and Environmental Policy Research* (*CEEP*) (CEEP 2006). The CEEP conducts scientific research on the areas of energy and environment and aims at providing energy scenario forecasting, energy system analysis and policy proposals for government and enterprises (CEEP 2006). The main projects include the Near Zero Emissions Coal (NZEC), China-UK joint project (2007-2009), the Cost Curve of China's Greenhouse Gas Abatement and Low-carbon Economic Policy Research (2009-2010). Beginning in 1999, the CASS began to annually draft and issue the Sustainable Development Report of China. The *China Research Society of Urban Development* (*CRSUD*) within the CASS (which was established in 1984), is a national community group specializing in urban economy, society and ecology development studies. Its aim is to provide services for urban reform, construction and management (CEEP 2006). The CRSUD established the first network focusing on low-carbon development at the local level—the Chinese Urban Low-carbon Economy Network (ULCEN) (http://www.cusdn.org.cn). This network emphasizes urban-level communication of best practices and low-carbon city development. RE development is one of the key fields for realizing urban low-carbon targets (CRSUD 2007) (see Appendix II).

6.2.1.3 Other governmental stakeholders

In the field of RE development, fiscal subsidy and technological R&D investment are two main supportive measures for guaranteeing the competitive capability and innovation of the RE power in the market. Therefore, the *Ministry of Finance* (*MOF*) and the *Ministry of Science and Technology* (*MOST*) have played a significant role in this area. As mentioned in Chapters 3 and 5, with the growing salience of climate change at the domestic level, especially once the carbon intensity reduction and RE development targets were tied together, pro-RE actors gained more fiscal subsidies and R&D investment from the national level.

The MOF, which is promoted by the NDRC, has issued many administrative regulations regarding the special fund, tax preferences and low-interest loans for RE generators since 2005. Examples include the Interim Measures on Special Fund Management of RE Development in 2006, the Import Tariff Adjustment for Large Wind Turbines, Key Components and Raw Materials in 2008, and the Interim Measure on the Management of Public Subsidies for Golden Sun Demonstration Projects in 2009 (see Chapter 3). In addition, the MOF is also the main agency in charge of the *Renewable Energy Development Special Fund*, which was set up according to the RE Law Amendment in 2009 (see Chapter 3).

In the R&D field, the national science and technology programs from the MOST are central to China's RE technology innovation. Most of the R&D funds for RE technology come from China's three main national programs: the 973 Program, the 863 Program, and the Key Technology R&D Program (Huang et al. 2012: 121). Furthermore, they play an active role in R&D financial support for the CDM programs. With the increasing concerns for environmental protection, the State Environmental Protection Administration (SEPA) was upgraded to the *Ministry of Environmental Protection* (*MEP*) in 2008. The role of the MEP in RE development cannot be underestimated, especially in the environmental assessment of RE projects.① The *Chinese Academy for Environmental Planning* (*CAEP*), which was founded in 2001 under the SEPA is a leading think tank of the Chinese environmental protection administration (CAEP 2012). When the SEPA was upgraded to the MEP in 2008, the CAEP began to play a significant role in providing technical support and consultation for environmental planning, project selection, tax designing (like carbon tax) and assessments for RE projects (CAEP 2012).

6.2.2 Key pro-RE societal actors in the RE governance system

Apart from governmental institutions involved in the RE policy making and policy implementation processes, more and more pro-RE societal actors have played an active role in the RE governance system, such as RE research centers in the universities, RE industry associations, environmental NGOs and professional RE websites. These new societal actors "try to sway official policy by providing new policy proposal and seek additional leverage by influencing public opinion" (Jakobson and Knox 2010: 1). Compared with western countries, the influence of societal actors in the policy-making process is rather limited and weak. However, with the increasing opening-up of national institutional channels, there has been more reporting of successful public environmental protests. Prof. Huan Qingzhi pointed out that "if we say that the results of the Nujiang dam construction project collective protest in 2003/2004 and Xiamen PX project collective protest in 2007 are uncertain (the former is shelved, the latter is relocated), then we have to admit that both the Shifang Molybdenum Copper Alloy Factory project protest and the Qidong sewage pipeline into the sea project protest in July 2012 have clearly realized their goals—the projects will not be built in

① Hydro power station construction has a potential risk as it can disrupt ecological systems. The heightened production levels of poly-silicon cells for PV power has led to serious local environmental pollution. That is why some Environmental-NGOs in China harshly question whether renewable energies are real "green" or not. As a result, the government began to focus more attention on environmental assessments of RE projects and started to control the disorderly RE development rather than merely promote quantity development of installed RE capacity.

the future."① Therefore, we can see an increasing pluralization of policy-making in China (Mertha 2009: 996). Chinese leaders have started to recognize that societal actors can "actually provide them with valuable resources, such as information about societal perceptions, policy alternatives and implementation capacity" (Schreurs 2002: 258). In addition, NGOs in China usually have a cooperative relationship with the government. Some of them are (partly) set up and organized by the government, and can be called GONGOs (government-organized NGOs). In the RE governance field, these societal actors have increasingly cooperative relations with governmental research institutions: to provide RE development reports, expose policy loopholes in the policy implementation process, and protect interests and rights of the RE power generators. This development is undeniably increasing the degree of cohesiveness of the pro-RE coalition. There are three kinds of societal actors playing an increasingly important role in the RE governance: societal academic institutions related to RE policy research, such as RE and low-carbon research centers in universities; RE industry associations and related environmental NGOs; and the RE media power, especially professional websites concerning RE development, CDM and low-carbon development.

6.2.2.1 Societal academic institutions focused on RE policy research

The universities, as "knowledge convergence clusters", have shown a proactive attitude in the frontier of RE development. Among these universities, three Beijing-based first-class universities, Tsinghua University, Peking University and Renmin University of China, have played significant role in providing policy proposals for governmental leaders, since they have more chances to get national-level research projects and various professors of these universities have been invited to the *Politburo Collective Study Sessions of the CPC* to hold lectures.② Since China issued its National Climate Change Program, more and more lectures concerning climate change mitigation, low-carbon strategies and RE development have been held there.

For instance, in the Politburo's collective study session of 27 June 2008, the researcher Luo Yong from the CMA and Professor He Jiankun from the Low-carbon Energy Center of Tsinghua University led the study session focusing on climate change

① Interview with Huan Qingzhi, Professor of Environmental Politics, in Centre for Environmental Politics Research, Peking University (7 March 2012, in Beijing).

② The Politburo of the CPC is the highest-level policy-making agency of China and the power within the Politburo is centralized in the Politburo Standing Committee. After former President Hu Jintao was appointed CPC general secretary in 2002, he started convening Politburo collective study sessions seven or eight times annually. See Jakobson and Knox (2010: 35). These are meetings at which top experts in the country are invited to deliver a lecture to members of the Politburo on a topic in which they specialize. Since the first study session on 26 December 2002, a total of 83 sessions covering a wide range of issues had taken place as of 30 January 2013. See Lu (2007).

and capacity building for responding to climate change (CPC People 2010). In the Politburo collective study session of 30 May 2011, the main study topic was related to the cultivation and development of strategic emerging industries (CPC People 2010). RE experts from Peking University and the CRES were also invited to hold a lecture before the Politburo. The RE industry has been treated as one of the key strategic emerging industries for realizing a low-carbon economic structural transformation. In the Politburo collective study session of 24 May 2013, President Xi Jinping invited experts from Tsinghua University, the CAS and the CASS to hold a lecture regarding ecological civilization, environmental protection and RE development (Xinhua News 2013). In sum, the Politburo Collective Study Sessions of the CPC has provided a significant channel for societal actors to meet with paramount leaders. It has a symbolic and demonstrational effect: setting an example for lower level officials and sending out signals about current policy foci (Lu 2007: 2-3). The study sessions are not solely meant to provide policy analysis and proposals to Politburo members; they also serve as a platform for the leadership to publicize and promote new policies in order to facilitate policy implementation (Jakobson and Knox 2010: 35).

Apart from special channels with paramount leaders, Tsinghua University has been playing a leading role in conducting research on new and renewable energy development, especially supporting CDM project research in the initial stage, like the establishment of the *Center for CDM Research and Development* in 2005. The *Research Center for China Studies* led by Hu Angang (2001) is a very influential academic institute for high-level consultation (like submitting Report of China Studies directly for high-level officials in Beijing). Hu is a leading scholar who has called for China to make emission reduction commitments as soon as possible and to pay more attention to RE development. In addition, Tsinghua University set up the *Institute of Low Carbon Economy* in 2008. In 2010, the *EU-China Institute for Clean and Renewable Energy* (*ICARE*) was established between Turin Polytechnic University (Italy) and Tsinghua University (China) under the cooperative framework of the "Sino-EU Clean Energy Center Joint Declaration", which was signed at the eleventh EU-China summit in May 2009 (ICARE 2012). The ICARE aims to fill the gap between China's priority in battling against climate change by adopting clean and RE and the lack of a critical mass of Chinese engineers in these new technologies (ICARE 2012).

Peking University set up the *Research Center for Contemporary China* as early as 1988. It conducts quantitative interdisciplinary research about sustainable development. In 2006, the *CDM Club*, *6E Plus* (*Environment*, *Energy*, *Economy*, *Ecosystem*, *Education*, *Equity*) (2006) was set up in Peking University to focus on the significant role of CDM projects focused on research and RE development for sustainable ecosystems.

The *China Center for Energy and Development* and the *Research Center for World New Energy Strategy* were established in 2011. The former puts more emphasis on new thinking in energy security, RE technology development and low-carbon markets; the latter aims to provide a national strategic vision of RE development for policy makers. These academic organizations have made efforts to provide more policy recommendations and proposals about RE development as well as low-carbon strategies for political leaders. Compared with the comprehensive research of Tsinghua University and Peking University, Renmin University researchers focus more on national strategies and relevant policy research. This is the case with the Center for International Energy Strategy Studies established in 2003. Furthermore, most universities have begun to build research institutes on climate change, RE development and low-carbon economy (see Appendix II).

6.2.2.2 RE industry associations and relevant environmental NGOs

Along with rapid RE development, more RE industry associations have emerged and their influence on RE governance has become increasingly strong. With a large membership network of RE enterprises, *RE industry associations* have become spokesmen on behalf of the core interests of the RE industry, and try to lobby government officials to win more favorable policy support. For instance, some RE industry associations can influence deputies of the National People's Congress (NPC) through their personal relations. Some leaders of RE industry associations are invited to become committee members of governmental research groups, such as Shi Dinghuan, the chairman of China Renewable Energy Society (CRES), who is a committee member of the State Expert Advisory Committee (SEAC). Relying on the establishment of new institutional channels in the bureaucratic system, societal actors have gained more chances to influence the RE policy-making process. At the same time, they also play a coordinating role within RE industries and enhance the implementation of RE technical standards and RE industry regulations.

The *Chinese Renewable Energy Society* (*CRES*) was developed out of the former Solar Energy Society, the earliest RE association in China which was established already in 1976. It has many institutional connections, including with the Solar Photovoltaic Society, the Solar Thermal Utilization Association, the Solar Photochemistry Association, the Solar Building Association, the Chinese Wind Energy Association and the Biomass Energy Association (CRES 2011). The CRES actively promotes academic exchanges, provides professional statistics and information of RE development, and develops all-around friendly cooperative relations with other academic institutions, local governments, RE enterprises and international institutions (CRES 2011). CRES's predecessor, the Solar Energy Society played a guiding role in promoting the rapid development of SWH from its founding through the late 1980s and 1990s. Furthermore, the Solar Photovoltaic Society of the CRES has exerted great social influence and appealed for the introduction of the feed-in tariff for PV. In 2011, the government finally issued the Notice on Feed-in Tariff Policy of Solar Photovoltaic to guarantee the PV fixed price to be 1 *yuan*/(kW · h) or 1.15 *yuan*/(kW · h).

Another influential RE industry association is the *Chinese Renewable Energy Industries Association* (*CREIA*), which was established in 2000 with the support of the UNDP, the GEF and the SETC in the cooperative framework of the climate change regime. The CREIA obtained its legal registration from the Ministry of Civil Affairs in 2002. It represents a range of RE manufacturers of wind, solar thermal, solar PV and biomass power. Its aims are to provide RE policy consultation for RE enterprises, promote RE development and utilization on a larger scale, and address the environmental problems caused by China's coal-dominated structure. The CREIA has been active in forming coalitions with environmental NGOs, such as Greenpeace and the WWF, in order to promote rapid RE development and has called for further RE policy change (Toke 2011: 161). Apart from the CRES and the CREIA, the significant RE industry associations also include the China Energy Conservation Association (CECA), which was established in 1989, the China Association of Rural Energy Industry (CAREI), which was set up in 1992 and the China Renewable Energy Industry Association (CHNREIA), which was founded in 2000.

In addition to the RE industry associations, some civil environmental protection organizations/environmental NGOs also have shown increasing concerns about RE development and utilization. They have given active support for RE policy implementation and supervised the environmental management of RE projects (Wang, Z. et al. 2010: 125-126). Among these NGOs, *Greenpeace* has taken the lead in launching pro-RE campaigns and made "some hard-hitting attacks on the impact of the coal industry in China" (Mao et al. 2008; Toke 2011). The main aim of Greenpeace China is to "push China to quit coal, which supplies 70% of the country's energy and produces 80% of its carbon dioxide emissions and to catalyze a RE revolution in China—which has vast untapped potential for solar and wind energy" (Greenpeace 2006). Although the feed-in tariff policy was enshrined in the RE Law, the concrete administrative regulation for the feed-in tariff of wind power did not appear until 2009, and the feed-in tariff of solar PV did not appear until 2011. In order to promote the RE campaign for the feed-in tariff, Greenpeace organized a series of seminars involving representatives of the RE industries and leading policy-makers and bureaucrats, especially including officials from the ERI within the NRDC (Toke 2011: 161). Through this way, Greenpeace can "boast influence to the extent that it has produced policy documents in collaboration with personnel from the ERI" (Toke 2011: 161).

Another significant green NGO to promote environmental information transparency and RE development is the *Institute of Public and Environmental Affairs (IPE)*. The IPE has taken a leading role in "expanding environmental information disclosure to allow communities to fully understand the hazards and risks in the surrounding environment and to promote widespread public participation in environmental governance" (IPE 2006). In order to encourage improvements in the control of urban air pollution, the Law School of Renmin University of China and the IPE jointly developed the Urban Air Quality Information Transparency Index (AQTI) in 2011 (IPE 2012). In the winter months of 2012-2013, the PM2.5 smog had a serious wide-ranging and long-lasting influence on central and northeastern China (covering 17 provinces).① This unprecedented large-scale air pollution event produced much more social concern than earlier incidents (Xu and Zhang 2013). The IPE issued a special research report on the PM2.5 situation—Small Particles, Big Breakthrough: 2012 Urban Air Quality Information Transparency Index (IPE 2012). This report provided comprehensive data on PM2.5 at the local level for the public and introduced policy suggestions for the government on how to reduce the PM2.5 smog. The measures should include both emergency response and focus on solving deep-rooted problems by developing RE in order to break the coal-dominated energy supply mix and reduce the dust emissions from the coal thermal plants and controlling the exhaust from vehicles and other pollution from heavy industries (the iron industry, ore refineries, concrete makers and the chemical sector) (Ma 2013).② Other green NGOs, such as the China Resource Recycling Association (CRRA), the China Association of Environmental Protection Industry (CAEPI) and the Friends of Nature all play an active role in environmental protection activities and promote a green transformation of energy consumption (see Appendix II).

---

① PM2.5 refers to the atmospheric particulate matter (air pollutants) with a diameter of 2.5 micrometers or less, which leads to smog formation in cities and causes serious harm to people's health. These PM2.5 particles mainly come from fossil fuel burning for electricity and heating as well as automobile exhaust (and industrial smelting, and metal processing). See IPE (2012).

② The PM2.5 smog event shows the links between climate change and domestic air pollution. China's climate change mitigation efforts have contributed to domestic environmental problem solving. At the same time, the deteriorating domestic air pollution has further simulated China to take major steps to reduce GHG, sulphur dioxide, nitrogen oxides emissions, industrial smoke, dust and volatile organic compound releases from key industries. In Beijing, coal and cars are the two main sources of air pollution. According to the city's environmental protection bureau, coal accounts for 16.7% of all air pollution, and vehicles for 22%. See Xu and Zhang (2013).

6.2.2.3 Mass media: professional websites concerning RE development

With the relatively high salience of climate change at the domestic level and with the rapid development of RE, "climate change", "low-carbon economy", and "renewable energy", have become buzz words in the mass media (newspaper, TV, Internet). *Renmin Ribao* (*People's Daily*) and Xinhua News Agency are the voice of the CPC. The frequency of the reports relating to climate change and RE development in these influential media venues has increased exponentially in the last decade. Further, the Internet version of these two significant media outlets, People Net (http://www.people.com.cn) and Xinhua News (http://www.news.cn) have both introduced climate change, energy and environmental protection columns. Supported by the Climate Change Department of the NDRC beginning in 2008, three key professional websites about climate change and clean energy were established to promote information exchange and policy transparency of the Chinese government: the *China Climate Change Info-Net* (http://www.ccchina.gov.cn/en), the *Clean Development Mechanism in China* website (http://cdm.ccchina.gov.cn/english/index.asp) and the *China CDM Fund* (*CDMFUND*) website (http://www.cdmfund.org/en/index.aspx). The CDM in China provides information about domestic policy and regulation on climate and RE, CDM project information, and up-to-date research reports. In these official websites, up-dated RE development and newly issued administrative regulations of relevance have a priority position in Internet columns. The priority is to keep RE policy transparency and send a positive signal for RE development to society.

Apart from governmental low-carbon and RE websites, unofficial professional RE websites also have played a significant role in providing concentrated, professional and systematical information on RE policy and development. The unofficial website of *Polaris Power* (http://www.bjx.com.cn) was established in 1999, and is the most influential website in China providing all-round information about energy industries and focusing on up-to-date RE policy and development. This website is not only a forum for market research, RE products advertisement, technological exchange, and relevant policy analysis of the RE industry, but also provides in-depth interviews with RE experts and governmental officials, professional RE industry reports and valuable RE industry outlooks. Through this website, the RE policy researchers/analysts, private RE enterprises and even common energy consumers can find useful information for their own purposes. Moreover, this website has become a social discussion and argumentation frontier related to RE policy making and policy implementation. Many RE experts and enterprises publicize their critiques of grid-connection and curtailment problems and call for further RE policy change through this website.

The website of *China Low-carbon* (http://www.ditan360.com) is China's first low-carbon network media. It has constructed a significant promotional platform and hosts carbon trading and financing discussions as well as carbon finance in China. The *China Dialogue* (http://www. china dialogue. net), which was founded in 2006, is a significant bilingual website and provides high-quality reports and in-depth interviews with key experts and officials in the fields of climate change, environmental protection and RE development (China dialogue 2006). It aims to stimulate common understanding of a green transformation in China, to promote environmental information transparency and to expose policy loopholes in environmental governance (China dialogue 2006). In addition, the websites of the New Energy & RE (http://www. crein. org. cn), the RE in China (http://www. cnecc. org. cn), the New Energy Net (http://www. newenergy. org. cn) and websites concerning local RE development have all contributed to the RE policy diffusion and increasing social acceptance to this field. In sum, these unofficial low-carbon and RE development websites have become significant green media avenues with the power to promote the diffusion of RE policy understanding among different societal actors, enhance the transparency of RE policy analysis and RE policy implementation, and expose RE policy loopholes through stimulating social discussion and argumentation (see Appendix II).

6.2.3 Conventional interest groups in the RE governance

One cannot overlook the role of large *state-owned enterprises*, such as five big electricity enterprises, two big grid enterprises, three big oil enterprises, coal enterprises, nuclear enterprises. They have strong vested interests in the energy sector. In order to keep their dominant place in energy regulation, they rely on their special status to influence the paramount leaders. There is a "*revolving door*" *mechanism* existing in the state-owned enterprises. Leaders of key state-owned enterprises have to be nominated by the central government. Therefore, these high-level leaders have a double-identity as enterprises leaders as well as semi-governmental officials as high as at the ministerial or vice-ministerial ranks. In the "revolving door" mechanism, the enterprise leaders also have a chance to be nominated to be key governmental officials when they show strong performance. Some serve as alternate members of the CPC Central Committee (Jakobson and Knox 2010: 25). Jakobson and Knox (2010) summarize the role of SOEs in the policy-making system:

> Large SOEs under the central government tend to have closer ties with Beijing's political elite than their smaller counterparts, particularly in strategic industries such as petroleum, minerals, nuclear power and defence... While SOEs are, in principle, subordinate to either central or local government, the pressure to maintain profitability

can at times provide an incentive for SOEs to define China's interests narrowly in contrast to the more extensive agenda that... policy officials must consider. (Jakobson and Knox 2010: 24)

In order to defend their own interests, SOEs attempt to influence the policy-making and policy implementation process. Even the NDRC, as the most powerful ministerial agency in macro-economic planning, has limited ability to constrain the behavior of SOEs. For instance, the National Energy Bureau (NEB) which was formed in 2003 was trapped in an embarrassing situation, since its rank (bureau-level) was even lower than many state-owned enterprises (ministry or vice-ministry-level agencies). Even when the NEB was upgraded to the National Energy Administration (vice-ministry-level), the authority of the NEA to regulate the behaviors of SOEs was not sufficient. Therefore, the role of SOEs has a significant influence on RE policy making and implementation. This role cannot be underestimated.

In the RE field, two large grid SOEs, the *State Grid Corporation of China* (*SGCC*) and the *China Southern Power Grid Company* (*CSG*), are significant stakeholders. After the electricity "Plant-Grid Separation" reform in early 2002, the assets of State Electric Power Corporation were divided into five power SOEs and two grid SOEs (SGCC 2010). The State Grid Corporation of China (SGCC) is the largest electric utility company transmitting and distributing power in China. This power distributor is headquartered in Beijing and manages distribution from subsidiaries in northern China, northeastern China, eastern China, middle China and northwestern China (SGCC 2010). The China Southern Power Grid Company (CSG), which is headquartered in Guangzhou, handles the investment, construction and management of power transmission, transformation and distribution covering China's five southern provinces of Guangdong, Guangxi, Yunnan, Guizhou and Hainan (CSG 2010). Compared to the profit they can obtain through integrating RE power into their grids, the grid SOEs gain more profit from cooperating with coal-fired plants. The price of electricity purchased by the grid operators from coal-fired plants can be as low as US $0.05, while wind power at government-dictated wholesale prices is US $0.08 to US $0.10 per kilowatt-hour (Asian Power 2012). The government subsidizes grid companies for selling RE power to help move China away from polluting coal, but the subsidies are not enough for grid companies to make a profit (Asian Power 2012). The grid connection problem and RE power curtailment have become bottlenecks for RE development. In 2011, about a third of RE power sources still could not access the national grid (Clean Biz 2012). Especially since the first half of 2012, grid operators are increasingly reluctant to distribute the costly and unpredictable RE power amid a sharp economic downturn (Clean Biz 2012). The CWEA secretary-general Qin

Haiyan said that the curtailment further worsened the situation: "the curtailment forced 20% to 30% of turbines to lie idle in wind farms in 2012 (doubled than that of 2011). In some areas, such as the eastern part of Inner Mongolia, the curtailment left more than 50% of turbines idle" (Wu 2013). Joseph Jacobelli, an independent energy analyst①, proposed the reasons behind these phenomena: "The key barrier is the current tariff-setting mechanism gives no commercial incentive whatsoever to the grids to connect and dispatch renewables... it would also take China several years to build ultra high-voltage lines needed to deliver the power produced at remote wind farms to users in the south and on the coast." (Clean Biz 2012) Therefore, grid SOEs strongly resisted the "full purchase policy" for RE power embodied in the feed-in tariff as well as the mandatory RE quota system, and lobbied paramount leaders to increase the RE transmission subsidy.

Compared with the grid SOEs' reluctance and resistance towards RE development, *five major stated-owned power generation groups*, *Huaneng*, *Datang*, *Huadian*, *Guodian and CPI*, have received more incentives to promote large-scale RE projects, especially after the issuing of the RE Law in 2005. There are two driving forces pushing them to play a leading role in RE development: *First*, they claim that they are interest losers in the energy sector compared with grid SOEs, mainly due to the low feed-in tariff for coal-thermal power. ② The grid SOEs tend to make a larger profit by lowering the purchase tariff for power enterprises and raising the retail tariff for electricity customers. Due to the promising prospect of RE development in the green market and increasingly favorable RE policies for guaranteeing a profitable space, major power SOEs have shown a strong willingness to bid for and invest in large-scale RE projects. *Second*, due to the strict requirements of the quota system, the quota for RE power in each power SOE will influence also coal thermal power development. As early as 2007, in the Mid- and Long-Term Plan for RE Development, it mentioned that "the power plants with equity installed capacity of over 5 GW shall have an equity installed capacity of non-hydro RE accounting for 3% of their total capacity by 2010, and over 8% by 2020" (State Council 9/2007). Although this regulation did not gain serious implementation and the draft RE quota system regulation did not appear until May 2012, big power enterprises have realized that a mandatory RE quota will be the key constraint for thermal power construction projects in the near future. Therefore, profitable RE projects and rich RE resources will also meet the long-run interests of

---

① He was the former head of global cleantech research at the HSBC Holdings PLC.

② Although the Pricing Department within the NDRC takes the main responsibility for energy price regulation, grid SOEs still have significant influence on the feed-in price. They try to lower the feed-in price for power generation actors and raise the retail price for consumers in order to maintain huge interest margins.

coal thermal power companies if they want to apply for more coal-thermal power projects.

Compared with other forms of RE, wind power has achieved the most rapid growth rate. When the carbon intensity reduction target was tied together with the RE development target in 2009 and RE development ranked as a key industry in the national low-carbon strategy in 2010, five big power SOEs and local SOEs competed with each other to invest in wind turbine manufacturing and large-scale wind farms with rich wind resources. Over 90% of wind power projects have been financed and constructed by the large central state-owned power enterprises and local state-owned power enterprises (REN21 2009a: 17). *China Longyuan Electric Power Group*, which is a subsidiary of Guodian Group, was the first one to hit the milestones of first, 1,000MW and later, 2,000MW in the installed capacity of wind power (REN21 2009a:17). As of the end of 2008, the total installed capacity of Longyuan was 2,800 MW, of which the 1,375 MW was newly added in 2008. Following Longyuan, Datang and Huaneng had installed capacity of 1,073 MW and 933 MW in 2008, respectively (REN21 2009a: 17). In 2011, the accumulative on-grid wind power of Guodian Group amounted to 9.81 GW, keeping it at the position of No. 1 in China. Huaneng and Datang Groups ranked second and third, respectively (Xinhua News 2012c).[①] By the end of 2011, there were approximately 60 SOEs (excluding their subsidiaries) involved in the investment and construction of wind power. Their cumulative on-grid capacity reached 37.98 GW, accounting for 79.4% of national total on-grid wind power capacity (Xinhua News 2012c). Among this, the cumulative on-grid capacity from the big five power SOEs amounted to 27.1 GW, accounting for 57% of national on-grid power (Xinhua News 2012c).

This kind of rapid expansion in wind power investment and wind farm construction by SOEs can be described as the "*wind power enclosure movement*" (Hexun News 2011). Some scholars have criticized the "wind power enclosure movement" which was initiated by SOEs and pointed out its negative impact on wind power development: due to an obviously favorable political background and a strong financial back-up, SOEs tend to seize wind farm construction rights regardless of their cost in the concession bidding projects. Large power SOEs offer a "bottom price" even lower than the production cost in the concession bidding in order to seize more wind-rich renewable energy projects. For instance, in the first off-shore wind power projects

---

① Some other power generation groups and large state-owned businesses which are new in this field, such as Three Gorges Group and Guohua Energy Investment Corporation, and also some local state-owned investors, such as Hebei Construction and Investment Group, put forward ambitious development plans with installed capacity goals of more than 10,000MW (REN21 2009a: 17).

concession bidding process, the bidding prices from the five big power SOEs were almost similar to that of the on-shore wind power (Ifeng 2013). But actually, the cost of off-shore wind power is twice that of on-shore wind power, due to its high construction and maintenance cost (Ifeng 2013). Therefore, this kind of vicious competition has led to the stagnation of off-shore wind power. ① In addition, due to the huge upfront investment, slow profit recovery, coupled with the grid-connection difficulty, the profitability of wind farms has been a serious problem plaguing the wind power industry. In this context, small- and middle-sized RE enterprises have lost ground in this vicious competition; they have been forced to retreat and face bankruptcy risks. To a certain degree, this enclosure movement constrains the innovation capacity of the RE industry and breaks the balanced-development of the RE industrial system. ②

In the 12th FYP period (2011-2015), the NEA introduced a new strategic approach for wind power development, emphasizing both centralized power grid development and distributed power grid development, in order to solve the grid-connection and curtailment problems. The distributed grid promotion will bring more chances for local small- and middle-sized RE enterprises. Nevertheless, it is undeniable that with the increasing proportion of RE, the RE branches of large power SOEs, will become active members in the pro-RE coalition and will promote RE policy change and try to overcome the grid-connection bottlenecks. It also should be noted that there is a kind of interest divergence among different power SOEs. Some power SOEs and local SOEs have invested more in coal thermal power plants and nuclear power plants, so they are laggards or on-lookers in RE policy change. Some SOEs have higher RE investment rates, and will show more willingness to promote RE policy change in order to guarantee profits.

Apart from grid and power SOEs, China's three major national oil companies—the *China National Petroleum Corporation* (*CNPC*), the *China Petroleum and Chemical Corporation* (*Sinopec*), and the *China National Off-shore Oil Corporation* (*CNOOC*) have also exerted influence on energy policy making and implementation. Since supply-biased

① In September 2010, the National Energy Administration (NEA) organized the first round of off-shore wind concession bidding projects in Jiangsu Province, aiming to build a total of 1-GW wind power capacity in near off-shore and inter-tidal areas. The winners were all state-owned enterprises (SOEs): China Datang Cooperation Renewable Power, China Power Investment, Shandong Luneng and Longyuan Power. The tariffs ranged from 0.62 *yuan*/(kW · h) to 0.74 *yuan*/(kW · h). However, as of the end of February 2012, construction had still not begun on any of the projects. See CGI (2012: 78).

② The power SOEs do not pay sufficient attention to R&D development for RE, and they have other profitability paths.

energy security is still dominant, the oil SOEs have been encouraged by the "go out" strategy to search for oil in Africa, Latin America, the Middle East and Central Asia (People Net 2005). During this process, these oil SOEs made a fortune from oil transportation and sales. In the meantime, this global oil search is seen as a significant approach for building up "national strategic oil reserves" (Finance Eastday 2011). These activities provide the opportunity for top corporate managers to interact with, as well as present proposals to, political leaders (Jakobson and Knox 2010: 27-28). However, the interests of oil SOEs are not always consistent with national objectives. ① Although the RE Law has stipulated that oil sales companies should purchase biofuels, it is hard for biofuels to enter the fuel transportation and fuel sales systems due to the strong hindrances from conventional interest groups in the state-owned oil enterprises.

Apart from oil interests, three large oil SOEs also control the transportation and sales of natural gas. With the "shale gas revolution" emerging in the U.S.②, these large oil SOEs started lobbying the paramount leaders to give shale gas exploration priority in the national energy strategy beginning in 2010 (CSGCN 2013). Shale gas is natural gas produced from shale, a type of sedimentary rock. In September 2010, Chatham House published a report entitled the "*Shale Gas Revolution*": *Hype and Reality*. According to the report, shale gas has become an increasingly important source of natural gas in the United States (CSGCN 2013) and greatly decreases the U.S.'s energy dependency on oil and natural gas imports. Based on the estimation of the U.S. Energy Information Administration, China has the world's largest reserves of the hard-to-reach gas trapped in shale rock (around 36 trillion cubic meters), even more than that of the United States (AIC News 2013). Encouraged by the "windfall of shale gas", the oil SOEs have accelerated cooperative steps with foreign energy

---

① Jakobson and Knox pointed out: "CNPC and Sinopec investments in Sudan have spurred accusations by Western governments and international human rights organizations that China is propping up the Sudanese Government, which is accused of not making concerted efforts to stop the atrocities in Darfur. Even after the NDRC's decision in 2007 to remove Sudan from a list of preferred countries for oil investments, the two Chinese oil companies purchased Sudanese assets" (Jakobson and Knox 2010: 29-30). In the RE development, there is a similar story.

② The "shale gas revolution" refers to a phenomenon that emerged in terms of domestic gas supply in the United States. Shale gas is part of what is described as "unconventional gas". Shale gas rose from less than 1% of domestic gas production in the United States in 2000 to over 20% by 2010. The Energy Information Administration projects that it will account for 46% of United States gas supply by 2035, which will lead to a kind of energy revolution. See Stevens (2012: 1).

companies owning shale gas exploration technology①, such as Royal Dutch Shell, BP and Chevron to explore for large-scale shale gas in China (AIC News 2013). For instance, CNPC, cooperating with Royal Dutch Shell launched large-scale shale gas exploration in western Sichuan Province in 2012 (CSGCN 2013). Lobbied by oil SOEs, the NEA announced the first FYP for the shale gas sector in March 2012, with output targets of 6.5 bcm in 2015 and 60-100 bcm in 2020 (Stevens 2012: 10). Then the special fund for shale gas exploration was founded in November 2012, with a subsidy level of 0.4 *yuan*/ cubic meter (Ifeng 2012). However, a new round of "Gold Rush" for shale gas would inhibit RE investment on the grounds that "the prospect of large volumes of cheap gas might appear to provide a cheaper route to a lower carbon economy than high-cost RE" (Stevens 2012: 2). In other words, the cheap shale gas will not be able to substitute for (cheap) coal but rather for (relatively expensive) RE (Stevens 2012: 1). Therefore, in the mid- to long-run, the shale gas policy promoted by the oil SOEs will have some influence on RE policy.

Growing opposition to shale gas is "driven by concerns over the environmental impact of hydraulic fracturing and the impact on greenhouse gas emissions" (Sudworth 2013). The Ministry of Environmental Protection (MEP) and environmental NGOs have increasingly spoken out on the negative environmental consequences of shale gas exploration. Wan Bentai, a general engineer of the MEP, argued that "China is a water-scarce country with large population. The fracking technology of shale gas needs a great amount of water and its chemicals injection will cause serious groundwater pollution. The shale gas projects should be undergone strict environmental impact assessment" (China News 2012b). Therefore, the pro-RE actors are making efforts to prove the environmental risks of shale gas exploration and emphasizing that shale gas can not be a substitute for RE development (see Appendix II).

Based on the special high position of SOEs, the supervisory role of the *State Electricity Regulatory Commission* (*SERC*) has been limited. As an independent supervisory agency, the SERC should be responsible for regulating China's electricity industry (power and grid enterprises), such as supervising the RE grid-connection. In 2007, the SERC issued Regulatory Measures on Off-take Purchase of Electricity from RE Sources by Grid Companies in order to foster grid-connection implementation. The SERC started requiring all power grid companies in China to preferentially purchase the maximum amount of "green" electricity generated from RE according to the above

---

① Two key technologies are especially relevant for shale gas. These are horizontal drilling and hydraulic fracturing (fracking), where water, sand and chemicals are injected into the horizontal borehole of the well at very high pressure to fracture the shale rocks and release the gas. Neither technology is new. Horizontal drilling emerged in the 1930s and the first well was fracked in the United States in 1947. See Stevens (2012: 1).

regulation (Chen 2009: 146). However, the power of this administrative regulation was rather limited mainly due to the strong resistance of two big grid SOEs. They put a one-sided emphasis on the instability of RE power and its negative impact on grid security. That is why there are increasing voices for amending the Electricity Law (which was issued in 1995), in order to guarantee grid connection and transmission of RE power in the long run.

6.3 Institutional characteristics of the pro-RE coalition in China

The authoritarian system of China is not a monolithic system. Instead, the "fragmented authoritarianism framework" is usually applied to illustrate the interaction among different institutions and stakeholders. As mentioned in Chapter 5, the absence of an Energy Ministry and an Energy Law has shown the weak institution building in the energy sector. Based on the analysis of key actors in the RE policy system, it can be seen that although institutional reform in the energy sector has not been as successful as expected, there are many newly-established institutions dealing with climate change, RE development and low-carbon economy. They have emerged through the climate change socialization process. These pro-RE actors emerged and became stronger through their institutional anchoring and ability to access more resources. Through institutional lock-in effects, these newly-established institutions gained more authority and political resources helping them to defend their own interests. They now have louder voice and power in the RE policy-making system, especially since the climate change and low-carbon economy concept have gained more political salience.

Apart from governmental actors, more and more societal actors are playing a proactive role in RE governance. They show their willingness to cooperate with governmental actors. They include RE research centers in universities, RE industry associations, environmental NGOs and media power. Figure 6.1 shows the key governmental and societal actors in the RE policy making system. I use text boxes with different colors to illustrate the newly-established institutions in the RE governance system. The white text boxes are original institutions in the RE governance already there in the early 1990s; the light-gray ones emerged when the SDPC/NDRC took main responsibility for the climate change negotiations in 1998; the dark-gray ones emerged after China issued the National Climate Change Program in 2007.

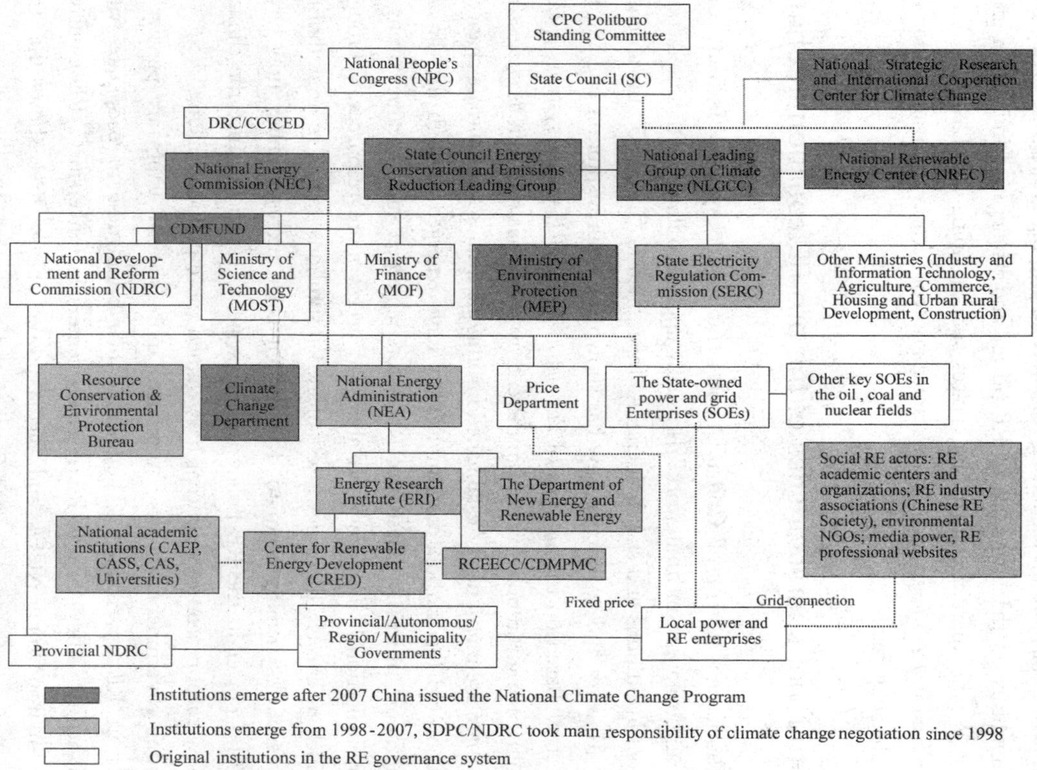

Figure 6.1 Key governmental and societal actors in the RE policy system of China

Abbreviations: RCEECC the Research Center for Energy Environment and Climate Change; CDMPMC the CDM Project Management Center within ERI; CCICED the China Council for International Cooperation on Environment and Development; CAEP the Chinese Academy for Environmental Planning; CASS the Chinese Academy of Social Science; CAS the Chinese Academy of Science

Source: Drawn by the author.

Based on the author's analysis of key governmental and societal actors in the RE policy system, this section summarizes five characteristics of the pro-RE coalition:

First, there has been obvious institutional change in the pro-RE coalition, not only in the increased number of pro-RE actors, but also in the upgrading of their hierarchical rank. Although China's climate change policy was criticized as being just a "supplement of energy policy" (the NDRC was criticized as a hardliner pursuing GDPism), the institutional change within the SDPC/NDRC has formed a stronger channel to bind China's climate change commitment and RE development together. A typical case is the establishment of the Center for Renewable Energy Development (CRED) in 1998 in parallel with the Research Center for Energy Environment and Climate Change (RCEECC) within the ERI, in order to provide knowledge support and policy proposals for the climate change negotiations and CDM project implementation. The ERI works as a key consulting agency to provide policy proposals and policy drafts for the NEA and the NDRC. The CRED in the ERI has played a significant role in taking the lead in RE research, especially in studying the RE experiences of pioneering countries and drafting key RE legislative documents and RE administrative regulations for the NDRC. Promoted by the research of the CRED, the NDRC introduced tendering policy to the large-scale wind-power concession bidding projects beginning in 2003. Apart from the CRED, the Department of New Energy and Renewable Energy (DNERE), which was established in 2001 under the NDRC, was also spawned from the socialization process of climate change, since the CRED is only a research institute and the NDRC needs a special bureaucratic agency to supervise RE development, set industrial standards for RE and coordinate policy implementation of large-scale RE projects. When the National Energy Bureau (NEB) was established in 2003, the DNERE became an important department of the NEB, influencing energy policy change towards RE. In addition, there have been more institutional changes in the high-level bureaucratic system related to energy regulation and RE governance. The emergence of high-level bureaucratic institutions, such as the NLGCC, the NCSC and the CNREC, has symbolized the unprecedented national attention given to climate change and RE development: these domestic bureaucracies/window agencies have been established according to the institutional requirements of the climate change negotiations and climate mitigation actions.

Second, the NDRC has remained in a central position and continues to coordinate RE governance. Although the influence of societal actors has increased as RE policy-making has become more pluralistic, governmental actors still play the most direct and significant role in promoting RE policy change. Since the NDRC is the most powerful governmental agency in the bureaucratic system responsible for macroeconomic planning and energy regulation, it plays a central role in the governmental coordination of RE policy-making and implementation. During the institutional anchoring process, the pro-RE coalition gained opportunities to strengthen its position, especially having its own interest representatives in the central governmental agencies, like the institutional change within the NDRC. China has gradually learned the significance of RE development in a green growth approach and the institutional lock-in effect has exerted its functional influence on RE policy change. Even though the NDRC still has a deep-rooted stance prone to economic development, once paramount leaders making a climate mitigation commitment at the international level, the NDRC has greater capacity to coordinate the implementation of climate change targets. The Pricing Department under the NDRC has played a significant role in cooperating with the Ministry of Finance (MOF) in putting the FIT policy into effect. A significant step was the introduction of the carbon-intensity reduction and RE proportion targets introduced before the Copenhagen Conference in 2009, which linked climate change directly with RE development. According to this general target, the NDRC has promoted the issuing of concrete RE targets under the 12th FYP for RE Development. Furthermore, since the NDRC has strong local branches, the general target has been broken down onto the provincial level in order to facilitate implementation. It also should be noted that the NDRC is not a monolithic agency; instead, there are many groups with different interest tendencies, such as grid SOEs and oil SOEs that have their own speakers within the NDRC. Along with the increasing institutional anchoring of climate change and RE agencies within the NDRC, the general stance of the NDRC has become less hardline and more flexible. To a certain degree, the climate change negotiations task taken on by the NDRC has pressured this agency to promote carbon reduction. This has gradually promoted the green policy integration process within the bureaucratic system.

Third, key governmental research institutes and think tanks have increasing influence on the RE policy-making process. While the NDRC has played a dominant role in the RE policy-making process, its subordinate research agency, the CRED under the ERI has played a pivotal and authoritative role in providing RE policy suggestions and taking the responsibility of drafting RE policies. Based on its comparative studies of best international practices in RE development as well as their own innovative RE policy instruments, the CRED began to investigate the feasibility of different policy instruments and promoted the formulation of the RE Law. Through offering RE policy drafts, annual reports and policy advice for the NEA and the NDRC, the CRED has played a key role in the RE policy-making process. These laws and regulatory drafts are submitted to the NEA first, and then handed to the NDRC. The NDRC has the authority to ratify RE administrative regulations with the permission of the State Council; the RE legislative drafts need the final ratification of the National People's Congress (NPC).① In 2012, the CRED was upgraded to a national-level research institution—the CNREC, which assists the State Council in promoting RE policy system improvement. In addition, other governmental research institutes as well as the social academic institutes and RE research centers in the universities have played a supportive role in promoting improvements in RE policy system and provide professional policy advice for governmental agencies. The NCSC established in 2011 is a high-level think tank working on climate change. It focuses on strategic research and international cooperation. It has close cooperative relations with the CNREC on RE development research. The CCICED is responsible for exchanging and disseminating successful international experiences and best practices in the field of environment and development, and putting forward policy recommendations to national leaders through its Annual General Meeting. The Chinese Academy for Environmental Planning (CAEP) under the SEPA has played an increasingly significant role in promoting the integration of environmental taxes, especially a carbon tax into the energy sector. Furthermore, the Chinese Academy of Science (CAS) and the Chinese Academy of Social Science (CASS), have played a leading role in drawing more academic resources for RE and low-carbon research: for instance, the CAS established the Center for Energy and Environmental Policy Research (CEEP) in 2006 to promote the environment-friendly energy system construction. The CASS established the Chinese Urban Low-carbon Economy Network (ULCEN) to promote local RE and low-carbon economy construction. In sum, the research institutes have gained more authoritative power in the policy-making process.

Fourth, societal actors have played an increasingly proactive role in RE governance, showing their willingness to cooperate with governmental research agencies as well as exerting societal power to expose RE policy weaknesses. Apart from the significant role of research agencies in RE policy change, the societal actors, like RE industry associations and professional RE websites also played an increasingly active role in the RE policy improvement process. For instance, the Chinese Renewable Energy Society (CRES) is the earliest-founded RE social association (1976) in China. Now it includes several sub-associations for different renewables, the Solar Photovoltaic Society (1976 the earliest association of Chinese RE Society), the Chinese Wind Energy Association (established in 1981), the Solar Thermal Utilization Association, the Solar Building Association and Biomass Energy Association. These associations are promoters and supervisors of RE

① The NPC rarely plays a veto role in the law which is supported by the NDRC.

industries. They promote technological innovation and the diffusion of advanced RE technology, the commercialization of RE, and RE industrial standards for orderly management. They also are interest representatives of RE industries, acting as a channeling bridge between governmental agencies and RE industries; they fight for a more favorable policy context for RE and reflect RE development problems as well as policy loopholes to the relevant governmental agencies in order to improve RE policy designing. The annual RE industry reports and professional special investigation reports provide more policy evaluation and assessment information for the RE policy maker, helping them to make relevant policy change to improve the RE policy system. With the development of RE industry associations, the role of the mass media, especially the professional RE websites, has also been strengthened. Compared to the TV, news and blogs, the professional RE websites, can provide lasting, stable, professional and systematical information about the RE industry. These websites have played an indispensable role in providing up-to-date RE policy information and keeping information transparency, especially in relation to RE policy implementation and grid-connection status at the local level. Some websites also provide expert analyses about RE policy and interviews with key figures in the government or research institutes. These send indispensable policy signals to RE industries. The policy implementation problems on the website stimulate heated social discussions and argumentation, which in turn can spur indirect but massive social influence on the RE policy change process.

Fifth, state-owned power enterprises (SOEs) have played a dominant role in RE generation. A special phenomenon in RE development is the dominant pattern of state-owned enterprises (SOEs), especially after the issuance of the RE Law. When CDM projects and wind-power concession bidding projects were launched around 2002-2003, some small- and middle-sized private enterprises became active investors in RE. Some local governments also showed their eagerness to green fixed assets investment, by investing in wind farms (China Venture 2011). The issuing of the RE Law sent a positive policy signal to the whole RE industry. It guaranteed a profitable space for the RE industry from a legal perspective. Since then, power SOEs have shown their interests in going after this "Green Gold". Large-scale RE projects are usually monopolized by the SOEs, which enjoy a more favorable political context and better financial support and have capital strength (China Venture 2011). Compared with small- and middle-sized private RE enterprises, these more powerful SOEs have much stronger capacities and financial advantages (easier access to national subsidies and bank loans), which are necessary to invest in large-scale RE projects, especially in concession bidding for RE projects. Due to the "special identity" of SOEs, they can take advantage of their greater political and market resources to promote RE development. ① Some scholars point out that there are two main aims for SOEs to invest in RE: the first are the cost and benefit concerns tied to the constraining effects of the mandatory RE quotas that will be coming in the future. The second stimulating factor is the expectation for profits from RE development (Hexun News 2011). With the electricity market reform, the dual-track coal price was abolished in the end of 2012. Power plants cannot buy coal under the market price as they could before. ② The production costs of coal thermal plants are mainly from their raw material input, that is coal. The rising price of coal will greatly increase the production cost of the thermal plants, and then leading to the rising price of coal electricity. ③ In this context, RE power will become more competitive due to decreasing production costs tied to technological innovation. Furthermore, the ambitious national target of RE power for 2015 has had a strong dynamic effect and drawn more investment from SOEs.

---

① It can be estimated that within the next few years China's large-scale RE investments (on-shore wind farm, off-shore wind farm, solar PV power and biomass power) will still mainly be occupied by the large SOEs; small- and middle-sized RE enterprises will only take a smaller market share.

② The dual-track coal price system in China ("planned coal" and "market coal") means that coal is sold at government-regulated contract prices and open-market prices, respectively. See Pu (2012). The main aim of dual-tracking in the past was to guarantee profits of coal thermal plants (ease their cost pressures) and to stabilize national electricity prices: the coal power companies can buy thermal coal at a contract price much lower than the market price. The contract price is usually set in an annual negotiation between power groups and coal producers held at the end of the year, and NDRC as a broker promotes consensus-reaching. See Want Chinatimes (2012).

③ The Chinese government formally issued a guideline to abolish administrative controls on coal prices for power generation in December 2012, including cancelling the regulations on a thermal coal price cap, preferences for the annual major coal supply contracts for power companies, as well as railway transportation quotas for thermal coal and emphasizing that local governments can not be allowed to interfere. See Pu (2012).

Chapter 7
The Role of the Strengthened Pro-RE Coalition in RE Policy Change: The Introduction of the Quota System to Combine with the FIT

After five years of rapid development from 2005 to 2010, more and more problems emerged in the RE policy system, such as grid connection bottlenecks, wind-turbine grid disconnection accidents, wind power curtailments and overcapacity of wind turbines and solar panels. These problems are linked to each other. If grid connection and transmission problems of wind and solar PV power are solved, the overcapacity of wind turbines and solar panels would be addressed in the domestic RE market. Since feed-in tariffs for wind power, biomass and solar PV power were settled after 2009, there has been increasing demand from pro-RE actors to introduce the mandatory quota system to combine with the feed-in tariff policy, with the aim of resolving the grid connection and transmission problems. The goal of this chapter is to explore the role of the pro-RE coalition in RE policy change by means of policy-oriented learning and argumentative persuasion. The analysis focuses on the introduction of the quota system to the RE policy system: how the pro-RE coalition competes with conventional actors to introduce the mandatory RE quota system to combine it with the FIT policy and what this means to a green transformation of China.

7.1 From the feed-in tariff policy to introducing the quota system

Wang Zhongying, the director of the China National Renewable Energy Center (CNREC) and the deputy director of Energy Research Institute (ERI) of the NDRC, proposed that "the current RE policy making has entered 'a deep water area': problems of current RE development are more likely caused by the imperfect policy system rather than technical hindrance, although the technological innovation is also a key factor influencing RE development" (Xie 2012). With the rapid development of large-scale RE projects in the past decade, the interest confrontation between the pro-RE coalition and the conventional interest groups (such as state grid companies, coal-fired power stations, the state-owned oil enterprises and nuclear power companies, local actors) has been reinforced. For instance, more and more RE development problems have emerged: the grid connection problem, wind power curtailment, wind-turbine grid disconnection accidents, and sales channel blockage of bio-fuels. The core question at this stage is how to break the systematic hindrance of the coal-dominated energy mix and integrate RE into the current energy system. Further RE development still needs continuous supportive RE policies from the central government, such as fostering the implementation of the mandatory quota system.

7.1.1 Comparing the three RE policy instruments used in China

Apart from RE fiscal subsidies (special fund, favorable tax rates, low-interest loans), there are three main RE policy instruments being applied in China as mentioned in Chapter 3: the tendering system (since 2003 and based on the former U.K. model), the feed-in tariff system (FIT) (beginning in 2005 and based on the German model) and the quota system (based on the U.S. model and combined with the FIT beginning in 2009). A comparison of these three policy instruments is found in Table 7.1.

Table 7.1 Comparison of three RE policy instruments used in China

	Tendering	Feed-in tariff	RPS/ quota system
Basic functional mechanism	Governmental project-led. Based on the lowest bid price.	Price-based. Providing a long-term guaranteed price for RE generators (such as 20 years).	Market-based. Requiring quite mature market for green certificate trading.
General advantages	A transition policy to provide a relatively high degree of certainty and stability for RE development in the early stage.	The FIT guarantees a profitable space for RE generators; ensures RE diversity and local industry infrastructure development.	The RPS realizes price minimization; promotes inter-regional complementarities of capital and resources through a green certificate trading system.
Main purpose behind adoption	To establish a price-base for the FIT or the RPS through bidding competition.	To secure sufficient profit space for RE generators; promote rapid RE development within a short time.	To solve the grid-connection and curtailment problems based on a market-based tool.
Main RE structural problems in China	Vicious competition leading to bid prices that are lower than the cost price; the monopoly of state-owned power enterprises.	Grid-connection and curtailment problems; the monopoly of state-owned grid enterprises.	The market economy system in China is immature, hard to apply Green Certificate System; only as a complement for the FIT at the current stage.

Source: Drawn by the author.

The tendering policy is "using competitive bidding process to select projects that offer the best price" (Wiser et al. 2002: 7). The main goal of a tendering policy is to promote large-scale RE development with concession bidding projects even if vicious price competition occurs. In China, large state-owned power enterprises have a great advantage over small- and middle-sized RE enterprises and can more easily win in the bidding process as they can introduce lower price. Since the FIT for wind power was finally settled in 2009, the tendering policy is still only applied to off-shore wind park construction and large-scale solar PV projects, whose generation prices are comparatively high. The feed-in tariff policy (FIT) refers to a price-based policy which offers RE developers a guaranteed power sales price, coupled with a purchase obligation (a guaranteed market) by electric utilities in a relatively long time (such as 20 years) (Mendonça et al. 2010; Wiser et al. 2002). The RE Law which was issued in 2005, stipulated three key principles to promote the implementation of the feed-in tariff policy: a mandatory connection and purchase policy; fixed feed-in electricity prices for different RE power generators; and a cost-sharing mechanism, which is funded by a surcharge on electricity sales in order to support the RE feed-in tariff and grid connection projects. Of these three principles, only the fixed feed-in electricity price for wind power generators was realized by 2009, and bottlenecks in grid-connection and curtailment continued to impede RE development. ①

The quota system is defined as a market-based mechanism that generally places an obligation on electricity supply companies to produce a specified fraction of their electricity from RE sources (Jaccard 2004; Wiser et al. 2002). Compared with the FIT, the quota system relies more on the private market for its implementation and claims that "market implementation will result in competition, efficiency and innovation that will deliver RE at the lowest possible cost" (Chen et al. 2007; Cory and Swezey 2007). Two main supportive mechanisms for a quota system are the trading of green certificates/RE certificates (RECs) and the cost-sharing mechanism in the electricity market. The quota system needs a more mature market than the FIT to

① The NDRC has officially set the feed-in tariff for wind power through issuing the Notice on Policy to Improve Grid-Connected Power Pricing for Wind Power in 2009 [0.51 *yuan*/(kW · h), 0.54 *yuan*/(kW · h), 0.58 *yuan*/(kW · h), 0.61 *yuan*/(kW · h) for four different wind-resources regions respectively]; set the feed-in tariff for biomass [0.75 *yuan*/(kW · h)] through issuing the Standard for Feed-in Policy of National Unified Agricultural and Forestry Biomass in 2010, and set feed-in tariff for solar PV power through issuing the Notice on Feed-in Policy of Solar Photovoltaic in 2011 [1 *yuan*/(kW · h), 1.15 *yuan*/(kW · h)].

guarantee the operationalization of RECs. ①

Both the FIT and the quota system aim to solve the problem of high generation cost in RE development, therefore they usually do not coexist within one RE policy system. However, China has its own special national conditions. Although China has an FIT policy to guarantee profits for RE generators, the grid-connection problem and curtailment problem became worse due to the strong resistance from the state-owned power and grid enterprises. Through introducing a quota system combined with the FIT, the pro-RE coalition aims to set a mandatory RE quota for the grid and power SOEs and to coordinate RE planning between the central and the provincial governments. There are three main advantages to combine the quota system with the FIT: *First*, the quota system sets concrete mandatory RE quotas for the power and grid enterprises, which forces conventional interest groups to integrate RE generation and transmission into the carbon lock-in system, such as pressing the grid enterprises to accelerate the construction of RE-friendly smart power grids. *Second*, the implementation of the quota system will spur an electricity market reform and a reliance on market forces to drive RE development. Especially once the NDRC issued the Notice on Carbon Trading Trials Scheme in 2011 to initiate carbon-trading trials (Wang, T. 2012b), RE quotas could be transferred to RE certificates directly and enhance the carbon-trading system. *Third*, the quota system is conducive to the sharing of the benefits and responsibilities of RE production between the western and eastern regions of China (Langniss and Wiser 2003). ② Eastern electricity companies can achieve their RE quota by buying tradable RE certificates or by exploiting RE resources in western regions (Langniss and Wiser 2003).

Based on the comparison in Table 7.1, there are three tendencies in China's RE policy change: *first*, from the single RE policy instrument (tendering system) to a comprehensive RE policy system (FIT as the main RE policy instrument, which is complemented by the RE quota system and the tendering policy); *second*, from only putting emphasis on the installation capability of RE to focusing on both "quantity" and "quality" dimensions of RE development, and aiming to solve the grid-connection and curtailment problems by introducing the mandatory quota system. At the same

① RECs is a market-based mechanism, in which certified RE generators earn certificates for every unit of electricity they produce and can sell these certificates along with their electricity to supply companies. Supply companies then pass the certificates to some form of regulatory body to demonstrate their compliance with their regulatory obligations.

② Western China has rich renewable resources, especially strong wind and much space for solar PV; however, the economic development of western China has fallen far behind the eastern coastal areas, where there is high demand for large amounts of energy.

time, the government has begun to limit the disorderly development of local RE; and *third*, turning from mainly governmental project-led RE projects (concession bidding projects for wind power and solar PV power) to promoting the market-oriented reform of RE development, especially attempting to combine the RE quota system with the carbon trading pilot trials in order to enhance the GHG emission reductions and stimulate further RE development through market forces. After the 2009 Copenhagen Conference, the carbon-intensity reduction target and RE development target were tied together according to the national leader's commitment. Against this backdrop, pro-RE actors are finding a more favorable political atmosphere to promote RE policy change and electricity market reform, although they still have a bumpy path ahead of them since they are confronted with strong resistance from the conventional interest groups in the energy sector.

7.1.2 The bumpy path to the introduction of the mandatory RE quota system

To a certain degree, the RE Law in 2005 was a kind of compromised policy outcome, since it did not clarify the mandatory quota for grid enterprises to purchase RE as well as a penalty for deviations. Although some actors in the pro-RE coalition once attempted to introduce the quota system into a RE draft law in the earlier stage, this proposal was rejected due to strong resistance from grid enterprises and coal thermal plants. When the RE Law came into effect in 2006, some pro-RE actors in the ERI and in other research institutes began to explore the feasibility of combining the RE quota system with the FIT, considering the immature condition of China's market economy. In 2007, Xie Zhenhua, the former director of the State Environmental Protection Administration (SEPA) was nominated as the deputy director of the NDRC to take charge of the climate change negotiations. The first National Climate Change Program was issued by the NDRC in the same year. Stimulated by this context, the voice from the pro-RE coalition to introduce the quota system to combine with the feed-in tariff emerged again in 2007, which was embodied in the mandated market share (MMS) regulation in the Mid- and Long-Term Development Plan for Renewable Energy. This plan was the first national mid- and long-term plan for RE development (State Council 9/2007). According to the MMS, "It is required that the power plants with equity installed capacity of over 5 GW shall have an equity installed capacity of non-hydro RE accounting for 3% of their total capacity by 2010, and over 8% by 2020" (State Council 9/2007). However, the RE quota regulation in MMS was not taken seriously by conventional stakeholders. It was not carried into implementation effectively and failed to constrain the behavior of the main power and grid actors.

Since then, the pro-RE actors have begun to take advantage of international as well as domestic resources to promote further RE policy change. At the international level, with the increasing reputational pressure from the climate change regime, the pro-RE coalition has taken efforts to prove that RE is one of the most effective ways to reduce GHG emissions. Especially due to the successful performance of RE development beginning in 2005, national leaders have become more confident about linking the carbon intensity target with the RE development target. At the domestic level, more and more investigative reports and expert critiques on RE development from the pro-RE coalition (RE industry associations, low-carbon and RE research institutes, and professional RE websites) have emerged and attracted societal concern. These investigative reports and professional online critiques from experts have exposed policy loopholes in the RE system. Most of the problems can be summarized as grid connection and transmission bottlenecks. These domestic resources have been applied by the pro-RE coalition to challenge the validity of conventional energy forces. The Regulation for Management of Renewable Power Quota (Exposure Draft) was finally released by the NDRC in May 2012. Whether the draft will be ratified in the future or not depends on the competition among pro-RE coalition and conventional energy forces.

From 2007 to 2015, the nine-year long efforts have shown that introducing the quota system to assure that grid operators are accepting a certain amount of electricity generated from wind or other renewable resources was confronted with many forces of resistance. At first sight, the argumentation in favor of the FIT and the quota system only relates to the RE policy instruments level, however, introducing and fostering the implementation of the RE quota system will have a greater impact on constraining the behavior of conventional interest groups in the energy sector. Without the strong political support from the national carbon-intensity reduction strategy and the 12th Five-Year Plan for RE development, the Regulation for Management of Renewable Power Quota (Exposure Draft) could not have come into being. In the interest game and resources-reallocation process, the role of the pro-RE coalition in trying to introduce the quota policy draft for social discussion is indispensable. In the process of drafting the mandatory RE quota system, the pro-RE coalition endeavors to clarify the concrete RE quota for power generation enterprises, grid enterprises as well as provincial actors. As Meng Xiangan, the vice-president of the China Renewable Energy Society (CRES) said, "the quota mechanism is exactly designed to solve the problem of who will generate wind power, who will buy wind power, and who will use wind power" (CRES 2012).

7.2 Policy-oriented learning in RE policy change

According to Sabatier's ACF framework, policy-oriented learning refers to "relatively enduring alterations of thought or behavioral intentions that result from experience and which are concerned with the attainment or revision of the precepts of the belief system of individuals or of collectivities" (Sabatier and Jenkins-Smith 1993b: 42). China has a "learning by doing" tradition, which could be traced back to the Deng Xiaoping era that began in the late 1970s. Deng encouraged an incremental policy reform and policy innovation relying on the trial and error exercise of policy experimentations. China is a latecomer in RE development field, and pro-RE actors have become main supporters leading the RE policy-oriented learning and promoting rapid RE development. With increasing pluralization of the policy-making process in the "fragmented authoritarianism" framework, new actors, such as research institutes, social RE industry associations, environmental NGOs and professional RE websites, have used their voices to call for policy change. Policy-oriented learning normally "entails experimenting with a variety of guidance instruments and other implementing mechanisms" (Sabatier and Jenkins-Smith 1993b: 44), and these pro-RE actors have attempted to increase the feasibility and the scientific basis of their policy proposals through learning. This has been done in order to solve problems in the RE policy system and promote rational RE development in the coal-dominated energy mix.

7.2.1 Implications of the "learning by doing" way for RE policy change

The "learning by doing" way of China dates back to the early stage of opening-up policy in the Deng Xiaoping era. In 1979, Deng proposed the creation of special economic zones with favorable economic policies in order to speed up the market economy reform trials and accumulate more experience with reform for use in other areas in China. In 1980, the 15th meeting of the Fifth National People's Congress Standing Committee decided to approve the decision of the State Council to establish special economic zones in four cities: Shenzhen, Zhuhai and Shantou in Guangdong Province, as well as Xiamen in Fujian Province (China Gate 2012). Later, the successful performance of these trial cities set good examples for other places. Problems that emerged could be solved in time due to relatively quick feed-back (China Gate 2012). It was felt that the prosperous development of the trial cities might subsequently be a basis for the promotion of large-scale market economic reforms. In the policy-making process, the "learning by doing" pattern presents an incremental process: learning from the experience of pioneering countries, policy entrepreneurs in

China attempt to prove the feasibility of new policies to solve newly emerging problems and promote innovative policy instruments to be integrated into the policy system. Due to interest conflicts among different stakeholders in the policy-making system, paramount national leaders typically conduct policy trials on a small-scale in order to gain experience before introducing change on a large scale.

This ideological path can also explain the abstract characteristics of the legislative framework in China. As discussed in Chapter 3, basic laws like the RE law are usually "considered vague and abstract, and leave much room for interpretation when it comes to policy implementation" (Lee 2012: 15). There is more flexibility for policy improvement; the effective implementation of basic laws depends on the support of subsequent administrative regulations. During the policy implementation process, different interest groups and advocacy coalitions have more space to influence a law's interpretation and translate their own willingness into administrative regulations. Pro-RE actors attempt to take the lead to expose RE policy loopholes and errors in policy experimentation and provide more policy improvement proposals, although anti-RE actors have different interpretations of policy implementation results. Liu (2013) summarizes this way of "learning by doing" in China:

> In China, the policy-making process can be concluded as incremental, and heavily relies on the trial and error exercise of policy experimentation. Ineffective laws were amended and new regulations were revised and added to the policy mix. In addition, decentralizing is a very important part of reform, but policy experimentation and change are heavily directed by the central government and remain to be under its control. (Liu 2013: 10)

In the field of RE development, as a late comer, China also followed a "learning by doing" pattern, putting much emphasis on policy trials of demonstration and pilot projects. In order to avoid unnecessary mistakes and setback failures, pilot programs and demonstration projects introduced on a small scale were seen as a better approach to carry out innovative RE policies, to correct errors in a timely manner, and to accumulate experience through learning by doing. The successful performance achieved in the pilot programs and demonstration projects boosted national confidence that an expansion to a larger scale, even to a nation-wide scale could be successful. As early as 2003, the CRED introduced the tendering policy (concession bidding policy) to China and suggested the NDRC apply this policy to promote large-scale wind power. By the end of 2009, six rounds of concessional biddings for wind power had been executed; they have greatly pushed forward the development of wind power. With this successful experience, the pattern of concession bidding was applied in the development of large-scale grid-connected solar PV power stations and off-shore wind power projects. In addition, the NDRC launched the Low-Carbon Pilot Cities and Provinces Project in August 2010; five provinces (Guangdong, Liaoning, Hubei, Shaanxi, Yunnan) and eight cities (Tianjin, Chongqing, Shenzhen, Xiamen, Hangzhou, Nanchang, Guiyang, Baoding) have acted as low-carbon pilots to demonstrate the feasibility of low-carbon development plans and RE application in urban life. In 2011, the Ministry of Transport (MOT) initiated pilot projects for the construction of low-carbon transport systems, through employing low-carbon vehicles, optimizing transport planning and operating methods, improving public transport information services, and establishing and improving carbon emissions management (NDRC 11/2012). Ten cities—Tianjin, Chongqing, Shenzhen, Xiamen, Hangzhou, Nanchang, Guiyang, Baoding, Wuxi and Wuhan—were selected to carry out the initial trials. A further 16 cities—Beijing, Kunming, Xi'an, Ningbo, Guangzhou, Shenyang, Harbin, Huai'an, Yantai, Haikou, Chengdu, Qingdao, Zhuzhou, Bengbu, Shiyan and Jiyuan—were named the second batch of pilot cities in February, 2012 (NDRC 11/2012). During the 12th FYP, the NEA announced that they are intending to build 100 new energy demonstration cities to promote the development and application of new energy in cities (Wang, Z. et al. 2012: 187-188).

In the "learning by doing" process, comprehensive policy design and policy assessment are of great importance. Due to insufficient experience and relatively weak policy research, RE development targets which were set in the Mid- and Long-Term Development Plan for RE in 2007 were rather un-scientific. According to the plan, the installation capacity target of wind energy was set at 10 GW by 2010 and 30 GW by 2020 (State Council 9/2007). However, these targets severely underestimated the rapid development of wind energy; the installed capacity of wind energy in 2010 reached 44.7 GW, even surpassing the 2020 target and in 2011 reached 62.36 GW (Wang, Z. et al. 2010: 235). In contrast to the rapid development of wind energy, it has proven to be rather difficult to achieve the targets set for bio-liquid fuels and biomass power. Neither biogas nor bio-ethanol achieved the 11th FYP targets. The development of bio-liquid fuel is constrained by the immature second generation bio-fuel technology and the national "non-grain" policy. There is a great gap between biomass objectives and raw material availability for their generation. The original target for biomass power was 30 GW by 2015 (Wang, Z. et al. 2010: 235), but the installed capacity target for biomass power was reduced to 13 GW by 2015 in the 12th FYP (NEA 8/2012). In summary, the designing of RE development targets as well as policy instruments application should be based on scientific research assessments and feed-back error correction mechanisms in the "learning by doing" process.

7.2.2 Policy-oriented learning promoted by the pro-RE coalition: combining the quota system with the FIT

The Center for Renewable Energy Development (CRED) under the ERI is the key pro-RE actor leading RE policy-oriented learning and taking charge of drafting the RE policy regulations and providing policy recommendations for the NDRC. As a governmental research institution, the CRED has launched a series of comparative research projects on various RE policy instruments in different western countries (especially the former U.K. model, the German model, and the U.S. model), in order to explore the effectiveness and feasibility of measures to stimulate the industrialization process of large-scale RE development and provide policy proposals for governmental decision making (for direct submission to the NDRC). Since China ratified the Kyoto Protocol in 2002, this research team took the main responsibility for drafting the RE Law and the Catalogue for the Guidance of RE Industry Development in April 2003, which laid a foundation for the establishment of a RE policy system (Schuman and Lin 2012: 95). In the transition to a combined quota system and FIT, the CRED became the main governmental research agency promoting policy-oriented learning. It explored effective methods for constraining the behavior of stakeholders blocking RE grid connection and transmission and investigating the compatibility of the mandatory RE quota plus the FIT system beginning in 2007.

The CRED also paid attention to promoting cooperation with international institutions, such as the GEF, the World Bank, the UNDP, the IEA, and the Asia Development Bank (ADB) (CRED 2009). The most important cooperative project influencing the policy-oriented learning and RE policy change process is the China Renewable Energy Scale-up Program (CRESP), which is supported by the WB and the GEF under the climate change regime beginning in 2006. In addition to providing international material incentives to stimulate RE development, another aim of the CRESP is to improve the RE Law cooperating with the CRED (CRESP 2010). The CRESP made it feasible to combine policy studies with international experience and invited international experts to participate in the study (WPO 2009). Cooperating with the CRESP, the CRED began to absorb best practices of RE policy instruments and explore the feasibility of the quota system and its compatibility with the FIT in order to overcome the grid-connection bottleneck for RE development. The CRESP and the CRED carried out the Implementation of RE Quota System (Exposure Draft) (CRESP 2010). Furthermore, the CRESP proposed amendments and recommendations for 5 supporting regulations, including the Mid- and Long-Term Development Planning of RE, the RE Electricity Price and Cost Distribution Management Methods, and the RE Industrial Guidance Directors for NPC's social discussion, in order to modify and improve the RE law (CRESP 2010).

Some societal pro-RE actors, such as academic research institutes in the universities, RE industry associations and professional RE websites played an active role in promoting policy-oriented learning in RE governance. These societal actors called to amend the RE Law in order to address policy loopholes, especially to explore a feasible way to combine the quota system with the FIT in order to guarantee RE grid-connection. The idea was to arm the RE Law with more "teeth" to constrain conventional energy forces. The efforts of pro-RE actors were reflected in the RE Law Amendment in 2009. However, the most important principle "guarantee the system of safeguards for the purchase of the full amount of power generated from RE" is still subject to administrative rules.

With the efforts of the pro-RE coalition, the quota system was highlighted in the Decision on Accelerating the Cultivation and Development of Strategic Emerging Industries in 2010. In 2012, the CRED was upgraded to the high-level national think tank—CNREC, which has more authority and power in RE policy making, as it can submit policy change proposals directly to the State Council. Based on the policy-oriented learning of the CNREC, the Management of Renewable Power Quota (Exposure Draft) was issued by the NDRC in May 2012. After the six-year long effort to introduce a mandatory RE quota into the RE policy system promoted by the pro-RE coalition, this regulation set a concrete RE quota that constrains the conventional energy forces: it proposes a 15% RE power quota for power enterprises and 5% for grid enterprises by 2015 and different RE quotas for local actors. Nevertheless, this is still draft legislation for social discussion and not a formal regulation. Different stakeholders hold different views about the fixed RE quotas, and conventional interest groups have tried to block the ratification of this regulation.

During policy-oriented learning, the policy transition to introducing a mandatory RE quota to combine with the FIT also leaned on the national energy intensity reduction targets and carbon intensity reduction strategies embodied in the Five-Year Plan. In the FYP designing process, some high-level advisory agencies played a significant role in promoting China's policy innovation in low-carbon development and green economic transformation. Under Li Keqiang's leadership, the CCICED established Task Forces and Special Policy Studies, composed of many domestic and foreign experts, who work on key issues on ecological process of development and put forward policy recommendations for the FYP based on their research. At the high-level Annual General Meeting, the leaders in the State Council attend the meeting to listen to the policy recommendations directly (CCICED 2012a). In the CCICED's annual reports, RE development has gained an increasingly higher priority. These reports introduced many recommendations for RE policy improvement based on best international practices and the promotion of successful policy learning and innovation, such as China's Low-Carbon Industrialization Strategy (CCICED 2012a), the Development Mechanism and Policy Innovation of China's Green Economy (CCICED 2011b). ①

The CCICED is an influential organization building a bridge to link key figures in the State Council (especially the officials from Ministry of Foreign Affairs, the NDRC, the Ministry of Finance, and the Ministry of Commerce) and the experts in the sustainable and low-carbon development fields. Therefore, it has great influence on the Five-Year Plan. In 2012, under efforts from the CNREC and the CCICED, the issuing of 12th FYP for RE Development by the NDRC symbolized a significant cognitive transition from a green transformation in the RE policy system. It makes clear ambitious RE development targets, especially proposing that electricity generation from renewable sources should account for more than 20% of total electricity generation by 2015. Soon after, a series of 12th FYP policies for wind, solar and biomass power, and new energy automobiles were drafted by the CNREC. In the current RE policy system, mandatory RE quotas have put significant constraints on conventional energy forces.

7.3 Argumentative persuasion and RE policy change

According to Sabatier's ACF analysis, different advocacy coalitions compete with each other and attempt to translate their own beliefs and policy proposals into the governmental programs in the subsystem (Sabatier 1988; Sabatier 2007; Sabatier and Jenkins-Smith 1993b). As mentioned in the theoretical chapter, apart from policy-oriented learning, argumentative persuasion is also a significant strategy for the advocacy coalition to realize its policy target. This book defines argumentative persuasion as the newly strengthened coalition challenging the validity and causal assumptions of the conventional coalition's policy initiatives and stimulating the inner reflection process by criticizing the defects and limitations of former policy strategies, and attempting to provide convincing policy strategy alternatives (see Chapter 2).

---

① On the CCICED Annual General Meeting in December 2012, premier minister Li Keqiang delivered an important opening speech related to building a modern China based on the idea of an ecological civilization. He pointed out that the promising market prospects in green industry sectors, such as RE applications and energy-saving building construction, have led to the emergence of a prosperous large-scale ecological industry, which further accelerated the development of the recycling economy, green low-carbon industry as well as environmental protection. See Li and Cao (2012).

7.3.1 Consensus-building mechanisms in China's policy-making system

Although China is regarded as an authoritarian country, it is undeniable that the policy-making process is influenced by different stakeholders in the bureaucratic system rather than merely controlled by one or two national leaders. In this political structure of "*fragmented authoritarianism*", the policy-making arena is "governed by incremental change via bureaucratic bargaining" (Mertha 2009: 996). Based on this understanding, Jakobson and Knox highlight the importance of the "*consensus building*" mechanism in China's central government's decision making (or the need to create at least the perception of consensus) (Jakobson and Knox 2010: 1). Consensus building "encourages actors both inside and outside the official policy establishment to find ways to influence the views of top leaders. Informal channels based on personal relationships and institutional allegiances are important. Furthermore, a mosaic of other factors also affect the mindset of decision makers in China" (Jakobson and Knox 2010: 1).

The consensus building process is more like a bargaining process among different actors. Bargaining occurs "horizontally between government ministries, agencies and state enterprises, as well as vertically between different levels of government" (Lieberthal and Lampton 1992; Lieberthal and Oksenberg 1988). Leaders of individual institutions are expected to argue for the interests of their own institutions and "competition between institutions is deliberately encouraged" (Andrews-Speed 2012: 128). During the consensus building process, different bureaucratic actors endeavor to persuade paramount leaders to take their policy proposals through many political channels. Although the policy-making process in China is a "black box", it is undeniable that the policy outcome is an interest competition or comprising result influenced by many stakeholders through regular high-level meetings. "The progressive introduction of rules and procedures over the last two decades has strengthened consensus-based policy making in a way which has reduced the influence of individuals, has constrained factionalism and competition, and has enhanced cooperation and compromise" (Andrews-Speed 2012: 128).

The logic of consensus building is based on argumentative persuasion in the policy-making system. To be more specific, with the institution building of the pro-RE coalition, more pro-RE actors in the bureaucratic system attempt to exert more influence on energy policy making and persuade paramount leaders in order to defend their own interests. No doubt, if the final policy outcome is based on pro-RE consensus-building, the pro-RE actors will get more political resources. The pre-RE coalition takes advantage of international and domestic policy research results to challenge the validity of conventional energy actors, and to point out policy loopholes in the current energy policy system through comprehensive investigation, in order to translate its innovative RE policy proposals into governmental programs. In this collective argumentation, key policy brokers tend to achieve a communicative consensus according to their understanding and judgment. Due to the existence of fixed influencing channels, outcomes of argumentative persuasion can be eventually translated into policy outcomes. In the RE case, argumentative learning has not been a totally elite-driven process of change; some societal actors, such as research centers in universities, professional RE websites, and key RE innovation entrepreneurs, also have used argumentative persuasion to promote RE policy.

7.3.2 Relations between policy-oriented learning and argumentative persuasion

There are three key steps for RE policy-oriented learning: the first step is to perceive the problem in the current system, and pro-RE actors identify causes and look for policy solutions by policy-oriented learning; in the second step, the minority coalition exposes policy loopholes in policy implementation to the public and documents performance gaps in existing governmental programs; the final step is the proposal of policies to deal with problems and prepare for analytical debate with conventional interest groups in the energy sector. Sabatier identifies this analytical debate as a "persuasion" process, in which "each side attempts to persuade or convince the others—as well as neutral parties, particularly potential policy brokers—of the validity of its claims" (Sabatier and Jenkins-Smith 1993b: 55). Therefore, the aim of the policy-oriented learning promoted by pro-RE actors is to prepare sufficient policy resources for the argumentative persuasion stage, then eventually endeavor to lever RE policy change. In the stage of policy-oriented learning, this book mainly focuses on learning within the pro-RE coalition; and in the stage of argumentative persuasion, this book highlights the competition of the pro-RE coalition and conventional energy forces in the RE governance subsystem.

Different from introducing a simple policy instrument to launch large-scale RE projects in the earlier stage, deeper change such as the "adjustment period" when a mandatory RE quota system was combined with the FIT, poses a greater challenge to conventional energy forces. This process relates closely with the larger economic structural adjustments and energy systematic reforms underway, including the national grid reform, electricity market reform, and coal consumption pattern reform. The implementation of the quota system could further break the interest allocation pattern of different stakeholders in the current system and lead to an interest re-balancing among different actors: RE developers, state-owned grid enterprises, local government and renewable power consumers. Therefore, compared with the FIT, the introduction of a quota system has encountered greater resistance. This kind of deeper RE policy change has required the use of argumentative persuasion by the pro-RE coalition.

Through policy-oriented learning process, the pro-RE coalition can take international resources (like international experience and know-how diffusion) and domestic resources (convincing reports and statistics about policy loopholes) to challenge conventional stakeholders and persuade policy brokers to make a policy outcome based on the pro-RE consensus-building. Through argumentative persuasion, the pro-RE coalition endeavors to persuade the paramount leaders to recognize the strategic position of RE development and pay attention to severe policy loopholes which need to be rectified as soon as possible. Armed with convincing statistics and feasible policy proposals for addressing climate change and energy problems, the pro-RE coalition is in a better position to make an inroad into a system dominated by conventional energy forces.

7.3.3 Argumentative persuasion promoted by the pro-RE coalition: combining a quota system with the FIT

In the RE policy-making system, the pro-RE coalition not only takes the lead in policy-oriented learning, but also competes with conventional energy forces to introduce a mandatory RE quota policy to complement the FIT system. The goal is to solve the grid-connection and RE power curtailment bottlenecks. The way the pro-RE coalition has used argumentative persuasion can be summarized as follows:

7.3.3.1 Supervising the RE industry development and exposing RE policy loopholes

Actors in the pro-RE coalition have played a significant role in supervising RE industry developments and exposing RE policy loopholes to policy brokers. In this process, some societal actors, especially RE industry associations have taken more efforts to investigate the "real story" of RE development and expose policy loopholes through Internet or professional reports. Most societal actors have shown an increasingly constructive and cooperative stance to governmental research actors. The more open and pluralistic policy-making process has provided more channels for these societal actors to point out RE development problems. Through providing more convincing evidence that is based on their investigations and research, the pro-RE actors have been able to further challenge the validity of conventional energy forces and persuade policy brokers to choose a pro-RE policy proposal and to improve RE governance.

For instance, in the grid disconnection accidents, the China Wind Energy Association (CWEA), cooperating with the National Energy Administration (NEA), launched a large-scale survey on the quality of wind turbines covering the entire wind industry in November 2011 (CNB Daily 2011). The investigation included accident-site survey, comprehensive survey of domestic wind turbine manufacturers (Goldwind, Sinovel and Guodian United Power Technology), the main foreign wind turbine manufactures (Vestas and Suzlon) and wind farm developers. Through in-depth investigation, the CWEA drafted a report based on primary materials and submitted it to the NEA. In this report, the CWEA emphasized that the weakness of national grid construction and the ill management of wind farms led to the accidents, although the SERC and state grid enterprises both attributed the main responsibility of grid disconnection accidents to wind turbine manufacturers. They emphasize that the lack of low voltage ride through (LVRT) technology of wind turbines posed a threat to grid stability and security.① The experts in the CWEA showed that even though some wind turbines were equipped with the qualified LVRT, there were still grid disconnection accidents happening, mainly due to the weak reliability management of the power grids. Therefore, grid SOEs should also take on the responsibility for these accidents. The equipment of LVRT capability for wind turbines cannot solve all the problems, unless the grid companies improve the grid compatibility for RE power. In addition, the CWEA has established an online discussion website for grid disconnection accidents (http://www.cnwp.org.cn/zhuanti/show.php?itemid=13). This website aims to draw more social attention to wind power accidents and accelerate standardization in the wind power industry, and urge improvements in RE-friendly grid-connection management.

In addition to greater social attention to wind turbine accidents, the China Wind Power Outlook 2012, exposed the serious situation of wind power curtailment in China. According to the report, more than 10 billion kW·h of wind-generated power was curtailed in surveyed regions, accounting for 12% of these regions' total wind energy (CREIA et al. 2012). As a result of curtailment, wind farm operators suffered losses of more than 5 billion RMB (USD 712 million), halving the sector's profits. The curtailed energy amounts could have replaced the burning of 3.3 million tons of coal, which in turn equals 10 million tons of carbon dioxide emissions (CREIA et al. 2012). It clearly points out that although wind turbine manufactures and wind power generators are taking efforts to develop grid-friendly wind equipment and wind farms, the grid companies are not developing wind-friendly or RE-friendly grids. Their efforts are not sufficient. Grid planning and construction are lagging behind and the gap between wind power generation and grid transmission has enlarged. This has led to

---

① Low voltage ride through capability allows wind turbines to continue operating during and after voltage dips and temporary faults by maintaining uninterrupted grid connection, so the grid can adjust more quickly, which improves entire power grid safety and stability. See CNB Daily (2011).

more grid-disconnection accidents as well as wind power curtailment (CREIA et al. 2012). If more large-scale capacity was connected to the grid, it might mean that even more wind energy would be curtailed, even if wind energy generators invest a great amount of money in optimizing low voltage ride through (LVRT) technology (CREIA et al. 2012: 67-69). Under the support of Greenpeace and the GWEC, the CREIA released Wind Power 21 in China and the China Wind Power Outlooks for 2007, 2008, 2009, 2010, 2011 and 2012. These professional reports exposed these kinds of problems in wind energy development and stimulated much social discussion, which has in turn been used by the pro-RE coalition in its argumentative persuasion.

In addition to RE industry associations, research centers in universities, professional RE website as well as some green NGOs also have played an increasingly active role in RE governance, such as releasing key experts' critiques and proposals by the RE industry online, publishing professional RE industry reports, launching a large-scale RE development survey (including an online questionnaire) and releasing up-dated statistics about the RE industry. Here I want to emphasize the role of professional RE websites in argumentative persuasion, a role which has been enhanced due to the rapid development of the Internet in China. By June 2012, there were 538 million Internet users in China, accounting for 39.9% of the total population and ranking first in the world (Sina News 2012). Surfing online has become a significant means of obtaining new information (Sina News 2012). That is why the role of professional RE and low-carbon websites cannot be underestimated, such as the Polaris Power website (http://www.bjx.com.cn), the Newenergy Net (http://www.newenergy.org.cn) and the China Dialogue (http://www.china dialogue.net). These websites provide up-to-date information about RE development and RE policy (especially new RE legislative documents and administrative regulations) for RE developers and different social communities; they also provide argumentative persuasion forums to expose RE development potential predicaments as well as RE policy implementation loopholes to society. This has been especially important for attracting the attention of policy brokers as heated online social discussions and arguments can not easily be ignored. The experts from grid enterprises and the experts from RE industry associations have different stories/voices on websites. In addition, Polaris Power website has hosted a discussion column since 2010 concerning wind power development problems in China (BJX 2010). Through argumentative persuasion, there has been growing social voice behind the introduction of the RE quota system as it is seen as a way to constrain the behavior of grid and power SOEs as well as provincial actors.

7.3.3.2 Initiating feasible RE policy proposals to break the "policy deadlock"

In the RE policy making, conventional forces have tried to block the issuing of new pro-RE policies with technical and financial excuses, which had led to a kind of "political impasse". Using argumentative persuasion, actors in the pro-RE coalition have introduced various policy proposals and attempted to demonstrate their feasibility. Sometimes, the pro-RE actors provide compromise solutions in an effort to weaken the opposition of conventional forces. They do this in order to move beyond "policy deadlocks" and to persuade key policy brokers of the importance of supporting RE.

The China National Renewable Energy Center (CNREC) has various channels it can use to try to influence policy brokers in the RE subsystem. Wang Zhongying, the director of the CNREC pointed out that "the technological difficulties emphasized by the grid enterprises are no more than superficially technological problems, there are deeper reasons for the grid-connection problem" (Chinapower Net 2012). Wang introduced three main reasons. *First* is the cognitive problem. Different interest groups have different understandings and often find it quite hard to reach a full consensus on the question of whether wind power as well as other RE forms should be vigorously developed or not. Even within the NDRC, leaders from different departments hold different views, including opinions questioning the prospects of RE (Chinapower Net 2012). *Second* is the problem of political institutions. In the energy system, the state-owned enterprises occupy monopoly positions in the energy market and they are not sufficiently supervised (the role of SERC is quite limited) (Chinapower Net 2012). *Third*, interest allocation is still a core problem. As a newly emerging industry, RE development has broken the balance of the old interest pattern, but the new balance of interest has not yet been established. Therefore, there are trade-offs in the interest game that takes place among different stakeholders (Chinapower Net 2012). The CNREC was critical in persuading policy brokers to introduce the mandatory RE quota system to run in parallel with the FIT, as a way of further forcing resource reallocation among different stakeholders and guaranteeing grid-connection for RE power.

The interest game pattern in the pro-RE coalition's use of argumentative persuasion is very obvious. In arguing against the positions held by conventional energy forces and in trying to persuade policy brokers to believe in the urgency of further policy change, the pro-RE coalition has worked to weaken or restrict the power of those trying to slow the new RE implementation process. The role of argumentative persuasion becomes salient in cases of "policy deadlock", which tend to be entangled with the many interests of various stakeholders. There are two approaches to argumentative persuasion commonly used by pro-RE actors to break "policy deadlocks". *First*, actors in the pro-RE coalition make full use of survey statistics as well as the international experiences of pioneering countries to enhance the persuasive power of their argumentation, especially exposing the falsity of the technical or financial excuses of conventional forces; *second*, to provide some feasible and flexible innovative proposals (sometimes putting forwards a compromise transition policy proposal to reduce resistance) to promote the process of RE policy change, rather than being trapped or paralyzed in "policy deadlock".

For instance, during efforts to overcome the grid-connection bottleneck, the state-owned enterprises emphasized technological constraints of systematic peak load regulation and adjustment and smart grid deployment as a means of enhancing grid stability. These technological excuses have been used to explain wind power curtailment. Grid owners claim that overly high percentages of RE power threaten the grid security of an entire region. The pro-RE actor, the CREIA has drawn attention to wind power curtailments in its reports and has turned to international experiences to challenge the validity of the grid enterprises' arguments. The experts from the CREIA point out that the rates of national wind power installation in Denmark, Germany and Spain are respectively, 40%, 15% and 20% and the proportion of wind power in the national electricity production, respectively, 22%, 10% and 18% (CREIA et al. 2012: 67-69). Compared with these countries, wind power proportions in total electricity consumption of most regions in China are much lower. For example, the proportion of wind power in total electricity supply is only 6.32% in Jilin Province, 5.57% in Heilongjiang Province and 7.68% in Gansu Province; only the proportion of wind power installation in Inner Mongolia has exceeded 20% in 2011 (CREIA et al. 2012: 67-69). Therefore, the China Wind Energy Association (CWEA) suspects the excuses given by the state grid company for wind power curtailment. The low proportion of wind power in China today should not have such a great impact on grid stability (CREIA et al. 2012: 67-69). Therefore, there is no reason for state-owned grid enterprises to restrict the connection of wind farms to the grid or force them to cut off their production.

The CREIA and other pro-RE actors have claimed that the RE curtailment problem can be solved through two main approaches: *first*, improving integration of RE power through *priority dispatch*, especially enhancing the policy implementation of

Measures on Energy-saving Power Dispatch①; *second*, defining conditions of permissible curtailment by grid companies and *clarifying the compensation due to RE generators and penalty regulations for violations.* For dealing with the policy deadlock, the pro-RE scholars, like Schuman and Lin (2012), suggest to learn from Spain's priority dispatch model and Germany's curtailment controlling model. According to the Spanish model, "it is necessary to increase the amount of flexible, peaking generation sources such as natural gas power plants that can be used to balance the variable generation from wind and solar. In addition, RE generators such as wind and solar farms will also need to provide real-time information and forecasting of generation to the dispatcher [...]" (Schuman and Lin 2012: 102). In other words, the information coordination between the RE generators and dispatchers is of great importance. Due to the efforts of the CREIA and other pro-RE actors, RE power curtailment has begun to draw more social attention; however, there are still no special administrative regulations in place that can be used to constrain grid operators. This problem is closely related to priority dispatch. If the RE power cannot get a priority position for transmission through the grid (e. g. through a merit order system), RE curtailment cannot be avoided, especially if there are no regulations identifying the compensation level for RE developers or penalties for grid companies that do not comply. In the German model, there are clear regulations concerning priority purchase and curtailment compensation for RE generators. The regulations are embodied in the national legislative framework—the German Renewable Energy Sources Act Amendments (EEG). Schuman and Lin point out that "the German model stipulates a mandatory purchase policy for renewable power and identifies the deviation conditions. It requires grid companies to compensate the renewable electricity generator even in those circumstances where the deviation is justified" (Schuman and Lin 2012: 102).② In sum, a fundamental approach to solving the dispatch priority and RE

---

① In August 2007, in order to enhance the grid-connection and priority dispatch for renewable power, the NDRC issued the Measures on Energy-saving Power Dispatch and carried it out in five southern provinces (Guangdong, Jiangsu, Henan, Sichuan, Guizhou) as trial operation (People Net 2010b). According to the statistics of the SERC, in Guizhou Province, the dispatch for thermal power decreased 3.5% while the dispatch amount for hydro power and other RE power increased by 40.1% in 2007. This showed the effectiveness of priority dispatch (People Net 2010b). However, efforts to spread this policy in northern China has encountered much resistance from the large coal thermal plants that have strong vested interests and political influence in the energy sector. They have close interest relations with the grid companies and tend to be allocated dispatch priority leaving RE generators at a disadvantage.

② The purpose of the German provision is to hold the grid operators responsible for grid overload situations, thereby encouraging investment in upgrading the grid infrastructure as well as ensuring a greater degree of predictability for renewable power generators. See Schuman and Lin (2012: 102).

curtailment problems is to promote mandatory RE quotas for the power and grid companies. This would foster mandatory responsibilities for priority dispatch and curtailment compensation in the near future.

The resistance from grid SOEs, however, is still quite strong. In order to foster the implementation of mandatory RE quotas in wind and solar PV power, developing a distributed power generation system is the most effective way to stimulate the domestic solar PV power market in the short run. This policy was proposed by the CNREC and other pro-RE actors in 2012. A *distributed power generation system* is a form of compromise with grid SOEs, since they are less resistant to it even though they still have to coordinate the distributed power grid in the long run to guarantee the power stability of the distributed grid. ① Meng Xiangan, the deputy director of the China Renewable Energy Society (CRES), proposed that "the most important thing for supporting solar PV manufacturing industry is to expand the domestic PV power installation and to promote the distributed solar-power generation" (SolarF 2012). Chu Junhao, as the deputy of the National People's Congress (NPC) and an academician of the Chinese Academy of Sciences (CSS), pointed out that in order to improve the overly heavy reliance on the overseas market, such as solar panel manufacturing, China should encourage the development of its domestic RE market, to generate and transmit more RE power for energy demand. Developing small-scale distributed power grids is an effective way to encourage the generation of more wind and solar power for regional power utilization (NPC Net 2012). Therefore, pro-RE actors have asked the central government to subsidize distributed solar-power generation and regulate the benchmark price of solar electricity in various places according to weather and geographic conditions (SolarF 2012). The ERI suggests that China could develop 15 GW of distributed solar-power generation capacity by the end of 2015 (SolarF 2012). Through the efforts of the pro-RE coalition, the distributed electricity generation pattern was embodied into the 12th FYP for RE Development (NEA and CNREC 2012):

> Applications of distributed RE will be scaled-up. Establishing [a] rid supporting system and management system in favor of distributed electricity generation such as solar power; establishing 30 new energy micro-grid demonstration projects; integrating diversified RE technologies, such as distributed electricity generation (solar power, etc.) and RE for heating and fuel applications; [e]stablishing 100 New-Energy City

---

① The State Grid Corp, China's largest state-owned power utility company, in November 2012 began to provide a service that allows distributed PV solar-power producers to connect to the national grid for free. See SolarF (2012).

> and 200 Green-Energy County for pilot [projects]. Take advantage of distributed energy to supply electricity to areas [which the] grid cannot cover. Energy supplies of more than 50% rural households will get access to renewable energies such as biogas, solar energy and biomass-gasification. (NEA and CNREC 2012)

In addition, a distributed power generation system is also a flexible and feasible approach to promote small-scale wind power development and assure its connection to the grid. In the China Wind Power Outlook 2012, the CREIA pointed out that until 2011, rich wind resources areas such as northwestern China have been the main investment focus for wind power projects (CREIA et al. 2012). However, due to the problems of grid connectivity and curtailment, a reasonable step for wind developers is to switch to the central and eastern parts of China (CREIA et al. 2012). ① Although these places do not have rich wind resources (except coastal regions), these regions "feature a dense population, heavy power demand and good grid connectivity" (CREIA et al. 2012). Therefore, compared with building large-scale wind power farms in the remote west, small- and middle-scale distributed wind power has more potential to solve grid connectivity problems and transmit RE power to heavy power demand regions. ②

7.3.3.3 Boosting expectations for a green transformation through RE

As mentioned in Chapter 3, RE development has been confronted with challenges and constraints both from the international and domestic levels since the end of 2010. These include the downturn of the global carbon market, the depression of CDM projects, the anti-dumping duty and anti-subsidy tariff on solar panels imposed by the U.S. and the EU, wind-turbine grid disconnection accidents, wind power curtailment, and resistance to bio-fuels in the fuel sales and transportation system. Forces of resistance usually have pessimistic expectations about RE development. They

---

① By the end of 2011, Guangxi, Qinghai, Guizhou, Shaanxi, Henan, Ningxia, Tianjin, Yunnan and Anhui had seen two-fold growth in installed wind power capacity as compared to 2010. Except for Qinghai and Ningxia, all the other provinces are non-traditional markets. Coastal regions such as Shandong, Jiangsu, Guangdong and Fujian all passed the 1 GW milestone, forming a group of tier-2 wind power development provinces following the "Sanbei" region. See CREIA et al. (2012).

② Confronted with great resistance from grid SOEs in the policy transition to the quota system, the distributed power generation pattern has become a compromising choice to solve the RE grid connection problem in the short- to mid-run. Nevertheless, there are still two problems regarding the development of distributed power generation. First, distributed power generation needs supportive technological development. For solar PV power, this means improving the power conversion efficiency of PV roof projects (CREIA et al. 2012). Second, distributed power generation can be treated as a transitional solution to the promotion of on-grid renewable power development. It cannot, however, replace the necessary creation of a national smart grid and long-distance transmission lines from large-scale RE projects, such as large-scale wind farms and large-scale desert PV power farms, in the northwest.

believe that developing RE is too politically and economically costly for China. They argue China's technical capacity and economic strength are not sufficient to support an ambitious RE policy target. In contrast, the pro-RE coalition emphasizes the sector's positive prospects drawing on scientific research and countering the negative discourses of the conventional energy actors. Their aim is to boost expectations tied to a green transformation through RE development.

The governmental research institutes, especially the Center for Renewable Energy Development (CRED) in the ERI, have played a significant role in proving the technological feasibility of ambitious targets in wind and solar power. In October 2011, supported by the Sino-Danish Renewable Energy Development Program (RED) and the IEA, the CRED issued the *Technology Roadmap: China Wind Energy Development Roadmap 2050* (ERI and IEA 2011). The aim of this roadmap is "to compile and analyze key factors and issues encountered during wind power development, and propose feasible solutions. Such analysis and solutions will provide a valuable reference to wind power, power system strategy and policy making" (ERI and IEA 2011). Different from the 2007 roadmap①, this roadmap sets ambitious targets for a longer time period (2011-2050), which is conducive to boosting expectations for RE strategic development in the long run. This roadmap foresees wind power capacity reaching 200 GW by 2020, 400 GW by 2030 and 1,000 GW by 2050. Wind power will be one of five main power sources, and will meet 17% of electricity demand (ERI and IEA 2011).② Investment costs per unit of wind power will gradually fall; the costs of wind power are expected to be the same as or close to the cost of coal power in 2020 (ERI and IEA 2011). Environmental and social benefits will be considerable if the above targets are realized. Annual CO_2 emission mitigation will be 1.5 billion tonnes in 2050, and an estimated 720,000 jobs will be created (ERI and IEA 2011).

The 2050 roadmap also provides concrete action measures for different stages: solving the grid connection and transmission bottlenecks and promoting demonstration of smart grid technologies. In the middle and long term, a reform of the electric power

---

① With the support of the REEEP project, the CRED issued the Roadmap for China's Wind Power Development in March 2007 (CRED 2007), which paved the way for the issuing of the Mid- and Long-Term Development Plan for RE (2007-2020) by the NDRC in August 2007. In the 2007 Roadmap, the targets for wind power were raised to 5 GW in 2010, 30 GW (try to reach 50 GW) in 2020 and 100 GW by 2030, which were also reflected in the Mid- and Long-Term Development Plan.

② Before 2020, land-based wind power will dominate, with off-shore wind power at the demonstration stage; from 2021 to 2030, both land and off-shore wind power will be developed, and far off-shore wind power will be in a demonstration stage; after 2030, wind power will be developed further on land and off-shore. To realize the above targets, the total investment in wind power will be CNY 12,000 billion (ERI and IEA 2011).

sector should be promoted, and a pro-RE electric power market should be established. After 2030, advanced RE technologies will be widely deployed, including advanced and cost-effective storage technologies and smart grids (ERI and IEA 2011). Since the CRED has a close cooperative relation with the Department of New Energy and Renewable Energy (DNERE) in the NDRC, the positive impact of the RE long-term roadmap cannot be underestimated. Some of the suggestions in the 2050 roadmap have been embodied into the 12th FYP for RE Development, which was issued in 2012.

In addition to the reports from the key governmental research institutes, some societal pro-RE actors, such as the RE industry associations, have provided reports and roadmaps promising RE development as a means to stimulate high national expectations for RE development. The China Wind Power Outlook which was issued by Greenpeace, GWEC and CREIA predicted China's installed wind power capacity could reach 122 GW by 2020, and if the Chinese government could give a favorable policy support to wind power, then the installed capacity of wind energy could exceed 120 GW by 2020(Greenpeace et al. 2007). This report urged China to set a more ambitious target in order to seize an opportunity of massive uptake of wind power. Compared with the 2007 official target embodied in the Mid- and Long-Term Development Plan for RE (30 GW wind power by 2020), the target in this report seems more in line with reality (Greenpeace et al. 2007). The successful experience of wind power development in the past decade has further proved the feasibility of ambitious targets, and heightened expectations for a green transformation.

Compared with wind power, solar power development has undergone unprecedented tough challenges in 2012: the anti-dumping duty and anti-subsidy tariff, which were imposed by the U. S. and the EU further worsened the overcapacity and depressed the solar equipment sector, hurting enterprises. The pro-RE actors, especially solar energy industry associations and solar energy enterprises expected the government to raise solar PV power installation targets in the 12th FYP, since the increased targets would help struggling domestic manufactures better face the challenging overseas market (CGI 2012: 76). Conventional energy forces anticipated that the "winter time" for solar power would mean that even national banks would not loan more to solar power enterprises. The pro-RE coalition tried to prove that 2012 was not a doom year for solar energy development, but a strategic turning point or "an opportunity time period" for solar PV power growth. In the field of solar PV power, solar energy development targets were elevated several times, as promoted by pro-RE actors, such as the CRED, RE industry associations, solar energy developers and some research institutes within universities. The NDRC raised the solar PV target four times within one year. The NEA first released a solar PV target in the FYP in

February 2012 of 5 GW by 2015 (Sustainable Business News 2012). ① Then the target was changed to 10 GW, adjusted to 15 GW, and finally the target was fixed at 21 GW by 2015 and 50 GW by 2020 in the 12th FYP for Solar PV Power Development. ② According to the Strategic Action Plan for Energy Development(2014-2020) issued by State Council in 2014, when the PV installed capacity reaches 100 GW by 2020, the photovoltaic power price will equal to general sales price of national grids by then. The ambitious solar PV target has strongly boosted the solar PV industry and sent a positive signal for solar energy investment.

7.4 Influence of the mandatory RE quota system for a low-carbon transformation of China

After a six-year long effort, the NEA issued the Regulation for Management of Renewable Power Quota (Exposure Draft) in May 2012. With this act, a mandatory RE quota system was officially introduced into the RE policy system and combined with the FIT policy. China has undergone a deep transition of market-oriented reform, and interest conflicts among different stakeholders have increased. The FIT policy mainly aims to protect the profitability of RE generators in the long run, especially for small- and middle-sized RE producers; the mandatory RE quota system mainly targets to constrain the behavior of grid SOEs, power SOEs and local governments.

7.4.1 Impact of the mandatory RE quota system on key RE stakeholders

According to the Regulation for Management of Renewable Power Quota, the RE quota for State Grid (China's largest grid operator) will be 5% by 2015, while the smaller China Southern Power Grid will have a quota of 3.2% (NDRC 5/2012). The four grid companies will be required to purchase a certain percentage of their total

① In February 2012, China released its Solar Five-Year Plan, which includes a target for its domestic manufacturers of 5 GW a year by 2015. The plan also targets a reduction in solar panel prices to $1,111 per kilowatt (kW) by 2015, and $794 per kW by 2020.

② Analysts even see this new target as very conservative, expecting actual solar installations to surpass 30 GW (Renewable Energy 2012). Researchers from the Energy Research Institute hold more optimistic expectations for solar PV power, and anticipate it might reach 30-40 GW by 2015.

generation from non-hydro RE generators in their area (Schuman and Lin 2012: 93). ①

Table 7.2 Renewable power purchase quotas for four grid companies

Company	Provincial Coverage	Target 2015 RE power quota purchase (%)	Total forecast power purchase in 2015 (TW · h)	Forecast RE power purchase in 2015 (TW · h)
State Grid	Inner Mongolia East, Liaoning, Shaanxi (70% market share), Gansu, Xinjiang, Heilongjiang, Jilin, Ningxia, Shandong, Hebei, Shanxi, Beijing, Tianjin, Qinghai, Jiangsu, Hunan, Henan, Sichuan, Fujian, Shanghai, Anhui, Jiangxi, Zhejiang, Hubei, Chongqing	4.8	5,196	249
South Grid	Guangxi, Guangdong, Yunnan, Guizhou, Hainan	3.2	1,024	33
Inner Mongolia Power (Grid)	Inner Mongolia West	14.9	168	25
Shaanxi Provincial Power (Grid)	Shaanxi (30% market share)	9.9	48	5
Average / Total		4.8	6,436	312

Source: Schuman and Lin (2012: 93).

① Even the two big state-owned grid companies have begun to enter the field of wind power development since 2012. In 2012, the National Grid established its New Energy Limited Company which mainly takes care of developing wind and solar power (Polarispower Net 2012). Later, in June 2012, the Comprehensive Energy Limited Company, which is affiliated to Southern Grid, cooperated with 8 other power enterprises to set up Southern Off-shore Wind Power Joint Company. This company focuses on investing in off-shore wind power, even though they know that off-shore wind projects are currently stagnant. See Polarispower Net (2012).

The power enterprises shall undertake a maximum 15% RE power quota by 2015. ① Since the northwestern area is the most significant place for wind power generation, the Inner Mongolia Power Company's (covering Inner Mongolia West) quota will be 14.9% and Shaanxi Electric Power Company (covering 30% of Shaanxi) will have a quota of 9.9% (NDRC 5/2012; Schuman and Lin 2012: 93). The draft regulation requires the power companies, which generate more than 5 GW, to generate RE sources accounting for 11% of their installed capacity (NDRC 5/2012). And in the meantime, 6.5% of their gross power generation will also come from non-hydro RE (Schuman and Lin 2012: 92). ② This means that the largest 14 generators, accounting for 66% of China's annual power generation (2,786 TW · h) will be required to generate an average of 6.5% of their total electricity generation from non-hydro RE by 2015 (Schuman and Lin 2012: 92). ③ Although the regulation draft has not been ratified yet, its signaling effect has played a significant role in stimulating the power companies to develop RE. Power companies, which have a generation capacity of more than 5 GW, are usually state-owned power enterprises. The five big stated-owned power enterprises have taken over the lead in RE development. From January to May 2012, the approved power generation projects of the five big power enterprises were 138, among which wind power projects accounted for 95% (Polarispower Net 2012).

Table 7.3 Renewable energy quotas for six largest covered generators

Company	2010 electricity generation (TW · h)	2010 RE generation (TW · h)	2010 RE generation quota (%)	Forecasted 2015 electricity generation (TW · h)	Forecasted 2015 RE generation with a 6.5% quota (TW · h)
Huaneng	538	6.3	1.2	817	53
Datang	473	6.2	1.3	718	47
Guodian (including Longyuan)	420	11.9	2.8	638	41
Huadian	360	2.5	0.7	546	35

① It includes wind power, solar power, and biomass but excludes hydropower.

② Guodian Corporation, one of the top five state-owned power companies, already has enough RE generation to meet the target, with 22% of its total installed capacity coming from renewables by the end of 2011. See Schuman and Lin (2012).

③ At the end of 2010, the 14 power companies generated an average of just 1.34% (37.3 TW · h) of their power generation from RE, so this will mean increasing generation from renewable sources to 276 TW · h of their forecasted total 4,235 TW · h total generation in 2015. See Schuman and Lin (2012:92).

China Power Investment	294	2.1	0.7	447	29
Shenhua	160	3.0	1.9	244	16

Source: Schuman and Lin (2012: 92).

For provincial actors, the regulation sets four types of regions with different quota requirements for their RE consumption rate (NDRC 5/2012). The classification standards cover the RE sources, total electric power consumption, and electric power transmission capacity of the different provinces (NDRC 5/2012):

The quotas for the first group are 10%-15%, including the eastern part of Inner Mongolia (15%), the western part of Inner Mongolia (15%), Xinjiang (10%), Gansu (10%), Ningxia (10%), Shaanxi (10%), Liaoning (10%), Jilin (10%), Heilongjiang (10%) (NDRC 5/2012). Most of these provinces are northwestern and northeastern provinces with rich wind resources although their total electricity consumption is not very high compared with the eastern coastal provinces (NDRC 5/2012). The quota for the second group is 6%, including Beijing, Tianjin, Hebei, Shanxi, Shandong, Qinghai, Yunnan (NDRC 5/2012). The third group has quotas of 3%-4%, including Jiangsu (4%), Hunan (4%), Guizhou (4%), Shanghai (3%), Fujian (3%), Guangdong (3%), Henan (3%), Sichuan (3%), Anhui (3%), Jiangxi (3%) (NDRC 5/2012). And the fourth group, including Zhejiang, Hubei, Guangxi, Chongqing, Hainan, is only required to meet a 1% quota (NDRC 5/2012). The average RE consumption target across all of the provinces is 5%. If counting from the absolute amount of RE consumption, Shandong, Hebei, Inner Mongolia, Liaoning and Jiangsu are the top five provinces in this area (Schuman and Lin 2012: 93).

Table 7.4 Ten provinces with the largest forecast absolute renewable power purchase obligations in 2015

Province/Municipality	Target RE power consumption in 2015(%)	Total forecast electricity consumption in 2015 (TW·h)	Forecast RE power consumption target (TW·h)
Shandong	6	502	30
Hebei	6	425	26
Inner Mongolia West	15	168	25
Liaoning	10	247	25
Jiangsu	4	546	22

Guangdong	3	571	17
Shanxi	6	250	15
Inner Mongolia East	15	84	13
Shaanxi	10	123	12
Beijing	6	189	11
Average and total for top 10	6	3,105	196
Average and total for all provinces	5	6,335	323

Source: Schuman and Lin (2012: 93).

The ratification of the Regulation for Management of Renewable Power Quota has nevertheless still encountered quite strong resistance. The grid SOEs, power SOEs and provincial-level actors have big differences in terms of their interests in relation to the allocation of the mandatory RE quotas (EEO 2013). Some western provinces complain that although they have rich wind and solar sources, their comparatively large RE quota cannot be realized without effective grid-connection and more fiscal subsidies (EEO 2013). Furthermore, the effective supervision of the implementation of these mandatory RE quotas needs to be improved. Currently, the SERC is still not sufficiently high in the power hierarchy to effectively supervise the grid and power SOEs, not to mention the performance of provincial actors.

In order to enforce the ratification and execution of the Regulation for Management of Renewable Power Quota, NDRC issued The Assessment Measure for Renewable Power Quota (Trial Implementation) in September 2014. It emphasized three principles: The eastern region should take more responsibility for RE development and further improve the quota target of eastern region; enforce the power grid enterprises to complete the quota responsibility; the assessment measure indicators for renewable power quota include two levels: the basic indicators and advanced indicators (such as following provincial assessment indicators for 2020 RE power quotas). Based on principles above, it clarified the responsibility of concrete RE power quota for every provincial government, as well as national and provincial power grid enterprises, with a target to alleviate the curtailment situation of RE power.

Table 7.5 Basic provincial assessment indicators for 2020 RE power quotas

	Total social power consumption	Local RE Power Generation Capacity (Ten Million kW · h)						
		Wind power	Solar power	Biomass power	Total	Input (+) Output (−)	RE power consumption	Quota indicator
Huabei Region								
Beijing	1,250	12	18	5	35	90	125	10
Tianjin	1,020	15	18	10	43	59	102	10
Hebei	4,830	372	61	63	496	−13	483	10
Shanxi	2,770	238	46	30	313	−36	277	10
Inner Mongolia	3,635	840	54	30	924	−452	473	13
Dongbei Region								
Liaoning	3,000	171	26	12	210	180	390	13
Jilin	975	205	18	60	283	−156	127	13
Heilongjiang	1,240	121	18	72	211	−50	161	13
Huadong Region								
Shanghai	1,670	13	14	37	64	53	117	7
Jiangsu	7,200	156	70	128	354	150	504	7
Zhejiang	5,380	37	50	97	184	85	269	5
Anhui	2,850	38	33	58	129	70	200	7
Fujian	2,800	135	25	41	201	−5	196	7
Jiangxi	1,821	50	25	28	103	−12	91	5
Shandong	6,310	296	66	127	489	142	631	10

Zhongnan Region								
Henan	4,762	43	50	60	152	181	333	7
Hubei	2,725	45	26	78	149	42	191	7
Hunan	2,174	70	21	51	142	24	166	7
Guangdong	6,930	88	50	78	216	269	485	7
Guangxi	1,950	14	10	14	38	42	80	5
Hainan	380	17	20	14	50	−24	27	7
Xinan Region								
Chongqing	1,605	14	10	14	38	42	80	5
Sichuan	3,325	40	26	21	87	80	166	5
Guizhou	1,860	76	15	12	103	−10	93	5
Yunnan	2,330	228	56	28	312	−79	233	10
Tibet	83	4	15	0	19	−8	11	13
Xibei Region								
Shaanxi	1,800	94	60	13	167	13	180	10
Gansu	1,582	444	98	6	548	−342	206	13
Qinghai	1,074	7	105	1	112	−5	107	10
Ningxia	1,166	131	53	6	189	−38	152	13
Xinjiang	3,400	432	105	4	541	−99	442	13
Total/Average	84,097	4,466	1,272	1,201	6,939			

Source: *21st Century Economic Report* (2014).

Therefore, apart from setting concrete quotas for provincial actors, The Assessment Measure for Renewable Power Quota (Trial Implementation) also has proposed three mechanisms to foster implementation effectiveness:

First, RE quota completion will become the *key standard for governmental official performance evaluation* (including the leaders of state-owned enterprises). The RE quota will be incorporated into the comprehensive evaluation index system of energy saving and emission reduction as well as the energy consumption cap requirement. These green evaluation indexes/indicators (especially the GHG emission reduction index and energy consumption cap index related to climate change mitigation) have gained importance since China issued its 12th FYP in 2011. In addition, the performance of the RE quota will be publicized by the NEA, and this will have a significant impact on the political career promotion chances of local officials. Furthermore, as one kind of economic incentive, the power enterprises can obtain green power certificates from the RE generation quota. If a domestic carbon trading market is launched in the near future, these green certificates will be tradable (NDRC 5/2012).

Second, the regulation stipulates the *supervision and penalty mechanism* for RE quota implementation. Deviant behavior will be subject to economic and political penalties, including direct economic fines, which will influence economic resource allocation as well as new power project applications; publicization of incidents of malpractice; and, the use of the political performance evaluation system to punish the main responsible officials who will be given low grades. Of course, these aspects of the regulations are still broad and abstract. That is why the CNREC has been busy with drafting the Management Methods for RE Power Quota for further RE development (NDRC 5/2012).

Third, in order to reduce strong resistance from the grid companies, the regulations also imply that a related *interest compensation mechanism* will be introduced. The RE quota mechanism will force the grid companies to buy the relatively higher priced electric power from RE and set up proper subsidizing mechanisms for grid companies (NDRC 5/2012). The NEA issued the Interim Measure on Management of Funds Subsidizing Feed-in Tariff from RE Sources in April 2012. The government will subsidize grid companies for constructing and maintaining grid systems transmitting RE generated electric power, including wind power. The subsidies are CNY 0.01/(kW · h) [$0.002/(kW · h)] for transmission lines within 50 kilometers, CNY 0.02/(kW · h) for transmission lines from 50-100 kilometers, and CNY 0.03/(kW · h) for transmission lines over 100 kilometers. In the regulation, this mechanism has gained much more attention than before.

It is said that the enforcement of RE quotas among different energy stakeholders will bring more dynamics for further electricity market reform. It is interesting that the foreseeable reform in the electricity market has begun even before the formal ratification of the Regulation for Management of Renewable Power Quota. In March 2015, NDRC and NEA issued the Guidance on Power Operation Adjustment Optimization to Improve Renewable Power Grid Access. All provinces should enhance full-time generation and trans-provincial transmission of RE power by guaranteeing full-time RE grid access, especially to promote benefit compensation mechanism so as to enlarge the market space for RE power consumption; give priority for increasing the RE power generation in new electricity demand; and encourage direct transaction between RE producer and user. Undoubtedly, this reform in the electricity market will accelerate the official ratification of RE quota system; then the implementation of quota system will foster and enhance the further reform process in the electricity market in the long run.

7.4.2 Coupling the quota system with the carbon trading system and its implications for a green transformation

Designing a harmonized global carbon market was not only a main strategy of the EU under the Kyoto Protocol, but also a key goal (Sterk and Mersmann 2011: 1). The EU ETS is the largest carbon trading entity in the world. However, the goal for global carbon market construction at the international level cannot be achieved without the development of a domestic carbon trading market in different countries. Although China issued its first National Climate Change Program in 2007 and played an increasingly active role in CDM projects, the central government still held a conservative and negative attitude towards a domestic carbon trading market at that time. 2010 was a key turning point for ETS development. In the Decision on Accelerating the Cultivation and Development of Strategic Emerging Industries which was issued in October 2010, the central government for the first time mentioned that China will gradually create an emissions trading market over the coming five years (Sterk and Mersmann 2011: 9). Stimulated by hopes of a bright future for a carbon market, there were 100 carbon exchanges in operation or under preparation as of late 2011 (Wang, T. 2012).

Since the end of 2011, China has formally taken a positive stance toward the establishment of the carbon trading market at the domestic level. Despite the adverse context of the global carbon market slump, the NDRC issued the *Notice on Carbon Trading Trials Scheme* in October 2011, initiating a group of city and provincial-level carbon-trading trials (Wang, T. 2012). In this scheme, five cities and two provinces are fixed as carbon trading pilots: the cities of Beijing, Tianjin, Shanghai, Chongqing and Shenzhen and the provinces of Hubei and Guangdong. Beijing, Tianjin, Shanghai have more experience gained from earlier environmental exchanges in these cities (Lin and Yang 2012). ① According to the scheme, these pilot cities and provinces need to organize and compile an implementation plan for the carbon emission trading pilot program, including defining the objectives and key tasks; calculating overall caps for greenhouse gas emissions in their regions; and formulating plans for distributing specific emissions targets (NDRC 11/2012). Beijing, Shanghai and Guangdong launched their pilot programs on March 28, August 16, and September 11, 2012, respectively (NDRC 11/2012). ② Chinese leaders have held on to a relatively optimistic plan to launch a national-level market carbon trading market by 2015, based on the successful experience of these ETS pilots cities and provinces. In addition, including a domestic carbon trading and carbon tax system into the legislative framework is one of the key targets of the Climate Change Law. The issuing of the Climate Change Law (Exposure Draft) in 2012 guaranteed the legislative position of the carbon trading system for climate change mitigation.

In June 2012, the NDRC issued the *Interim Regulation of Voluntary Greenhouse Gas Emission Trading* on the official website of the Clean Development Mechanism in China, paving the way for the national carbon trading system and market building. It implied that the government tended to revive the confidence of CDM developers through initiating the domestic carbon trading market. This regulation made clear that the NDRC is the national authority taking charge of the voluntary GHG emissions trading activities. ③ The regulation sets out the "basic management framework, trading procedures and supervisory measures of the voluntary trading, establishes a registration and recording system and an information disclosure system, and encourages project-based voluntary greenhouse gas emissions trading" (NDRC 6/2012). In order to further enrich the guidance principles, the NDRC also issued the

① China's three main carbon markets—the Beijing Environment Exchange, Shanghai Environment Energy Exchange and Tianjin Climate Exchange—were all formed within two months of each other, towards the end of 2008.

② Among these pilot cities and provinces, Guangdong is the most active actor to take the lead in "designing a trading system based on absolute emission caps, Tianjin and Beijing have indicated that their trading scheme might be based on energy saving credits. Shanghai has not yet decided on which route to follow—absolute caps on carbon dioxide, carbon and energy intensity-based credits are all being considered." See Sterk and Mersmann (2011: 9). Guangdong, China's second-most populated province and one of its most economically developed, announced the start of a voluntary industrial sector carbon trading scheme by 2012 or 2013 in order to reduce its levels of carbon intensity by 30% against 2005. See Sterk and Mersmann (2011).

③ The regulation is applied to the trading activities of the following 6 GHG emissions: CO_2, CH_4, N_2O, HFCs, PFCs and SF_6.

Guide on Validation and Certification of Voluntary Greenhouse Gas Trading in October 2012.

Since the start of China's efforts to transition toward a more green growth and low-carbon oriented society, the domestic carbon trading market has taken on a core position. The launch of the domestic carbon trading market is not only an innovative policy change, but also has close relations with a systematic green transformation. From the discursive perspective, the governmental discourse has begun to emphasize taking "climate change as an opportunity to promote the economic structure transformation" rather than "only treating climate change as challenge and burden" (Xinhua News 2009b). For China, a carbon trading system can be a flexible and cost effective policy tool to promote a green transformation. Andrew Steer, the president of the World Resources Institute, proposed that "carbon trading is not a panacea for solving all the problems, but by allowing trading to take place, it's cheaper to address the overall problem" (Lan 2012). Furthermore, under the international pressure of the climate change regime as well as domestic energy and environmental challenges, there is a high expectation that carbon trading trials will stimulate deep economic structural reform in the energy sector and electricity market and will aid in the transformation towards more green growth. Steer also holds an optimistic attitude towards China's emissions trading system, which "is likely to be the world's second-largest carbon market by 2015, and may be a major player if it is connected to the proposed world system" (Lan 2012). ①

Xie Zhenhua, the deputy director of the NDRC, argued that through establishing and improving its own carbon market, China can obtain more experience to participate in rule formulation for an international carbon trading market (People Net 2012). In order to guarantee the successful performance of the carbon trading trials, China also is paying attention to international relations, such as cooperating with Australia in the development of low-carbon cities and learning lessons from the use of market mechanisms since 2011 (Climate Connect 2011). And in the same year, China has been one of the first to receive an initial grant of 350,000 USD under the World Bank's Partnership for Market Readiness for the development of its planned provincial systems and to build up domestic capacities in the carbon market field (Sterk and Mersmann 2011: 9).

Since the launching of the carbon trading system involves a series of systemic

---

① Andrew Steer thinks that Europe, China, Japan, Republic of Korea, South Africa and Australia could trade with each other and have a credible, working market, even if some countries, like the United States, decide not to join the mechanism. See Lan (2012).

policy changes, it has great implications for further RE policy change, even stimulating the transition to major policy change. For instance, in the Technology Roadmap: China Wind Energy Development Roadmap 2050 (ERI and IEA 2011), which was issued in October 2011 by the CRED, the carbon trading system is treated as central to boosting wind power growth in the middle- to long-term. The great efforts to push RE policy change—introducing a quota system in combination with the FIT—are closely tied with launching the domestic carbon trading market. The Regulation for Management of Renewable Power Quota (Exposure Draft) does not directly lead to the trading of RE Certificates in the current stage. This makes sense "given that China will need to gain experience with tracking progress in meeting the quotas by generators, grid companies and provincial-level governments" (Schuman and Lin 2012: 102). However, with the growth and maturity of a domestic carbon trading system, the RE quota could be directly transferred to the *Chinese Certified Emission Reduction* (*CCER*). In other words, the carbon trading mechanism could increase economic efficiency in meeting RE generation targets by increasing the flexibility of grid companies and generators to meet their targets through the carbon market measures (Schuman and Lin 2012: 102). It is also conducive for decreasing the economic development imbalance among different regions, especially between the rich renewable resource regions in northwestern China and the heavy energy demand regions in the eastern coastal areas of China. For example, it "would allow grid companies and generators in areas with less renewable resources, such as Beijing and Shanghai, to meet their target obligations by purchasing CCERs from areas with rich renewable resources, such as Inner Mongolia" (Schuman and Lin 2012: 102). The RE quota system could then be combined perfectly with the carbon trading system to promote a green transformation, which would also be a big stimulus for electricity market reform.

Chapter 8
Conclusion

The energy supply mix in China is dominated by coal: over 70% of energy was coal based and over 82% of electricity consumption was from coal thermal plants in 2010 (IEA 2011b). This coal-dominated energy structure has contributed to China's high GHG emissions and environmental pollution. China became the largest GHGs emitter globally in 2007. Due to its rapid economic growth and related high energy consumption, China exceeded the U. S. to become the largest energy consumer in 2010. This "energy giant" needs systematic energy regulation and effective energy policy to support its fast-speed economy. However, institution building related to energy policy is still quite weak in China. There is neither Energy Ministry nor Energy Law. The characteristic of "fragmented authoritarianism" in energy policy is obvious, since conventional energy actors, such as large state-owned enterprises, strongly articulate their own vested interests in the energy sector. Although there have been increasing demands to change the "black energy" consumption pattern, energy supply sources have kept very stable in past decades. Conventional state-owned energy enterprises have great vested interests in the coal-dominated energy structure. In order to guarantee their interests, they have hindered major institutional reforms in terms of new energy regulations or the structure of the electricity market. For instance, the second largest energy source for China is from oil. ① Due to the dominant "supply-oriented" energy security concept, the Chinese government has used active oil diplomacy to guarantee the oil supply and to enlarge the "national strategic oil reserves". State-owned oil companies have earned their "windfall profits" under the national "go-out" strategy and gained more influence on the energy policy-making process.

---

① Along with the rapid growth of the private automobile consumption, the oil dependence rate of China increased to 57% in 2012 (IEA 2012b).

The large state-owned oil enterprises also control natural gas production and transportation. Beginning in 2012, three large state-owned oil enterprises launched a large-scale shale gas projects in Sichuan Province (CSGCN 2013). There is a real fear that "shale gas may substitute not for coal but for renewable energy" (Stevens 2012: 3).

Against this background, it has been difficult to develop large-scale RE projects. Historically speaking, China was a latecomer compared with western pioneering countries and was without experience in RE development. Before the 1990s, the development of biogas, hydropower, solar cookers, and off-grid small-scale wind power was merely treated as a supplementary measure for the rural energy supply. There was no specific institution taking charge of RE development and RE policy promotion. Even entering the 1990s, RE development was still in a dispersed, small-scaled situation with merely sporadic policy support. Large-scale wind, solar PV power and biomass power projects hardly made any progress because there was no favorable policy support and lack of high R&D investment. Even when the Law of Science and Technology Progress was issued in 1993, which aimed to support R&D on RE development to enhance energy diversification and energy security, RE development still did not get sufficient promotion. The historical watershed for RE development emerged when the SDPC/NDRC became the leading actor responsible for the climate change negotiations and signed the Kyoto Protocol in 1998. In the decade after China ratified the Kyoto Protocol in 2002 and launched CDM projects, the country made great progress in RE development. Beginning in 2010, China surpassed the U. S. and Germany to become the leading country in RE investment, wind power installation capacity, solar panel manufacturing and solar water heating utilization. According to the ambitious RE targets in the 12th Five-Year Plan, wind power generation will reach 100-150 GW by 2015 and solar PV power will achieve 21 GW by 2015 (State Council 3/2011). Later, Strategic Action Plan for Energy Development (2014-2020) issued in 2014 further proposed that the wind power installed capacity will reach 200 GW and the PV installed capacity will reach 100 GW by 2020 (State Council 11/2014).

This book aims to solve the following puzzle: Against the backdrop of a heavy carbon lock-in in the energy mix, why has China made such remarkable progress in RE development over the past decade and what are the hidden dynamic mechanisms of energy policy change towards RE? There are several factors that the literature points to as explaining this domestic RE policy change: energy security concerns, economic growth concerns and environmental protection concerns at the domestic level, the climate change regime and the global competition for the booming global market for environment and low-carbon technologies at the international level. Domestic factors like energy security, environmental protection and economic growth concerns are treated as the main variables to explain the rapid RE development in China. However, international factors like the climate change regime have not received due attention in the literature. Energy security and economic interests in the development of climate-friendly technologies definitely are significant factors behind the promotion of RE. Nevertheless, to break the dominance of vested "fossil" interests in the energy sector and to get RE onto the mainstream of the political agendas cannot be explained without understanding the external driving force of the international climate change regime. Climate change is an indispensable factor to understand why China has achieved substantial progress in RE development within such a short time and how the interaction of domestic actors is influenced by external factors.

8.1 Returning to the research question and research variables

This book explores why and how China's participation in the climate change regime exerts an influence on domestic energy policy change towards RE. For this purpose, the theoretical approach attempts to combine socialization theory and the advocacy coalition framework to explain the influence from the climate change regime on domestic energy policy change by integrating RE. With the deeper involvement of China in the climate change regime and stronger reputational pressure from the international level, China's changing response to climate change has increasingly becoming a major driving force for promoting domestic RE development (Lema and Ruby 2007: 3888). I define the climate change regime in a broad sense and treat it as a comprehensive external social context to influence domestic policy change. In the climate change socialization process, the capacity building of the pro-RE coalition is key to understanding how international factors have had a concrete impact on domestic energy policy change towards RE. One of the most difficult tasks in analyzing RE policy change in China is to understand how it is made, that is, how the actors shape and determine policy outcomes, especially how the pro-RE coalition has strengthened its position in the RE policy-making system. The green transformation process in China has been rather complex, since the energy policy system is entangled with many stakeholders with differing interests.

A main factor behind the rapid development of RE has been energy policy change. The *dependant variable* of this book is identified as energy policy change through integrating RE, as specified in Chapter 3. There has been an incremental process of change in RE policy instruments; however, the deeper major policy change or systematic shift in energy regulation has still a long way to go. According to the in-depth process-tracing analysis conducted above, there have been five developmental stages in China's RE policy. Before the end of the 1990s, there was nearly no specific renewable energy policy, except some sporadic regulation clauses embodied in some energy policies. A serious consideration on designing RE policy did not enter onto the political agenda until 2003. A national tendering system for wind power was introduced. Through several government-led wind concession bidding projects some large-scale wind farm construction developed rapidly. This successful experience laid the foundation for further RE policy making. The issuing of the Renewable Energy Law in 2005 symbolized the start of a comprehensive RE policy system. The German model of feed-in tariff policy was enshrined in the Renewable Energy Law and supported by subsequent administrative regulations from different governmental institutions. The issuing of the Renewable Energy Law had a signpost effect for RE investment by guaranteeing a favorable environment for RE generation. RE development has realized rapid growth over the last decade and China has become a leading country in the RE industry. After Five Years of soaring growth (2006-2010), some potential problems such as grid-connection bottlenecks, wind turbine grid disconnection accidents, RE power curtailment and solar panel production overcapacity have emerged to challenge RE development. The downturn of the carbon market, the depression of CDM projects and the anti-dumping duty for solar panels from the U. S. and the EU have had deleterious effects on RE development. However, even despite these adversities on two levels, China still holds to its ambitious RE targets. In order to overcome the grid-connection and curtailment problems, the Renewable Energy Law Amendment was issued in 2009 to introduce the mandatory quota system combined with the FIT, setting a milestone for improving the effectiveness of the whole RE policy system. The mandatory quota system was reaffirmed in the 12th FYP for RE Development in 2011 and more specific regulations were embodied in the Regulation for Management of Renewable Power Quota (Exposure Draft) in May 2012. Later The Assessment Measure for Renewable Power Quota (Trial Implementation) was issued by NDRC in order to set basic and advanced assessment measure indicators for renewable power quota.

The influence mechanism of the climate change socialization process can be identified as the *independent variable* in this book. The research aim was to explore the causal relationship between the independent variable and the dependant variable, that is to say, why and how the climate change socialization process makes a significant impact on domestic RE policy change and through which specific approaches. Through process-tracing, Chapter 4 explored five stages in China's participation in the international climate change regime and showed how socialization into the regime influenced domestic climate change policy. With a deeper involvement in the climate change regime, China's stance has undergone a gradual change, becoming more flexible and proactive. This kind of evolution through socialization was caused not only from its adaptive role-playing (establishing new bureaucratic agencies and a low-carbon discourse shift) to gain more diplomatic support, but also from its strategic calculation in the international regime. China was influenced by visible material incentives (financial support, know-how and technology transfer) and invisible social influences: national reputation and credibility, and especially the effects of continuous international pressure for China to act due to its high and rapidly growing GHG emissions. While treating the international climate regime (together with the climate change discourse) as a significant social context, the influence of international pressures on China to reduce its carbon emissions on domestic energy policy cannot be underestimated. In August 2008, the Standing Committee of the NPC issued the Resolution on Actively Responding to Climate Change, which symbolized the legislative start of climate policy legislation. The Exposure Draft of the Climate Change Law was issued in March 2012 and the ratification process will be conducted by the NPC in following three years. Since the carbon intensity target and the RE development target are the two main goals in China's climate change mitigation framework, the Climate Change Law will provide stronger legislative support for the implementation of a mandatory RE quota system.

Through in-depth process tracing of RE policy change and China's participation in the climate change regime in the past two decades, this book has argued that there is a diachronic covariance of climate change regime influence and the domestic RE policy development. Since the NDRC became the main negotiator in the climate change regime and signed the Kyoto Protocol in 1998, China began to design its RE policy. It introduced tendering policy/concession projects beginning in 2003, just after the ratification of the Kyoto Protocol in 2002. When the Kyoto Protocol came into force in 2005, China issued the Renewable Energy Law in the same year to introduce the feed-in tariff policy. After the 2009 Copenhagen Climate Conference, the quota system policy, combined with the FIT system, was introduced to the RE policy system through issuing the RE Law Amendment in the same year. In order to confront with the international requirement for signing legally-binding agreement in Paris Conference, China submitted its Intended Nationally Determined Contribution (INDC) Document to UN in July 2015. The ambitious RE target embodied in INDC has significant implications to the exposure draft of 13th Five-Year Plan issued in October 2015.

In this context, the concept of the pro-RE coalition based on Sabatier's advocacy coalition framework (ACF) has been introduced into the analysis, to investigate the coalition building of the proponents of RE and to analyze the interaction of different stakeholders in RE policy change. The pro-RE coalition includes various governmental and societal actors who share a set of similar normative and causal values related to sustainable development, green growth, climate protection and RE development and who often act in concert to promote RE policy change. During the intensified societal interaction with the international climate change regime, the pro-RE coalition in China gained a favorable political opportunity structure and more power, through institutional anchoring and resource reallocation. Chapter 5 has explored these micro-processes of climate change socialization and provides a comprehensive picture of the strengthening of the pro-RE coalition. Actors in the pro-RE coalition have more voice to challenge the validity of the conventional energy forces and promote RE policy change. Chapters 5 and 6 summarized the characteristics of the pro-RE coalition, and analyzed its role in competing with conventional forces to introduce a RE quota system to combine with the feed-in tariff policy. Therefore, although energy security concerns and the interest in a growing domestic "climate industry" are strong factors to drive RE development, without the external dynamics from the climate change regime, the pro-RE coalition would not have been able to grow so rapidly and gain enough political resources to break the coal-based lock-in pattern.

8.2 Theoretical perspectives

The goal of this book is to analyze how the capacity building of the pro-RE coalition was strengthened through the climate change socialization process and how the coalition competed with conventional energy forces to promote RE policy change. In order to link the influence of the international regime with the domestic energy policy change, I combined socialization theory with Sabatier's advocacy coalition framework (ACF), aiming to investigate how international factors, such as external impetus, impacted on domestic RE policy development.

The active role of the state in the socialization process

In the socialization process, the government is not a passive receiver of international rules; instead, the domestic structure decides whether the international regime matters and how it matters. Socialization theory should not be treated as "top-down" unidirectional theory and the international regime is not a "normative teacher" to guiding government behavior. On the contrary, government institutions have played an autonomous role in identifying their interests and national policy preferences at the international level. Their international positions are influenced by their domestic interest calculations and the interactions among different stakeholders. Jeffrey T. Checkel (2001, 2005) and Alastair I. Johnston (2003, 2008) attempt to interlink the rationalist approach and the constructivist approach to explain the compliance behavior of governments in international institutions. There is an international political game that takes place in climate negotiations. States are attempting to maximize their domestic political benefits and to minimize the negative effects of the international agreement. It is undeniable that during the strategic calculation process, the agenda-setting and signaling mechanisms provide an external impetus that can facilitate a reallocation of resources among domestic actors. In addition, due to the bounded rationality of novices in a context of uncertainty, governments tend to adapt their behavior in order to fit into the new atmosphere smoothly. The state imitates in a "non-reflective" way the institutional arrangement, procedural and behavioral rules, and discourses embodied in the international regime. This in turn can to a certain degree have an institutional anchoring effect. Checkel titles this process "role playing" (Checkel 2005: 810) and Johnston calls it "mimicking" (Johnston 2005: 1021-1022). Based on the institutional lock-in effect, the international regime has chances to exert more impact on the state and gradually stimulate "normative turning" or "pro-norm" behavior. Checkel and Johnston resort to institutionalism and functionalism to bridge the "logic of consequences" of rationalism and the "logic of appropriateness" of constructivism. However, the degree of institutional anchoring in the bureaucratic system will finally decide the degree of influence of the international regime. In other words, whether the new bureaucratic agencies have sufficient power and authority to influence the policy-making process is the key standard to judge the effectiveness of the socialization process.

Capacity building of the advocacy coalition interlinking the international regime and domestic policy-making

This book does not focus on the compliance of the state with the international climate regime. My approach has been to explore how certain domestic stakeholders take advantage of international sources to gain influence in the policy-making system. If the state joins in the international regime for whatever purpose, its role-playing behaviors and interest strategic calculation at the international level will inevitably influence institutional arrangements and resource reallocation at the domestic level. Some stakeholders will gain and some stakeholders will lose in this two-level game. Sabatier argues that the capability of an advocacy coalition to promote policy change in the policy-making system depends upon its resources (money, expertise, number of supporters, and legal authority) (Sabatier and Jenkins-Smith 1993b: 29). Therefore, the strengthening of the capacity of the advocacy coalition—in our case related to the international socialization process—is the key to bridging between the external influence of the international regime and domestic policy change. Although Sabatier also mentions that "the advocacy coalition and the external events out of the subsystem will play a significant role in the resource reallocation in the direction of the advocacy coalition framework" (Sabatier and Jenkins-Smith 1993b: 29), he does not pay due attention to the domestic coalition building process under the influence of international socialization. Regarding domestic RE policy development, this book treats the capacity building of the pro-RE coalition as the significant link to understanding how the pro-RE coalition gets strengthened by the climate change socialization process. The main argument of this book can be summarized as follows: through the institutional anchoring and resource reallocation that resulted from socialization into the climate change regime, the pro-RE coalition gained more political resources and increased its authority and thereby its ability to compete successfully with the conventional energy forces by means of policy-oriented learning and argumentative persuasion.

A two-step model illustrating the influence of socialization on domestic policy change

Checkel introduces three micro-processes, strategic calculation, role playing and normative suasion in his study of the socialization process in international regimes (Checkel 2005). Based on an analysis of the active role of one state in the socialization process, I argue that the international regime is not the main "teacher" or "persuader" using normative suasion to influence state behavior. Instead, the domestic actors at the sub-national level should be given more attention in the normative persuasion process. Through strengthening their capacity in the socialization process, some advocacy coalitions have played a significant role in competing with the dominant coalition and promoting policy change through argumentative persuasion. The analytical model in this book deals with two aspects: *First*, I explore how role playing and strategic calculation tied to the international climate change socialization process influence the strength of the pro-RE coalition. *Second*, I investigate how the strengthened pro-RE coalition promotes RE policy change through policy-oriented learning and argumentative persuasion. There is no strict sequential order between the two steps in the climate change socialization process. Instead, they are reinforcing relations that coexist in different stages of RE policy change.

The theoretical analysis was based on institutionalism and rationalism. In order to explore how role playing and strategic calculation influence the capacity building of different actors at the domestic level, I investigated micro-logic-chains in the socialization process. Here I start from two hypotheses: *first*, the stronger the institutional, procedural and discursive lock-in effect in the role playing process of the climate change regime, the more supporters of the pro-RE coalition will emerge and the more institutional anchoring will be achieved; *second*, the more material incentives (financial support and technology transfer) and social influence (especially reputational pressure) emanate from the climate change regime into the strategic calculation process, the more resource reallocation in the direction of the pro-RE coalition will take place.

The second aspect relates to the role of the strengthened pro-RE coalition in energy policy change towards RE. I start from the following hypothesis: the more effectively policy-oriented learning and argumentative persuasion are promoted by the strengthened pro-RE coalition, the more possibility there will be for the pro-RE coalition to influence RE policy change. According to the ACF framework, different advocacy coalitions compete with each other in order to translate their own belief into the final policy output. Through policy-oriented learning, the pro-RE coalition can learn from best practices, enhance the causal understanding of emerging problems and improve the plausibility of the new policy proposal. Based on policy-oriented learning, the pro-RE further challenges the validity of conventional energy forces and exposes the loopholes in existing RE policy. It then attempts to persuade key policy brokers (like the State Council and paramount leaders) to solve the problem and offers them a policy proposal. In the climate change socialization process, the pro-RE coalition gains more supporters, receives more R&D investment and financial support to conduct policy research and to promote a hierarchical upgrading of pro-RE institutions, which provides more channels for the pro-RE coalition to influence the central decision-making agencies and paramount leaders.

8.3 Main empirical findings

To combine the socialization theory and the ACF provides us with a new theoretical perspective to study domestic policy change under the influence of international socialization. In order to examine the theoretical hypotheses, this book applies the theoretical model to a "within case study" of RE policy change in China. The *main empirical findings* include:

The climate change regime matters due to the salience of climate change and effective links with bureaucratic processes at the domestic level

I emphasize the significant role of the climate change socialization process, as an indispensable external impetus that made it possible to break through China's domestic carbon lock-in dependence. It thus, indirectly spawned new institutions and promoted resource reallocation among different stakeholders. Treating the climate change regime as a main explanatory factor behind domestic RE policy change does not mean I follow a "top-down" unidirectional normative persuasion approach or treat a state as a "passive receiver" of the "teaching role" of the climate change regime. On the contrary, I go beyond rationalist and constructivist approaches to focus on the interaction among different sub-national stakeholders in the RE policy-making system.

In the coal-dominated energy supply system of China, the capacity building of the pro-RE coalition is the central key to understanding the influence of the climate change regime on domestic RE policy change. However, a precondition to analyzing the role of climate change socialization is to go deep into the domestic level to see why and how international climate policy matters. The influence of the climate change regime depends on its salience in the domestic structure. There needs to be a powerful bureaucratic agency working as a "window agency", to translate the international climate change commitment into national economic planning and energy regulation. In the pro-RE coalition, the special role of the NDRC in energy regulation and the climate change negotiations should be attached much more importance. Before the Kyoto Protocol was signed in 1997, climate change did not get due political attention. The National Group of Co-ordination on Climate Change, which was led by the China Meteorological Administration (CMA) and the State Environmental Protection Administration (SEPA), was no more than a weak and dispersed institution; it did not involve key economic actors. When the SDPC/NDRC, a powerful agency in macro-economic planning and energy regulation, took the main responsibility for the climate change negotiations in 1998, it symbolized that climate change had gained significantly more attention and a higher place on the policy agenda. The empirical analysis has proven that new RE and climate change institutions emerged within the NDRC. They have built an effective institutional channel between climate change policy and RE development. This has further influenced the designing and application of RE policy instruments in the Five-Year Plan.

The climate change regime has necessitated significant institutional change in the Chinese government in order for it to deal with the consequences of its involvement in the climate regime negotiations

According to the empirical research done here, China's role playing in the climate change negotiations, a form of socialization, has led to obvious institutional, procedural and discursive lock-in effects in the bureaucratic system. Along with this institutional anchoring, the pro-RE coalition has gained support from more key governmental actors. When the SDPC/NDRC took over the full responsibility for the climate change negotiations, several institutions were established within the SDPC/NDRC, such as the Center for Renewable Energy Development (CRED) and the Research Center for Energy Environment and Climate Change (RCEECC) within the

Energy Research Institute (ERI), to deal with the climate change negotiations and CDM project implementation. In 2001, the Department of New Energy and Renewable Energy (DNERE) was established and in 2008, the Department of Climate Change. At first, these institutions did not gain much power; however, along with the rising salience of climate change as an issue and low-carbon development priorities, they gained more legal authority and political resources and as a result could better defend their own interests in the bureaucratic system. In addition, pro-RE actors not only grew in number but also in the power hierarchy. After China issued the National Climate Change Program in 2007, the National Leading Group on Climate Change (NLGCC) and the State Council Energy Conservation and Emissions Reduction Leading Group were established. This showed the importance the Chinese government was placing on its voluntary climate change mitigation actions focused on energy conservation and RE development. Since the Copenhagen Conference (2009), China has been under unprecedented international reputational pressures from the climate change regime. In response, the NDRC established the China National Center for Climate Change Strategy and International Cooperation (NCSC) in 2011 and the CRED was upgraded to a national level think tank—the China National Renewable Energy Center (CNREC) in 2012. This symbolizes that climate change and RE development have gained priority places on the political agenda. In the procedural lock-in process, more administrative regulations and legislative documents regarding climate change and RE development have been integrated into governmental daily routines, especially after the issuing of the draft Climate Change Law. A green index has been gradually introduced into the local official performance evaluation system to break the one-sided orientation towards industrial growth. The discourses of climate change, carbon-intensity and low-carbon development now are used more frequently by paramount leaders. These concepts also were more prominent in the 12th Five-Year Plan. The integration of green policy at the institutional level has enhanced governmental coordination of RE development. The emergence of more RE research institutes, think tanks and RE industry associations has strengthened the capacity of the pro-RE coalition.

The increasing capacity of the pro-RE coalition is apparent from the emergence of organized societal supporters

Along with its institutional anchoring in the bureaucratic system, the increasing plurality of actors involved in RE policy making has stimulated the emergence of societal pro-RE forces. The pro-RE coalition has gained more key societal supporters. They include low-carbon and RE research centers as well as RE experts in universities (e. g., the Institute of Low Carbon Economy in Tsinghua University and the Research Center for World New Energy Strategy in Peking University); RE industry associations (e. g. , the Chinese Renewable Energy Society—CRES and the Chinese Renewable Energy Industries Association—CREIA); environmental NGOs (e. g. , Greenpeace in China and the Institute of Public and Environmental Affairs—IPE) and the organizers of professional RE websites (e. g. , Polaris Power, the New Energy Net and the bilingual China Dialogue). These societal actors played an increasingly active role in the process of RE policy improvements, especially in the exposing of grid-connection bottlenecks and RE power curtailments. They are representatives of the interests of renewable industries and act as a bridge between governmental agencies and RE industries. They fight for a more favorable policy context for RE and expose RE development problems as well as policy loopholes to policy brokers. In addition, societal actors have become more close to pro-RE governmental actors. There are increasingly cooperative relations between the CRED and the CRES and CREIA. This kind of tendency has increased the cohesiveness of the pro-RE coalition. For instance, in the grid disconnection accidents, the China Wind Energy Association (CWEA), cooperating with the National Energy Administration (NEA), launched a large-scale survey on the quality of wind turbines covering the entire wind industry in 2011 (CNB Daily 2011).

Strategic calculations have led to resource reallocations that have strengthened the pro-RE coalition's position

In the coal-dominated energy structure, China's strategic calculations vis-à-vis the climate change regime have focused on material incentives and social influence. These stimulated a reallocation of resources towards the pro-RE coalition. There is a two-stage "spiral model" of international material incentives in the strategic calculation: the outside-in oriented stage and domestic enhancement stage. When a state takes part in some kind of international regime, there is a positive correlation between the issue salience and the input of international supportive resources. For instance, the Clean Development Mechanism (CDM), the China Renewable Energy Development Project (REDP), the China Renewable Energy Scale-up Program (CRESP) and other multilateral or bilateral funds of the climate change regime have played a significant role in stimulating the development of the RE sector in the initial stage. The international incentives as well as the successful experience of RE development in China has pushed the RE issue onto the mainstream of the political agenda and it gained more attention. More and more domestic resources have been reallocated to the RE sector to further enhance the coalition building of the pro-RE coalition. Apart from the spiral model, a "signaling mechanism" has also played a significant role towards resource reallocation. Along with the increasing international reputational pressure placed on China, national leaders are being forced more and more to make (voluntary) commitments in the climate change regime. This in turn sends a positive signal regarding RE at the domestic level. Especially after the 2009 Copenhagen Climate Conference, the carbon-intensity target and RE development target were tied together and then broken down to the provincial level. Later, the Regulation for Management of Renewable Power Quota (Exposure Draft) set mandatory RE quotas for different provinces. These mandatory targets have made a breakthrough in the resource allocation pattern at the local level. In addition, national strategic targets in the Five-Year Plan play a signaling role in RE policy change. Particularly by the embodiment in the 12th FYP (2011-2015), the carbon-intensity reduction and low-carbon strategy has provided more dynamics to pro-RE actors and spurred further RE policy change.

Policy-oriented learning and argumentative persuasion promoted by the pro-RE coalition

Through institutional anchoring and resource reallocation, the capacity building of the pro-RE coalition has been enhanced (in terms of the number of supporters, national financial investments, legal authority, and research expertise) and become increasingly stronger in its ability to compete with conventional forces (like the state-owned grid enterprises, state-owned coal and oil enterprises, nuclear industry and some local forces of resistance to change) in the RE policy-making system. Through comparing the capacity of the pro-RE coalition in 2005 and 2009, it was shown that the pro-RE coalition has gained key governmental and societal supporters and more financing. The upgrading of RE and climate change institutions in the governmental hierarchy has provided the pro-RE coalition with more channels to influence the State Council and paramount leaders in the Politburo. The CRED within the NDRC has been presented as the "key learning agency" to lead RE policy research in China and to provide RE policy proposals directly to the NDRC. As a governmental research institution, the CRED has launched a series of comprehensive studies on various RE policy instruments in different western countries (especially the former U. K. , German and U. S. models), and explored effective measures to stimulate the industrialization process of large-scale RE development. In addition, the Department of Climate Change and the Department of New Energy and Renewable Energy (DNERE) in the NDRC and other governmental agencies related to RE policy have all played active roles as proponents of RE development. Led by the CRED, the pro-RE actors began to explore the feasibility of the quota system as well as its compatibility with the feed-in tariff policy. It also provided policy recommendations and feasible solutions for the NDRC to overcome the loopholes in this abstract legislative framework. In addition, the pro-RE societal actors have played an increasingly proactive role in terms of policy-oriented learning and argumentative persuasion. More RE experts have voice and influential authority in the RE policy making process as more political channels have opened up. They even have been invited to the Politburo Collective Study Sessions of the CPC to stimulate further RE policy-oriented learning. In terms of argumentative persuasion, pro-RE societal actors have challenged the validity of the arguments of conventional energy actors and begun to provide feasible policy proposals that boost expectations for RE development and can be used to persuade policy brokers. The report, China Wind Power Outlook 2012, which was jointly issued by Greenpeace, the Chinese Renewable Energy Industries Association (CREIA), and the Global Wind Energy Council (GWEC), exposed the serious situation of wind curtailment in China and stimulated heated social discussion and constrained the behavior of state-owned enterprises by introducing a quota system. Confronted with the anti-dumping tariff imposed by the U. S. and the EU, the China Renewable Energy Society (CRES) proposed to develop a distributed power generation system in order to quickly enlarge the domestic PV power market and save the PV panel industry. In addition, these societal actors cooperated with pro-RE governmental actors to lobby national leaders to set up more ambitious targets for PV power in the 12th FYP.

Implications of the RE quota system for China's green transformation

The influence of climate change socialization on RE policy change has been significant. China made carbon-intensity reduction and RE development commitments in 2009. It launched a carbon trading pilot and guaranteed the future role of this market-based instrument for GHG emission abatement when it issued the Climate Change Law in 2012. The 2013 FYP for Energy Development set a cap on energy consumption. The pro-RE coalition has taken advantage of this favorable atmosphere to promote further RE policy change. This process may stimulate a new round of reform in the energy sector in a spiral fashion. In order to solve the grid-connection and transmission bottleneck, the mandatory RE quotas system will be combined with the feed-in tariff policy. With the growth and maturity of the domestic carbon trading system, the renewable quotas could be directly transferred to the Chinese Certified Emission Reduction (CCER) system. The carbon trading mechanism can "increase economic efficiency in meeting renewable generation targets by increasing the flexibility of grid companies and generators to meet their targets through the market-based measures" (Schuman and Lin 2012: 102). The maintenance of carbon emission trading needs to be stimulated by an electricity market reform and a GHG emission cap. Although China emphasizes that it will be hard to reach its emission peak by 2020 or even 2030, if a legally binding climate change agreement covering all the member states is reached by 2015, setting a GHG emission cap will be a necessity (it might be a relative GHG emission cap first rather than an absolute cap). In this spiral process, rapid RE growth promoted by the pro-RE coalition and the coupling of the RE quota system with the domestic carbon trading system could further stimulate a series of green reforms and be a prelude to the strategic transformation of the energy sector in the middle- to long-run.

Appendix I
The Renewable Energy Policy System in China

First and second levels of the renewable energy policy system in China

Fields	Year	Title	Institution	Main Contents
National legislative framework	2005. 2 Effective 2006. 1	The Renewable Energy Law	NPC	The main aim is to introduce a FIT policy. Grid enterprises shall purchase all the RE power within the coverage of their power grid; a series of measures and goals related to price regulation, special funds and tax relief.
	2009. 12 Effective 2010. 4	The Renewable Energy Law Amendment	NPC	The amendment aims to set quota to require the state grid companies to purchase the RE power and to establish RE development fund, including dedicated money arranged from the national government's annual budget, and additional revenue from legally authorized levies on RE power prices.
	Other relevant laws: Air Pollution Law (NPC, effect. 1/2000); Circular Economy Promotion Law (NPC, effect. 1/2009); Electric Power Supervision Regulation (State Council, effect. 5/2005); Energy Law in progress (draft for comment, NDRC, issued 12/2007); Air Pollution Law Amendment (NPC, effect. 1/2016); Environmental Protection Taxes Law (draft for comment, State Council, issued 6/2015)			

National FYP strategic targets (mandatory target-driven policy)	2006.3	The 11th FYP (2006-2010)	State Council	To decrease the per-unit GDP energy consumption 20% by 2010 compared to 2005, targeting an annual savings rate of 4%. The total amount of major pollutants discharged will go down by 10%.
	2007.9	The Mid- and Long-Term Development Plan for Renewable Energy (2007-2020)	State Council	By 2010, China aims to raise the share of RE in total primary energy consumption to 10%. By 2020, it will aim to raise this share to 15%. Mandated market share (MMS) policies: It is required that the power plants with equity installed capacity of over 5 GW shall have an equity installed capacity of non-hydro RE accounting for 3% of their total capacity by 2010, and over 8% by 2020.
	2008.3	The Renewable Energy Development Plan under the 11th FYP	State Council	Raising the share of RE in total primary energy consumption to 10% by 2010. The annual RE utilization amounts to 300 million tons of standard coal; wind power total installed capacity reaching 10 million kilowatts, biomass power 5.5 million kilowatts and solar photovoltaic 300,000 kilowatts.
	2010.10	The Decision on Accelerating the Cultivation and Development of Strategic Emerging Industries	State Council	The RE has been listed as key-development strategic emerging industries in China. Fostering the implementation of the quota system to guarantee the system of safeguards for the purchase of the full amount of power generated from RE.
	2011.3	The 12th FYP (2011-2015)	State Council	The RE has been listed in the new strategic industry. The quota goals are embodied in the 12th FYP. By 2015, CO_2 emission per-unit GDP would be reduced by 17% and energy consumption per-unit GDP by 16% as compared with that in 2010; the proportion of consumption of non-fossil energy to the consumption of primary energy would be increased to 11.4%.

National FYP strategic targets (mandatory target-driven policy)	2011.9	The 12th FYP's Comprehensive Work Plan for Energy Conservation and Emission Reduction	State Council	Energy efficiency target for 2015 is a reduction in the national energy consumption per 10,000 *yuan* of GDP to 0.869 tons of standard coal, which represents a reduction of 16% compared with the 1.034 tons of standard coal in 2010 and 32% compared with the 1.276 tons of standard coal in 2005; achieving energy savings of 670 million tons of standard coal. Emissions reduction targets for 2015 are to control chemical oxygen demand and sulfur dioxide emissions at 23.476 million tons and 20.864 million tons respectively, representing a reduction of 8% on the 25.517 million tons and 22.678 million tons respectively recorded in 2010.
	2012.8	The 12th FYP for Renewable Energy Development	State Council	By 2015, the annual RE consumption will reach 478 million tce; including 400 million tce coming from commercialized RE, representing more than 9.5% in overall energy mix; the electricity generation from RE would account for more than 20% of total electricity generation by 2015; launching the green energy demonstration projects in 108 counties and the pilot projects of a large-scale utility of RE in buildings in 35 cities and 97 counties.
	2013.1	The 12th FYP for Energy Development	State Council	The total primary energy consumption and electricity consumption will be controlled within 4 billion tce and 6.15 trillion kW · h respectively. The coal consumption rate will decrease to 65%. The proportion of non-fossil energy consumption will increase to 11.4% and non-fossil energy power installation capacity will account for 30%.

National FYP strategic targets (mandatory target-driven policy)	2014.11	Strategic Action Plan for Energy Development	State Council	By 2020, non fossil energy accounts for 15% proportion of primary energy consumption, the proportion of coal consumption will be controlled within 62%. By 2020, the wind power installed capacity will reach 200 GW, wind power electricity price equals to the coal electricity price. By 2020, the PV installed capacity will reach 100 GW, the photovoltaic power price equals to general sales price of national grids.
National FYP relevant national climate change targets on RE	2007.6	China's National Climate Change Programme 2007	NDRC	This program defines guiding principles, main fields and key tasks concerning the work of addressing climate change. As required by this document, 31 provinces, autonomous regions and municipalities directly under the central government have all worked out their own programs to address climate change, and have put them into practice.
	2009. 11	China's Policies and Actions for Addressing Climate Change 2009	NDRC	Voluntary carbon-intensity commitment before the Copenhagen Conference: Reducing its carbon intensity (the amount of CO_2 emitted per unit GDP) by 40%-45% by 2020 compared to 2005 levels and obtaining 15% of all of its energy from non-fossil energy sources was expanded to encompass all non-fossil energy by 2020.
	2012.5	The Climate Change Law (Exposure Draft)	NPC	Including five important systems: climate change planning system; governmental responsibility system; coal consumption cap and domestic carbon trading system; carbon tax and its imposition principle system; and information disclosure system.

National FYP relevant national climate change targets on RE	2012. 11	China's Policies and Actions for Addressing Climate Change 2012	NDRC	Formulating and implementing the Work Plan for Greenhouse Gases Emission control during the 12th FYP Period. To promote low-carbon pilot projects in selected provinces and cities, launch carbon emission trading pilot programs, and explore the experience of different regions and industries in implementing low-carbon development through projects that encourage low-carbon products, transport systems and towns.
	2014. 11	China-U. S. Joint Statement on Climate Change	State Council	China plans to peak its CO_2 emissions before 2030 and will try to reach its peak at an early date, and plans to increase the proportion of non-fossil energy to 20% by 2030.
	2015. 7	Intended Nationally Determined Contribution (INDC)	NDRC	China plans to reduce the carbon intensity of its economy 60%-65% per unit of GDP by 2030, compared with 2005 levels, and reiterates a previously-announced aim that RE should make up 20% of its primary energy supply by the same date.

Abbreviations: NPC—National People's Congress; NDRC—National Development and Reform Commission.

Source: Compiled by the author.

Third level of the renewable energy policy system in China

Fields	Year	Title	Institution	Main Contents
Tendering policy	Beginning in 2003	The Interim Measure for wind power concession bidding projects	NDRC	Significant policy for initiating-stage renewable development, in order to explore the proper feed-in tariff. Beginning in 2003, it is mainly used in the large-scale wind power base project bidding, off-shore wind power project bidding, large ground-based photovoltaic power plant concession bidding.
Feed-in RE tariffs/prices	2006.1	The Management Regulation Related to RE Power Generation	NDRC	Grid connection tariffs should be set by the price regulatory department of the State Council according to the characteristics of different types of RE power generation and the circumstances of different localities.
	2009.7	The Notice on Policy to Improve Grid-Connected Power Pricing for Wind Power	NDRC	The grid-connected electricity price for different regions based on different resources and construction conditions: 0.51 *yuan*/(kW · h), 0.54 *yuan*/(kW · h), 0.58 *yuan*/(kW · h), 0.61 *yuan*/(kW · h) for four different wind-resources regions respectively.
	2010.1	The Interim Measure for the Management of Development and Construction of Off-Shore Wind Power	NEA, SOA	The price of off-shore is decided by the bidding price through the concession bidding projects.

Feed-in RE tariffs/prices	2010	The Standard for Feed-in Policy of National Unified Agricultural and Forestry Biomass	NDRC	Feed-in tariff for biomass was 0.25 *yuan*/(kW · h) higher than that of the electricity from the coal-fired power plants equipped with desulfurization facilities from January 2006 to June 2010. As of July 2010, the national feed-in tariff is equal to 0.75 *yuan*/(kW · h).
	2011.7	The Notice on Feed-in Tariff Policy of Solar Photovoltaic	NDRC	Solar PV FIT is 1.15 *yuan*/(kW · h) for all solar PV projects approved before July 1, 2011 and completed by December 31, 2011, and 1.00 *yuan*/(kW · h) for projects approved after July 1, 2011 or not completed by December 31, 2011. Tibet has a FIT of 1.15 *yuan*/(kW · h) for all projects.
Grid connection and RPS consideration	2007.7	The Regulatory Measure on Off-take Purchase of Electricity from RE Sources by Grid Companies	SERC	The power utilities must purchase renewable in a priority referring to the RE Law and provide grid-connection service. The grid connecting costs also could be shared in the power price levied towards the electricity users.
	2007.8	The Measure on Energy-saving Power Generation Dispatch	NDRC SERC NEB SEPA	Grid operation issues related to implementing priority dispatch; defining conditions for allowable curtailment by grid companies and appropriate compensation to generators; and developing renewable power technical standards.
	2012.5	The Regulation for Management of Renewable Power Quota (Exposure Draft)	NEA	The national RES quota index will be allocated to the regional or provincial power and grid companies, especially the State Grid and China Southern Power Grid will bear the associated quota. The State will set up RE development fund, and set aside a certain amount of subsidies to support the construction of power grids.

	2012.11	The Suggestion on Distributed Grid of Solar PV power	NDRC	Aim to improve China's photovoltaic solar industry by encouraging distributed power generation, or the use of small energy sources such as solar panels and wind turbines.
Grid connection and RPS consideration	2014.9	The Assessment Measure for Renewable Power Quota (Trial Implementation)	NDRC	The eastern region should take more responsibility for RE development and further improve the quota target of eastern region; enforce the power grid enterprises to complete the quota responsibility; the assessment measure indicators for renewable power quota include two levels: the basic index and advanced index.
	2015.3	Guidance on Power Operation Adjustment Optimization to Improve Renewable Power Grid Access	NDRC NEA	All provinces should enhance full-time generation and trans-provincial transmission of RE power by guaranteeing full-time RE grid access, especially to promote benefit compensation mechanism so as to enlarge the market space for RE power consumption; give priority for increasing the RE power generation in new electricity demand; and encourage direct transaction between RE producer and user.
Cost sharing	2006	The Interim Management Measure for Renewable Power Tariff and Cost Sharing	NDRC	The difference between the grid-connected power price of RE projects and of local desulfurized coal power constructed with state investment or subsidies and the average sale price of the local provincial power grid, as well as the cost of connecting RE power facilities to the grid, will be met by levying an additional surcharge on end users.

Cost sharing	2007	The Interim Measure on Allocation of Income from Surcharges on Renewable Power Prices	NDRC	The excess between the expenses incurred in the purchase of average power price generated with conventional energy shall be shared in the selling price; RE price difference shall be obtained from the provincial electricity sales revenue and adjusted by the State in a unified way.
Special fund	2006.6	The Interim Measure on Special Fund Management of RE Development	MOF	There are two main ways to provide special fund for promoting RE development: governmental grant and governmental discounted loan (loan with discounted interest).
	2008.8	The Interim Measure on Management of Special-Project Funds for Industrialization of Wind Power Generation Equipment	MOF	The industrial financial support aims to encourage industrialization and localization of wind turbine manufacturing: to provide subsidy of 600 *yuan*/kW for the first 50 megawatt wind turbines in the enterprises.
	2009.7	The Interim Measure on the Management of Public Subsidies for Golden Sun Demonstration Projects	MOF	In order to accelerate the industrialization and large-scale development of photovoltaic power generation, the government combines the financial assistance with the technology support and market driven approach. The grid-connected photovoltaic power generation project could get the financial subsidy equaling to the 50% of its total investment. The independent photovoltaic power generation system in remote areas could get subsidies to 70% of its total investment.
	Other regulations on special funds: the Interim Measure for Use of Public Finance Subsidy Funds Management for Solar Photovoltaic Use in Buildings (MOF, effect. 3/2009); the Notice on the Management of Construction of Golden Sun Demonstration Projects and Solar-PV Building-Application Demonstration Projects (MOF, et al. 9/2010).			

	2005	The Catalogue for the Guidance of RE Industry Development	NDRC	The Catalogue covers 88 RE development, utilization and system device/equipment manufacture of six regions. As for the project equipped with scale development and utilization, the relevant departments of the State Council will establish and perfect preferential policies concerning technological research and development, project model, financial taxation, product price, marketing, import and export.
	2008	The Catalog of Tax Preferences for Public Infrastructure Projects	MOF, SAT	Eligible enterprises developing RE projects pay no taxes on first three years of income from project, and 50% of the normal tax rate for the next three years.
Tax preference and low-interest loans	2008	The Import Tariff Adjustment for Large Wind Turbines, Key Components and Raw Materials	MOF	Cancellation of duty-free policy on the imported original wind turbine machine, and carrying out tariff incentives on import of key components and shortage materials of wind turbines in order to encourage the domestic R&D on wind turbines.
	2012	The Energy-Saving and New Energy Automotive Industry Development Plan (2012-2020)	NDRC	The energy-saving and new energy automotive industry and their key components production enterprises could enjoy the tax exemption policy of business tax. The new energy automobile demonstration projects and pilot programs could get governmental subsidies.
	Article 25 of the RE Law states that "national government and financial institutions may offer preferential loan with financial interest subsidy (low-interest loans) to RE development and utilization projects that are listed in the National RE Industrial Development Guidance Catalogue and qualified for the credit conditions". Article 26 of the RE Law states that "The Government grants tax benefits to projects listed in the National RE Industrial Development Guidance Catalogue and specific methods are to be prepared by the State Council". In the Mid- and Long-Term Development Plan for RE, it mentions that "The national government grants a favorable tax rate to renewable technology R&D and equipment manufacture".			

RE development standards	2006	The Technical Code for Solar Water Heating System of Civil Building	MOHURD	The technical code includes requirements for solar water heating system design, the architectural design, the installation steps and solar water heating system acceptance.
	2011	The Opinion on the Promotion for the Orderly Development of Wind Turbine Manufacturing	NDRC	Control the overcapacity and vicious competition in wind turbine manufacturing industry; improve the quality testing system, certification system and industry access system of wind turbine; promote the technological innovation and industrial upgrading; promote the off-shore wind turbine R&D.
	2012	The Technology Regulation for Wind Farm Connecting into Power System	AQSIQ	Setting relevant technical requirements for wind farms connecting to the national grid, especially specifying the general technical requirements for grid-connection design of large-scale wind farms.
	National or influential industrial standards, technical code for Solar Water Heating System of Civil Buildings, Bio-diesel for Blending Diesel Engine Fuel, Denatured Bio-ethanol, Ethanol Gasoline for Motor Vehicles; improve technical and product quality of RE through establishing testing and certification system.			

Abbreviations: NDRC—National Development and Reform Commission; NEA—National Energy Administration; NEB—National Energy Bureau (2003-2008); SOA—State Oceanic Administration; SERC—State Electricity Regulatory Commission of China; SEPA—State Environmental Protection Administration (1988-2008); MOF—Ministry of Finance; MOHURD—Ministry of Housing and Urban Rural Development of China; AQSIQ—General Administration of Quality Supervision, Inspection and Quarantine; SAT—State Administration of Taxation.

Source: Compiled by the author.

Appendix II
Key Governmental and Societal Actors in the Renewable Energy Policy System of China

Key governmental actors in the renewable energy policy system

Category	Institutions	Year	Functions
Key RE policy making agencies	The Politburo Standing Committee	1949	The CPC's highest body retains the ultimate decision-making power; the number of official actors vying to influence the top leadership's decisions has expanded considerably.
	The State Council Energy Conservation and Emissions Reduction Leading Group	2007	Regulating the national guide line and strategy for the energy conservation, emission reduction and low-carbon development.
	National Energy Commission (NEC)	2010	A high-level coordination body with ministerial rank, which is responsible for drafting national energy development plan, reviewing energy security and major energy issues as well as monitoring implementation.
	The National Development and Reform Commission (NDRC) (1952-1998 the State Planning Commission; 1998-2003 the State Development Planning Commission)	2003	Most powerful ministerial agency: As a macroeconomic management agency, formulating policies for economic and social development, and guiding the overall economic system restructuring, especially project approval and price-setting schemes.

Key RE policy making agencies	The National Energy Administration (2003-2008 the National Energy Bureau)	2008	Responsible for formulating and implementing energy development plans and industrial policies; promoting institutional reform in the energy sector, including planning for RE development. In charge of collecting funds from the RE surcharge and distributing them to grid companies.
	The Department of New Energy and Renewable Energy	2001	Supervising RE development, setting the industrial standards for RE, participating in the electricity system reform, coordinating the implementation of RE projects.
	The Pricing Department	1998	Responsible for setting prices for energy, among other economic goods, including setting the on-grid price for wind generated power, biomass power, solar PV power.
	The Climate Change Department of the NDRC	2008	Responsible for formulating the major strategic policy on climate change, fostering the implementation of tasks in the framework of the UNFCCC and the Kyoto Protocol.
	The Department of Resource Conservation and Environmental Protection	2003	After China ratified the Kyoto Protocol, this agency was established to promote the energy efficiency policy making and implementation.
Key governmental RE policy research agencies	The Center for Renewable Energy Development (CRED)	1998	Key RE research institute under the ERI. It aims to explore the feasibility of the RE Law formulation in China, study the innovative policy instruments to develop the RE industry and offer annual reports and policy proposals for the ERI and the NDRC.
	China National Renewable Energy Center (CNREC)	2012	The national key institution for assisting China's energy authorities in RE policy research, and industrial management and coordination. Main actor responsible for drafting the RE laws and regulations.

Key governmental RE policy research agencies	The Development Research Center of the State Council (DRC)	1981	A comprehensive policy research and consulting institution directly under the State Council.
	The National Strategic Research and International Cooperation Center for Climate Change (NCSC) in the NDRC	2012	The first national-level think tank on climate change to focus on strategic research and international cooperation, especially launching the comprehensive research on strategic planning, policy proposals and the carbon trading design.
	The State Expert Advisory Committee (SEAC)	2007	Established under the National Energy Leading Group, making suggestions on energy strategy and offering solutions for major problems in energy development.
	China Council for International Cooperation on Environment and Development (CCICED)	1992	The main task is exchanging and disseminating international successful experience in the field of environment and development; putting forward policy recommendations to the national leaders.
Key governmental RE policy research agencies	Chinese Academy for Environmental Planning (CAEP), under the SEPA/MEP	2001	To provide technical support and services for the environmental planning and consultation on environmental tax designing (like carbon tax).
	Chinese Academy of Science (CAS)	1949	Center for Energy and Environmental Policy Research (CEEP) conducts scientific research on the area of energy and environment, promotes the development and application of energy economics, policy and management science (established in 2006); Center for Sustainable Development: The China Sustainable Development Report (CSDR) since 1999.

Key governmental RE policy research agencies	Chinese Academy of Social Science (CASS)	1977	China Research Society of Urban Development (CRSUD) established Chinese Urban Low-carbon Economy Network (ULCEN) (http://www.cusdn.org.cn/en.php).
Key supportive agencies for RE policy-making	The Ministry of Finance (MOF)	1949	Promoting the special fund, tax preference and low-interest loans for RE generators and in charge of RE Development Special Fund and its supported programs.
	The Ministry of Science and Technology (MOST)	1949	Responsible for R&D financial support for RE: playing an important role in terms of technical support and expertise views, particularly in the areas of clean development mechanism (CDM) and other technology transfer development.
	The Ministry of Environmental Protection (MEP) (1998-2008 State Environmental Protection Administration—SEPA)	2008	Responsible for preventing and controlling environmental pollution, promoting environmental assessment of RE development.
Independent supervision	The State Electricity Regulatory Commission (SERC)	2003	Responsible for regulating China's electricity industry (power and grid enterprises), including the integration of renewable electricity into the grid.
SOEs and RE generators	Five large state-owned power enterprises	2002 power market reform	Huaneng, Datang, Huadian, Guodian and CPI, often referred to as the "Big Five", account for half of China's electricity generation and are all active in developing RE projects.

	RE power generators		Guodian's subsidiary, Longyuan, is currently the largest producer of wind in China in terms of installed capacity, with Datang, Huaneng, Huadian, and Guohua (a subsidiary of Shenhua) following in the rankings. The private sectors representing a smaller portion of renewables installed capacity and power generation.
SOEs and RE generators	Two state-owned grid enterprises①	2002 power market reform	Two main state-owned transmission and distribution companies that provide coverage for the entire country: State Grid Corporation of China and China Southern Grid.②
	Three state-owned oil enterprises	1988	the China National Petroleum Corporation (CNPC)
		2000	the China Petroleum and Chemical Corporation (Sinopec)
		1982	the China National Off-shore Oil Corporation (CNOOC)
	Other energy SOEs		Coal SOEs, Nuclear SOEs.

Other relevant actors	The Ministry of Industry and Information Technology (MOIIT) The State-owned Asset Supervision and Administration Commission (SASAC) The Ministry of Commerce (MOC) The Ministry of Agriculture (MOA) The Ministry of Housing and Urban Rural Development (MOHURD) The General Administration of Quality Supervision, Inspection and Quarantine (GAQSIQ) State Forestry Administration (SFA) China Meteorological Administration (CMA) The National Bureau of Statistics (NBS)
Local actors	Provincial NDRC, local power and RE industries

①State Grid's coverage accounts for about 80% of China's total electricity consumption. Covered provinces/municipalities are: Inner Mongolia East, Liaoning, Shaanxi (70% market share), Gansu, Xinjiang, Heilongjiang, Jilin, Ningxia, Shandong, Hebei, Shanxi, Beijing, Tianjin, Qinghai, Jiangsu, Hunan, Henan, Sichuan, Fujian, Shanghai, Anhui, Jiangxi, Zhejiang, Hubei, and Chongqing. Southern Grid operates in Guangdong, Guangxi, Guizhou, Hainan and Yunnan provinces through its subsidiaries.

②In addition, there are two smaller, local grid companies, the Inner Mongolia Power Grid (covering the western part of Inner Mongolia) and Shaanxi Provincial Power Grid (covering 30% of Shaanxi).

Source: Compiled by the author.

Key societal actors in the renewable energy governance system

Category	Institutions	Year	Working fields
Research centers regarding RE development in the universities	Tsinghua University		Research Center for China Studies led by Hu Angang (cooperated with Chinese Academy of Sciences 2001) Institute of Nuclear and New Energy Technology (2003) Center for CDM Research and Development (2005) Institute of Low-carbon Economy (2008) EU-China Institute for Clean and RE (ICARE) (2010) Research Center of International Environmental Policy (RCIEP)
	Peking University		Research Center for Contemporary China (1988) CDM Club, 6E Plus (Environment, Energy, Economy, Ecosystem, Education, Equity) (2006) National School of Development of Peking University (2008—based on China Center for Economic Research—CCER established in 1995) China Center for Energy and Development (2011) Research Center for World New Energy Strategy (2011)
	Renmin University of China		Center for International Energy Strategy Studies of Renmin University (2003)
	The similar research centers on climate change, RE and low-carbon economy have been set up in many universities in China.		
Key RES industry associations	Chinese Renewable Energy Society (CRES)	1976	The most important RE association in China, including Solar Photovoltaic Society (1976 the earliest association of Chinese RE Society) (http://www.cres.org.cn/index.html). Aims to unite the professionals throughout the field of RE for carrying out the research work on renewables policy, science and technology, and contribute the coordination of renewables, economy, society and environment in China.

Key RES industry associations	Chinese Renewable Energy Society (CRES)	1976	CRES includes: Chinese Wind Energy Association (CWEA established in 1981 http://www.cwea.org.cn); Solar Thermal Utilization Association; Solar Photochemistry Association; Solar Building Association; Biomass Energy Association.
	Chinese Renewable Energy Industries Association (CREIA)	2000	CREIA tends to promote the technological innovation of RE and the diffusion of advanced renewable technology; promote the commercialization of RE in China; enhance the communication and feed-back between the governmental agencies and RE industries, to reflect RE development problems to the relevant governmental agencies in order to improve the RE policy designing (http://www.creia.net).
	China Energy Conservation Association (CECA)	1989	CECA devotes itself to efficient utilization of energy, environment protection and advancing economic profit, and helps to enhance the energy efficiency technology and energy efficiency product of China to the world advanced level (http://www.cecaweb.org.cn/CN/english.html).
	China Association of Rural Energy Industry (CAREI)	1992	CAREI is a national non-profit organization affiliated with the Ministry of Agriculture, including: Small Power Source Association; Biogas Association; Biomass Energy Conversion Technology Association (http://www.carei.org.cn).

Key RES industry associations	China Association of Resource Comprehensive Utilization (CARCU)	1995	The mission of CARCU is to boost resource utilization efficiency, conserve energy, protect the environment, harmonize economic benefits, environmental benefits and social benefits, and push forward the sustainable social and economic development of China. It is dedicated to delivering comprehensive services to the relevant government agencies and member entities by way of extensive policy research, consultancy service, technical promotion, market development, professional training, conference and exhibition as well as international exchange and cooperation (http://www.carcu.org).
	China Renewable Energy Industry Association (CHNREIA)	2000	CHNREIA has played a representative role of the RE industry to reflect their demand to the government in order to get more policy support; organizing national RE industry conference to promote the green investment, editing the professional journal of *Renewable Energy* (http://www.chnreia.org).
Civil environmental protection organizations	Greenpeace in East Asia	1997	Greenpeace has been in East Asia since 1997 to fight climate change, stop toxic pollution, ensure food security, end illegal deforestation and defend the oceans. Its work focus in China is to push China to quit coal, which supplies 70% of the country's energy and produces 80% of its carbon dioxide emissions. Greenpeace is working to catalyze a renewable energy revolution in China—which has vast untapped potential for solar and wind energy (http://www.greenpeace.org/eastasia/about/history).

Civil environmental protection organizations	Institute of Public & Environmental Affairs(IPE)	2006	IPE has developed two pollution databases (water & air) to monitor corporate environmental performance and to facilitate public participation in environmental governance. The aim is to expand environmental information disclosure to allow communities to fully understand the hazards and risks in the surrounding environment, thus promoting widespread public participation in environmental governance (http://www.ipe.org.cn/En/index.aspx).
	Chinese Society for Environmental Sciences (CSES)	1978	The highest academic community in environmental science and largest environmental technology association in China. Responsible for editing the academic journal of *China Environmental Science*, mainly reporting the latest research process result for China's major environmental problems (http://www.chinacses.org/cn/index.html).
	China Resource Recycling Association (CRRA)	1992	Promoting the resource recycling, editing the professional journal of *Renewable Resources and Recycling Economy*, and establishing "renewable resource recycling network" (http://www.crra.org.cn).
	China Association of Environmental Protection Industry	1993	Actively involved in regulating the environmental protection industry plan, economic and technology policy and industry technical standards; promoting the product certification, technology assessment within the industry; promoting the industry coordination and fair competition (http://www.caepi.org.cn/).
	Other environmental NGOs: The Friends of Nature (1993), Green Earth Volunteers (1996)		

RE professional websites	Polaris Power website	http://www.bjx.com.cn
	Newenergy Net	http://www.newenergy.org.cn
	China Dialogue	http://www.chinadialogue.net
	New Energy & Renewable Energy website	http://www.crein.org.cn
	SolarF.net	http://www.solarf.org
	China New Energy Chamber of Commerce	http://www.cnecc.org.cn
	Renewable Energy in China	http://www.china-nengyuan.com
	Energy Research Observer Net	http://www.chinaero.com.cn/english/index.shtml
	China Low-carbon website	http://www.ditan360.com
	China Energy website	http://www.china5e.com
	Chinaenergy Net *	http://www.cnenergy.org
	China Climate Change Info-Net *	http://www.ccchina.gov.cn/en
	CDM in China website *	http://cdm.ccchina.gov.cn/english/index.asp
	China CDM Fund website *	http://www.cdmfund.org/en/index.aspx
	Other RE development and low-carbon economy websites	

* means the official website.

Source: Compiled by the author.

Bibliography

21st Century Economic Report. (2014). "The Assessment Measure for Renewable Power Quota (Trial Implementation)." Available HTTP: 〈http://guangfu.bjx.com.cn/news/20140925/549944.shtml〉 (accessed on 6 November 2014).

Abbott, K. W. and Snidal, D. (1998). "Why States Act through Formal International Organizations." *Journal of Conflict Resolution*, Vol. 42, No. 1, pp. 3-32.

Aden, N. T. and Sinton, J. E. (2006). "Environmental Implications of Energy Policy in China." *Environmental Politics*, Vol. 15, No. 2, pp. 248-270.

AIC News. (2013). "Shale Gas: China's Gold Rush?" Available HTTP: 〈http://www.thefinancialist.com/shale-gas-chinas-gold-rush/〉 (accessed on 18 March 2013).

Andrews-Speed, P. (2012). *The Governance of Energy in China: Transition to a Low-Carbon Economy*. London: Palgrave Macmillan.

Asian Power. (2012). "China to Force Grids to Buy Renewable Energy." Available HTTP: 〈http://asian-power.com/environment/in-focus/china-force-grids-buy-renewable-energy〉 (accessed on 16 November 2012).

Axelrod, R. (1986). "An Evolutionary Approach to Norms." *The American Political Science Review*, pp. 1095-1111.

Bach, D. and Newman, A. L. (2010). "Transgovernmental Networks and Domestic Policy Convergence: Evidence from Insider Trading Regulation." *International Organization*, Vol. 64, No. 3, pp. 505-528.

Bearce, D. H. and Bondanella, S. (2007). "Intergovernmental Organizations, Socialization, and Member-State Interest Convergence." *International Organization*, Vol. 61, No. 4, pp. 703-733.

Benford, R. D. and Snow, D. A. (2000). "Framing Processes and Social

Movements: An Overview and Assessment." *Annual Review of Sociology*, Vol. 26, pp. 611-639.

Bennett, A. and Elman, C. (2008). "Case Study Methods." In D. Snidal and C. Reus-Smit (eds.), *The Oxford Handbook of International Relations*. Oxford: Oxford University Press, pp. 499-517.

Bennett, C. J. (1997). "Understanding Ripple Effects: The Cross National Adoption of Policy Instruments for Bureaucratic Accountability." *Governance*, Vol. 10, No. 3, pp. 213-233.

Bennett, C. J. and Howlett, M. (1992). "The Lessons of Learning: Reconciling Theories of Policy Learning and Policy Change." *Policy Sciences*, Vol. 25, No. 3, pp. 275-294.

Benton, M. and Frazier, P. J. (1976). "The Agenda Setting Function of the Mass Media at Three Levels of 'Information Holding'." *Communication Research*, Vol. 3, No. 3, pp. 261-274.

Bernstein, S. (2012). "The Clean Tech and Renewables Market." Available HTTP: 〈http://www.goldmansachs.com/our-thinking/focus-on/clean-technology-and-renewables/bernstein/index.html〉 (accessed on 18 November 2012).

Betz, J. (2013). "The Reform of China's Energy Policies." GIGA Working Papers, Vol. 216, pp. 1-35.

BJX. (2010). "Social Discussion Column on Wind Power in China." Available HTTP: 〈http://fd.bjx.com.cn/〉 (accessed on 21 June 2011).

BJX. (2012). "The Operating Rate of PV Polysilicon Enterprises Less than 20% Due to the Dropping Price (the Website of Polaris Power)." Available HTTP: 〈http://guangfu.bjx.com.cn/news/20121010/393180.shtml〉 (accessed on 16 October 2012).

BJX. (2013). "The Distributed Grid Connection Power Promoted by Li Keqiang." Available HTTP: 〈http://news.bjx.com.cn/html/20130318/423160.shtml〉 (accessed on 16 April 2013).

BNEF. (2011). *Global Renewable Energy Market Outlook: Executive Summary*. Report from Bloombery New Energy Finance.

Bourdieu, P. and Thompson, J. B. (1991). *Language and Symbolic Power*. Cambridge: Harvard University Press.

Boyd, O. (2012a). "China's Energy Reform and Climate Policy: The Ideas Motivating Change." CCEP Working Papers, Centre for Climate Economics & Policy, Crawford School of Public Policy, The Australian National University.

Boyd, O. (2012b). "The Motivations for China's New Energy and Climate

Policies." Available HTTP: 〈http://www.eastasiaforum.org/2012/08/14/the-motivations-for-chinas-new-energy-and-climate-policies/〉 (accessed on 16 September 2012).

Boyd, O. (2012c). "A Rise in Confucianism will Make China's Leaders More Eco-conscious." Available HTTP: 〈http://www.chinadialogue.net/article/show/single/en/5312-A-rise-in-Confucianism-will-make-China-s-leaders-more-eco-conscious〉 (accessed on 10 November 2012).

Brzezinski, Z. (2009). "The Group of Two That Could Change the World." *Financial Times*, Vol. 13, No. 1.

Buckley, C. (2012). "China Report Spells out 'Grim' Climate Change Risks." Available HTTP: 〈http://www.reuters.com/article/2012/01/18/us-china-climate-idUSTRE80H06J20120118〉 (accessed on 17 September 2012).

Busch, P.-O. and Jörgens, H. (2005). "The International Sources of Policy Convergence: Explaining the Spread of Environmental Policy Innovations." *Journal of European Public Policy*, Vol. 12, No. 5, pp. 860-884.

Busch, P.-O., Jörgens, H. and Tews, K. (2006). "The Global Diffusion of Regulatory Instruments: The Making of a New International Environmental Regime." In M. Jänicke and K. Jacob (eds.), *Environmental Governance in Global Perspective: New Approaches to Ecological Modernisation.* Berlin: FFU Report—Special edition on the occasion of the 20th anniversary of the Environmental Policy Research Centre, pp. 123-145.

CAEP. (2012). "The Overview of The Chinese Academy for Environmental Planning (CAEP)." Available HTTP: 〈http://www.caep.org.cn/toptypeEN.asp? typeid=43〉 (accessed on 26 August 2012).

Carraro, C. and Tavoni, M. (2010). "Looking Ahead from Copenhagen: How Challenging is the Chinese Carbon Intensity Target?" Available HTTP: 〈http://www.voxeu.org/article/china-s-copenhagen-commitment-business-usual-or-climate-leadership〉 (accessed on 17 July 2011).

Carrapatoso, A. (2011). "Climate Policy Diffusion: Interregional Dialogue in China-EU relations." *Global Change, Peace & Security*, Vol. 23, No. 2, pp. 177-194.

Cary, E. (2011). "China's Policy Impasse: The Case of the Green GDP Initiative." Available HTTP: 〈http://www.jamestown.org/single/? no_cache=1&tx_ttnews%5Btt_news%5D=37901#.VxNvMuwQifE〉 (accessed on May 17 2012).

Casey, J. and Koleski, K. (2011). "US-China Economic and Security Review Commission." *Backgrounder: China's 12th Five-Year Plan.*

CBC News (2011). "European Court of Justice Expected to Approve Tax on

International Flights." Available HTTP: 〈http://www.cbc.ca/news/business/story/2011/12/20/airline-european-greenhouse.html〉 (accessed on 16 July 2012).

CCICED. (2010). "The Overview of Chinese Government, China Council for International Cooperation on Environment and Development (CCICED)." Available HTTP: 〈http://www.cciced.net/encciced/aboutus/overview/〉 (accessed on 16 June 2012).

CCICED. (2011a). *China's Low-Carbon Industrialization Strategy*. The China Council for International Cooperation on Environment and Development (CCICED), Policy Research Report in 2011 Annual General Meeting.

CCICED. (2011b). *Development Mechanism and Policy Innovation of China's Green Economy*. The China Council for International Cooperation on Environment and Development (CCICED), Policy Research Report in 2011 Annual General Meeting.

CCICED. (2012a). "Overview for the China Council for International Cooperation on Environment and Development (CCICED)." Available HTTP: 〈http://www.cciced.net/encciced/aboutus/overview/〉 (accessed on 17 July 2012).

CCICED. (2012b). "Policy Mechanisms toward Environmental Targets for the 12th Five-Year Plan: Strategies and Policy Studies on Medium-to-Long-Term Efforts to Reduce Pollution." Available HTTP: 〈http://www.cciced.net/encciced/event/AGM_1/2012agm/meetdoc/201211/P020121206409938261681.pdf〉 (accessed on 17 December 2012).

CDMFUND. (2012). "The Macro-policy Research of CDM Fund." Available HTTP: 〈http://www.cdmfund.org/eng/about_us.aspx? m = 20121025103734327589〉 (accessed on 16 June 2012).

CEEP. (2006). "The Overview of Center for Energy and Environmental Policy Research (CEEP)." Available HTTP: 〈http://www.ceep.cas.cn/en/〉 (accessed on 29 June 2012).

CGI. (2012). *The China Greentech Report 2012: Faced with Challenges, China Accelerates Greentech Growth*. The China Greentech Initiative (Strategic Insights, Industry Collaboration, Market Acceleration).

Chan, G. (2006). *China's Compliance in Global Affairs: Trade, Arm Control, Environmental Protection, Human Rights*. New Jersey, London and Singapore: World Scientific Publishing Co.

Chang, S., Zhao, L., Timilsina, G. R. and Zhang, X. (2012). "Biofuels Development in China: Technology Options and Policies Needed to Meet the 2020 Target." *Energy Policy*, Vol. 51, pp. 64-79.

Chayes, A. and Chayes, A. H. (1993). "On Compliance." *International Organization*, Vol. 47, No. 2, pp. 175-205.

Chayes, A. and Chayes, A. H. (1998). *The New Sovereignty: Compliance with International Regulatory Agreements.* Cambridge, MA: Harvard University Press.

Checkel, J. T. (1997). "International Norms and Domestic Politics: Bridging the Rationalist-Constructivist Divide." *European Journal of International Relations*, Vol. 3, No. 4, pp. 473-495.

Checkel, J. T. (2001). "Why Comply? Social Learning and European Identity Change." *International Organization*, Vol. 55, No. 3, pp. 553-588.

Checkel, J. T. (2005). "International Institutions and Socialization in Europe: Introduction and Framework." *International Organization*, Vol. 59, No. 4, pp. 801-826.

Chen, C., Wiser, R. and Bolinger, M. (2007). "Weighing the Costs and Benefits of State Renewables Portfolio Standards: A Comparative Analysis of State-Level Policy Impact Projections." *Ernest Orlando Lawrence Berkeley National Laboratory, LBNL-61580.*

Chen, G. (2009). *Politics of China's Environmental Protection: Problems and Progress.* World Scientific Publishing Co. Pte. Ltd.

Cheng, J. Y. S. (2008). "A Chinese View of China's Energy Security." *Journal of Contemporary China*, Vol. 17, No. 55, pp. 297-317.

China Daily. (2009). "Climate Change Law to Bring Teeth to Emissions Mandates." Available HTTP: 〈http://www.chinadaily.com.cn/china/2009-08/26/content_8617151.htm〉 (accessed on 27 July 2011).

China Daily. (2011). "China to Establish Climate Change Think Tank." Available HTTP: 〈http://china.org.cn/environment/2011-11/22/content_23975275.htm〉 (accessed on 26 May 2012).

China Daily. (2012). "Ecological Civilization is Meaningful to China." Available HTTP: 〈http://www.chinadaily.com.cn/opinion/2012-11/19/content_15942603.htm〉 (accessed on 26 November 2012).

China dialogue. (2006). "The Overview of China dialogue: Mission, Status and Contact." Available HTTP: 〈http://www.chinadialogue.net/static/about〉 (accessed on 27 June 2011).

China dialogue. (2012). *China's Green Revolution: Energy, Environment and the 12th Five-Year Plan.* China dialogue Report.

China dialogue. (2015). "China Aims to Cut Carbon Intensity 60%-65% in National Climate Plan." Available HTTP: 〈https://www.chinadialogue.net/article/show/single/en/7985-China-aims-to-cut-carbon-intensity-6-65-in-national-climate-plan〉(accessed on 27 July 2015).

Chinafaqs. (2011). "Propelling the Durban Climate Talks—China Announces Willingness to Consider Legally Binding Commitments Post-2020." Available HTTP: 〈http://www.chinafaqs.org/blog-posts/propelling-durban-climate-talks-china-announces-willingness-consider-legally-binding-comm〉 (accessed on 17 July 2012).

China Gate. (2012). "China's Special Economic Zones." Available HTTP:〈http://cn.chinagate.cn/economics/tequ/node_7099387.htm〉 (accessed on 16 September 2012).

China News. (2008). "The Policy Proposal of Low-Carbon Economy from CPPCC Member Wu Xiaoqing." Available HTTP: 〈http://www.china.com.cn/2008lianghui/2008-03/05/content_11616175.htm〉 (accessed on 16 July 2012).

China News. (2011). "The Establishment of the National Strategic Research and International Cooperation Center for Climate Change (NCSC)." Available HTTP: 〈http://www.chinanews.com/gn/2011/12-07/3513116.shtml〉 (accessed on 12 June 2012).

China News. (2012a). "Climate Change Response Law (Draft Version for Discussion)." Available HTTP: 〈http://news.china.com.cn/txt/2012-03/18/content_24923504.htm〉 (accessed on 18 July 2012).

China News. (2012b). "The Environmental Risk of the Shale Gas Exploration in China." Available HTTP: 〈http://www.ce.cn/cysc/ny/gdxw/201305/30/t20130530_49524.shtml〉 (accessed on 30 June 2013).

China News. (2012c). "The Explanation to the Climate Change Response Law (Draft Version)." Available HTTP: 〈http://www.china.com.cn/news/txt/2012-03/18/content_24923468.htm〉 (accessed on 12 August 2012).

China News. (2012d). "The Growth Rate of China's Wind Power Installation Will Be Slowed Down." Available HTTP: 〈http://www.chinanews.com/ny/2011/03-25/2932152.shtml〉 (accessed on 15 June 2012).

Chinapower Net. (2012). "The Renewable Energy Development Needs the Efforts from the Whole Society: Interviewing with Wang Zhongying, the Director of China National Renewable Energy Center." Available HTTP: 〈http://www.chinapower.com.cn/article/1210/art1210466.asp〉 (accessed on 6 September 2012).

Chinastakes. (2009). "China Criticizes US Carbon Tariff Protectionism, Considers Domestic Carbon Tax Policy." Available HTTP: 〈http://www.chinastakes.com/2009/9/china-criticizes-us-carbon-tariff-protectionism-considers-domestic-carbon-tax-policy.html〉 (accessed on 16 March 2012).

China Venture. (2011). "The Monopolization of Power State-owned Enterprises in the Wind Power." Available HTTP: 〈http://news.chinaventure.com.cn/3/20111107/68723.shtml〉 (accessed on 17 July 2012).

Clémençon, R. (2008). "The Bali Road Map: A First Step on the Difficult Journey to a Post-Kyoto Protocol Agreement." *The Journal of Environment & Development*, Vol. 17, No. 1, pp. 70-94.

Clean Biz. (2012). "China Ordering 15% Renewables as Wind Sector Struggles." Available HTTP: 〈http://www.cleanbiz.asia/news/china-ordering-15-renewables-wind-sector-struggles#.UezfqvAtttw〉 (accessed on 17 November 2012).

ClimateWire. (2011). "After Explosive Growth, Global Carbon Markets Stall and Begin to Shrink." Available HTTP: 〈http://www.nytimes.com/cwire/2011/06/02/02climatewire-after-explosive-growth-global-carbon-markets-64850.html?pagewanted=all〉 (accessed on 17 August 2012).

CNB Daily. (2011). "Chinese Wind Farm Power Grid Disconnection Accident." Available HTTP: 〈http://deblockconsulting.com/blog/china-news/chinese-wind-farm-power-grid-disconnection-accident/〉 (accessed on 15 December 2011).

CNREC. (2012). "The Inaugural Ceremony of China National Renewable Energy Centre Held in Beijing." Available HTTP: 〈http://www.cnrec.org.cn/zxdt/2012-02-24-159.html〉 (accessed on 17 May 2012).

Constantin, C. (2007). "Understanding China's Energy Security." *World Political Science Review*, Vol. 3, No. 3, pp. 1-32.

Cortell, A. P. and Davis Jr., J. W. (1996). "How Do International Institutions Matter? The Domestic Impact of International Rules and Norms." *International Studies Quarterly*, Vol. 40, No. 4, pp. 451-478.

Cortell, A. P. and Davis Jr., J. W. (2000). "Understanding the Domestic Impact of International Norms: A Research Agenda." *International Studies Review*, Vol. 2, No. 1, pp. 65-87.

Cortell, A. P. and Peterson, S. (2001). "Limiting the Unintended Consequences of Institutional Change." *Comparative Political Studies*, Vol. 34, No. 7, pp. 768-799.

Cory, K. S. and Swezey, B. G. (2007). "Renewable Portfolio Standards in the States: Balancing Goals and Rules." *The Electricity Journal*, Vol. 20, No. 4, pp. 21-32.

Couture, T. and Gagnon, Y. (2010). "An Analysis of Feed-in Tariff Remuneration Models: Implications for Renewable Energy Investment." *Energy Policy*, Vol. 38, No. 2, pp. 955-965.

CPC People. (2010). "The Politburo Collective Study Sessions of CPC." Available HTTP: 〈http://cpc.people.com.cn/GB/64162/111911/〉 (accessed on 17 September 2012).

CRED. (2007). *Roadmap for China's Wind Power Development.* Available HTTP: 〈http://toolkits.reeep.org/file_upload/10303002_1.pdf〉 (accessed on 29 July 2012).

CRED. (2009). "Projects of Center for Renewable Energy Development." Available HTTP: 〈http://www.cred.org.cn/cn/project.asp〉 (accessed on 15 July 2011).

CREIA, GREENPEACE and GWEC. (2012). *China Wind Power Outlook 2012.* Available HTTP: 〈http://www.greenpeace.org/eastasia/publications/reports/climate-energy/2012/wind-energy-report-2012/〉 (accessed on 16 October 2012).

CRES. (2011). "About the China Renewable Energy Society (CRES)." Available HTTP: 〈http://www.cres.org.cn/english/20110116112.html〉 (accessed on 16 March 2012).

CRES. (2012). "News of China Renewable Energy Society." Available HTTP: 〈http://www.cres.org.cn/html/xhxw/tztg/〉 (accessed on 16 September 2012).

CRESP. (2010). "Introduction to China Renewable Energy Scale-up Programme." Available HTTP: 〈http://www.cresp.org.cn/english/about.asp〉 (accessed on 6 April 2012).

CRESP. (2011). "Exclusive Interview with Han Wenke Director of Energy Research Institute." Available HTTP: 〈http://www.cresp.org.cn/english/content.asp?id=1771〉 (accessed on 18 March 2012).

CRSUD. (2007). "The Overview of China Research Society of Urban Development (CRSUD)." Available HTTP: 〈http://www.cusdn.org.cn/en.php〉 (accessed on 27 July 2012).

CSG. (2010). "The Overview of the China Southern Power Grid Company." Available HTTP: 〈http://www.csg.cn/〉 (accessed on 18 December 2012).

CSGCN. (2013). "The Large-Scale Shale Gas Project in Sichuan Province." Available HTTP: 〈http://www.csgcn.com.cn/article/show/20558.aspx〉 (accessed on 16 July 2013).

Dai, X. (2007). *International Institutions and National Policies.* Cambridge: Cambridge University Press.

Danish, K. W. (2007). "An Overview of the International Regime Addressing Climate Change." *Sustainable Development Law & Policy*, Vol. 7, No. 2, pp. 10-15.

Davis, C. L. (2004). "International Institutions and Issue Linkage: Building Support for Agricultural Trade Liberalization." *American Political Science Review*, Vol. 98, No. 1, pp. 153-169.

DCCEE. (2011). "Breakthrough at Durban Climate Change Conference." Available HTTP: 〈http://www.climatechange.gov.au/media/whats-new/durban-breakthrough.aspx〉 (accessed on 16 December 2011).

Deng, L. (2014). "China Needs to Scale up Wind and Solar in 13th Five-Year Plan." Available HTTP: 〈https://www.chinadialogue.net/blog/7349-china-needs-to-scale-up-wind-and-solar-in-13th-five-year-plan/en〉 (accessed on 17 July 2015).

Deng, Y. (2008). *China's Struggle for Status: The Realignment of International Relations.* Cambridge and New York: Cambridge University Press.

Ditan360. (2012). "First Successful CDM Project in China." Available HTTP: 〈http://www.ditan360.com/lib/Info-105401.html〉 (accessed on 17 July 2012).

Dolan, C. J. (2003). "Economic Policy and Decision Making at the Intersection of Domestic and International Politics: The Advocacy Coalition Framework and the National Economic Council." *Policy Studies Journal*, Vol. 31, No. 2, pp. 209-236.

Dolowitz, D. and Marsh, D. (1996). "Who Learns What from Whom: A Review of the Policy Transfer Literature." *Political Studies*, Vol. 44, No. 2, pp. 343-357.

Dolowitz, D. and Marsh, D. (2000). "Learning from Abroad: The Role of Policy Transfer in Contemporary Policy-making." *Governance*, Vol. 13, No. 1, pp. 5-23.

Downs, E. (2004). "The Chinese Energy Security Debate." *The China Quarterly*, Vol. 177, No. 1, pp. 21-41.

Downs, E. (2006). *Energy Security Series: China.* The Brookings Institution, the Brookings Foreign Policy Studies.

DRC. (2011). "The Overview of the Development Research Center of the State Council (DRC)." Available HTTP: 〈www.drc.gov.cn/about us/〉 (accessed on 17 July 2012).

Ebert, J. (2012). "REEEP Funds Energy Projects in China, India." Available HTTP: 〈http://biomassmagazine.com/articles/1248/reeep-funds-energy-projects-in-china-india〉 (accessed on 18 July 2012).

EC. (2012). "EU Initiates Anti-Dumping Investigation on Solar Panel Imports from China." Available HTTP: 〈http://europa.eu/rapid/press-release_MEMO-12-647_en.htm〉 (accessed on 28 September 2012).

EC2. (2010). "Know More About EC2." Available HTTP: 〈http://www.ec2.org.cn/about-us〉 (accessed on 17 May 2012).

Economy, E. (2001). "The Impact of International Regimes on Chinese Foreign Policy-making: Broadening Perspectives and Policies ... but Only to a Point." In D. M. Lampton (ed.), *The Making of Chinese Foreign and Security Policy in the Era of Reform, 1978-2000.* Stanford: Stanford University Press.

Economy, E. and Schreurs, M. A. (1997). "Domestic and International Linkages in Environmental Politics." In M. A. Schreurs and E. Economy (eds.), *The Internationalization of Environmental Protection.* Cambridge: Cambridge University Press, pp. 1-18.

Eder, K. (1992). *Framing and Communicating Environmental Action. A Discourse Analysis of Environmentalism.* Firenze: European University Institute.

EEO. (2013). "The Bumpy Way to Ratify the Regulation for Management of Renewable Power Quotas." Available HTTP: ⟨http://www.eeo.com.cn/2013/0419/242781.shtml⟩ (accessed on 20 April 2013).

Eimer, T., Lütz, S. and Verena, S. (2013). "Norm Diffusion through Advocacy Coalitions: Implementing International Intellectual Property Norms in India and Brazil." Presented at the ISA 54th Annual Convention 2013 in San Francisco.

Ellison, B. A. (1998). "Intergovernmental Relations and the Advocacy Coalition Framework: The Operation of Federalism in Denver Water Politics." *Publius: The Journal of Federalism*, Vol. 28, No. 4, pp. 35-54.

Entman, R. M. (1993). "Framing: Toward Clarification of a Fractured Paradigm." *Journal of Communication*, Vol. 43, No. 4, pp. 51-58.

ERI and IEA. (2011). *Technology Roadmap: China Wind Energy Development Roadmap 2050.* Available HTTP: ⟨http://www.china.tu-berlin.de/fileadmin/fg57/SS_2012/Umwelt/IEAchina_wind_2050.pdf⟩ (accessed on 18 December 2011).

European Commission. (2005). *EU and China Partnership on Climate Change.* Available HTTP: ⟨http://europa.eu/rapid/pressReleasesAction.do? reference=MEMO/05/298⟩ (accessed on 12 January 2011).

European Commission. (2005-2012). *EC-China Energy Dialogue.* Available HTTP: ⟨http://ec.europa.eu/energy/international/bilateral_cooperation/china/dialogue_en.htm⟩ (accessed on 16 May 2011).

European Commission. (2013). "EU Imposes Provisional Anti-dumping Tariffs on Chinese Solar Panels." Available HTTP: ⟨http://europa.eu/rapid/press-release_IP-13-501_en.htm⟩ (accessed on 6 June 2013).

Fearon, J. D. (1994a). "Domestic Political Audiences and the Escalation of International Disputes." *American Political Science Review*, Vol. 88, No. 3, pp. 577-592.

Fearon, J. D. (1994b). "Signaling Versus the Balance of Power and Interests."

Journal of Conflict Resolution, Vol. 38, No. 2, pp. 236-269.

Fearon, J. D. (1998). "Domestic Politics, Foreign Policy, and Theories of International Relations." *Annual Review of Political Science*, Vol. 1, No. 1, pp. 289-313.

Feldman, D. C. (1997). "Socialization in an International Context." *International Journal of Selection and Assessment*, Vol. 5, No. 1, pp. 1-8.

Feng, J. (2010). "The Alternative of Green GDP." Available HTTP: 〈http://www.infzm.com/content/41415〉 (accessed on 21 March 2012).

Finance Eastday. (2011). "Capacity of National Strategic Oil Reserves in China." Available HTTP: 〈http://finance.eastday.com/economic/m1/20110118/u1a5676242.html〉 (accessed on 16 June 2012).

Finnemore, M. (1993). "International Organizations as Teachers of Norms: The United Nations Educational, Scientific, and Cultural Organization and Science Policy." *International Organization*, Vol. 47, No. 4, pp. 565-597.

Finnemore, M. (1996). *National Interest in International Society*. Ithaca and London: Cornell University Press.

Finnemore, M. and Sikkink, K. (1998). "International Norm Dynamics and Political Change." *International Organization*, Vol. 52, No. 4, pp. 887-917.

Flockhart, T. (2004). "'Masters and Novices': Socialization and Social Learning Through the NATO Parliamentary Assembly." *International Relations*, Vol. 18, No. 3, pp. 361-382.

Flockhart, T. (2006). "'Complex Socialization': A Framework for the Study of State Socialization." *European Journal of International Relations*, Vol. 12, No. 1, pp. 89-118.

Florini, A. (1996). "The Evolution of International Norms." *International Studies Quarterly*, Vol. 40, No. 3, pp. 363-389.

Gao, H., Wang, Z. and Ren, D. M. (eds.) (2009). *Reader for Knowledge on Renewable Energy Technology and Industrial Development*. Beijing: Chemical Industry Press, Series issued by China Renewable Energy Scale-up Programme (CRESP).

Gilly, B. (2009). *The Right to Rule: How States Win and Lose Legitimacy*. New York: Columbia University Press.

Givner, M. J. (2010). *The Story Behind the Boom: International and Domestic Sources of Influence on Chinese Renewable Energy Policy-Making*. Thesis of Wesleyan University.

Goertz, G. and Diehl, P. F. (1992). "Toward a Theory of International Norms: Some Conceptual and Measurement Issues." *Journal of Conflict Resolution*, Vol. 36, No. 4, p. 634.

Gold, T. and Guthrie, D. (2002). *Social Connections in China: Institutions, Culture, and the Changing Nature of Guanxi.* Cambridge: Cambridge University Press.

Goodman, R. (2004). "International Law and State Socialization: Conceptual, Empirical, and Normative Challenges." *Duke LJ*, Vol. 54, p. 983.

Goodman, R. and Jinks, D. (2004). "How to Influence States: Socialization and International Human Rights Law." *Duke Law Journal*, Vol. 54, No. 3, pp. 621-703.

Gourevitch, P. (1978). "The Second Image Reversed: The International Sources of Domestic Politics." *International Organization*, Vol. 32, No. 4, pp. 881-912.

Green Dialogue. (2011). "Li Junfeng: Climate Change Negotiations Promoting the Defusion of the Low-Carbon Development Concept." Available HTTP: 〈http://news.qq.com/a/20111226/001131.htm〉 (accessed on 18 October 2012).

Greenpeace. (2006). "The History of Greenpeace." Available HTTP: 〈http://www.greenpeace.org/eastasia/about/history/〉 (accessed on 17 March 2012).

Greenpeace. (2007). "Climate Change and Energy in China." Available HTTP: 〈http://www.greenpeace.org/china/zh/publications/reports/climate-energy/2007/〉 (accessed on 23 July 2012).

Greenpeace, CREIA and GWEC. (2007). *China Wind Power Report 2007*. Available HTTP: 〈http://www.greenpeace.org/eastasia/publications/reports/climate-energy/2007/wind-power-report/〉 (accessed on 18 July 2011).

GWEC. (2012). "China Wind Energy Development Update 2012." Available HTTP: 〈http://www.gwec.net/china-wind-market-update/〉 (accessed on 16 December 2012).

Haas, E. B. (1975). "On Systems and International Regimes." *World Politics: A Quarterly Journal of International Relations*, Vol. 27, No. 2, pp. 147-174.

Haas, E. B. (1980a). "Technological Self-Reliance for Latin America: The OAS Contribution." *International Organization*, Vol. 34, No. 4, pp. 541-570.

Haas, E. B. (1980b). "Why Collaborate? Issue-Linkage and International Regimes." *World Politics*, Vol. 32, No. 3, pp. 357-405.

Haas, E. B. (1990). *When Knowledge Is Power: Three Models of Change in International Organizations.* Berkeley, Los Angeles and Oxford: University of California Press.

Haas, E. B. (2004). "Introduction: Institutionalism or Constructivism?" *The Uniting of Europe*, pp. xiii-lvi.

Haas, P. M. (1989). "Do Regimes Matter? Epistemic Communities and Mediterranean Pollution Control." *International Organization*, pp. 377-403.

Haas, P. M. (1990). "Obtaining International Environmental Protection Through Epistemic Consensus." *Millennium: Journal of International Studies*, Vol. 19, No. 3, pp. 347-363.

Haas, P. M. (1992). "Banning Chlorofluorocarbons: Epistemic Community Efforts to Protect Stratospheric Ozone." *International Organization*, Vol. 46, No. 1, pp. 187-224.

Haas, P. M. (2000). "International Institutions and Social Learning in the Management of Global Environmental Risks." *Policy Studies Journal*, Vol. 28, No. 3, pp. 558-575.

Haas, P. M. and Haas, E. B. (2002). "Pragmatic Constructivism and the Study of International Institutions." *Millennium-Journal of International Studies*, Vol. 31, No. 3, pp. 573-601.

Haggard, S. and Simmons, B. A. (1987). "Theories of International Regimes." *International Organization*, Vol. 41, No. 3, pp. 491-517.

Hajer, M. A. (1997). *The Politics of Environmental Discourse: Ecological Modernization and the Policy Process.* Oxford: Oxford University Press.

Hall, P. A. (1993). "Policy Paradigms, Social Learning, and the State: The Case of Economic Policymaking in Britain." *Comparative Politics*, Vol. 25, No. 3, pp. 275-296.

Hallding, K., Han, G. and Olsson, M. (2009). "China's Climate- and Energy-Security Dilemma: Shaping a New Path of Economic Growth." *Journal of Current Chinese Affairs*, Vol. 38, No. 3, pp. 119-134.

Han, J. (2009). *Renewable Energy Development in China: Policies, Practices and Performance.* Wageningen University Doctoral Book.

Harris, P. G. (ed.) (2003). *Global Warming and East Asia: The Domestic and International Politics of Climate Change.* London and New York: Routledge.

Harris, P. G. (2006). "Environmental Perspectives and Behavior in China." *Environment and Behavior*, Vol. 38, No. 1, pp. 5-21.

Harris, P. G. (2007). "Collective Action on Climate Change: The Logic of Regime Failure." *Nature Resources Journal*, Vol. 47, p. 195.

Harris, P. G. (ed.) (2009). *China and Global Climate Change.* Hongkong: Proceedings of the conference held at Lingnan University, 18-19 June 2009.

Harris, P. G. (2011a). "Diplomacy, Responsibility and China's Climate Change Policy." In P. G. Harris (ed.), *China's Responsibility for Climate Change: Ethics, Fairness and Environmental Policy.* Bristol: The Policy Press, pp. 1-25.

Harris, P. G. (2011b). "Peace, Security and Global Climate Change: The Vital Role of China." *Global Change, Peace & Security*, Vol. 23, No. 2, pp. 141-145.

Harris, P. G. and Yu, H. (2005). "Environmental Change and the Asia Pacific: China Responds to Global Warming." *Global Change, Peace & Security*, Vol. 17,

No. 1, pp. 45-58.

Hatch, M. T. (2003). "Chinese Politics, Energy Policy, and the International Climate Change Negotiations." In P. G. Harris (ed.), *Global Warming and East Asia: The Domestic and International Politics of Climate Change.* London and New York: Taylor & Francis Group, pp. 43-67.

Heberer, T. (2009). "How Stable is China Currently?" Available HTTP: 〈http://www.europarl.europa.eu/meetdocs/2009_2014/documents/d-cn/dv/d-cn20100520_heberer_/d-cn20100520_heberer_en.pdf〉 (accessed on 16 November 2012).

Heggelund, G. (2007). "China's Climate Change Policy: Domestic and International Developments." *Asian Perspective*, Vol. 31, No. 2, pp. 155-191.

Hexun News. (2011). "The Enclosure Movement of Wind Farms by State-owned Power Enterprises." Available HTTP: 〈http://news.hexun.com/2011-03-11/127881415.html〉 (accessed on 18 March 2012).

Hilton, I. (2014). "Growing Business Commitment to Low Carbon Growth is a Bright Spot at UN Talks in Lima." Available HTTP: 〈https://www.chinadialogue.net/article/show/single/en/7591-Growing-business-commitment-to-low-carbon-growth-is-a-bright-spot-at-UN-talks-in-Lima〉 (accessed on 30 December 2014).

Hodgson, A. (2011). *Climate of Change: A Foreign Policy Analysis of China's Participation in International Environmental Agreements.* Master Thesis of the University of Kansas.

Hong, J., Guo, X., Marinova, D., Jia, R. and Yang, F. (2011). "Distribution Characteristics and Prospects for CDM Projects in China's 19th International Congress on Modelling and Simulation." Perth, Australia, 12-16 December 2011.

Hooghe, L. (2005). "Several Roads Lead to International Norms, but Few via International Socialization: A Case Study of the European Commission." *International Organization*, Vol. 59, No. 4, pp. 861-898.

Horii, N. (2012). "Transformation of China's Energy Structure from Dependence on Coal During the 12th Five-Year Plan Period." Presented at 2012 International Conference on Clean and Green Energy, Singapore.

Howlett, M. and Joshi-Koop, S. (2011). "Transnational Learning, Policy Analytical Capacity, and Environmental Policy Convergence: Survey Results from Canada." *Global Environmental Change*, Vol. 21, No. 1, pp. 85-92.

Hu, A. and Hilton, I. (2010). "Deng would back Green Growth: Interview with Hu Angang from China Dialogue." Available HTTP: 〈http://www.chinadialogue.net/article/show/single/en/3744--Deng-would-back-green-growth-〉 (accessed on 16 April 2011).

Huang, C., Su, J., Zhao, X., Sui, J., Ru, P., Zhang, H. and Wang, X. (2012). "Government Funded Renewable Energy Innovation in China." *Energy Policy*, Vol. 51, pp. 121-127.

ICARE. (2009). "Master Renewable Energy: ICARE China-EU program." Available HTT: 〈http://www.master-renewable-energy.com/en/icare.php〉 (accessed on 17 July 2011).

ICARE. (2011). "Overview of ICARE China-EU program." Available HTTP: 〈http://www.master-renewable-energy.com/en/icare.php? PHPSESSID = d8730a1b86f745f8e2337ae2e75fe7ce〉 (accessed on 18 July 2012).

ICARE. (2012). "Inauguration of China-EU Institute for Clean and Renewable Energy at Huazhong University of Science and Technology (30/10/2012)." Available HTTP: 〈http://eeas.europa.eu/delegations/china/press_corner/all_news/news/2012/20121030_en.htm〉 (accessed on 18 May 2012).

ICTSD. (2012). "China Publishes Draft Climate Change Law." Available HTTP: 〈http://ictsd.org/i/news/biores/133382/〉 (accessed on 1 June 2012).

IEA. (2010). *World Energy Outlook 2010*. Paris: International Energy Agency.

IEA. (2011a). *Clean Energy Progress Report*. Paris: International Energy Agency.

IEA. (2011b). *World Energy Outlook*. Paris: International Energy Agency.

IEA. (2012a). *Facing China's Coal Future: Prospects and Challenges for Carbon Capture and Storage*. Paris: International Energy Agency.

IEA. (2012b). *Key World Energy Statistics 2012*. Paris: International Energy Agency.

IEA. (2012c). *Medium-Term Renewable Energy Market Report 2012: Market Trends and Projections to 2017*. Paris: International Energy Agency.

Ifeng. (2012). "The Special Fund for the Shale Gas Exploration." Available HTTP: 〈http://finance.ifeng.com/stock/roll/20121106/7259159.shtml〉 (accessed on 17 December 2012).

Ifeng. (2013). "The Stagnation of Off-Shore Wind Power and Critiques for Concession Bidding Policy." Available HTTP: 〈http://news.ifeng.com/shendu/nfzm/detail_2013_01/18/21340452_0.shtml〉 (accessed on 16 March 2012).

IISD. (2011). "Summary of the Durban Climate Change Conference." Available HTTP: 〈http://www.iisd.ca/vol12/enb12534e.html〉 (accessed on 23 March 2012).

IISD. (2012). "Summary of the Doha Climate Change Conference." Available HTTP: 〈http://www.iisd.ca/vol12/enb12567e.html〉 (accessed on 28 December 2012).

Ikenberry, G. J. and Kupchan, C. A. (1990). "Socialization and Hegemonic

Power." *International Organization*, Vol. 44, No. 3, pp. 283-315.

Ikenberry, J. G. (1996). "The Intertwining of Domestic and International Politics." *Polity*, Vol. 29, No. 2, pp. 293-298.

IRENA. (2011). "About IRENA." Available HTTP: 〈http://www.irena.org/Menu/index.aspx? PriMenuID = 13&mnu = Pri〉 (accessed on 19 December 2012).

IRENA. (2013). "China to Join International Renewable Energy Agency." Available HTTP: 〈http://www.irena.org/News/Description.aspx? NType = N&News_ID =287〉 (accessed on 17 January 2013).

IPCC. (2012). *Renewable Energy Sources and Climate Change Mitigation.* Special Report of the Intergovernmental Panel on Climate Change, published by Cambridge University Press.

IPE. (2006). "The Overview of the Institute of Public and Environmental Affairs (IPE)." Available HTTP: 〈http://www.ipe.org.cn/En/about/about.aspx〉 (accessed on 18 March 2011).

IPE. (2012). *Small Particles, Big Breakthrough: 2012 Urban Air Quality Information Transparency Index.* Available HTTP: 〈http://www.ipe.org.cn/Upload/Report-AQTI-2012-EN.pdf〉 (accessed on 6 November 2012). Report from Institute of Public & Environmental Affairs.

Jänicke, M. and Jacob, K. (eds.) (2006). *Environmental Governance in Global Perspective: New Approaches to Ecological Modernization.* FFU Report Special Edition on the Occasion of the 20th Anniversary of the Environmental Policy Research Centre, Free University of Berlin.

Jaccard, M. (2004). "Renewable Portfolio Standard." *Encyclopedia of Energy*, Vol. 5, pp. 413-421.

Jachtenfuchs, M. (1996). *International Policy-Making as a Learning Process? The European Union and the Greenhouse Effect.* Aldershot and Brookfield: Ashgate Publishing Company.

Jakobson, L. and Knox, D. (2010). *New Foreign Policy Actors in China* (SIPRI Policy Paper). Stockholm: Stockholm International Peace Research Institute.

James, O. and Lodge, M. (2003). "The Limitations of 'Policy Transfer' and 'Lesson Drawing' for Public Policy Research." *Political Studies Review*, Vol. 1, No. 2, pp. 179-193.

Jänicke, M. (2012a). "Dynamic Governance of Clean-Energy Markets: How Technical Innovation Could Accelerate Climate Policies." *Journal of Cleaner Production*, Vol. 22, No. 1, pp. 50-59.

Jänicke, M. (2012b). "'Green Growth': From a Growing Eco-Industry to

Economic Sustainability." *Energy Policy*, Vol. 48, pp. 13-21.

Jänicke, M. and Lindemann, S. (2010). "Governing Environmental Innovations." *Environmental Politics*, Vol. 19, No. 1, pp. 127-141.

Jänicke, M. and Zieschank, R. (2011). "Environmental Tax Reform and the Environmental Industry." In P. Ekins and S. Speck (eds.), *Environmental Tax Reform (ETR)—A Policy for Green Growth.* Oxford: Oxford University Press, pp. 313-319.

Jenkins-Smith, H. C. (1988). "Analytical Debates and Policy Learning: Analysis and Change in the Federal Bureaucracy." *Policy Sciences*, Vol. 21, No. 2, pp. 169-211.

Jervis, R. (1997). *System Effects: Complexity in Social and Political Life.* Cambridge: Cambridge University Press.

Jiang, Z. (2008). "Reflections on Energy Issues in China." *Journal of Shanghai Jiaotong University (Science)*, Vol. 13, No. 3, pp. 257-274.

Johnston, A. I. (1998). "China and International Environmental Institutions: A Decision Rule Analysis." In M. B. McElroy (ed.), *Energizing China: Reconciling Environmental Protection and Economic Growth.* Cambridge: Harvard University Press.

Johnston, A. I. (2001). "Treating International Institutions as Social Environments." *International Studies Quarterly*, Vol. 45, No. 4, pp. 487-515.

Johnston, A. I. (2002). "International Institutions and Impact on National Behaviour." *World Economics and Politics*, No. 12, pp. 21-27.

Johnston, A. I. (2003). "Socialization in International Institutions." In G. J. Ikenberry and M. Mastanduno (eds.), *International Relations Theory and the Asia Pacific.* New York: Columbia University Press, pp. 107-162.

Johnston, A. I. (2005). "Conclusions and Extensions: Toward Mid-Range Theorizing and Beyond Europe." *International Organization*, Vol. 59, No. 4, pp. 1013-1044.

Johnston, A. I. (2008). *Social States: China in International Institutions, 1980-2000.* Princeton and Oxford: Princeton University Press.

Jones, B. D. and Baumgartner, F. R. (2005). *The Politics of Attention: How Government Prioritizes Problems.* Chicago: University of Chicago Press.

Katzenstein, P. J. (1976). "International Relations and Domestic Structures: Foreign Economic Policies of Advanced Industrial States." *International Organization*, Vol. 30, No. 1, pp. 1-45.

Kang, X. (2010). "Perception of Interests and Internalization of International Norms: A Case Study on China's Internalization of Norms in International Climate Cooperation." *World Economics and Politics*, No. 1, pp. 66-83.

Karch, A. (2007). "Emerging Issues and Future Directions in State Policy Diffusion Research." *State Politics & Policy Quarterly*, Vol. 7, No. 1, pp. 54-80.

Kennedy, A. B. (2010). "China's New Energy-Security Debate." *Survival*, Vol. 52, No. 3, pp. 137-158.

Kent, A. (2007). *Beyond Compliance: China, International Organizations, and Global Security*. Stanford: Stanford University Press.

Keohane, R. O. (1988). "International Institutions: Two Approaches." *International Studies Quarterly*, Vol. 32, No. 4, pp. 379-396.

Keohane, R. O. and Milner, H. V. (eds.) (1996). *Internationalization and Domestic Politics*. Cambridge: Cambridge University Press.

Keohane, R. O. and Victor, D. G. (2010). "The Regime Complex for Climate Change." The Harvard Project on International Climate Agreements, Discussion Paper 10-33, pp. 1-34.

Kim, S. H., Scheufele, D. A. and Shanahan, J. (2002). "Think About It This Way: Attribute Agenda-Setting Function of the Press and the Public's Evaluation of a Local Issue." *Journalism & Mass Communication Quarterly*, Vol. 79, No. 1, pp. 7-25.

Kingdon, J. (1995). *Agendas, Alternatives, and Public Policies* (2nd edn). New York: Addison-Wesley.

Krasner, S. D. (1982). "Structural Causes and Regime Consequences: Regimes as Intervening Variables." *International Organization*, Vol. 36, No. 2, pp. 185-205.

Lacity, M. C., Willcocks, L. P. and Khan, S. (2011). "Beyond Transaction Cost Economics: Towards an Endogenous Theory of Information Technology Outsourcing." *The Journal of Strategic Information Systems*, Vol. 20, No. 2, pp. 139-157.

Lan, L. (2012). "Global Carbon Trading 'Near': Interviewing with Andrew Steer." Available HTTP: 〈http://usa.chinadaily.com.cn/epaper/2012-10/29/content_15854194.htm〉 (accessed on 6 November 2012).

Langniss, O. and Wiser, R. (2003). "The Renewables Portfolio Standard in Texas: An Early Assessment." *Energy Policy*, Vol. 31, No. 6, pp. 527-535.

Lazarus, M. and Polycarp, C. (2011). "International Mechanisms for Greenhouse Gas Mitigation Finance and Investment." In G. Fan et al. (eds.), *The Economics of Climate Change in China: Towards a Low-Carbon Economy*. London and Washington DC: Earthscan, pp. 301-354.

Lecours, A. (2005). *New Institutionalism: Theory and Analysis*. Toronto: University of Toronto Press.

Lee, M. (2012). "Analyzing the Influence of Major Actors in China's Renewable Energy Policy as a Means of Predicting Future Chinese Renewable Energy Policy

Trends." Available HTTP: 〈https://deepblue.lib.umich.edu/bitstream/handle/2027.42/90860/? sequence=1〉.

Leeds, B. A. (1999). "Domestic Political Institutions, Credible Commitments, and International Cooperation." *American Journal of Political Science*, Vol. 43, No. 4, pp. 979-1002.

Legro, J. W. (1997). "Which Norms Matter? Revisiting the 'Failure' of Internationalism." *International Organization*, Vol. 51, No. 1, pp. 31-63.

Lema, A. and Ruby, K. (2007). "Between Fragmented Authoritarianism and Policy Coordination: Creating a Chinese Market for Wind Energy." *Energy Policy*, Vol. 35, No. 7, pp. 3879-3890.

Leone, S. (2012). "31 Percent Anti-Dumping Tariffs Announced for Chinese Solar Panels." Available HTTP: 〈http://www.renewableenergyworld.com/rea/news/article/2012/05/31-percent-anti-dumping-tariffs-announced-for-chinese-solar-panels〉 (accessed on 19 May 2012).

Leung, G. C. K. (2011). "China's Energy Security: Perception and Reality." *Energy Policy*, Vol. 39, pp. 1330-1337.

Lewis, J. I. (2008). "China's Strategic Priorities in International Climate Change Negotiations." *Washington Quarterly*, Vol. 31, No. 1, pp. 155-174.

Lewis, J. I. (2009). "Climate Change and Security: Examining China's Challenges in a Warming World." *International Affairs*, Vol. 85, No. 6, pp. 1195-1213.

Lewis, J. I. (2011). "Energy and Climate Goals of China's 12th Five-Year Plan." *Pew Center on Global Climate.*

Levy, M., Young, O. and Zürn, M. (1995). "The Study of International Regimes." *European Journal of International Relations*, Vol. 1, pp. 267-330.

Li, J. and Xu, J. (2010). "Climate Change in China: Policy Evolution, Actions Taken and Options Ahead." *Journal of Natural Resources Policy Research*, Vol. 3, No. 1, pp. 23-35.

Li, S. (2013). "UN Climate Talks Can Spur Emission Cuts in China." Available HTTP: 〈http://www.chinadialogue.net/blog/6117-UN-climate-talks-can-spur-emission-cuts-in-China/en〉 (accessed on 20 June 2013).

Li, V. and Lang, G. (2010). "China's 'Green GDP' Experiment and the Struggle for Ecological Modernisation." *Journal of Contemporary Asia*, Vol. 40, No. 1, pp. 44-62.

Li, X. (2010). "Social Rewards and Socialization Effects: An Alternative Explanation for the Motivation Behind China's Participation in International Institutions." *The Chinese Journal of International Politics*, Vol. 3, pp. 347-377.

Li, Y. and Cao, W. (2012). "Framework of Laws and Policies on Renewable

Energy and Relevant Systems in China under the Background of Climate Change." *Vermont Journal of Environmental Law*, Vol.13, pp.823-863.

Liang, W. (2010). "Changing Climate? China's New Interest in Global Climate Change Negotiations." In J. J. Kassiola and S. Guo (eds.), *China's Environmental Crisis: Domestic and Global Political Impacts and Responses.* Basingstoke and New York: Palgrave Macmillan, pp.61-84.

Lieberthal, K. and Lampton, D. M. (1992). *Bureaucracy, Politics, and Decision Making in Post-Mao China.* Berkeley: University of California Press.

Lieberthal, K. and Oksenberg, M. (1988). *Policy Making in China: Leaders, Structures, and Processes.* Princeton, NJ: Princeton University Press.

Lin, A. and Yang, F. (2012). "Design Tips for a Carbon Market." Available HTTP: 〈http://www.chinadialogue.net/article/show/single/en/4797〉 (accessed on 16 July 2012).

Lin, L. (2013). "Will China's New Premier Li Keqiang Improve the Environment?" Available HTTP: 〈http://www.chinadialogue.net/article/show/single/en/5847-Will-China-s-new-premier-Li-Keqiang-improve-the-environment-〉 (accessed on 26 July 2013).

Lin, M. (2009). "Domestic Audience Cost and International Cooperation." *Teaching and Research*, No.2, pp.81-89.

Lindlof, T. R. and Taylor, B. C. (2011). *Qualitative Communication Research Methods* (3rd edn). London: Sage.

Litfin, K. T. (2000). "Advocacy Coalitions Along the Domestic-Foreign Frontier: Globalization and Canadian Climate Change Policy." *Policy Studies Journal*, Vol.28, No.1, pp.236-252.

Liu, J. and Diamond, J. (2008). "Revolutionizing China's Environmental Protection." *Science*, Vol.319, No.5859, pp.37-42.

Liu, L. (2013). "Institutions of Renewable Energy Governance in China." Available HTTP: 〈http://tokyo2013.earthsystemgovernance.org/wp-content/uploads/2013/01/0199-Liguang-Liu.pdf〉 (accessed on 15 February 2013).

Liu, Q. (2015). "China's Cadres Ready Greener Five Year Plan." Available HTTP: 〈https://www.chinadialogue.net/article/show/single/en/8267-China-s-cadres-ready-greener-Five-Year-Plan〉 (accessed on 26 December 2015).

Liu, S. and Xu, N. (2012). "Data Gaps Hobble Carbon Trading." Available HTTP: 〈http://www.chinadialogue.net/article/show/single/en/5093-Data-gaps-hobble-carbon-trading〉 (accessed on 29 September 2012).

Liu, Z., Shi, Y., Yan, J., Ou, X. and Lieu, J. (2012). "Research on the Decomposition Model for China's National Renewable Energy Total Target."

Energy Policy, Vol. 51, pp. 110-120.

Long, T. E. and Hadden, J. K. (1985). "A Reconception of Socialization." *Sociological Theory*, Vol. 3, No. 1, pp. 39-49.

Lovaglia, M. J. (1995). "Power and Status Exchange, Attribution, and Expectation States." *Small Group Research*, Vol. 26, No. 3, pp. 400-426.

Lovinfosse, I. D. (2008). *How and Why Do Policies Change? A Comparison of Renewable Electricity Policies in Belgium, Denmark, Germany, the Netherlands and the UK.* Brussels: P. L. E. Peter Lang.

Lu, N. (1997). *The Dynamics of Foreign-Policy Decision-making in China.* Boulder: Westview Press.

Lu, Y. (2007). "The Collective Study Sessions of the Politburo: A Multipurpose Tool of China's Central Leadership." *Briefing Series of China Policy Institute (The University of Nottingham)*, No. 27, pp. 1-13.

Luo, X. and Wang, W. (2008). "Renewable Energy Development Project in China: Bring Affordable, High-quality Solar Lighting to Rural China." Available HTTP: 〈http://siteresources. worldbank. org/INTEAPREGTOPENERGY/ Publication sand Reports/21874077/Case_Study. pdf〉 (accessed on 28 June 2012).

Lü, X. and Liu, D. (eds.) (2004). *Clean Development Mechanism in China: Taking a Proactive and Sustainable Approach.* Beijing: Tsinghua University Pressing House.

Ma, J. (2013). "We're Winning the Air Pollution Data Battle: So What Next?" Available HTTP: 〈http://www. chinadialogue. net/article/show/single/en/5593-We-re-winning-the-air-pollution-data-battle-so-what-next-〉 (accessed on 10 January 2013).

Ma, Z. (2011). Information from the Interview with MA Zhong, Dean and Professor in School of Environment and Natural Resources, Renmin University of China, 10 March 2011, Beijing.

Mah, D. N.-Y. and Hills, P. (2012). "Collaborative Governance for Sustainable Development: Wind Resource Assessment in Xinjiang and Guangdong Provinces, China." *Sustainable Development*, Vol. 20, No. 2, pp. 85-97.

March, J. G. and Olsen, J. P. (1984). "The New Institutionalism: Organizational Factors in Political Life." *The American Political Science Review*, Vol. 78, No. 3, pp. 734-749.

March, J. G. and Olsen, J. P. (2006). "The Logic of Appropriateness." In M. Moran, et al. (eds.), *The Oxford Handbook of Public Policy.* Oxford: Oxford University Press, pp. 689-708.

Marsh, D. and Sharman, J. C. (2009). "Policy Diffusion and Policy Transfer." *Policy Studies*, Vol. 30, No. 3, pp. 269-288.

Mao, Y., Sheng, H. and Yang, F. (2008). *True Cost of Coal.* The Report of Greenpeace.

McCombs, M. (2005). "A Look at Agenda-setting: Past, Present and Future." *Journalism Studies*, Vol. 6, No. 4, pp. 543-557.

McCombs, M. E. and Shaw, D. L. (1972). "The Agenda-Setting Function of Mass Media." *Public Opinion Quarterly*, Vol. 36, No. 2, pp. 176-187.

McGarrity, J. (2015). "China's GHG Emissions Likely to Reach 'Early' Peak by 2025." Available HTTP: 〈https://www.chinadialogue.net/blog/7965-China-s-GHG-emissions-likely-to-reach-early-peak-by-2-25-says-new-report/en〉 (accessed on 16 October 2015).

McKinsey and Company. (2012). "China's Green Revolution: Prioritizing Technologies to Achieve Energy and Environmental Sustainability." Available HTTP: 〈http://citeseerx.ist.psu.edu/showciting?cid=11387380〉 (accessed on 19 May 2013).

Meijerink, S. (2005). "Understanding Policy Stability and Change: The Interplay of Advocacy Coalitions and Epistemic Communities, Windows of Opportunity, and Dutch Coastal Flooding Policy 1945-2003." *Journal of European Public Policy*, Vol. 12, No. 6, pp. 1060-1077.

Mendonça, M. and Jacobs, D. (2009). "Feed-in Tariffs Go Global: Policy in Practice." *Renewable Energy World*, Vol. 12, No. 4, pp. 1-6.

Mendonça, M., Jacobs, D. and Sovacool, B. K. (2010). *Powering the Green Economy: The Feed-in Tariff Handbook.* London and Sterling: VA Earthscan/James & James.

Meng, S. (2012). "An Insight into the Green Vocabulary of the Chinese Communist Party." Available HTTP: 〈http://www.chinadialogue.net/article/show/single/en/5339-An-insight-into-the-green-vocabulary-of-the-Chinese-communist-party〉 (accessed on 16 November 2012).

Mercer, J. (1996). *Reputation and International Politics.* Ithaca and London: Cornell University Press.

Mercer, J. (2005). "Rationality and Psychology in International Politics." *International Organization*, Vol. 59, No. 1, pp. 77-106.

Mertha, A. (2008). *China's Water Warriors: Citizen Action and Policy Change.* Ithaca: Cornell University Press.

Mertha, A. (2009). "Fragmented Authoritarianism 2.0: Political Pluralization in the Chinese Policy Process." *China Quarterly*, Vol. 200, pp. 995-1012.

Michonski, K. and Levi, M. A. (2010). *Harnessing International Institutions to Address Climate Changes.* New York: Council on Foreign Relations, Incorporated.

Milner, H. V. (1997). *Interests, Institutions and Information: Domestic Politics and International Relations.* Princeton: Princeton University Press.

Miriam, S. (2009). "Utilizing the Clean Development Mechanism for the Deployment of Renewable Energies in China." *Applied Energy*, Vol. 86, No. 2, pp. 237-242.

Mitchell, C. (2000). "The England and Wales Non-fossil Fuel Obligation: History and Lessons." *Annual Review of Energy and the Environment*, Vol. 25, No. 1, pp. 285-312.

Moore, S. (2011). "Strategic Imperative? Reading China's Climate Policy in Terms of Core Interests." *Global Change, Peace & Security*, Vol. 23, No. 2, pp. 147-157.

Morse, R., Rai, V. and He, G. (2009). "The Real Drivers of Carbon Capture and Storage in China and Implications for Climate Policy." Program on Energy and Sustainable Development (PESD) Working Paper, No. 88.

NCOCC. (2007). "Final Reporting Workshop on GEF/UNDP: Enabling China to Prepare Its Second National Communication Project Held in Beijing." Available HTTP: 〈http://nc.ccchina.gov.cn/english/column.asp?ColumnId=11〉 (accessed on 17 July 2012).

NCOCC. (2009). "Enabling China to Prepare Its Second National Communication to the UNFCCC Subprojects Launched." Available HTTP: 〈http://nc.ccchina.gov.cn/english/NewsInfo.asp?NewsId=200〉 (accessed on 23 August 2012).

NCOCC. (2011). "Compilation of the Second National Communication on Climate Change of China Launched." Available HTTP: 〈http://nc.ccchina.gov.cn/english/NewsInfo.asp?NewsId=617〉 (accessed on 27 July 2012).

NDRC. (2003). The Wind Power Concession Programme.

NDRC. (7/2009). Notice on Policy to Improve Grid-Connected Power Pricing for Wind Power. Available HTTP: 〈http://www.sdpc.gov.cn/zcfb/zcfbtz/2009tz/t20090727_292827.htm〉 (accessed on 8 August 2011).

NDRC. (9/2011). Comprehensive Work Plan for Energy Conservation and Emission Reduction in the 12th Five-Year Plan (2011-2015) Period. Available HTTP: 〈http://www.gov.cn/zwgk/2011-09/07/content_1941731.htm〉 (accessed on 10 November 2011).

NDRC. (5/2012). Regulations for Management of Renewable Power Quotas (Draft Version).

NDRC. (6/2012). The Interim Regulation for Voluntary Greenhouse Gas Emission Trading. Available HTTP: 〈http://thecleanrevolution.org/_assets/files/Interim-Regulation-of-Voluntary-Greenhouse-Gases-Emission-Trading-in-China(1).pdf〉 (accessed on 29 June 2012).

NDRC. (11/2012). China's Policies and Actions for Addressing Climate Change 2012. Available HTTP: 〈http://www.ccchina.gov.cn/WebSite/CCChina/UpFile/File1324.pdf〉 (accessed on 28 November 2012).

NDRC. (1/2013). 12th Five-Year Plan for Energy Development. Available HTTP: 〈http://www.xinhuanet.com/energy/jiage/jg9.htm〉 (accessed on 29 January 2013).

NEA. (2007). The Overview of the State Expert Advisory Committee. Available HTTP: 〈http://www.nea.gov.cn/nyzjzx/〉 (accessed on 17 June 2012).

NEA. (8/2012). 12th Five-Year Plan for Renewable Energy Development. Available HTTP: 〈http://news.bjx.com.cn/html/20120810/379617.shtml〉 (accessed on 16 September 2012).

NEA and CNREC. (2012). Key Information at a Glance: China 12th Five-Year Plan for Renewable Energy Development. China National Energy Administration, with the support of the Europe-China Clean Energy Centre.

Newenergy Net. (2012). "The Dilemma of Biomass Power Industry Should Be Solved by the Government." Available HTTP: 〈http://www.newenergy.org.cn/html/0127/7251247379.html〉 (accessed on 27 July 2012).

NPC. (2/2005). Renewable Energy Law. Available HTTP: 〈http://www.chinacleanenergydb.com/renewable-energy/legislation〉 (accessed on 8 January 2012).

NPC. (12/2009). Renewable Energy Law Amendment. Available HTTP: 〈http://www.chinacleanenergydb.com/renewable-energy/legislation〉 (accessed on 15 June 2011).

NPC Net. (2012). "Suggestions to Amend the Electricity Law to Pave the Way for Further Renewable Energy Development." Available HTTP: 〈http://www.npc.gov.cn/npc/dbdhhy/11_5/2012-03/05/content_1699765.htm〉 (accessed on 29 May 2012).

Oberheitmann, A. and Sternfeld, E. (2011). "Global Governance, Responsibility and A New Climate Regime." In P. G. Harris (ed.), *China's Responsibility for Climate Change: Ethics, Fairness and Environmental Policy*. pp. 195-222.

Ojekunle, Z. O., Lin, Z., Xin, T., Harrer, G., Martins, A. O. and Bangura, H. (2009). "Global Climate Change: The Empirical Study of Sensitivity Model in China's Sustainable Development." *Energy Sources, Part A: Recovery, Utilization, and Environmental Effects*, Vol. 31, No. 19, pp. 1777-1789.

Olivier, J. G. J., Janssens-Maenhout, G. and Peters, J. A. H. W. (2012). *Trends in Global CO_2 Emissions: 2012 Report*. PBL Netherlands Environmental Assessment Agency.

People Net. (2005). "The Go-out Strategy of Three Large Oil SOEs: 60 Projects All Over the World." Available HTTP: 〈http://finance.people.com.cn/GB/1038/3705933.html〉 (accessed on 17 June 2012).

People Net. (2010a). "Carbon Reverse Pressure Mechanism Leads to A Low-Carbon Path in China." Available HTTP: 〈http://politics.people.com.cn/GB/1026/11907981.html〉 (accessed on 12 May 2011).

People Net. (2010b). "Why It Is Easy for Trial Operation But Difficult for Policy Spreading." Available HTTP: 〈http://paper.people.com.cn/zgnyb/html/2010-07/26/content_579562.htm〉 (accessed on 9 November 2011).

People Net. (2012). Xie Zhenhua: China Will Participate in the Rulemaking of International Carbon Market. Available HTTP: 〈http://finance.people.com.cn/n/2012/1122/c70846-19662593.html〉 (accessed on 16 December 2012).

PEW. (2010). Who's Winning the Clean Energy Race: Growth, Competition and Opportunity in the World's Largest Economies. The Pew Charitable Trusts.

Point Carbon. (2012). "China Drafts First Climate Law, Eyes ETS." Available HTTP: 〈http://www.pointcarbon.com/news/1.1796448〉 (accessed on 27 July 2012).

Polarispower Net. (2012). "The Wind Power Enclosure Movement of the Large State-owned Enterprises." Available HTTP: 〈http://news.bjx.com.cn/html/20120802/377551.shtml〉 (accessed on 17 August 2012).

Pralle, S. B. (2009). "Agenda-Setting and Climate Change." *Environmental Politics*, Vol. 18, No. 5, pp. 781-799.

Princen, S. (2007). "Advocacy Coalitions and the Internationalization of Public Health Policies." *Journal of Public Policy*, Vol. 27, No. 1, p. 13.

Pu, J. (2012). "China to End Price Cap on Coal." Available HTTP: 〈http://english.caixin.com/2012-12-25/100476669.html〉 (accessed on 31 December 2012).

Putnam, R. D. (1988). "Diplomacy and Domestic Politics: The Logic of Two-Level Games." *International Organization*, Vol. 42, No. 3, pp. 427-460.

Qin, Y. (2005). "Core Problem of International Relations Theory and the Construction of a Chinese School." *Social Sciences in China*, No. 3, pp. 165-176.

Qin, Y. (2007). "Why is There No Chinese International Relations Theory?" *International Relations of the Asia-Pacific*, Vol. 7, No. 3, pp. 313-340.

Qin, Y. (2011). "Rule, Rules, and Relations: Towards a Synthetic Approach to Governance." *The Chinese Journal of International Politics*, Vol. 4, No. 2, pp. 117-145.

Qin, Y. and Wei, L. (2007). "Structures, Processes, and the Socialization of

Power: China and Regional Cooperation in East Asia." *World Economics and Politics*, No. 3, pp. 7-15.

RED. (2009). "Sino-Danish Renewable Energy Development Programme." Available HTTP: 〈http://www.cnred.org.cn/english/manageInfo.do?action=showColumn&typeId=-6&type=tag〉 (accessed on 27 September 2011).

REEEP. (2009a). "Renewable Energy & Energy Efficiency Partnership (REEEP) Project Database." Available HTTP: 〈http://www.reeep.org/projects〉 (accessed on 17 March 2012).

REEEP. (2009b). "Renewable Energy & Energy Efficiency Partnership (REEEP): A Brief Overview." Available HTTP: 〈http://www.reeep.org/reeep-brief-overview〉 (accessed on 21 August 2012).

REN21. (2006). *Changing Climates: The Role of Renewable Energy in a Carbon-Constrained World.* Report of Renewable Energy Network for the 21st Century. Available HTTP: 〈http://www.ren21.net/Portals/97/documents/Publications/REN21_Changing_Climates_report.pdf〉 (accessed on 2 January 2012).

REN21. (2009a). *Background Paper: Chinese Renewables Status Report 2009.* Report of Renewable Energy Network for the 21st Century. Available HTTP: 〈http://www.ren21.net/Portals/97/documents/Publications/Background_Paper_Chinese_Renewables_Status_Report_2009.pdf〉 (accessed on 6 January 2012).

REN21. (2009b). *Recommendations for Improving the Effectiveness of Renewable Energy Policies in China.* Report of Renewable Energy Network for the 21st Century. Available HTTP: 〈http://www.ren21.net/Portals/97/documents/Publications/Recommendations_for_RE_Policies_in_China.pdf〉 (accessed on 2 January 2012).

REN21. (2011). *Renewables 2011 Global Status Report.* Report of Renewable Energy Network for the 21st Century. Available HTTP: 〈http://www.ren21.net/Portals/97/documents/GSR/REN21_GSR2011.pdf〉 (accessed on 6 January 2012).

REN21. (2012). *Renewables 2012 Global Status Report.* Report of Renewable Energy Network for the 21st Century. Available HTTP: 〈http://www.map.ren 21.net/GSR/GSR2012.pdf〉 (accessed on 6 September 2012).

REN21. (2013). *Renewables 2013 Global Status Report: Key Findings.* Report of Renewable Energy Network for the 21st Century. Available HTTP: 〈http://www.ren21.net/Portals/0/documents/Resources/GSR/2013/KeyFindings_2013_lowres.pdf〉 (accessed on 16 June 2013).

REN21 and UNEP. (2012). *Global Trends in Renewable Energy Investment 2012.* Available HTTP: 〈http://fs-unep-centre.org/sites/default/files/media/globaltrendsreport2012_3.pdf〉 (accessed on 16 October 2012).

Ren, D., Wang, Z. and Gao, H. (eds.) (2009). *The Reader for Knowledge on Renewable Energy Policies and Regulations.* Beijing: Chemical Industry Press.

Renewable Energy. (2012). "China Quadruples 2015 Solar Energy Target to Aid Demand, Prices." Available HTTP: 〈http://www.renewableenergyworld.com/rea/news/article/2012/07/china-quadruples-2015-solar-energy-target-to-aid-demand-prices〉 (accessed on 19 August 2012).

REUTERS. (2013). "Goldman Sees China Becoming Biggest Oil Importer." Available HTTP: 〈http://www.reuters.com/article/2012/01/09/us-oil-china-imports-idUSTRE80815H20120109〉 (accessed on 17 March 2012).

Richerzhagen, C. and Scholz, I. (2008). "China's Capacities for Mitigating Climate Change." *World Development*, Vol. 36, No. 2, pp. 308-324.

Risse-Kappen, T. (1991). "Public Opinion, Domestic Structure, and Foreign Policy in Liberal Democracies." *World Politics*, Vol. 43, No. 4, pp. 479-512.

Risse-Kappen, T. (1994). "Ideas Do not Float Freely: Transnational Coalitions, Domestic Structures, and the End of the Cold War." *International Organization*, Vol. 48, No. 2, pp. 185-214.

Risse-Kappen, T. (1995a). "Bringing Transnational Relations Back in: Introduction." In T. Risse-Kappen (ed.), *Bringing Transnational Relations Back in: Non-state Actors, Domestic Structures, and International Institutions.* Cambridge: Cambridge University Press.

Risse-Kappen, T. (ed.) (1995b). *Bringing Transnational Relations Back in: Non-state Actors, Domestic Structures, and International Institutions.* Cambridge: Cambridge University Press.

Risse, T. (1999). "International Norms and Domestic Change: Arguing and Communicative Behavior in the Human Rights Area." *Politics & Society*, Vol. 27, No. 4, p. 529.

Risse, T. (2000). "'Let's Argue!': Communicative Action in World Politics." *International Organization*, Vol. 54, No. 1, pp. 1-39.

Risse, T., Ropp, S. C. and Sikkink, K. (eds.) (1999). *The Power of Human Rights: International Norms and Domestic Change.* Cambridge: Cambridge University Press.

Risse, T. and Sikkink, K. (1999). "The Socialization of International Human Rights Norms into Domestic Practices: Introduction." In T. Risse et al. (eds.), *The Power of Human Rights: International Norms and Domestic Change.* Cambridge: Cambridge University Press, pp. 1-38.

Rochefort, D. A. and Cobb, R. W. (1994). *The Politics of Problem Definition: Shaping the Policy Agenda.* Lawrence, KS: University Press of Kansas.

Rose, R. (1993). *Lesson-Drawing in Public Policy: A Guide to Learning Across Time and Space.* Cambridge: Cambridge University Press.

Ross, L. (1998). "China: Environmental Protection, Domestic Policy Trends, Patterns of Participation in Regimes and Compliance with International Norms." *The China Quarterly*, pp. 809-835.

Sabatier, P. (1988). "An Advocacy Coalition Framework of Policy Change and the Role of Policy-oriented Learning Therein." *Policy Sciences*, Vol. 21, pp. 129-168.

Sabatier, P. (ed.) (2007). *Theories of the Policy Process.* Boulder: Westview Press.

Sabatier, P. and Jenkins-Smith, H. C. (eds.) (1993a). "The Advocacy Coalition Framework: Assessment, Revisions, and Implications for Scholars and Practitioners." In P. Sabatier and H. C. Jenkins-Smith (eds.), *Policy Change and Learning: An Advocacy Coalition Approach.* Boulder: Westview Press, pp. 211-235.

Sabatier, P. and Jenkins-Smith, H. C. (eds.) (1993b). *Policy Change and Learning: An Advocacy Coalition Approach.* Boulder: Westview Press.

Sabatier, P. and Jenkins-Smith, H. C. (1999). "The Advocacy Coalition Framework: An Assessment." In P. Sabatier (ed.), *Theories of the Policy Process.* Boulder: Westview Press, pp. 118-188.

Sabatier, P. and Weible, C. (2007). "The Advocacy Coalition: Innovations and Clarifications." In P. Sabatier (ed.), *Theories of the Policy Process.* Boulder: Westview Press, pp. 189-220.

Scheufele, D. A. (1999). "Framing as a Theory of Media Effects." *Journal of Communication*, Vol. 49, No. 1, pp. 103-122.

Scheufele, D. A. (2000). "Agenda-setting, Priming, and Framing Revisited: Another Look at Cognitive Effects of Political Communication." *Mass Communication & Society*, Vol. 3, No. 2, pp. 297-316.

Scheufele, D. A. and Tewksbury, D. (2007). "Framing, Agenda Setting, and Priming: The Evolution of Three Media Effects Models." *Journal of Communication*, Vol. 57, No. 1, pp. 9-20.

Schimmelfennig, F. (2000). "International Socialization in the New Europe: Rational Action in an Institutional Environment." *European Journal of International Relations*, Vol. 6, No. 1, pp. 109-139.

Schimmelfennig, F. (2005). "Strategic Calculation and International Socialization: Membership Incentives, Party Constellations, and Sustained Compliance in Central and Eastern Europe." *International Organization*, Vol. 59, No. 4, pp. 827-860.

Schreurs, M. A. (2002). *Environmental Politics in Japan, Germany, and the United States.* Cambridge: Cambridge University Press.

Schreurs, M. A. (2008). "From the Bottom up Local and Sub-national Climate Change Politics." *The Journal of Environment & Development*, Vol. 17, No. 4, pp. 343-355.

Schreurs, M. A. (2010). "Multi-Level Governance and Global Climate Change in East Asia." *Asian Economic Policy Review*, Vol. 5, No. 1, pp. 88-105.

Schroeder, M. (2009). "Utilizing the Clean Development Mechanism for the Deployment of Renewable Energies in China." *Applied Energy*, Vol. 86, No. 2, pp. 237-242.

Schuman, S. and Lin, A. (2012). "China's Renewable Energy Law and Its Impact on Renewable Power in China: Progress, Challenges and Recommendations for Improving Implementation." *Energy Policy*, Vol. 51, pp. 89-109.

SGCC. (2010). "Overview of the State Grid Corporation of China." Available HTTP: 〈http://www.sgcc.com.cn/index.shtml〉 (accessed on 17 November 2012).

Shankar, U. (2012). "The Parallels Between EU Financial Crisis and Carbon Market Collapse." Available HTTP: 〈http://re.indiaenvironmentportal.org.in/blogs/parallels-between-eu-financial-crisis-and-carbon-market-collapse〉 (accessed on 28 October 2012).

Shor, E. (2008). "Conflict, Terrorism, and the Socialization of Human Rights Norms: The Spiral Model Revisited." *Social Problems*, Vol. 55, No. 1, pp. 117-138.

Simon, H. A. (1978). "Rationality as Process and as Product of Thought." *The American Economic Review*, Vol. 68, No. 2, pp. 1-16.

Sina News. (2007). "President Hu Jiaotao Attended the APEC Summit." Available HTTP: 〈http://news.sina.com.cn/z/hjt07cfadly/〉 (accessed on 18 July 2011).

Sina News. (2010). "Involving the Green GDP Index into the Climate Change Law." Available HTTP: 〈http://news.sina.com.cn/green/p/2010-11-11/135021454382.shtml〉 (accessed on 23 July 2012).

Sina News. (2012). "Internet Users in China Reaching 538 Million." Available HTTP: 〈http://news.sina.com.cn/m/2012-11-02/102025495863.shtml〉 (accessed on 16 December 2012).

Slater, M. D. (2007). "Reinforcing Spirals: The Mutual Influence of Media Selectivity and Media Effects and Their Impact on Individual Behavior and Social Identity." *Communication Theory*, Vol. 17, No. 3, pp. 281-303.

Solarbuzz. (2012). "The 'Major Reshuffle' of PV Equipment Industries in 2012 to Reduce the Overcapacity." Available HTTP: 〈http://www.solarbuzz.com/cn/

news/recent-findings/PV_new_phase〉(accessed on 17 October 2012).

SolarF. (2012). "Solar Industry to Get Jolt from New Policies." Available HTTP: 〈http://www.solarf.org/html/news/policy/2012/1220/3663.html〉(accessed on 16 December 2012).

Soutar, R. (2015). "A 'Less Defensive' China Can Help Spur Global Climate Deal." Available HTTP: 〈https://www.chinadialogue.net/article/show/single/en/8248-A-less-defensive-China-can-help-spur-global-climate-deal〉(accessed on 16 October 2015).

State Council. (3/2006). 11th Five-Year Plan on National Economic and Social Development. Available HTTP: 〈http://www.chinacleanenergydb.com/general-strategic-plans/Five-Year-Plans〉(accessed on 18 January 2012).

State Council. (9/2007). The Mid- and Long-Term Development Plan for Renewable Energy (2007-2020). Available HTTP: 〈http://www.china.com.cn/policy/txt/2007-09/04/content_8800358.htm〉(accessed on 28 July 2012).

State Council. (2007). White Paper on China's Energy Conditions and Policies. Available HTTP: 〈http://www.gov.cn/zwgk/2007-12/26/content_844159.htm〉(accessed on 17 March 2011).

State Council. (3/2011). 12th Five-Year Plan on National Economic and Social Development. Available HTTP: 〈http://www.ce.cn/xwzx/gnsz/gdxw/201103/16/t20110316_22305305.shtml〉(accessed on 17 May 2012).

State Council. (1/2013). The 12th Five-Year Plan for Energy Development. Available HTTP: 〈http://news.xinhuanet.com/energy/2013-01/24/c_124272433.htm〉(accessed on 25 January 2013).

State Council. (11/2014). Strategic Action Plan for Energy Development (2014-2020). Available HTTP: 〈http://news.xinhuanet.com/energy/2014-11/20/c_127231835.htm〉(accessed on 27 March 2015).

Sterk, W. and Mersmann, F. (2011). *Domestic Emission Trading Systems in Developing Countries: State of Play and Future Prospects*. Wuppertal Institute for Climate, Environment and Energy.

Stevens, P. (2012). The "Shale Gas Revolution": Developments and Changes (Briefing Paper of Chantham House). Available HTTP: 〈http://www.chathamhouse.org/sites/default/files/public/Research/Energy,%20Environment%20and%20Development/bp0812_stevens.pdf〉(accessed on 16 December 2012).

Stone, D. (1999). "Learning Lessons and Transferring Policy Across Time, Space and Disciplines." *Politics*, Vol. 19, No. 1, pp. 51-59.

Stone, D. (2004). "Transfer Agents and Global Networks in the

'Transnationalization' of Policy." *Journal of European Public Policy*, Vol. 11, No. 3, pp. 545-566.

Stryker, S. and Statham, A. (1985). "Symbolic Interaction and Role Theory." In G. Lindzey and E. Aronson (eds.), *The Handbook of Social Psychology*. New York: Random House, pp. 311-378.

Su, C. (2002). "China and International Institution: A Research Agenda." *World Economics and Politics*, No. 10, pp. 5-10.

Su, C. (2005). "Discovering the New Diplomacy of China: Multilateral International Institutions and New Diplomatic Perspective of China." *World Economics and Politics*, No. 4, pp. 11-16.

Su, C. (2007). "The Political Economy of the Mutual Transformation of the Domestic and International Systems: Implications for China and the International System (1978-2007)." *World Economics and Politics*, No. 11, pp. 6-13.

Su, W. (2012). "Grasping the Opportunity of Green Low-Carbon Development and Promoting the Social Sustainable Development in China." Available HTTP: 〈http://www.cbcsd.org.cn/sjk/qushi/infor/20130416/download/swch.pdf〉 (accessed on 16 June 2012).

Sudworth, J. (2013). "China's Ambitious Quest for Shale Gas." Available HTTP: 〈http://www.bbc.co.uk/news/world-asia-22023464〉 (accessed on 8 April 2013).

Sustainable Business News. (2012). "China Boosts 2015 Solar Energy Target Again." Available HTTP: 〈http://www.sustainablebusiness.com/index.cfm/go/news.display/id/23836〉 (accessed on 20 September 2012).

Tang, S. (2011). *A General Theory of Institutional Change*. London and New York: Routledge.

Tanquintic-Misa, E. (2011). "China Leads Global Investments in Renewable Energy." Available HTTP: 〈http://au.ibtimes.com/articles/261083/20111205/china-leads-global-investments-renewable-energy.htm#.UdhPoJktttw〉 (accessed on 21 June 2012).

Teng, F. and Gu, A. (2007). "Climate Change: National and Local Policy Opportunities in China." *Environmental Sciences*, Vol. 4, No. 3, pp. 183-194.

Tews, K. (2005). "The Diffusion of Environmental Policy Innovations: Cornerstones of an Analytical Framework." *European Environment*, Vol. 15, No. 2, pp. 63-79.

Tian, Y. (2011). "The Impact of International Institutions on Domestic Politics: From the Perspective of Rational Choice Institutionalism." *World Economics and Politics*, No. 1, pp. 5-24.

Tingley, D. H. and Walter, B. F. (2011). "The Effect of Repeated Play on

Reputation Building: An Experimental Approach." *International Organization*, Vol. 65, No. 2, pp. 343-365.

Toke, D. (2011). *Ecological Modernisation and Renewable Energy*. Hampshire and New York: Palgrave Macmillan.

Tomz, M. (2007). "Domestic Audience Costs in International Relations: An Experimental Approach." *International Organization*, Vol. 61, No. 4, p. 821.

Tsang, S. and Kolk, A. (2010). "The Evolution of Chinese Policies and Governance Structures on Environment, Energy and Climate." *Environmental Policy and Governance*, Vol. 20, No. 3, pp. 180-196.

Tujan, T. (2010). "The North's Destructive Model." Available HTTP: 〈http://www.dandc.eu/articles/166521/index.en.shtml〉 (accessed on 12 March 2011).

UNEP. (2012). "Doha Climate Conference Opens Gateway to Greater Ambition and Action on Climate Change." Available HTTP: 〈http://www.unep.org/newscentre/default.aspx? DocumentID =2700&ArticleID =9353〉 (accessed on 28 December 2012).

Vandenbergh, M. P. (2007). "Climate Change: The China Problem." *Southern California Law Review*, Vol. 81, pp. 905-958.

Wang, F., Yin, H. and Li, S. (2010). "China's Renewable Energy Policy: Commitments and Challenges." *Energy Policy*, Vol. 38, No. 4, pp. 1872-1878.

Wang, H. (2012). "Where Should Bio-diesel Go?" Available HTTP: 〈http://paper.people.com.cn/zgnyb/html/2012-06/18/content_1069602.htm〉 (accessed on 21 August 2012).

Wang, Q. and Chen, Y. (2010). "Barriers and Opportunities of Using the Clean Development Mechanism to Advance Renewable Energy Development in China." *Renewable and Sustainable Energy Reviews*, Vol. 14, No. 7, pp. 1989-1998.

Wang, T. (2012). "China's Carbon Market Challenge." Available HTTP: 〈http://www.chinadialogue.net/article/show/single/en/4936-China-s-carbon-market-challenge〉 (accessed on 6 July 2012).

Wang, Y., Gao, G. and Li, M. (2012). "The Analysis of Carbon Finance Based on the Angle of Sustainable Development." *Advances in Applied Economics and Finance*, Vol. 3, No. 2, pp. 527-532.

Wang, Z., Ren, D. and Gao, H. (eds.) (2010). *The Renewable Energy Industrial Development Report 2009*. Beijing: Chemical Industry Press.

Wang, Z., Ren, D. and Gao, H. (eds.) (2012). *The Renewable Energy Industrial Development Report 2011*. Beijing: Chemical Industry Press.

Want Chinatimes. (2012). "China Considers Market-Driven Mechanism for Coal Prices." Available HTTP: 〈http://www.wantchinatimes.com/news-subclass-cnt. aspx? id =20120822000027&cid =1102〉 (accessed on 19 September 2012).

Watanabe, R. (2011). *Climate Policy Changes in Germany and Japan: A Path to Paradigmatic Policy Change.* London and New York: Routledge.

Weeks, J. L. (2008). "Autocratic Audience Costs: Regime Type and Signaling Resolve." *International Organization*, Vol. 62, No. 1, pp. 35-64.

Weible, C. M., Sabatier, P. A. and McQueen, K. (2009). "Themes and Variations: Taking Stock of the Advocacy Coalition Framework." *Policy Studies Journal*, Vol. 37, No. 1, pp. 121-140.

Weiss, E. B. and Jacobson, H. K. (2000). *Engaging Countries: Strengthening Compliance With International Environmental Accords.* Cambridge: MIT press.

Wendt, A. (1999). *Social Theory of International Politics.* Cambridge and New York: Cambridge University Press.

Wiener, J. B. (2007). "Climate Change Policy and Policy Change in China." *UCLA L. Rev.*, Vol. 55, pp. 1805-1826.

Williams, T. (2010). "Why Commit? International Socialization Theory and China's Climate Change Policy." Available HTTP: 〈http://papers. ssrn. com/sol3/papers. cfm? abstract_id =1676207〉.

Wingfield, B. (2012). "U. S. Sets Anti-Dumping Duties on China Solar Imports." Available HTTP: 〈http://www. bloomberg. com/news/2012-10-10/u-s-sets-anti-dumping-duties-on-china-solar-imports. html〉 (accessed on 29 October 2012).

Wiser, R., Hamrin, J. and Wingate, M. (2002). "Renewable Energy Policy Options for China: A Comparison of Renewable Portfolio Standards, Feed-in tariffs, and Tendering Policies." *Center for Resource Solutions*, Vol. 16.

World Bank. (2010). *Project Performance Assessment Report: China's Renewable Energy Development Project (REDP).* Available HTTP: 〈http://cleanenergysolutions. org/content/project-performance-assessment-report-chinas-renewable-energy-development-project-redp〉 (accessed on 15 March 2012).

World Bank. (2011). "Seizing the Opportunity of Green Development in China (Supporting Report 3 of World Bank)." *China 2030: Building a Modern, Harmonious, and Creative High-Income Society.* Washington, D. C. The World Bank, pp. 229-292.

WPO. (2009). "Public Attitudes toward Climate Change: Findings from a Multi-Country Poll (Report from World Public Opinion. org)." Available HTTP: 〈http://www. worldpublicopinion. org/pipa/articles/btenvironmentra/649. php〉 (accessed on 16 March 2011).

Wu, Q. (2013). "Analysis—Chinese Wind Curtailments Double in 2012." Available HTTP: 〈http://www. windpowermonthly. com/article/1171987/

analysis---chinese-wind-curtailments-double-2012〉(accessed on 17 March 2013).

Xia, C. and Song, Z. (2009). "Wind Energy in China: Current Scenario and Future Perspectives." *Renewable and Sustainable Energy Reviews*, Vol. 13, No. 8, pp. 1966-1974.

Xie, D. (2012). "The Renewable Energy Policy-making in China Has Entered the 'Deep Water Area'." Available HTTP: 〈http://www.infzm.com/content/71057〉(accessed on 9 September 2012).

Xinhua News. (2009a). "The Important Speech of President Hu Jintao in the UN Climate Change Summit." Available HTTP: 〈http://news.xinhuanet.com/world/2009-09/23/content_12098929.htm〉(accessed on 29 July 2012).

Xinhua News. (2009b). "Stance and Measures of China in Climate Change Mitigation." Available HTTP: 〈http://news.xinhuanet.com/ziliao/2009-09/16/content_12063193.htm〉(accessed on 17 June 2011).

Xinhua News. (2011a). "The Conference of National Leading Group on Climate Change Led by Premier Wen Jiabao." Available HTTP: 〈http://news.xinhuanet.com/2010-11/19/c_12795533.htm〉(accessed on 17 May 2012).

Xinhua News. (2011b). "The Frequent Occurence of Wind Turbine Grid Disconnection Accidents and the Rectification Requirement for the Wind Power Industry." Available HTTP: 〈http://news.xinhuanet.com/fortune/2011-06/07/c_121502833.htm〉(accessed on 16 March 2012).

Xinhua News. (2012a). "China Says Energy Consumption is Controllable." Available HTTP: 〈http://news.xinhuanet.com/english/china/2012-01/11/c_131355042.htm〉(accessed on 16 July 2012).

Xinhua News. (2012b). "CPC Advocates Building 'Beautiful' China." Available HTTP: 〈http://www.chinadaily.com.cn/china/2012cpc/2012-11/08/content_15897936.htm〉(accessed on 18 November 2012).

Xinhua News. (2012c). "The Development Status of Wind Power Industry in China." Available HTTP: 〈http://news.xinhuanet.com/energy/2012-09/29/c_123779235.htm〉(accessed on 16 November 2012).

Xinhua News. (2012d). "The Energy-Saving Emission Reduction Targets of 12th Five-Year Plan." Available HTTP: 〈http://news.xinhua08.com/a/20120520/958604.shtml〉(accessed on 16 June 2012).

Xinhua News. (2013). "The Politburo Collective Study Session of 24 May 2013 held by President Xi Jinping." Available HTTP: 〈http://news.xinhuanet.com/video/2013-05/24/c_124761554.htm〉(accessed on 26 May 2013).

Xu, N. and Zhang, C. (2013). "How Did China's Air Pollution Crisis Get This Bad?" Available HTTP: 〈http://www.chinadialogue.net/article/show/single/

en/5604-How-did-China-s-air-pollution-crisis-get-this-bad-⟩ (accessed on 16 January 2013).

Xu, W. (2012). "Ecological Civilization Emphasized at Party Congress." Available HTTP: ⟨http://www. morningwhistle. com/html/2012/PoliticsSociety_1113/215294. html⟩ (accessed on 27 November 2012).

Yamin, F. and Depledge, J. (2004). *The International Climate Change Regime: A Guide to Rules, Institutions and Procedures*. Cambridge: Cambridge University Press.

Yan, S. and Xiao, L. (2010). "Evolution of China's Position in International Climate Talks." *Journal of Contemporary Asia-Pacific Studies*, No. 1, pp. 80-90.

Yan, Y. (2012). "China Targets Renewables to Cut Energy Dependence." Available HTTP: ⟨http://www. rsc. org/chemistryworld/2012/09/china-renewables-five-year-plan-biomass⟩ (accessed on 21 November 2012).

Ye, Q., Li, M. and Lingyun, Z. (2007). "Climate Change Governance in China: A Case Study." *Chn Popu Res Envi*, Vol. 17, No. 2, pp. 8-12.

Young, O. R. (2001). "Inferences and Indices: Evaluating the Effectiveness of International Environmental Regimes." *Global Environmental Politics*, Vol. 1, No. 1, pp. 99-121.

Young, O. R. (2010). *Institutional Dynamics: Emergent Patterns in International Environmental Governance*. Cambridge and London: The MIT Press.

Yu, H. (2004a). "Global Environment Regime and Climate Policy Coordination in China." *Journal of Chinese Political Science*, Vol. 9, No. 2, pp. 63-77.

Yu, H. (2004b). "Knowledge and Climate Change Policy Coordination in China." *East Asia*, Vol. 21, No. 3, pp. 58-77.

Yu, H. (2008). *Global Warming and China's Environmental Diplomacy*. New York: Nova Science Publishers, Inc.

Yuan, X. and Zuo, J. (2011). "Transition to Low-carbon Energy Policies in China: From the Five-Year Plan Perspective." *Energy Policy*, Vol. 39, No. 6, pp. 3855-3859.

Zürn, M. and Checkel, J. T. (2005). "Getting Socialized to Build Bridges: Constructivism and Rationalism, Europe and the Nation-state." *International Organization*, Vol. 59, No. 4, pp. 1045-1079.

Zeng, M., Lü, C., Ma, M., Peng, L., Yan, B., Li, N. and Xue, S. (2012). "Renewable Energy Development Thrives During China's 12th Five-Year Plan." Available HTTP: ⟨http://www. powermag. com/issues/features/Renewable-Energy-Development-Thrives-During-Chinas-12th-Five-Year-Plan_5187. html⟩ (accessed on 6 January 2013).

Zhang, Z. (2003). "The forces behind China's Climate Change Policy: Interests, sovereignty and Prestige." In P. G. Harris (ed.), *Global Warming and East Asia: The Domestic and International Politics of Climate Change.* London and New York: Taylor & Francis Group, pp. 66-86.

Zha, D. (2005). "China's Energy Security and Its International Relations." *The China and Eurasia Forum Quarterly*, Vol. 3, No. 3, pp. 39-54.

Zha, D. (2006). "China's Energy Security: Domestic and International Issues." *Survival*, Vol. 48, No. 1, pp. 179-190.

Zhang, C. (2015). "Pilot Scheme to Grade Officials on Environmental Protection." Available HTTP: 〈http://www.chinadialogue.net/article/show/single/en/8198-Pilot-scheme-to-grade-officials-on-environmental-protection〉 (accessed on 28 September 2015).

Zhang, H. (2006). "China's Position in the Negotiations on International Climate Change: Continuities and Changes." *World Economics and Politics*, No. 10, pp. 36-43.

Zhang, H. (2007). "China and International Climate Change Negotiation." *International Politics Quarterly*, No. 1, pp. 21-36.

Zhang, P., Yang, Y., Shi, J., Zheng, Y., Wang, L. and Li, X. (2009). "Opportunities and Challenges for Renewable Energy Policy in China." *Renewable and Sustainable Energy Reviews*, Vol. 13, No. 2, pp. 439-449.

Zhang, X., Chang, S. and Eric, M. (2012). "Renewable Energy in China: An Integrated Technology and Policy Perspective." *Energy Policy*, Vol. 51, pp. 1-6.

Zhang, Z. (2003). "The forces behind China's Climate Change Policy: Interests, Sovereignty and Prestige." In P. G. Harris (ed.), *Global Warming and East Asia: The Domestic and International Politics of Climate Change.* London and New York: Taylor & Francis Group, pp. 66-86.

Zhang, Z. (2010a). "China in the Transition to a Low-carbon Economy." *Energy Policy*, Vol. 38, No. 11, pp. 6638-6653.

Zhang, Z. (2010b). "Copenhagen and Beyond: Reflections on China's Stance and Responses." In E. Cerda and X. Labandeira (eds.), *Climate Change Policies: Global Challenges and Future Prospects.* Cheltenham and Northampton: Edward Elgar.

Zhao, Z. Y., Zuo, J., Feng, T. T. and Zillante, G. (2011). "International Cooperation on Renewable Energy Development in China: A Critical Analysis." *Renewable Energy*, Vol. 36, pp. 1105-1110.

Zhou, S., Tong, Q., Yu, S., Wang, Y., Chai, Q. and Zhang, X. (2012). "Role of Non-fossil Energy in Meeting China's Energy and Climate Target for 2020." *Energy Policy*, Vol. 51, pp. 14-19.

Zhuang, G. (2009). "Copenhagen Climate Game and Re-Understanding of China's Role." *Foreign Affairs Review*, No. 6, pp. 13-21.

图书在版编目(CIP)数据

中国可再生能源政策变迁机制研究:国际气候变化机制与国内可再生能源政策倡议联盟的互动/李昕蕾著.—济南:山东大学出版社,2016.3
ISBN 978-7-5607-5530-4

Ⅰ.①中… Ⅱ.①李… Ⅲ.①再生资源-能源政策-研究-中国
Ⅳ.①F426.2

中国版本图书馆 CIP 数据核字(2016)第 075739 号

责任策划:谭学秋
责任编辑:王 潇 谭学秋
封面设计:牛 钧

出版发行:山东大学出版社
社 址 山东省济南市山大南路 20 号
邮 编 250100
电 话 市场部(0531)88364466
经 销:山东省新华书店
印 刷:济南华林彩印有限公司
规 格:720 毫米×1000 毫米 1/16
21.25 印张 348 千字
版 次:2016 年 3 月第 1 版
印 次:2016 年 3 月第 1 次印刷
定 价:38.00 元
